CW01213680

Yearbook of Transnational History

Yearbook of Transnational History

(2023)

Volume 6

Edited by Thomas Adam
Assisted by Austin E. Loignon

FAIRLEIGH DICKINSON UNIVERSITY PRESS
Vancouver • Madison • Teaneck • Wroxton

Editorial Board

Sven Beckert, *Harvard University, Boston, USA*
Tobias Brinkmann, *Penn State University, Philadelphia, USA*
Daniela Caglioti, *Universita di Napoli, Naples, Italy*
Pilar Gonzalez, *Université Paris I, Paris, France*
Frank Jacob, *Nord University, Norway*
Paul Kerry, *Brigham Young University, Provo, USA*
Axel Korner, *Universität Leipzig, Germany*
Alan Lessoff, *Illinois State University, Normal, USA*
Gabriele Lingelbach, *Christian-Albrechts-Universität, Kiel, Germany*
Kris K. Manjapra, *Tufts University, Medford, USA*
Kiran Klaus Patel, *University of Maastricht, Maastricht, The Netherlands*
Pierre-Yves Saunier, *Université Laval, Quebec City, Canada*
Axel Schaefer, *Johannes Gutenberg Universität, Mainz, Germany*
Ian Tyrrell, *University of New South Wales, Sydney, Australia*

Yearbook of Transnational History

(2023)

Volume 6

Special Theme: Heritage Without National Boundaries

Guest editor: Barry L. Stiefel and Shelley-Anne Peleg

FAIRLEIGH DICKINSON UNIVERSITY PRESS

Vancouver • Madison • Teaneck • Wroxton

Published by Fairleigh Dickinson University Press
Copublished by The Rowman & Littlefield Publishing Group, Inc.
4501 Forbes Boulevard, Suite 200, Lanham, Maryland 20706
www.rowman.com

86-90 Paul Street, London EC2A 4NE, United Kingdom

Copyright © 2023 by The Rowman & Littlefield Publishing Group, Inc.

All rights reserved. No part of this book may be reproduced in any form or by any electronic or mechanical means, including information storage and retrieval systems, without written permission from the publisher, except by a reviewer who may quote passages in a review.

Fairleigh Dickinson University Press gratefully acknowledges the support received for scholarly publishing from the Friends of FDU Press.

British Library Cataloguing in Publication Information Available

Library of Congress Cataloging-in-Publication Data Available

ISBN 9781683933786 (cloth) | ISBN 9781683933793 (epub)

Contents

Editorial Board		iv
1	Heritage Without National Boundaries *Barry L. Stiefel and Shelley-Anne Peleg*	1
2	Crossing Borders with Crusader Heritage *Shelley-Anne Peleg*	31
3	YU-NESCO: The Role of World Heritage in Making and Breaking Boundaries in Yugoslavia and Its Successor States: Croatia, Montenegro, and North Macedonia *Josef Djordjevski*	53
4	The Labor Movement as UNESCO World Heritage: Claiming a Seat for Workers through Assembly Halls *Marie Brøndgaard*	77
5	Approaching Balkan Dark/Dissonant Cultural Heritage Places through Visual Arts: The Case of the ECHO Project *Nikos Pasamitros*	97
6	The Champlain Quadricentennial: Celebrating 400 years of…? *Anastasia L. Pratt*	123
7	Fugitives No More: A Multinational Comparative Study of Maroon Heritage Preservation *Barry L. Stiefel*	145
8	Rediscovering the Roots That Remained Abroad: Challenges and Methods in Teaching Transborder Genealogy *Izabella Parowicz*	167

9	Stateless Heritage: The Sealing Sites of the South Shetland Islands, Antarctica *Michael Pearson and Melisa A. Salerno*	195
10	Aerospatial Heritage Sites: A Borderless, Transnational Heritage of Valued, Meaningful Sites at Altitude *Ryan N. Sisak*	223
Index		255
About the Editors and Contributors		271

Chapter 1

Heritage Without National Boundaries

Barry L. Stiefel and Shelley-Anne Peleg

Cultural heritage is the legacy received from the past, lived in the present, and passed on to future generations. Cultural heritage (tangible and intangible), its origins, and its practices are often confined to the boundaries of a nation-state. Tangible cultural heritage refers to material things, such as historical and archaeological monuments, landscapes, artifacts, and objects. Intangible cultural heritage refers to practices, representations, living expressions, knowledge, and skills inherited from the past considered to be part of a place's cultural heritage. Various heritage aspects are connected via common themes, regional climate zones or cultures, and spatial movement, and not necessarily by superimposed national borders. Borders change over time and space, and states also appropriate cultural heritage differently. Multinational frameworks attempt to reclaim all fields of heritage as global experiences and universal projects. International frameworks are focused on built and tangible heritage, as well as intangible and living heritage from across the globe and beyond (considering such things as the Space Race). Multicultural heritage frameworks adopt themes that cross boundaries and cover ideas, which are not exclusive and relate to people of many different nationalities. Therefore, transnational heritage conceptions are based on the understanding that aspects of culture are interconnected, including ties with natural heritage, which entails biodiversity, ecosystems, geological structures, and other natural resources. This means that tangible and intangible cultural heritage, as well as natural heritage, are often intersectional, and experts in the heritage field are encouraged to engage in international debates and discussions that address understanding heritage and its management in a diversity of ways. Some shared heritage practices, such as materials, ideas, and morals, are interpreted, "used," or presented in different ways.

Transnational History as a distinct field of study emerged during the early 2000s, as described by Pierre-Yves Saunier and Thomas Adam.[1] Saunier suggested that "[w]henever the historians' sources go 'beyond words,' and this is the case when you adopt a transnational perspective, archaeology is a card to be counted on."[2] Material culture can convey messages about life in the past as alternative evidence that historical documents are not always able to express, and hence enhance our understanding of history. Within some academic circles, archaeology is a subbranch of anthropology, which is often those engaged in the study and documentation of intangible heritage. So, archaeologists and anthropologists are highly intersectional with the recording and interpretation of cultural heritage, whether in its tangible or intangible forms, and the transnational nature of these early discourses is reflected in the work of these disciplines in addition to museum curators, naturalists, and others involved with heritage-related scholarship. Thus, the heritage preservation field is a multidisciplinary enterprise that reflects these many practices through the knowledge transfers that have occurred between practitioners and educators.

THE EMERGENCE OF MULTINATIONAL HERITAGE PRESERVATION BEFORE TRANSNATIONAL HISTORY

Cultural traditions and, by extension, heritage have existed long before the concept of the nation-state came into being. With the conglomeration of ancient city-states into the world's first empires (Egypt, Sumer, Babylonia, Assyria, etc.), multiple peoples and their associated cultures created multicultural societies. So, for a significant part of human history, cultural heritage has *not* always been defined or delineated by political borders. We find the evidence for this situation in the archaeological record as material remains also transcend national borders.[3] However, to better comprehend the current state of transnational heritage preservation, an understanding of recent historical developments is necessary. Knowledge of the history of transnational heritage preservation can help inform current trajectory and what future directions should be considered. While cultural and natural heritage can be created anywhere and everywhere (even in extraterrestrial locations like the moon), the development of its official documentation and preservation procedures has occurred within a transnational framework, primarily under the directive of multinational charters, conventions, and agreements as authorized heritage. The earliest document was the 1931 Athens Charter for the Restoration of Historic Monuments, which emerged under the guidance of the First International Congress of Architects and Technicians of Historic Monuments and was not driven by government-associated representatives of the respected countries. The attendees of the Congress significantly encouraged "acting in the spirit of the Covenant of the League of Nations," and collaboration between countries with the goal of furthering the preservation of "artistic and historic monuments."[4] The Second Congress of Architects, Conservationists and Technicians of Historical Monuments that convened in Venice, May 1964, established two important international frameworks that produced the infrastructure for preservation ethics and specified conservation and restoration procedures. The first is the establishment of the International Council on Monuments and Sites, ICOMOS, as a global nongovernmental organization, which is dedicated to promoting the application of theory, methodology, and scientific techniques for the conservation of architectural and archaeological heritage. The idea of a nongovernmental organization like ICOMOS, dedicated to heritage preservation from one end of the world to the other, was conceived long before by professionals in Europe, the United States, Brazil, Mexico, Japan, and India.[5] With a network of over ten thousand experts from all over the world, ICOMOS benefits from the interdisciplinary exchange of its members from many nation-states who collectively contribute to the improvement of the preservation of heritage and the standards and the techniques for each type of cultural heritage property.[6] The congress also ratified the Venice Charter for the Conservation and Restoration of Monuments and Sites, which also became an international framework. This Charter posed the concept of historic monuments and sites as common heritage and designated a common responsibility to safeguard their authenticity for future generations. The Venice Charter defined the basic principles that have since served and guided the conservation and restoration procedures of ancient and historic buildings all over the world, with each country being responsible for applying the framework according to its own culture and tradition.

Saving the Abu Simbel temple of Egypt in the 1960s initiated yet another revolutionary idea in heritage preservation. This was the first act to launch an international campaign to save a monument from being flooded by the waters of Lake Nasser. This co-spearheaded international operation became the drive for establishing a transnational convention with the main goal of establishing a worldwide force—the UNESCO World Heritage Convention—that could create and strengthen a sense of kinship and act as a single, global community to protect both cultural and natural heritage.[7] The World Heritage Convention of 1972, which defines UNESCO's multinational program of identifying and protecting the world's cultural and natural heritage sites found to be of Outstanding Universal Value, designates certain sites as having a cultural and/or natural significance that are so exceptional that they transcend national boundaries and are of general importance.

However, the 1972 Convention only covered tangible aspects of cultural, natural, and cultural-natural mixed heritage and did not address the intangible aspects of cultural heritage. Intangible cultural heritage includes traditions or living expressions inherited from our ancestors and passed on to our descendants, such as oral traditions, performing arts, social practices, rituals, festive events, knowledge and practices concerning nature and the universe, or the knowledge and skills to produce traditional crafts. These aspects are a means to maintain cultural diversity in the face of growing globalization, as well as represent the wealth of knowledge that is transmitted from one generation to the next. With this understanding, in 2003, UNESCO established the Convention for the Safeguarding of the Intangible Cultural Heritage.[8] With the goal of raising awareness and ensuring mutual appreciation at local, national, and international levels, the convention provides international cooperation and assistance to safeguard intangible cultural heritage and ensure respect of the communities, groups, and individuals concerned.[9]

Natural heritage preservation was included in the Convention of 1972, but it was not part of the charters of Athens or Venice. In 1971, there had been the Ramsar Convention on Wetlands by the United Nations, which was an intergovernmental treaty that created a framework for the conservation of wetlands, but it had a negligible influence on the UNESCO heritage convention the following year, even regarding natural heritage.[10] The modern concept of protecting nature emerged in the United States in 1872, a century earlier, with the establishment of Yellowstone National Park as the first such national park in the world and was a key step in the way preservation of natural heritage was approached administratively within state and interstate authorities. The purpose of a national park, for which Yellowstone was the prototype, was to set aside land in its natural state for the enjoyment of future generations, a novel concept in the nineteenth century.[11] The national park concept soon attracted tourists as well as drew the attention of other countries, spreading quickly to other parts of the world due to the same economic motivations as the United States, initiating the establishment of The Royal National Park (Australia, 1879), Banff National Park (Canada, 1885), Sarek National Park (Sweden, 1909), Virunga National Park (Congo, 1925), and Nahuel Huapi National Park (Argentina, 1934).[12] National park creation continued steadily with two coincidentally being established near each other along an international border, first in 1895 with Waterton Lakes National Park in Alberta, Canada, and then Glacier National Park by the United States in 1910, Montana. The siting of these two national parks was not at first planned or coordinated, though the reasons for respectively establishing both were the same regarding the protection of their awe-inspiring natural beauty.[13] However, further east, along the same international borderline at Boissevain-Morton, Alberta, and Rolette County, North Dakota, an intentional 3.65-mile^2 (5.87 kilometer^2) International Peace Garden was jointly established in 1929 due to its near-location as the geographical center of the American-Canadian border, though its purpose is recreational instead of natural or cultural heritage preservation. While the establishment of the International Peace Garden was influenced by a Rotary Club meeting in Waterton, Alberta, two years later both the Montana and the Alberta chapters were jointly in attendance. At the meeting, the members of the Rotary clubs from both countries introduced the idea that Waterton Lakes and Glacier national parks should be jointly managed together as a symbol of peace and friendship between their neighboring countries, in addition to nature conservation. Both Rotary chapters then petitioned their respective members of Congress and Parliament to formally create the first international peace park, which was completed in 1932. Seven years later, a Peace Arch Park was also created between Canada and the United States at Blaine, Washington/ Surrey, British Columbia, which, as an architectural monument, introduced a new kind of collaboration through the built environment.[14]

A striking contrast between the Athens and Venice charters with the parks/gardens discussed along the Canadian-American border is that the charters were policy-focused on anywhere whereas the parks were localized activities that an international boundary just so happened to bisect. This dichotomy is considered in chapters 3, 6, and 8 in this volume. The emergence of early transnational preservation of cultural sites also began very differently with the onset of the historic center of Rome. From 1929 to 1931, the Italian fascist government of Benito Mussolini both ratified the Lateran Treaty that re-established the Vatican as a sovereign papal state and unilaterally approved the Master Plan of Rome, which was the city's first major plan to address the preservation of ancient monuments.[15] Some of the ancient monuments are within the jurisdiction of the Holy See, technically making the Historic Centre of Rome a transnational heritage site. Thus, this early instance of transnational heritage preservation collaboration was born out of a top-down, authoritarian situation that was purposely created instead of grassroots-transborder multinationalism promoted through a nongovernmental organization. We have observed transnational heritage organized around the following circumstances: contiguous sites and intangible traditions that are bisected by a border (e.g., a Borderlands culture); discontiguous sites and traditions that transcend a national boundary; sites that transcend all national spaces by being stateless (e.g., Antarctica, international waters and extraterrestrial spaces); sites and traditions of indigenous and other conquered peoples that have had their lands unwilfully absorbed and borders nullified by a colonizing state, creating an intranational-transnational situation (e.g., indigenous peoples in the Americas, Australia, New Zealand, etc.); intangible cultural heritage and traditions that have spatially moved from one state to another within frameworks of immigration (e.g., the case of the Maroons, and Eastern European Genealogy) as well as the connection between nationalism, politics, and heritage (e.g., the crusader sites and the sites of violence in former Yugoslavia); joint collaborations targeted at documenting heritage, preserving heritage, and using heritage as a means to dialogue between nations (e.g., the ECHO project in the Balkans and the Champlain Quadricentennial celebrations); and shared heritage (e.g., Antarctica, the labor movement, and Aerospatial Heritage). Transnational heritage preservation circumstances can also be born out of circumstances that drive people apart instead of bringing them together, as we shall learn from chapter 5 in this volume.

THE STATE OF UNESCO TRANSNATIONAL HERITAGE PROGRAMS: TANGIBLE AND INTANGIBLE

Underscoring transnational heritage preservation are the dominating paradigms articulated in the World Heritage Convention of 1972, with its regulations establishing two forms of transnational listings: transboundary sites and serial sites.[16] Transboundary sites, according to the convention, are "on the territory of all concerned States Parties having adjacent borders" with proposals "prepared and submitted by States Parties jointly" as well as it being "highly recommended that the States Parties concerned establish a joint management committee or similar body to oversee the management of the whole of a transboundary property."[17] As of 2023 there were 1,154 properties on the World Heritage List, with forty-three sites that were transnational. This represents only 4 percent of the world's officially recognized heritage sites of outstanding universal value. However, of the 167 countries who participate in the World Heritage program created by the 1972 convention, sixty-seven countries have at least one site that is part of a transnational listing, with Germany having the most with ten. Twenty-six of the forty-three transnational World Heritage listings are cultural, with fifteen listed as natural and two sites as mixed cultural-natural. The distribution of transnational World Heritage Sites by continent places Europe at the highest with twenty-six, followed by Africa at six, Latin America with four, Asia with four, and North America with two. This breakdown reflects the political borders of these continents, where there are many nation-states in Europe and Africa, and fewer in Asia, Latin America, and North America, where countries such as Russia, Canada, the United States, China, and Brazil take up large land areas. Noticeably missing are Australia and the Pacific Ocean region where countries often only have aquatic instead of terrestrial land boundaries. However, compiling transnational World Heritage Sites by continent is complicated because listings can be dis-contiguous and spread across multiple continents, such as the Architectural Work of Le Corbusier, which is found in Europe, Asia, and South America, making this a truly transnational World

Heritage listing. Therefore, the continental tabulation is higher because serial properties located on multiple continents, as with Le Corbusier architectural sites, are counted more than once. Presently, the only transboundary World Heritage Site that is endangered is the Mount Nimba Strict Nature Reserve, between Côte d'Ivoire and Guinea, due to illegal poaching and human-caused wildfires to turn forested lands into agricultural land.

In 1979, the second year of listing properties to the World Heritage List, the natural heritage site of Kluane/Wrangell-St. Elias/Glacier Bay/Tatshenshini-Alsek between Canada and the United States became the first transboundary site recognized by UNESCO, and its establishment between the sub-jurisdictions of Alaska, British Columbia, and Yukon shared many parallels with the Waterton Lakes-Glacier International Peace Park model. Earlier in the 1970s, Waterton Lakes-Glacier was jointly recognized by UNESCO as a biosphere reserve, but not until 1995 was the International Peace Park added to the World Heritage List.[18] In 1980, the Historic Centre of Rome was jointly nominated by Italy and the Holy See as the first transboundary cultural site. As quickly as transboundary listings for natural and cultural heritage occurred after the World Heritage List's establishment in 1978, it was not until 2013 that the Maloti-Drakensberg Park in South Africa and Lesotho created the first mixed heritage listing.

The World Heritage Convention regulations designate that "[e]xtensions to an existing World Heritage property located in one State Party may be proposed to become transboundary properties."[19] The first instance was the proposal of the Białowieża Forest as a natural heritage site by Poland in 1979. Following the disintegration of the Soviet Union in 1991, relations improved with Belarus to extend the World Heritage listing across the border between Poland and Belarus. Both the Maloti-Drakensberg Park and Białowieża Forest examples show similarities with the Waterton Lakes-Glacier International Peace Park model of exceptional natural heritage in a location that just so happens to be bisected by a border that separated two countries and where the people from each respective side came together for collaboration. This one form of transboundary properties on the World Heritage List can also span across more than one state boundary, which the natural heritage W-Arly-Pendjari Complex demonstrated when it was expanded from Niger (first listed in 1996) to also include Benin and Burkina Faso in 2017.

The second form of transnational World Heritage listings are serial properties, but these can also occur within one nation such as the Wieliczka and Bochnia Royal Salt Mines, which are located exclusively in Poland (1979). The exemplar instance of a serial multinational cultural heritage nomination is the Architectural Work of Le Corbusier as well as the Struve Geodetic Arc, which was created in 2005 and comprises thirty-four sites distributed between ten countries, including Belarus, Estonia, Finland, Latvia, Lithuania, Norway,

Moldova, Russia, Sweden, and Ukraine. However, the most expansive serial site listing is the Ancient and Primeval Beech Forests of the Carpathians and Other Regions of Europe, first created in 2007 and extended in 2011 and 2017, which now entails a dozen countries across the continent including Albania, Austria, Belgium, Bulgaria, Croatia, Germany, Italy, Romania, Slovakia, Slovenia, Spain, and Ukraine. While having fewer listing examples in number, the multinational serial site listings of the Architectural Work of Le Corbusier, the Struve Geodetic Arc, and the Ancient and Primeval Beech Forests of the Carpathians and Other Regions of Europe take a very thorough approach to transnational tangible cultural and environmental history as conceptualized by Saunier and Adam. But what brings meaning to tangible heritage are cultural-based intangible heritage values, which must also be explored regarding UNESCO undertakings.

A third form of unique transnational listings are the few situations in which nominations created by a state for a site in another country or by authorities that are not yet recognized states. Although not a state, three Palestinian sites were inscribed on the UNESCO list and immediately recognized as sites in danger. As of 2023, the UNESCO World Heritage list includes fifty-two endangered sites, with the goal of informing the international community of conditions that threaten the very characteristics for which a property was inscribed on the World Heritage List, and to encourage corrective action.

Intangible Cultural Heritage is defined as an expression, knowledge, practice, representation, or skill that is part of a place's cultural heritage.[20] Intangible heritage is community-based and depends on those whose knowledge of traditions, skills, and customs are passed on to the rest of the community, from generation to generation, or to other communities. Various aspects of intangible heritage evolve in response to their environments and contribute to a sense of identity and continuity. The UNESCO Convention for the Safeguarding of the Intangible Cultural Heritage was created in 2003 because of the "deep-seated interdependence between the intangible cultural heritage and the tangible cultural and natural heritage,"[21] which was not sufficiently recognized by the World Heritage List and led to the creation of the Lists of Intangible Cultural Heritage and the Register of Good Safeguarding Practices with their first listings in 2008. These lists comprise the List of Intangible Cultural Heritage in Need of Urgent Safeguarding, the Representative List of the Intangible Cultural Heritage of Humanity, and the Register of Good Safeguarding Practices.[22] As of 2023, there were 628 intangible heritage elements on these three lists from 139 countries, with sixty being multinational by ninety-three countries. Therefore, nearly 10 percent of intangible heritage elements recognized by UNESCO are multinational, which is a significantly higher proportion compared to the tangible sites on the World Heritage List. This translates that two-thirds of

Table 1.1. Transboundary Sites on the UNESCO World Heritage List (as of January 2023)

Year	Site Name	Type	First Country	Second Country	Third Country and More
1979	Kluane / Wrangell-St. Elias / Glacier Bay / Tatshenshini-Alsek	Natural	Canada	USA	
1979/1992	Białowieża Forest	Natural	Poland	Belarus	
1979/2019	Natural and Cultural Heritage of the Ohrid region	Mixed	North Macedonia (Yugoslavia)	Albania	
1980	Historic Centre of Rome	Cultural	Holy See	Italy	
1981	Mount Nimba Strict Nature Reserve	Natural	Côte d'Ivoire	Guinea	
1983	Jesuit Missions of the Guaranis	Cultural	Brazil	Argentina	
1983/1990	Talamanca Range-La Amistad Reserves / La Amistad National Park	Natural	Costa Rica	Panama	
1987/2005/2021	Frontiers of the Roman Empire	Cultural	United Kingdom	Germany	Austria, Slovakia, Netherlands
1989	Mosi-oa-Tunya / Victoria Falls	Natural	Zambia	Zimbabwe	
1995	Caves of Aggtelek Karst and Slovak Karst	Natural	Hungary	Slovakia	
1995	Waterton Glacier International Peace Park	Natural	Canada	USA	
1996	W-Arly-Pendjari Complex	Natural	Benin	Burkina Faso	Niger
1998	Prehistoric Rock Art Sites in the Côa Valley and Siega Verde	Cultural	Portugal	Spain	
1999/2005	Belfries of Belgium and France	Cultural	Belgium	France	
2000	Curonian Spit	Cultural	Lithuania	Russia	
2000	High Coast / Kvarken Archipelago	Natural	Finland	Sweden	
2000	Maloti-Drakensberg Park	Mixed	Lesotho	South Africa	
2001	Fertö / Neusiedlersee Cultural Landscape	Cultural	Austria	Hungary	
2003/2010	Monte San Giorgio	Natural	Italy	Switzerland	
2004	Muskauer Park / Park Mużakowski	Cultural	Germany	Poland	
2005	Struve Geodetic Arc	Cultural	Belarus	Estonia	Finland, Latvia, Lithuania, Norway, Moldova, Russia, Sweden, Ukraine
2006	Stone Circles of Senegambia	Cultural	Gambia	Senegal	

(continued)

Table 1.1. (Continued)

Year	Site Name	Type	First Country	Second Country	Third Country and More
2007	Ancient and Primeval Beech Forests of the Carpathians and Other Regions of Europe	Natural	Albania	Austria	Belgium, Bulgaria, Croatia, Germany, Italy, Romania, Slovakia, Slovenia, Spain, Ukraine
2008	Rhaetian Railway in the Albula / Bernina Landscapes	Cultural	Italy	Switzerland	
2011	Prehistoric Pile Dwellings around the Alps	Cultural	Austria	France	Germany, Italy, Slovenia, Switzerland
2012	Heritage of Mercury. Almadén and Idrija	Cultural	Slovenia	Spain	
2012	Sangha Trinational	Natural	Cameroon	Central African Republic	Congo
2013	Wooden Tserkvas of the Carpathian Region	Cultural	Poland	Ukraine	
2014	Qhapaq Ñan, Andean Road System	Cultural	Argentina	Bolivia	Chile, Colombia, Ecuador, Peru
2014	Silk Roads: the Routes Network of Chang'an-Tianshan Corridor	Cultural	China	Kazakhstan	Kyrgyzstan
2016	Stećci Medieval Tombstone Graveyards	Cultural	Bosnia and Herzegovina	Croatia	Montenegro, Serbia
2016	The Architectural Work of Le Corbusier	Cultural	Argentina	Belgium	France, Germany, India, Japan, Switzerland
2016	Western Tien-Shan	Natural	Kazakhstan	Kyrgyzstan	Uzbekistan
2017	Landscapes of Dauria	Natural	Mongolia	Russia	
2017	Venetian Works of Defence between the sixteenth and seventeenth centuries: Stato da Terra-Western Stato da Mar	Cultural	Croatia	Italy	Montenegro
2019	Erzgebirge/Krušnohoří Mining Region	Cultural	Czechia	Germany	
2021	Colonies of Benevolence	Cultural	Belgium	Netherlands	
2021	The Great Spa Towns of Europe	Cultural	Austria	Belgium	Czechia, France, Germany, Italy, United Kingdom

https://whc.unesco.org/en/list/&&transboundary=1&order=year

state parties in the Convention of 2003 are also involved in the protection of a multinational intangible cultural heritage element. Multinational intangible heritage elements were equally representative from the onset of the Lists of Intangible Cultural Heritage program's establishment, starting with nine out of the first ninety in 2008, which was also the most robust year of listing. Presently, France participates with the most multinational intangible heritage elements, for a total of nine. Most multinational intangible heritage elements comprise two or three countries, representing a regionalized traditional cultural practice. However, Falconry, a Living Human Heritage, has eighteen countries spread across Africa, Asia, and Europe. Because of the number of transcontinental, multinational intangible heritage elements the data tabulation by continent is complicated and only shows that intangible heritage is more transnational than tangible heritage. Reflecting the history of Iberian colonialism, elements such as the Artisanal Talavera of Puebla and Tlaxcala, the Ceramics of Talavera de la Reina, and the El Puente del Arzobispo Making Process between Spain and Mexico are even transoceanic. Since countries such as Australia, Canada, the United Kingdom, and the United States have not ratified the Convention for the Safeguarding of the Intangible Cultural Heritage, large areas of the globe—especially the Anglophone world—are noticeably missing from UNESCO's Intangible Cultural Heritage programs.

Extra-jurisdictional heritage sites do exist, most notably in Antarctica and in outer space. However, the Historic Sites and Monuments program of the Antarctic Treaty System is not part of UNESCO, and a counterpart for heritage documentation in outer space has yet to be officially created.[23] Nonetheless, it should be recognized that there are other trans-global world heritage properties and intangible elements that UNESCO is involved with and that are not transboundary because they fall within a singular geopolitical entity with a colonial past and/or because the engagement of heritage preservation with UNESCO is being used as a political means over complicated sovereignty rights. Examples of the first instance are certain cultural and natural World Heritage Sites of the United Kingdom, with the sites of Gough and Inaccessible Islands (South Atlantic), Henderson Island (South Pacific), Historic Town of St. George and Related Fortifications (Bermuda), and Gorham's Cave Complex (Gibraltar) far from the metropole of the British Isles. France also has its own World Heritage Sites scattered away from Europe, including Piton's cirques and ramparts (Reunion Island), Taputapuātea (South Pacific), Lagoons of New Caledonia (South Pacific), and the French Austral Lands and Seas (South Indian Ocean). The same holds true for the Netherlands (Historic Area of Willemstad, Curaçao). For intangible heritage elements there is also France's Martinique yole (a boat building tradition) in the Caribbean. Within these geopolitical frameworks

Table 1.2. Transnational Intangible Heritage (as of 2021)

Year	Site Name	List	1st Country	2nd Country	3rd Country and More
2021	Arabic calligraphy: knowledge, skills, and practices	Representative	Saudi Arabia	Algeria	Bahrain, Egypt, Iraq, Jordan, Kuwait, Lebanon, Mauritania, Morocco, Oman, Palestine, Sudan, Tunisia, United Arab Emirates, Yemen
2021	Congolese rumba	Representative	Democratic Republic of the Congo	Congo	
2021	Nordic clinker boat traditions	Representative	Denmark	Finland	Iceland—Norway—Sweden
2020	Art of crafting and playing Mbira/Sansi, the finger-plucking traditional musical instrument	Representative	Malawi	Zimbabwe	
2020	Art of miniature	Representative	Azerbaijan	Iran	Turkey, Uzbekistan
2020	Camel racing, a social practice and a festive heritage associated with camels	Representative	United Arab Emirates	Oman	
2020	Craftsmanship of mechanical watchmaking and art mechanics	Representative	Switzerland	France	
2020	Knowledge, know-how, and practices pertaining to the production and consumption of couscous	Representative	Algeria	Mauritania	Morocco, Tunisia
2020	Musical art of horn players, an instrumental technique linked to singing, breath control, vibrato, resonance of place, and conviviality	Representative	France	Belgium	Luxembourg, Italy
2020	Ong Chun/Wangchuan/Wangkang ceremony, rituals and related practices for maintaining the sustainable connection between man and the ocean	Representative	China	Malaysia	

2020	Pantun	Representative	Indonesia	Malaysia	
2020	Pilgrimage to the St. Thaddeus Apostle Monastery	Representative	Iran	Armenia	
2020	The art of glass beads	Representative	Italy	France	
2020	Traditional intelligence and strategy game: Togyzqumalaq, Toguz Korgool, Mangala/Göçürme	Representative	Kazakhstan	Kyrgyzstan, Turkey	
2020	Traditional weaving of Al Sadu	Representative	Saudi Arabia	Kuwait	
2020	Tree beekeeping culture	Representative	Poland	Belarus	
2020	Craft techniques and customary practices of cathedral workshops, or Bauhütten, in Europe, know-how, transmission, development of knowledge, and innovation	Good Safeguarding	Germany	Austria	France, Norway, Switzerland
2019	Alpinism	Representative	France	Italy	Switzerland
2019	Artisanal talavera of Puebla and Tlaxcala (Mexico) and ceramics of Talavera de la Reina and El Puente del Arzobispo (Spain) making process	Representative	Mexico	Spain	
2019	Byzantine chant	Representative	Cyprus	Greece	
2019	Date palm, knowledge, skills, traditions and practices	Representative	Bahrain	Egypt	Iraq, Jordan, Kuwait, Mauritania, Morocco, Oman, Palestine, Saudi Arabia, Sudan, Tunisia, United Arab Emirates, Yemen
2019	Transhumance, the seasonal droving of livestock along migratory routes in the Mediterranean and in the Alps	Representative	Austria	Greece	Italy

(continued)

Table 1.2. (Continued)

Year	Site Name	List	1st Country	2nd Country	3rd Country and More
2018	Art of dry stone walling, knowledge and techniques	Representative	Croatia	Cyprus	France, Greece, Italy, Slovenia, Spain, Switzerland
2018	Avalanche risk management	Representative	Switzerland	Austria	
2018	Blaudruck/Modrotisk/Kékfestés/ Modrotlač, resist block printing and indigo dyeing in Europe	Representative	Austria	Czechia	Germany, Hungary, Slovakia
2018	Heritage of Dede Qorqud/Korkyt Ata/ Dede Korkut, epic culture, folk tales and music	Representative	Azerbaijan	Kazakhstan	Turkey
2018	Traditional Korean wrestling (Ssirum/ Ssireum)	Representative	North Korea	South Korea	
2017	llano work songs	Urgent Safeguarding	Colombia	Venezuela	
2017	Art of crafting and playing with Kamantcheh/ Kamancha, a bowed string musical instrument	Representative	Azerbaijan	Iran	
2017	Cultural practices associated to the first of March	Representative	Bulgaria	North Macedonia	Moldova, Romania
2017	Spring celebration, Hıdrellez	Representative	North Macedonia	Turkey	
2016/2021	Falconry, a living human heritage	Representative	Germany	Saudi Arabia	Austria, Belgium, United Arab Emirates, Spain, France, Hungary, Italy, Kazakhstan, Kyrgyzstan, Morocco, Mongolia, Netherlands, Pakistan, Poland, Portugal, Qatar, Spain, Syria, South Korea, Czechia
2016	Flatbread making and sharing culture: Lavash, Katyrma, Jupka, Yufka	Representative	Azerbaijan	Iran	Kazakhstan, Kyrgyzstan, Turkey

2016	Nawrouz, Novruz, Nowrouz, Nowrouz, Nawrouz, Nauryz, Nooruz, Nowrouz, Navruz, Nevruz, Nowruz, Navruz	Representative	Afghanistan	Azerbaijan	India, Iran, Iraq, Kazakhstan, Kyrgyzstan, Uzbekistan, Pakistan, Tajikistan, Turkmenistan, Turkey
2016	Puppetry	Representative	Slovakia	Czechia	
2016	Traditional wall-carpet craftsmanship	Representative	Moldova	Romania	
2015	Aitysh/Aitys, art of improvisation	Representative	Kazakhstan	Kyrgyzstan	
2015	Al-Razfa, a traditional performing art	Representative	United Arab Emirates	Oman	
2015	Arabic coffee, a symbol of generosity	Representative	United Arab Emirates	Saudi Arabia	Oman, Qatar
2015	Majlis, a cultural and social space	Representative	United Arab Emirates	Saudi Arabia	Oman, Qatar
2015	Marimba music, traditional chants and dances	Representative	Colombia	Ecuador	
2015	Summer solstice fire festivals in the Pyrenees	Representative	Andorra	Spain	France
2015	Tugging rituals and games	Representative	Cambodia	Philippines	South Korea, Viet Nam
2014	Al-Ayyala, a traditional performing art of the Sultanate of Oman and the United Arab Emirates	Representative	United Arab Emirates	Oman	
2014	Traditional knowledge and skills in making Kyrgyz and Kazakh yurts (Turkic nomadic dwellings)	Representative	Kazakhstan	Kyrgyzstan	
2013	Mediterranean diet	Representative	Cyprus	Croatia	Spain, Greece, Italy, Morocco, Portugal
2013	Men's group Colindat, Christmas-time ritual	Representative	Moldova	Romania	

(continued)

Table 1.2. (Continued)

Year	Site Name	List	1st Country	2nd Country	3rd Country and More
2013	Practices and knowledge linked to the Imzad of the Tuareg communities	Representative	Algeria	Mali	Niger
2012	Al-Taghrooda, traditional Bedouin chanted poetry	Representative	United Arab Emirates	Oman	
2012	Cultural practices and expressions linked to the balafon of the Senufo communities	Representative	Mali	Burkina Faso	Côte d'Ivoire
2009	Tango	Representative	Argentina	Uruguay	
2009	Safeguarding intangible cultural heritage of Aymara communities	Good Safeguarding	Bolivia	Chile	Peru
2008	Baltic song and dance celebrations	Representative	Estonia	Latvia	Lithuania
2008	Gule Wamkulu	Representative	Malawi	Mozambique	Zambia
2008	Kankurang, Manding initiatory rite	Representative	Gambia	Senegal	
2008	Language, dance, and music of the Garifuna	Representative	Belize	Guatemala	Honduras, Nicaragua
2008	Oral heritage and cultural manifestations of the Zápara people	Representative	Ecuador	Peru	
2008	Oral heritage of Gelede	Representative	Benin	Nigeria	
2008	Processional giants and dragons	Representative	Belgium	France	Togo
2008	Shashmaqom music	Representative	Uzbekistan	Tajikistan	
2008	Urtiin Duu, traditional folk long song	Representative	China	Mongolia	

https://ich.unesco.org/en/lists?text=&multinational=2&display1=inscriptionID#tabs

the transglobal management of heritage sites and elements are recognized but single-nationally since no international borders are involved.[24]

In the Middle East another situation has emerged where several geopolitical entities are using UNESCO heritage program recognition as a means to further a sovereignty agenda. The Convention of 1972 states that the "inclusion of a property in the World Heritage List requires the consent of the State concerned,"[25] but when there is a dispute over such a property there are always at least two or more sides to consider. The first such example is the Old City of Jerusalem and its Walls, which was nominated by Jordan in 1981. The issue with Jerusalem is that its territorial sovereignty in 1981 was disputed.[26] In summary, the Jordanian government believed Jerusalem was their city even though they had lost police power in 1967 because it was (and continues to be) under the control of the Israeli government. The Israeli government felt that its sovereignty was being violated by Jordan's nomination because Jerusalem was under its control, and it was never asked nor gave consent as a concerned state party to the nomination. In contrast to both claims, neutral Switzerland interjected during the discussion for the World Heritage nomination because of "the special status of Jerusalem (*corpus separatum* according to the 1947 partition plan of the United Nations). The Swiss government contended that, according to this agreement, the City of Jerusalem is situated neither on Jordanian nor on Israeli territory,"[27] and thus neither party could solely nominate it to the World Heritage List. The transnational and trans-religious importance of the Old City of Jerusalem and its Walls to Christians, Muslims, and Jews was never disputed. A bi- or multinational nomination for Jerusalem with Jordan and Israel was never proposed, though to this day the Old City of Jerusalem and its Walls remain a "Site proposed by Jordan" but officially unassigned to any state party, with the area managed by the Israel Antiquities Authority and the Jordanian-sponsored Jerusalem Islamic Waqf.

In 1988, Jordan renounced its claims to Jerusalem and signed a peace treaty with Israel in 1994 that also recognized Jordan as a stakeholder in the Old City's Muslim Holy shrines, with another agreement in 2013 between Jordan and the Palestinian Authority confirming the previous Jordanian-Israeli agreements. Thus, a convoluted, yet successful transnational system of heritage management has been created between Jordan and Israel for the Old City of Jerusalem and its Walls in relation to the UNESCO World Heritage List program. Unfortunately, since 2012 there has emerged and continues to exist a contentious situation between Israel and the Palestinian Authority's three sites that it has nominated to the World Heritage List.[28] The Palestinian Authority has been involved with UNESCO's Lists of Intangible Cultural Heritage programs since 2008, when it nominated Hikaye (a narrative expression of storytelling). The other intangible element of the

Palestinian Authority recognized by UNESCO is the multinational Date Palm, Knowledge, Skills, Traditions and Practices listing that also includes Bahrain, Egypt, Iraq, Jordan, Kuwait, Mauritania, Morocco, Oman, Saudi Arabia, Sudan, Tunisia, the United Arab Emirates, and Yemen. Notably missing is Israel, which does have a date palm tradition, but like several other countries mentioned previously has not ratified the 2003 UNESCO Convention.[29] Due to strained political relations between Israel and several of its Arab neighbors it is unlikely that Israel will be included in this intangible transnational cultural heritage element listing either. The Old City of Jerusalem and its Walls as well as two of the three cultural heritage sites nominated by the Palestinian Authority were also identified by UNESCO as in danger, which signifies that when there are contentions between state parties over sovereignty or territory, this can imperil the future of such heritage sites and associated cultural traditions.

ORGANIZATION OF THIS VOLUME

Scholars from a variety of countries have worked alone as well as collaborated in examining case studies of transnational-related heritage preservation, creating a very large body of knowledge. Covering the full extent of heritage scholarship associated with a transnational situation is beyond the scope of this volume. However, *Towards World Heritage: International Origins of the Preservation Movement, 1870–1930*, edited by Melanie Hall, provides a valuable prologue to this volume in how heritage practitioners arrived at their current theories and methodologies. Within *Towards World Heritage* is a survey of the transnational history of heritage preservation case studies that covers (the present countries of) Canada, France, Germany, Israel, Sri Lanka, Sweden, the United Kingdom, and the United States.[30] *Towards World Heritage* is an exceptional history of transnational heritage preservation collaboration and knowledge sharing that is very specific to the decades between 1870 and 1930, with Yellowstone National Park and the Athens Charter serving as a symbolic beginning and ending. Other recent transnational-specific heritage-related publications include *Cultural Heritage, Transnational Narratives, and Museum Franchising in Abu Dhabi* by Sarina Wakefield, *Mobilizing Heritage: Anthropological Practice and Transnational Prospects* by Samuels K. Lafrenz and Paul A. Shackel, and *Regulating Transnational Heritage: Memory, Identity, and Diversity* by Merima Bruncevic. These publications are very contemporary-focused case studies on examples of heritage preservation related to museums and public history, which is another intersectional interest of Heritage Studies scholars.[31]

Within this volume, we begin our investigation with the history of transnational cultural landscapes and associated conservation efforts of Crusader heritage by Shelley-Anne Peleg. This chapter concentrates on the Crusader fortifications and castles in historic urban landscapes throughout the Eastern Mediterranean. Examples from Greece, Cyprus, Lebanon, Syria, and Israel illustrate common features in these monuments and demonstrate that although geographically separated, these fortifications and castles share many architectural characteristics and are expressions of one culture. This chapter shows that even strong current borders cannot prevent the common place of these remnants in modern cities. The fortifications and structures presented in this chapter are now touristic destinations in historic urban landscapes and protected heritage spaces. The chapter suggests that although these fortifications and castles have lost their original functions as systems that physically protected a city, they have obtained a new task in the current historic urban landscapes: the physical means to safeguard aspects of historic urban landscapes mentioned in the UNESCO Recommendations on the historic urban landscapes. Therefore, fortifications and castles in these cities are not only iconic historic attributes of the past but constitute in the present an important duty of preserving cultural heritage, civic pride, and identity. The chapter also draws attention to the relationship between nationalism and heritage, especially in national and colonial projects, and shows how in a region of competing claims, sites connected to the history of the Crusades attracted the attention of major European powers. These cross-cutting linkages allow us to use the Crusader sites as a prism for understanding the connection between heritage and transnationalism. However, imperial actors were not the only ones interested in these sites. Greek, Arab, and Israeli nationalists also used their own agendas for preserving this heritage.

Josef Djordjevski reveals in the third chapter the vital importance of world heritage to Yugoslavia and its successor states by examining historical and contemporary contingencies in three major settings. The sites addressed in this chapter are both UNESCO World Heritage Sites and important tourist destinations in each respective country: Dubrovnik in Croatia, Kotor in Montenegro, and Ohrid in North Macedonia. With the induction of these three sites into the World Heritage List in 1980, Yugoslavia became unique on the world stage, as a Socialist Federation, for the amount of protected natural and built heritage sites. The recognition of these sites by UNESCO coincided with a dramatic rise in mass tourism to the country and the continued significance of Yugoslavia's geopolitical position in Cold War relations between East and West. However, after the collapse of the Yugoslav Federation in 1991 and the bloody civil wars that followed, each of these sites were suddenly divided between and confined within the borders of three different, newly independent countries. The question addressed in this chapter is the role these World Heritage Sites played in both transcending and (re)creating boundaries and identities for each respective nation in times of dramatic change and transformation. The author argues that by examining the interconnections and interdependencies between nation branding, tourism, and the environment in these three cases, it becomes possible to see how they have transcended boundaries by coproducing cultural, economic, and environmental bridges between local, transnational, interethnic, and global contexts. The chapter also exposes their potential to create or reinforce internal divisions as well as establish connections between the former Yugoslavia, Europe, and the world. These sites that were once meant to show the commonalities between the Yugoslav peoples now served to reify national and ethnic prescriptions in the post-socialist nation building processes in Croatia, Montenegro, and North Macedonia.

In the fourth chapter, Marie Brøndgaard discusses the place of UNESCO and World Heritage as a global instrument using workers' assembly halls as a case study. She suggests that the labor movement should be a UNESCO World Heritage and argues that the workers' assembly halls from across many parts of the world are significant in the way they brought together workers for political, social, cultural, and educational purposes. These buildings bear testimony to the daily work and organization of the labor movement as a major force in shaping democracy and welfare across the world and have been instrumental in the organization of workers in the socialist labor movement, a still living tradition. Tied together through common ideological values and organizational practicalities, workers' assembly halls confirm the labor movement as a global phenomenon and cultural practice. Simultaneously, the individual characteristics of the buildings demonstrate how the labor movement has manifested itself in different parts of the world and adapted to local conditions. Brøndgaard explores a unique, untraditional approach to identifying workers' assembly halls that illustrate intangible values of the labor movement. This chapter suggests that a transnational serial nomination of these buildings contributes to a balanced heritage practice by applying a bottom-up approach. Such a call could serve as an invitation across political and cultural organizations, history networks, and the general public, uniting all regions of the world where the labor movement was or is present, thus introducing international collaboration. This research elucidates a different interpretation to shared heritage by exploring impacts of international frameworks on formalized heritage preservation and highlights shared heritage as a transnational matter.

In chapter 5, Nikos Pasamitros shows how different contexts influence the way that cultural heritage is viewed and used. The chapter presents the European Cultural Heritage Onstage (ECHO) creative project as an example of an alternative approach to the collective traumatic experiences of

European/Balkan communities (also regarded as dark heritage) and discusses how Authorized Heritage Discourse (AHD) has favored national management and use, while the universal framework subscribes and considers this heritage as an object of world value. These frameworks have been criticized for excluding and marginalizing sub-ethnic groups and subgroups as well as sub-national groups and subgroups. Critical approaches call for the inclusion of these groups and for community involvement in heritage management and for the broadening of perceptions of intangible heritage to meet the needs of local communities. The chapter presents the ECHO project as a guide to an alternative approach, one that promotes a multilayered view of heritage as local and at the same time as Balkan and European. Using dark heritage as a common feature, the ECHO program brought together communities and people from different Balkan countries through a joint artistic project, starting from the common European and Balkan identity of the communities, regardless of their national identity. It enabled local communities to reflect on intergenerational trauma and to speak about it through the process of co-creation and the artistic expression of people who did not belong to the local communities and demonstrated that such creative projects can provide an alternative that has a significant impact on the domestic communities and artists involved. Undertaking a transnational, pan-European approach, this project gave priority to organizations and, through them, to local communities to avoid the trap of the universalist approach. Thus, it increased the local involvement and ownership, and tried to incorporate the perceptions of nondominant, sub-ethnic groups and subgroups. The project shows that traumatic experiences can be an aspect of common heritage between locals and foreigners.

In the sixth chapter, Anastasia L. Pratt presents the Quadricentennial celebrations in 2008 and 2009 throughout Quebec, Ontario, New York, and New England celebrating Samuel de Champlain's arrival in North America. Ranging from conferences and publications to exhibitions and the creation of works of art, this chapter shows how the commemorations tended toward a shared version of history that recognizes Champlain as a kinder, gentler sort of explorer and that characterizes interactions between Champlain and Indigenous peoples as friendly and cooperative. Unlike most earlier commemorations, these events formally recognized Indigenous communities, but it seems clear that they did not go far enough in representing the cultural heritage shared by all of those who inhabited lands explored by Champlain. Through a description of the commemorative activities involved in the Quadricentennial Celebrations and a careful analysis of how those activities expressed a shared cultural heritage, this chapter probes questions of representation. The connections between the various peoples (American, Canadian, and First Nations) and the role of Lake Champlain itself, as well as the valley surrounding it, are considered major factors in the creation of a shared heritage. Since representation matters, this analysis also leads to suggestions about how to remember Champlain and his actions and how to remember the Indigenous people, communities, and cultures he encountered. The chapter looks at the history and heritage of the communities built along Lake Champlain and examines the representation of (shared) ownership of a heritage that is commemorated regularly and that has many physical manifestations in the form of statues, exhibitions, and historical markers.

In chapter 7, Barry L. Stiefel provides a comparative analysis of four case studies in the United States, Mauritius, Jamaica, and Suriname involving the preservation of maroon heritage. The four cases presented in this chapter view the heritage of run-away slaves who liberated themselves by escaping their masters and finding refuge in isolated locations as diasporic (dispersed through the slave trade) and migratory (due to their ancestor's escape from bondage) heritage. The discussion addresses how each respective country perceives and manages this diasporic group's heritage in respect to their own preservation policies. It also considers how countries with maroon heritage interface with the international heritage preservation programs of UNESCO. Bringing together this assemblage of maroon heritage sites, this chapter provides new insights into the management of maroon culture and the reasons for why its preservation is more visible in some places as compared to others—a comprehensive approach to maroon heritage preservation that has not been taken before. Assessing the differences in approach and treatment of maroon heritage preservation between countries is important to understand where and why successes and failures are occurring. From these findings an exchange of knowledge can lead to improvements in practice regarding maroon heritage preservation among other cultures that could learn from these approaches. This chapter explores the strengths, weaknesses, opportunities, and threats posed by various national preservation policies to a shared cultural heritage. Rarely does the public understand that maroon heritage is diasporic across a vast geographic expanse, though having a common African root, and that all maroons share the experience of multiple migrations.

In chapter 8, Izabella Parowicz provides insights into a teaching project at the European University Viadrina in Frankfurt an der Order (Germany) that focuses on genealogy. This university attracts numerous students from Central and Eastern Europe. Students who took the course on genealogy engage with exploring their own family histories that included ancestors of various ethnic, linguistic, and religious background. This chapter addresses how students of trans-border genealogy confront the complex history of Polish territories that were annexed in the eighteenth century by the three partitioning powers of Prussia, Russia, and Austria, and their navigation through issues such as researching in a foreign country and language, deciphering metrics written in at least four languages (Polish, Russian, Latin, and German), and unfamiliarity with local bureaucratic procedures. Parowicz demonstrates how personal genealogy research can lead to rethinking and redefining one's own identity, how one's own heritage can supersede national boundaries, and that family history is frequently very complex and cannot be contained within the context of one nation only.

Michael Pearson and Melisa A. Salerno take us beyond the nation-state paradigm in their chapter on stateless heritage in Antarctica. This chapter looks at the statelessness of Antarctica, the origin of this status, and how it is perpetuated. It further discusses how the Antarctic Treaty system might yet be used to protect and conserve cultural sites in Antarctica along with other aspects of the natural environment and that it likewise protects heritage in the absence of national boundaries. Pearson and Salerno examine the influence of the sealing industry in the early nineteenth century and the closely associated whaling industry as a global enterprise. Both authors describe how sealers discovered the South Shetland Islands in the Antarctic Peninsular region of Antarctica and, thereby, triggered a sealing boom which saw vessels from the United Kingdom, the United States, Australia, Chile, and Argentina landing sealing gangs to gather fur seal pelts and elephant seal oil. Sealer camp sites set up on the islands, consisting of occupied caves and stone-walled shelters, are now being located and studied by archaeological survey, excavation, and recording. While originating mainly from British and American occupants, these sites are not claimed by or protected by those nations—as the 1961 Antarctic Treaty specifically sets aside any national territorial claims. This chapter also presents how the Antarctic Treaty's national parties have tended to ignore the heritage value and conservation needs of these highly important sealing sites for a variety of reasons, including the fact that they reflect a bloody exploitative industry that sits uneasily within the Antarctic Treaty ideals of Antarctica as a nature reserve dedicated to science and peace, and, as such, the sealing sites do not advance the unstated nationalistic aspirations of the nations involved. In addition, the chapter discusses how, in view of the lack of national interest or responsibility, and the uneasy fit with Antarctic Treaty priorities, the sealing sites have not received sufficient consideration in terms of their protection and conservation. Therefore, the work of studying the sealing sites has been carried out by university and museum-based archaeological teams (none of which were based in the United Kingdom or United States), and while these have had logistical support from their respective national Antarctic program managers, no nation has proposed that the sites be protected as Antarctic heritage.

For the last chapter by Ryan N. Sisak, we leave the confines of Earth and explore options for the widespread recognition, designation, and interpretation of heritage sites in outer space. The entire concept of Sisak's work focuses on quasi-immaterial locations, paths, and regions in outer space or at altitude, exploring sites that are entirely untethered from a celestial object or any other tangible object (as most would understand tangible to imply). Aerospatial Heritage Sites contribute to the broader cultural landscapes created by the history of aeronautics and spaceflight—from just outside the Earth's atmosphere, where humans first left Earth en route to the Moon, to the place where humans first orbited and landed on another celestial body. Recognizing significant places in outer space as Aerospatial Heritage Sites transforms ordinary, unremarkable places into notable, remarkable heritage sites. As places in outer space have yet to be officially recognized as heritage, Sisak demonstrates their heritage potential by engaging in a synthetic phenomenology of place and landscape. He investigates places and landscapes visited in outer space, conveying the unique nature of these heritage sites, terming them Aerospatial Heritage Sites. This chapter demonstrates how Sisak's approach can facilitate heritage management practices that are less institutional and more personal, thereby aiding to circumvent and weaken the politics of the Authorized Heritage Discourse.

REFLECTIONS AND FINDINGS: HOW TRANSNATIONAL ARE UNESCO'S WORLD HERITAGE PROGRAMS?

To be recognized by UNESCO a cultural/natural tangible property or intangible cultural element must have Outstanding Universal Value, which means that it "is so exceptional as to transcend national boundaries and to be of common importance for present and future generations of all humanity."[32] Therefore, UNESCO's World Heritage programs are inherently transnational in their established purpose. Previous studies have debated the subjective aspect of "outstanding universal value" and the implications for heritage that is "less than outstanding," and, therefore, unworthy of UNESCO's recognition or frameworks for protection.[33] There is a gray area on what constitutes a transnational heritage management framework even outside of extra-territorial locations (Antarctica and outer space), such as the sites and elements under the colonial jurisdiction of the United Kingdom, France, the Netherlands, and Denmark, as well as the complicated situation between Israel and its neighbors, Jordan and the Palestinian Authority, but otherwise far less subjective.

In response to Saunier's inspired approach of inquiry, transnational heritage is everywhere but more often than not listings that entail more than one state party are localized in a borderlands' situation, as exemplified by the US-Canada International Peace Park model. Most transborder intangible cultural heritage practices also reflect this dynamic of localization. This is not too surprising considering that 96 percent of cultural and natural World Heritage Sites are *not* transboundary, as well as 90 percent of intangible cultural elements. Therefore, transnational heritage as represented through UNESCO's listing programs is primarily place-specific, which greatly reflects the mantra that in order to think globally one really has to act locally. Large-scale transboundary sites as recognized by UNESCO are in the minority, to which the Architectural Work of Le Corbusier, the Struve Geodetic Arc, the Ancient and Primeval Beech Forests of the Carpathians and Other Regions of Europe, and Falconry, A Living Human Heritage testify. However, this does not mean that other transnational heritages do not exist—they simply have gone unrecognized by UNESCO. For instance, there are already more than a dozen cathedrals and churches on the World Heritage List due to their Gothic architecture. There is also a plethora of historic places associated with colonial empires as well as transoceanic trades, slavery, and industrialization.[34] These many sites could be consolidated into a single World Heritage Listing, which would not only be transnational but also better reflect the purpose of Outstanding Universal Value as well as the goals of the *Global Strategy* for a World Heritage List that is better balanced and representative. Another transnational, bioregional version of Europe's Primeval Beech Forests presently unrecognized by UNESCO is the Taiga, the world's largest biome that spans across northern Eurasia and North America.

Intangible cultural heritage listings also mostly focus on heritage homelands with little connection to their associated diasporas. Christa Kearns, a former student of Stiefel, did her North American-based thesis on her ancestral Italian culinary heritage, tying it directly to the multinational intangible tradition of the Mediterranean Diet, which, besides Italy, includes Cyprus, Croatia, Spain, Greece, Morocco, and Portugal.[35] Kearns noted that the "Mediterranean diet involves a set of skills, knowledge, rituals, symbols and traditions concerning crops, harvesting, fishing, animal husbandry, conservation, processing, cooking, and particularly the sharing and consumption of food [as well as e]ating together [which creates] continuity of communities throughout the Mediterranean basin,"[36] and also found that her family continued these traditions after migrating to the United States.[37] Thus, intercultural transfers of cultural heritages across borders is largely being unrecognized by UNESCO's programs, and this is a hypothetical modification for the program to consider.[38]

UNESCO's World Heritage programs are a product of the state parties that created them through the convention process, which is why the emphasis of all forms of heritage is reflected with the state party as the fundamental unit, and not the physicality of the heritage site or element. The administrative structure based on the state party structure is also the reason for the organization of UNESCO World Heritage programs by sovereign territories even in transnational instances. Because of this organizational setup, heritages of the commons (Antarctica, outer space, etc.) are absent from the UNESCO World Heritage programs. To approach heritage recognition in any other way would necessitate ignoring the importance of sovereignty so that it is beyond the nation-state. The denationalization and deterritorialization of global heritage administration has not occurred and likely could only happen in a nongovernmental organizational structure or academia where nationality could be made unimportant. But, then, if heritage were to be denationalized, can it remain transnational if there are no borders to transcend?[39]

NOTES

1. Pierre-Yves Saunier, *Transnational History*, New York: Palgrave Macmillan, vii; and Thomas Adam, *Intercultural Transfers and the Making of the Modern World, 1800–2000*, New York: Palgrave Macmillan, 2011, 1–7.

2. Saunier, *Transnational History*, 128.

3. See Eric H. Cline and Mark W. Graham, *Ancient Empires: From Mesopotamia to the Rise of Islam*, Cambridge: Cambridge University Press, 2011.

4. *Charter for the Restoration of Historic Monuments*, Article VII, Section a), Athens, the 1st International Congress of Architects and Technicians of Historic Monuments, 1931.

5. *The First General Assembly of ICOMOS-1965 Cracow, Poland, Regulations, by-laws and national committees*, in: SJ Thirty Years of ICOMOS (https://www.icomos.org/publications/JS5_1.pdf, accessed May 20, 2022).

6. Information about ICOMOS comes from: https://www.icomos.org/en/about-icomos/mission-and-vision/mission-and-vision.

7. *Abu Simbel: The Campaign that Revolutionized the International Approach to Safeguarding Heritage*, UNESCO (https://en.unesco.org/70years/abu_simbel_safeguarding_heritage?, accessed May 20, 2022).

8. *Convention for the Safeguarding of the Intangible Cultural Heritage*, Preamble, Paris, 32nd Session of UNESCO, 2003.

9. *Text of the Convention for the Safeguarding of the Intangible Cultural Heritage*, (https://ich.unesco.org/en/convention, accessed May 20, 2022).

10. "A brief history," *International Union for Conservation of Nature* (2021) (https://www.iucn.org/about/iucn-a-brief-history, accessed May 13, 2021).

11. Barry L. Stiefel, "A Tale of Two Plains: Natural Heritage Conservation on North America's Prairie," in: Anthony Amato (ed.), *Conservation on the Northern Plains: New Perspectives*, Sioux Falls: Augustana College's Center for Western Studies, 2017, 74–92.

12. Christina Djossa, *These Are the World's First National Parks* (5 November 2020) (https://www.nationalgeographic.co.uk/2018/09/these-are-worlds-first-national-parks-1, accessed May 13, 2021).

13. Stiefel, "A Tale of Two Plains," 74–92.
14. Stiefel, "A Tale of Two Plains," 74–92.
15. See Borden W. Painter, *Mussolini's Rome: Rebuilding the Eternal City*, New York: Palgrave Macmillan, 2005.
16. The data on UNESCO World Heritage Sites comes from "World Heritage List," *UNESCO World Heritage Centre* (2021) (https://whc.unesco.org/en/list/, accessed May 20, 2021).
17. *Convention Concerning the Protection of the World Cultural and Natural Heritage*, Article III, Section C, Clauses 134–135, Paris, 17th Session of UNESCO, 1972.
18. Graham MacDonald, *Where the Mountains Meet the Prairies: A History of Waterton Country*, Calgary: University of Calgary Press, 2000, 90.
19. *Convention Concerning the Protection of the World Cultural and Natural Heritage*, Article III, Section C, Clauses 136, Paris, 17th Session of UNESCO, 1972.
20. The data on UNESCO intangible cultural heritage comes from "Browse the Lists of Intangible Cultural Heritage and the Register of good safeguarding practices," *Intangible Cultural Heritage* (2021) (https://ich.unesco.org/en/lists/, accessed May 20, 2021). Also see *Convention for the Safeguarding of the Intangible Cultural Heritage*, Paris, 32nd Session of UNESCO, 2003.
21. *Convention for the Safeguarding of the Intangible Cultural Heritage*, Preamble, 2nd Considering, Paris, 32nd Session of UNESCO, 2003.
22. "The List of Intangible Cultural Heritage in Need of Urgent Safeguarding (see criteria) is composed of intangible heritage elements that concerned communities and states parties consider require urgent measures to keep them alive. Inscriptions on this List help to mobilize international cooperation and assistance for stakeholders to undertake appropriate safeguarding measures. The Representative List of the Intangible Cultural Heritage of Humanity (see criteria) is made up of those intangible heritage elements that help demonstrate the diversity of this heritage and raise awareness about its importance. The Register of Good Safeguarding Practices contains programs, projects and activities that best reflect the principles and the objectives of the Convention." "Purpose of the Lists of Intangible Cultural Heritage and of the Register of Good Safeguarding Practices," and "Browse the Lists of Intangible Cultural Heritage and the Register of good safeguarding practices," *Intangible Cultural Heritage* (2021) (https://ich.unesco.org/en/purpose-of-the-lists-00807, accessed May 20, 2021).
23. The data for this section comes from "World Heritage List," *UNESCO World Heritage Centre* (2021) (https://whc.unesco.org/en/list/, accessed May 20, 2021); and "Browse the Lists of Intangible Cultural Heritage and the Register of good safeguarding practices," *Intangible Cultural Heritage* (2021) (https://ich.unesco.org/en/lists/, accessed May 20, 2021).
24. For example, see Francesca Cigna, Deodato Tapete, and Kathryn Lee, "Geological Hazards in the UNESCO World Heritage Sites of the UK: From the Global to the Local Scale Perspective," *Earth-Science Reviews* 176, no. XX (2018): 166–194.
25. *Convention Concerning the Protection of the World Cultural and Natural Heritage*, Article 11, Section 3, Paris, 17th Session of UNESCO, 1972.

26. See Michael Dumper and Craig Larkin, "The Politics of Heritage and the Limitations of International Agency in Contested Cities: A Study of the Role of UNESCO in Jerusalem's Old City," in: *Review of International Studies* 38, no. 1 (2012): 25–52.

27. UNESCO, "Analysis and Conclusion by World Heritage Centre and the Advisory Bodies in 1982," *State of Conservation* (1982) (https://whc.unesco.org/en/soc/1518, accessed May 20, 2021).

28. Tzvi Ben Gedalyahu, "PA Tells UNESCO Dead Sea an Arab 'Heritage Site'," *Arutz Sheva: Israel National News* (November 2, 2011) (https://www.israelnationalnews.com/News/News.aspx/149341, accessed May 20, 2021); and Khaldun Bshara, "Preservation of Heritage in Palestine: A Rising Awareness of an Imperiled Treasure," *Palestinian Journeys* (2021) (https://www.paljourneys.org/en/timeline/highlight/10524/preservation-heritage-palestine, accessed May 20, 2021).

29. "Culinary Traditions: History," *Intangible Cultural Heritage of Israel Center* (2019) (https://www.ich-israel.com/culinary-traditions, accessed May 20, 2021).

30. See Melanie Hall (ed.), *Towards World Heritage: International Origins of the Preservation Movement, 1870–1930*, London: Routledge, 2016.

31. Sarina Wakefield, *Cultural Heritage, Transnational Narratives, and Museum Franchising in Abu Dhabi*, London: Routledge, 2021; Samuels K. Lafrenz and Paul A. Shackel, *Mobilizing Heritage: Anthropological Practice and Transnational Prospects*, Gainesville: University Press of Florida, 2018; and Merima Bruncevic, *Regulating Transnational Heritage: Memory, Identity, and Diversity*, London: Routledge, 2021.

32. "Operational Guidelines," *World Heritage Policy Compendium* (2021) (https://whc.unesco.org/en/compendium/action=list&id_faq_themes=962, accessed May 20, 2021).

33. Damna A. Alzahrani, "The Adoption of a Standard Definition of Cultural Heritage," in: *International Journal of Social Science and Humanity* 3, no. 1 (2013): 9–12.

34. Barry L. Stiefel, "Rethinking and Reevaluating UNESCO World Heritage Sites: Lessons Experimented within the USA," *Journal of Cultural Heritage Management and Sustainable Development* 8, no. 1 (2018): 47–61.

35. Christa Kearns, "My Big Fat Italian Heritage," in: Barry L. Stiefel (ed.), *What is Your Heritage and the State of its Preservation? Volume 2: Collaborations with Storyboard America*, Berwyn Heights: Heritage Books, 2016, 83–114.

36. "Mediterranean Diet," *Intangible Cultural Heritage* (2013) (https://ich.unesco.org/en/RL/mediterranean-diet-00884, accessed May 21, 2021).

37. Kearns, "My Big Fat Italian Heritage," 83–114.

38. Thomas Adam, "New Ways to Write the History of Western Europe and the United States: The Concept of Intercultural Transfer," *History Compass*, 11, no. 10 (2013): 880–892.

39. Thomas Adam, "Transnational History: A Program for Research, Publishing, and Teaching," *Yearbook of Transnational History* 1 (2018): 1–8.

BIBLIOGRAPHY

Adam, Thomas. *Intercultural Transfers and the Making of the Modern World, 1800–2000*. New York: Palgrave Macmillan, 2011.

———. "New Ways to Write the History of Western Europe and the United States: The Concept of Intercultural Transfer." *History Compass* 11, no. 10 (2013): 880–892.

———. "Transnational History: A Program for Research, Publishing, and Teaching." *Yearbook of Transnational History* 1 (2018): 1–8.

Alzahrani, Damna A. "The Adoption of a Standard Definition of Cultural Heritage." *International Journal of Social Science and Humanity* 3, no. 1 (2013): 9–12.

Bruncevic, Merima. *Regulating Transnational Heritage: Memory, Identity, and Diversity*. London: Routledge, 2021.

Cline, Eric H., and Mark W. Graham. *Ancient Empires: From Mesopotamia to the Rise of Islam*. Cambridge: Cambridge University Press, 2011.

Dumper, Michael, and Craig Larkin. "The Politics of Heritage and the Limitations of International Agency in Contested Cities: A Study of the Role of UNESCO in Jerusalem's Old City." *Review of International Studies* 38, no. 1 (2012): 25–52.

Hall, Melanie, ed. *Towards World Heritage: International Origins of the Preservation Movement, 1870–1930*. London: Routledge, 2016.

Kearns, Christa. "My Big Fat Italian Heritage." In *What Is Your Heritage and the State of Its Preservation? Volume 2: Collaborations with Storyboard America*, edited by Barry L. Stiefel, 83–114. Berwyn Heights: Heritage Books, Inc., 2016.

Lafrenz, Samuels K., and Paul A. Shackel. *Mobilizing Heritage: Anthropological Practice and Transnational Prospects*. Gainesville: University Press of Florida, 2018.

MacDonald, Graham. *Where the Mountains Meet the Prairies: A History of Waterton Country*. Calgary: University of Calgary Press, 2000.

Saunier, Pierre-Yves. *Transnational History*. New York: Palgrave Macmillan, 2013.

Stiefel, Barry L. "Rethinking and Reevaluating UNESCO World Heritage Sites: Lessons Experimented Within the USA." *Journal of Cultural Heritage Management and Sustainable Development* 8, no. 1 (2018): 47–61.

———. "A Tale of Two Plains: Natural Heritage Conservation on North America's Prairie." In *Conservation on the Northern Plains: New Perspectives*, edited by Anthony Amato, 74–92. Sioux Falls: Augustana College's Center for Western Studies, 2017.

Wakefield, Sarina. *Cultural Heritage, Transnational Narratives, and Museum Franchising in Abu Dhabi*. London: Routledge, 2021.

Chapter 2

Crossing Borders with Crusader Heritage

Shelley-Anne Peleg

During the medieval period, the Latin Catholic Church in Europe initiated, supported, and sometimes led a series of religious wars and armed pilgrimages, known as Crusades, across the Eastern Mediterranean to Jerusalem in the Holy Land. Their original objective was to stop the spread of Islam and to retake control of the Holy Land in the Eastern Mediterranean. The Crusades were regarded by many of their participants as a means of redemption and expiation for sins. The outcome of these campaigns was the establishment of four Crusader states, which were the County of Edessa (1098–1150), the Principality of Antioch (1098–1287), the County of Tripoli (1102–1289), and the Kingdom of Jerusalem (1099–1291), in what is now Israel, the West Bank, the Gaza Strip, and adjacent areas.[1]

In 1291, after a period of almost two hundred years, the Latin Christians were finally expelled from the Kingdom of Jerusalem. However, different military Crusader orders and sea merchants continued these military campaigns, conquering and recapturing former Christian territories in the Eastern Mediterranean, in parts of Greece, Cyprus, and other areas nearby. Especially notable are the Knights Hospitaller who established new cities such as Bodrum, together with castles on Rhodes, Kos, and other adjacent Greek islands.

The Crusade campaigns played an integral role in the expansion of medieval Europe and left prominent physical imprints in the vast geographical space they covered. Upon arriving in the East, Crusaders encountered new concepts and gained access to knowledge, ideas, and possibilities that had been lost in Europe during the Dark Ages. This is well reflected in the architecture, sculpture, and an array of objects and artifacts that are hybrid in nature and cross regional boundaries.[2] The new architectural forms, urban layouts, and material culture of this period are a hybrid of Muslim art and building technologies intermingled with Crusader needs. These new forms are reflected in cities, castles, and fortresses; church and chapel structures; artistic and architectural features; baths, interior plumbing, and other advanced hygienic tools; and paintings, mosaics, and manuscripts—all reflecting this new mix of Western, Byzantine, and Islamic styles. The struggle of the European Crusaders to adapt to a strange environment and the degree to which that environment influenced and was changed by the newcomers are among the more fascinating aspects of this historical research.

This chapter will discuss fortifications in Historic Urban Landscapes and rural areas throughout the Eastern Mediterranean. Examples from Greece, Cyprus, Lebanon, Syria, and Israel illustrate common features in these monuments. This chapter will show that while separated by modern political borders, these fortifications share significant architectural characteristics. Although many of these territories are currently bounded by strong borders, they share a common crusader heritage. This includes built crusader remains, common architecture, building technologies, usage of various materials, and evidence of everyday life. This chapter will further discuss the present function of these fortifications and castles and show the influence of the spatial movement of the Crusades on the creation of a new heritage as well as how this new heritage includes both Eastern Islamic features and Western Latin features. In addition, this chapter shows how this heritage has been adopted in modern times by different nations as a means of representing ideology and identity and how despite strong borders between countries, they regard this heritage in the exact same way.

BACKGROUND OF CRUSADER HERITAGE

In 1095, Pope Urban II delivered a sermon at Clermont-Ferrand in which he summoned his followers to rescue the holy sites from the Muslims that at that time ruled over the Holy Land.[3] Many consider this as the spark that fueled a wave of military campaigns from Europe to the Holy Land, known as Crusades. Nobles and peasants responded in great number to the call and marched across Europe to Constantinople, the capital of the Byzantine Empire. With the support of the Byzantine emperor, knights, guided by Armenian Christians, marched to Jerusalem through Seljuq-controlled territories. In July 1099, after a five-week siege, Jerusalem fell and the Crusaders established the Latin Kingdom of Jerusalem. At their core was a desire to access monuments and memorials associated with the life of Jesus, and above all the Holy Sepulcher, the church in Jerusalem believed to be the tomb of Christ. On their route, the Crusaders overtook many cities and territories along the Eastern Mediterranean coast and established the four Crusader states with a fifth established after the Third Crusade, on the island of Cyprus.[4] In these territories, far away from Central Europe, the Crusaders always remained a minority. Therefore, the settlements and new churches were fortified—the walls replacing defenders.

CRUSADER FORTIFICATIONS

The Crusader period was an important stage—indeed one of the most important stages—in the development of the medieval castle.[5] The architectural and engineering achievements of this period fall chiefly into two categories: castle design and the introduction or improvement of specific elements in defenses. The main contribution of Western architects to Crusader fortification was the residential tower (*donjon*), a hallmark of Western feudal society not known in the East prior to the period of the Crusades. It dominated the castle and met the requirements of a noble ruler to demonstrate his power and social status.

Artisans, and farmers, known as Franks, from different places all over Western and Central Europe joined the knights and immigrated to the new states in the Eastern Mediterranean.[6] They settled as an elite Catholic minority, bringing with them new customs, institutions, and culture. Like most achievers, the Franks were enthusiastic adopters and innovators, and borrowed liberally from the rich and diverse Christian, Byzantine, and Muslim cultures.[7] Supported by skilled local craftsmen, of whom Armenians played an important role, they quickly adopted Eastern fortification schemes,[8] and learned indigenous customs, building technologies, and oriental qualities, which they adopted and adapted to their needs. The Franks met and became acquainted with the most advanced fortifications of the time: cities surrounded by double, if not triple, walls, protected by ample moats and gates that were commonly entered through an indirect access way. While their innovations were mainly in merging these elements—borrowing new and original combinations rather than inventing entirely new forms—the outcome was that in the Latin East the medieval castle evolved into a better-defended, more complex, and more effective instrument of defense and control. The needs and knowledge the Franks imported during the Crusades, along with their encounters with locals and skills they acquired in the East, were all translated and transformed into an extremely specific and defined material culture that was especially reflected in fortifications.

During the first seventy years of the Latin Kingdom, economic and geographic, rather than strategic, considerations determined the location of castles.[9] Crusaders did not always consider external dangers when deciding when and where to erect a castle. Very few were built in areas under danger of attack and were instead erected in relatively secure regions. There was nothing original in this. In Europe, more fortified sites were established in areas of relative calm than in those under potential attack. These can be regarded as core settlements and regional centers rather than military strongholds. These castles were small and relatively unsophisticated structures enclosed by a single wall, the width of which did not exceed 10 feet, with an average area that was smaller than that of a large manor or hall house. The major differences in the geographical layout of castles and large manors stemmed from the additional regional functions which the former filled and from the existence of extensive agricultural settlement outside their walls.

The character of the Crusader states gave castles a function that was more than a military mission. In both frontiers and heartlands, the construction of such buildings was invariably tied to the management and protection of newly conquered territories. In the beginning they served not only as post guards of borders and roads but also as a means of insuring governance over captured land and hostile populations as well as administrative centers.

The celestial European architecture brought to the Levant typical heavy Romanesque features. This style is characterized by its massive quality, thick walls, round arches, sturdy pillars, barrel vaults, large towers, and decorative arcading, which combines features of ancient Roman and Byzantine buildings and local traditions. But on the arrival in the Levant, the European architects, who were skilled in using wooden scaffoldings for the construction of arches and vaults, had to adapt to the new environment, where wood was scarce and expensive.[10] They developed new building techniques based essentially on ashlar and masonry, limiting the use of wooden scaffoldings, and imported some models and elements of former Islamic architecture. It can be said that this could have been the beginning of the Gothic style. This historiography of Romanesque and Gothic medieval architecture is a pan-European theme devoid of distinctive national characteristics and in many ways reflects migratory movements from Europe to the Levant and back.

Although they might differ in their specific plans, architectural details, or building materials, the Crusader castles, which include cutting-edge defensive elements and principles, became the visual expression of Frankish civilization in the Levant. They are dominant and monumental features of the landscape and are the most evident visual expressions of the cultural dialogue between the East and the West. Moving far beyond the achievements of contemporary European military architecture to include physical features new to European culture, these castles are not *just* a chapter in the history of architecture and should not be seen as solely military structures. They represent the outcome of a lengthy, ongoing dialogue between different schools of military tactics and approaches. As such, they show the creation of a new culture, one that crossed the historical and political boundaries of that period.

The evolution of crusader fortresses reflects migration movements across territories, functioning as a dialogue between Western and Eastern cultures, and illuminates cultural innovations. Although these structures are spread throughout several modern countries, I suggest viewing them as one *corpus*. Rather than seeing them as individual military structures, we should regard them as one group. As such, the entire corpus becomes tangible evidence to the Frankish holdings in the East and their instability, resourcefulness, innovation, and inventiveness.

In the modern Middle East—an area of conflict with uncrossable national borders—reviewing, researching, and investigating the full corpus of Crusader fortifications is almost an impossible mission. It is not uncommon that international projects cover only certain countries, which were often chosen because of the political climate. Project EAMENA (Endangered Archaeology in the Middle East and North Africa), for example, is a collaborative effort to create a database of Crusader sites in the Levant.[11] Inclusion depended on the geographical areas that were prioritized and the specific research interests or collaborative relationships of individual researchers. The project prioritized data entry for Lebanon as well as the State of Palestine and Jordan but excluded Israel. So, even if we view these structures as one heritage mass, the current political climate of the area prevents researchers from Syria, Lebanon, the Palestinian territories, and Israel from comparing notes, holding discussions, and conducting physical visits to the defensive structures spread throughout the territories of the four Crusader states. However, globalization, joint international research groups, and visits to Crusader sites in Cyprus, Greece, and Turkey make it possible to evaluate some of the connections between these structures.

ARCHITECTURAL FEATURES

Crusader fortifications include towers and different types of enclosed castles or fortresses, also referred to as castra.[12] While much can be said about differences between their architectural and physical details, these many rural castles and urban fortifications share similarities in their general appearance and novel design. Differing from each other in size, locations, and services they provided, medium-sized fortresses supplied services to nearby smaller ones and can be termed as "castles" or "fortresses." The term "city" can be applied to the larger and sometimes more fortified settlements.

The fortresses, castles, and fortifications were not built according to a known plan but grew gradually because of the expanding state in a reaction to challenges as they arose. Upon their enemy's arrival they became a deadly ring.[13] They separated urban from rural, inside from outside, known from unknown, and friendly from hostile, and became a sign of the Frankish presence and control over the local population.[14] The geographical weakness of the kingdom required that the fortifications include not only forts and castles but also churches and monasteries and even cities and villages in which most of the Frankish population lived. Security was the guiding factor in the life of the Franks, and fortifications protected and contained crusader life. As a minority at the time of the occupation, a continuing feature of Frankish rule was constant lack of manpower, thus, stone walls were used to fulfill the defense mission; out of the 1,000 settlements in the Holy Land, they fortified no less than 100 locations that dominated the landscape. This period, in which these massive defensive structures were built, can be called the Golden Ages of Citadels. The great number of fortresses, their size, and their defense infrastructure stimulate admiration.

These fortifications are also evidence of the development of the military orders—Christian religious societies of knights—that developed in the Holy Land and then spread to other countries. The Teutonic Knights, the Knights Hospitaller, and the Knights Templar overtook key strongholds, fortified them, and played a vital role in the defense of the Crusader states. Their fortresses became centers of power and administration, exemplifying patterns of traditional settlement. The communal lifestyle of a military order was influenced by a monastic template and facilitated by—and necessitated—a level of spatial integrity. In this respect, even the largest castles of the orders in the Latin East were more reminiscent of a monastery than a secular castle, with closely connected and shared interiors used by the entire community. Spatial analysis of these structures has reinforced how religious lifestyle prevailed over all other activities.

Inland sites tended to be compact and relatively inaccessible.[15] Fortifications set on hilltops, mountain spurs, or coastal headlands used naturally defensible features. Designers demonstrated considerable adaptability while responding to the nature of a site, the size, importance, function, and proposed garrison of a building. The fortifications' design was almost always a square or rectangular shape and consisted of two basic elements: walls with their towers and gates, and fortresses. Urban coastal fortifications were usually of an irregular shape and only some of them had a sea wall.[16] If the main fortress was incorporated into the main fortification system of the city, it was an independent unit, separated from the rest of the city with its own walls, towers, gates, and moats.

Towers were the majority of the fortifications, the most basic type of a fortification and the simplest ones throughout the Crusader-held territories.[17] The Crusaders built their first towers before they even set foot in the Holy Land.[18] In 1097 and 1098, during the Siege of Antioch, the Crusaders constructed three towers with the aim of preventing Turkish incursions.

Examples of over seventy-five such towers are listed throughout the Kingdom of Jerusalem (in modern-day Israel and Jordan) and more in the County of Tripoli (in the modern-day region of Tripoli, Northern Lebanon, and parts of western Syria), in the Kingdom of Cyprus, and in the Kingdom of Rhodes.[19] Built primarily by landowning nobles as centers of regional administration, they mostly served to guard the main roads and usually held within them just a small guard force. This explains why these towers are concentrated not in border areas but rather in the interior fertile areas where agricultural activity was intense. They were of the simple motte-and-bailey type, a tower on a hill with a bailey (outer wall) surrounded by a moat and stone walls.[20] The strength of the tower lay in its massive walls, often 10 to 14 feet wide, with few narrow openings and shooting slits. This was sufficient for protection against a raid of riding archers, but not strong enough to defend against a full enemy attack. These towers were mostly built to stand on their own but were often employed as an integral part of a larger castle and used as the keep or donjon—a massive building which was intended to serve as a final refuge if the enemy breached the castle walls.

New siege weaponry and the development of large-scale, powerful counterweight trebuchets greatly impacted defensive architecture as a counter-battery weapon was more effective when mounted on top of a tower.[21] This led to the appearance of larger, broader, and deeper towers serving as artillery emplacements. Some fortresses had one such great tower placed on the most vulnerable side, sometimes as a further development of the main keep. Where a larger area was enclosed, the result could be a series of massive towers linked by relatively traditional curtain walls. Another important development was a multiplication of existing defensive features such as doubled walls or thicker ones and the abundance of embrasures in the walls. Greater efforts were made to use naturally defensive features. Ancient columns were often laid horizontally through such walls, binding their inner and outer layers together, and there was increasing use of the Islamic talus or sloping additional base along the outer foot of a wall.

In response to specific defensive/offensive needs, the Crusaders adopted a type of fortress that was in common use in earlier periods: the enclosure castle or castrum.[22] The use of this castrum plan is known both from surviving examples and from written sources. Physical examples include structures such as Coliath, in the county of Tripoli (Syria), Castellum Regis and Qal'at Hunin in Northern Israel, Yavne (Ibelin), Blanchegarde (Tell es-Safi), Beit Govrin in Southern Israel, the castrum of Gaza, the sea castle in Sidon in Lebanon, a castrum in the small harbor town of Kyrenia, and the citadel of Famagusta in Cyprus. The plan of theses castles was generally larger than the tower and they remained simple in design. A classic castrum has a rectangular shape with higher corner towers and additional interval towers placed at regular distances at the mid-point of each wall except where the gate is situated between two small turrets.[23] The interior of the castrum included a few rooms such as kitchens, various service rooms, and halls and chapels often situated above the service rooms on a second story. Its advantages were that, on the one hand, the simple design allowed for easy and quick construction, and, on the other hand, the long stretches of curtain walls with numerous firing positions allowed this type of castle to play an active defensive role. The castrum was not new to the region. These four-cornered forts developed out of the Roman fortified camps and in the late Roman and Byzantine periods, and the design was used for frontier forts, notably those in North Africa. Several castra are contained within outworks that may have been intended to protect a settlement, which had developed outside the castle walls, perhaps as the result of some new threat.

From the inherited design of the castrum and under the influence of Byzantine double-line fortifications, the Franks derived a more sophisticated type of castle.[24] This was the double or concentric castrum, a castrum within a castrum, with the inner building almost identical to the outer one. Two castles, one in Israel (Belvoir, also known as Kohav Hayarden) and one in Syria (Crac des Chevaliers) are examples of his type. They include two lines of defense, thus creating an inner castrum, which contained a refectory (dining room), storerooms, and a kitchen as well as stables, a bakery, a forge, and a mill-room. The upper floor included service rooms, living quarters, and a chapel. This castrum was surrounded by an outer castrum with corner and interval towers. Concentric castles are regarded by modern Western scholarship as being typically Frankish in origin and were gradually transformed into visual icons representing the Crusades themselves. The silhouette of the larger castles became emblematic of Frankish presence in the hostile East. But the silhouettes are misleading, for much of what is identified as being a big castle are in fact external fortifications added by none other than the Muslim rulers after they took the castles from the Franks. This is even true of the external walls of the most typical castles of Kerak and Shaubak in modern-day Jordan, Beaufort in modern-day Lebanon, and Crac des Chevaliers in modern-day Syria.

Crac des Chevaliers and Qal'at Salah El-Din represent a significant example, illustrating the exchange of influences and documenting the evolution of fortified architecture in the Near East during the time of the Crusades. The Crac des Chevaliers was built by the Hospitaller Order of Saint John of Jerusalem from 1142 to 1271. With further construction by the Mamluks in the late thirteenth century, it ranks among the best-preserved examples of Crusader castles. The Qal'at Salah El-Din, even though partly in ruins, retains features from its Byzantine beginnings in the tenth century, the Frankish transformations in the late twelfth century, and fortifications added by the rulers of the Ayyubid dynasty (in the late twelfth to mid-thirteenth century). Both castles are located on high ridges in modern-day Syria that were key defensive positions. This well-known typical silhouette of the Crusader castle is to a large extent a Muslim castle identified as Crusader by later scholars or popular opinion. It seems that European scholars found it hard to believe that such beautiful fortresses were built by the Muslims themselves and not by the Crusaders.

Spur castles made use of a particular topographical feature, a high spur cut off from the surrounding countryside by two river valleys.[25] These castles were built in hilly regions and exploited steep cliffs on the sides of a ridge as a natural defense. The most vulnerable side that faced the ridge was strengthened by the construction of more extensive defenses such as parallel walls, towers, and a moat. Among the interesting details of military design is the rampart walk (chemin de ronde) around the curtain walls. These great spur castles often controlled major roads and valley passes. They could house a large garrison and contain supplies necessary for a major campaign. Smaller such castles served as administrative centers. The Montfort castle, situated in Northern Israel, the Kerak Castle located in Jordan, the Beaufort or Belfort (Qal'at al-Shaqif Arnun) situated in Southern Lebanon, and Crac des Chevaliers and Margat in Syria are all examples of such castles. While there is little similarity between the different hilltop examples, they are all impressive and massive structures enclosed by curtain walls, moats, and towers.

During the second period of the Latin Kingdom of Jerusalem, the Crusaders emphasized fortifying cities built along the shores of the Holy Land.[26] These cities included Ashkelon, Jaffa, Arsuf, Caesarea, and Akko (located in modern-day Israel), and Tyre, Sidon, and Beirut (located in modern-day Lebanon). The mission was a relatively easy one as most of these coastal cities had been already fortified in earlier periods. All cities contained two fortification units: the city walls and a citadel that functioned as the seat for the governor or commander and the garrison.

Local topography and the proximity of the sea were the decisive factors in the design of these fortifications and shaped the city walls. Ashkelon, for example, took advantage of a natural ridge and had a rainbow-like wall. In the city of Tyre, the battery that was built on the island hundreds of years before by Alexander the Great was swept away and sand accumulated on it, turning the island into a peninsula. Elsewhere, walls were usually trapezoidal.

The technique of fortifying cities was similar to that of forts. They contained a dry moat, an escarp, and walls with towers surrounding its top. Bridges built of wood led to the entrance gates. The design of the gates, a Muslim legacy, was built in a way that it was impossible to enter the city in a straight line. One had to pass one gate into a courtyard and then pass through another gate. The doors themselves rotated on hinges and were locked with a bolt and a huge beam.

After the mid-thirteenth century few new fortifications were built in the remaining Crusader states. The Mamluks in their effort to prevent the Crusaders from taking a hold on the Levantine coast had razed many of the harbors and their fortifications. The Kingdom of Cyprus survived because Mamluk attacks were rare and ineffective due to the lack of a powerful navy. Therefore, during the fourteenth and fifteenth century, the rulers of Cyprus felt no need to advance fortification schemes. The next step in the development of military architecture was the defense works of the Knights Hospitaller on Rhodes and the islands of the Dodecanese. Based on their experience in the Levant, the Knights Hospitaller created modern fortresses, which responded to new threats posed by the emergence of firearms.

THE CONNECTION BETWEEN POLITICAL AGENDAS AND PRESERVING AND RESTORING CRUSADER FORTIFICATIONS

The heritage of the Crusaders suits many national movements, especially those that admire chivalry, Catholic piety, and the willingness to die for a common cause.[27] Many European nations identify with memories of the Crusades. However, the Crusades do not belong to any specific European nation. No national movements can claim monopoly on the Crusades and no nation can claim that the Crusades are exclusively their history. The adoption of the Crusades as a Golden Era followed the disintegration of former common history and the creation of separate national identities. Narratives were broken down into parallel geographic histories and each nation appropriated its own share. The Belgians adopted Godfrey of Bouillon because he was born in a territory that was later incorporated into the Belgium state, just as the English claimed Richard the Lionheart because he ruled the territory which later became part of the English national space, and the French adopted Phillipe Auguste, King of the Franks later to become King of France.[28]

The process of the rehabilitation of the Crusades was influenced by how the Crusaders were viewed by nineteenth-century historians, and how these scholars understood their own history and collective identity. National connections to Crusader fortresses fit well with the process in which the Crusades became part of nationalist discourse. As early as the 1860s, French, English, and German archaeologists carried out projects that lent support to their nationalist conceptions, with each scholar utilizing Crusader archaeology to match the nationalist interpretation to which they were personally inclined.[29] French historians, for example, glorified relations between the Franks and the local population, attributing to the Frankish regime in the East qualities of tolerance and enlightened rule, claiming that these were characteristics of French Colonial rule. This assessment supported nineteenth-century French colonialism, which was represented as being different from the selfish aggression of other colonial powers such as Great Britain.[30]

As nationalist and colonialist discourses gained an increasingly stronger foothold in Crusade scholarship, they also left traces in studies devoted to medieval technological innovations. These viewpoints continued to influence historians in the twentieth century and manifested in modern interpretations of medieval settled space.[31] Thus, for example, we visualize the borders of the medieval state or the defense systems through modern nation-states that are defined by borders. The same can be said in relation to defensive strategies supposedly employed to protect the borders of a medieval state, or the role of castles in such a plan of defense.

Contemporary efforts to provide new data have initiated several European expeditions that are engaged in detailed archaeological and architectural surveys of Crusader and Muslim castles in the Levant. Each expedition has its own well-defined specific castle to study and publish its detailed plans. Ironically these archaeological efforts are strongly connected to geographical demarcation of the old colonialist's world: French expeditions work in Syria and Lebanon while British researchers survey Israel and Jordan.

Across the Mediterranean, historic cities are largely defined by the preservation of their medieval and early modern past. These urban entities maintain the physical evidence of their role as economic and cultural hubs, with their layered architectural heritage being integral to the experience of their urban fabric. They absorb the dense grid of a city, and their massive constructions physically engage citizens and visitors with wall facades, towers, and gates speaking a visual language that conveys a broad spectrum of information.

The socioeconomic, political, and cultural complexity of these cities' contemporary state reveals their historical transition. Monuments of the medieval and early modern period are instrumental for the subsequent growth and development of these cities. Among these, fortifications constitute the largest preserved examples, frequently having become iconic attributes of civic pride and identity. Although they have lost their protective function, their physical presence still influences the spatial experience of a city, and their preservation carries significance as a reflection of a range of spatial, social, and economic needs, as well as ideological and cultural perceptions of the past and how it affects both the present and future.

These fortifications are a synthesis of numerous building phases. In the city, they constitute an important part within the visual culture. They are a product of continuous, additive construction processes from their foundation through later periods. In later years, these defensive works underwent extensive restoration and preservation efforts due to wear and destruction caused by time, weather, and war. Continuous alterations, building, and restoration efforts were needed and became a primary task for local societies and their foremost members. This care is still visually evident on many of the fortification facades, but different building technologies and materials were employed to help keep the defense structures intact.

The preservation of crusader fortifications, and their development as tourist attractions, displays the national and colonial appropriation of the historical narrative and how we "see" the Crusades. The few examples presented here show how each individual site was intertwined with national and imperial interests. Due to the competition between colonial powers, states saw it as necessary to preserve these monuments of the past to establish themselves as civilized ruling powers. The sites show how the nationalization of heritage involves not just the construction of a national heritage but also other legacies both above and below the scale of the nation. These Crusader heritages are representative of a broader European interest in the Crusades, which manifested itself in explorations, restorations, and acquisitions. This interest emerged when the territories once conquered by crusaders and their successors "again" came under the rule of the expanding European powers during the modern colonization of the Mediterranean.

THE CASE OF NICOSIA

The city of Nicosia in Cyprus is defined by two medieval monuments, the iconic sixteenth-century Venetian fortification enclosure and at its center the massive Gothic cathedral of Hagia Sophia, transformed into the Selimiye Mosque in 1570. A short history of fortifications in Nicosia reveals the close relationship of defensive works to the very existence of the city, which from the late tenth century onwards became the island's capital. Cyprus was captured in 1191 by Richard the Lionheart during the Third Crusade to the Holy Land.[32] In 1192, the island was acquired by the ousted king of Jerusalem Guy de Lusignan who then established a dynasty that ruled Cyprus until 1489.

During the first century of Lusignan rule, Nicosia remained without a fortified enclosure, although an earlier existing fortress was enhanced. The construction of the city's walls only began about a hundred years later during the reign of Henry II, the last crowned king of Jerusalem. The fortification of the city seems to have continued for over another two hundred years, during which different rulers strengthened the original structures, added massive towers, fortified the entirety of the city, added many turrets, further improved and repaired the fortifications, and constructed a citadel. These successive campaigns to maintain and improve the defenses of Nicosia mirror the constant attention and necessary investment to protect the capital of Cyprus. The construction and maintenance of fortifications was a major priority for the medieval rulers of the island and a reality that shaped daily life and the spatial experience of the city. Not always successful in repelling sieges, one could say that these fortifications are evidence of the enemy's victory and serve as monuments commemorating these triumphs.

Succeeding the Lusignans in 1489, the Venetian rulers of Cyprus deemed the medieval walls to be outdated and unsuitable to meet the needs of siege warfare in the age of the cannon.[33] The Ottoman threat to Venetian possessions in the Mediterranean remained a constant challenge through the fifteenth and sixteenth century. Such concerns for the defense of Nicosia led to an ambitious new defensive scheme with the construction of an impressive fortification system built between 1567 and 1570, a fabrication that redefined the island's capital. Entire quarters of the medieval city and its existing walls were demolished in the late 1560s under the supervision of the experienced engineer Guilio Savorgnano. The refortification constituted a circular enclosure, surrounded by a moat, supported by a total of eleven heart-shaped bastions and three fortified gates.

During the Ottoman period (1571–1878), the walls of Nicosia were no longer used for defensive purposes, rather they served as an instrument to control the city and its inhabitants and continued to outline the daily experience of urban space.[34] The gates were guarded and closed every night, thus regulating the entry and overnight stay of merchants and travelers. No systematic efforts were made to preserve the city's defenses during those times. Limited restorations provided necessary stone facing and helped to protect and consolidate the dissolving upper parts of the earthwork ramparts. These defensive structures continued to define the spatial development of Nicosia.[35]

Even when the city expanded outside its medieval walls, the fortifications continued to keep their architectural integrity. In modern times, an increased interest in medieval heritage initiated investments and conservation programs of the historical fortifications. Many times, the walls were viewed as an obstacle for the city's growth and municipal authorities, or mayors, supported their demolition. Concerns about reusing parts of the fortifications for livestock markets, parking, or garbage disposal clashed with fanatic preservation believers. They objected to ideas of dismantling building materials from the walls as well as requests to cut new openings through the enclosure.

The identification of the fortifications as heritage worth protecting dates to the period of British rule on the island (1878–1960). The British administration of Cyprus invested in the preservation of the medieval monuments as a reflection of their colonial aspirations.[36] Heritage preservation was always a sensitive political matter as it was linked to Cypriot cultural identity, and the local island population consisted of Greek Cypriots, Turkish Cypriots,

Armenians, and Maronite Christians. In time, this became a highly contested issue between the British and the Greek-Cypriot majority whose aim was to unite the island with Greece. Driven by strong ideas about the importance of medieval heritage and its preservation, the British Curator of Ancient Monuments attempted to tackle the neglected condition of the deteriorating walls that surrounded the historic core. The British directed massive efforts to protect the walls while making every effort to create for them an appropriate landscape setting, proceeding with their gradual restoration and preserving the existing structure as much as possible. By declaring them monuments, the British secured their future care and solidified their historic importance and continued with systematic restorations and promotions of the fortifications as monuments worth protecting. Their efforts are an example of how medieval architectural ruins, originally intended for war and defense, became icons of civic identity and heritage.

Like the island itself, Nicosia, the capital of Cyprus, was divided in 1974, distorting the ideal geometrical form of the fortifications. As a divided city, and a capital city of two peoples, the use of space in Nicosia is burdened politically and symbolically. Strangely enough, the antiquated fortifications, neither of Ottoman nor Hellenic origin, are regarded as common built heritage that both sides have been able to agree upon.[37]

THE CASE OF THE OLD CITY OF AKKO

After the Crusaders, under the leadership of the king of England, Richard the Lionheart reconquered the Holy Land in 1191, and Akko became the capital of the Latin Kingdom of Jerusalem.[38] Historical sources and few archeological remains show the strength of the double wall fortification, the guard towers, and the entrance gates to the city.[39]

The Knights Hospitaller built a typical castrum as their headquarters adjacent to the city's northern walls. A pilgrim named Theodoric visited the city and, among his impressions of the Holy Land, he described the impressive, fortified Hospitaller compound. According to historical sources, this was one of the few castrums that were built in the city. Other castrums built in Akko served the king himself, the Knights Templar, and the Italian sea merchants that settled in the city. When the Frankish Kingdom of Jerusalem fell in 1291, these fortifications were destroyed and left deserted.[40]

In the eighteenth century, when the city was repopulated, the Ottoman rulers deposited endless amounts of soil on top of the Hospitaller castrum to gain height for a new palace, thus burying the Crusader compound below.[41] This palace, Burj el-Hazna (the Treasury Tower), was a fortified tower that served the new local Ottoman administration. Barracks (el-Qashla) secured the

Tower and a garden adjacent to them gave the ruler a retreat. Additionally, they were surrounded by a new set of fortifications built above parts of the Medieval fortifications. These walls constructed during the Ottoman period still surround the Old City of Akko and are wrongly thought of as Frankish fortifications.

During the British Mandate period (1917–1948) this structure was transformed into the northern central British prison, and the Treasury Tower and its barracks underwent extensive functional and material modification; gallows were installed, the barracks were adapted for prison cells, and the Treasury Tower itself became a jail for detainees. During this period, many officers and engineers visited the underground remnants of the Hospitaller castrum documenting parts of its massiveness and complexity.

The British showed a great deal of interest in the Old City of Akko and planned its new development.[42] They gave excessive attention to the fortifications of the city, surveyed them, conducted several restoration works on the walls,[43] and documented and prepared a new master plan for the development of the city of Akko, declaring it as an open air museum of the Crusader Period.[44] In many respects, the British saw themselves as the Crusaders of the modern era, and understood that their task was to rescue the Holy Land and the holy Christian sites from the Muslim hands that had previously controlled the country.[45] As the Holy Land—the land of the Bible, and the backdrop of Jesus's life and sacrifice, the lost Kingdom of Jerusalem, as well as the image of heavenly Jerusalem—Palestine was charged with meaning for any British citizen. The deep religious significance of the Holy Land to Christianity and the memory of the unfulfilled crusader quest endowed the possessive sentiment toward Palestine with an unparalleled religious dimension. This notion is reflected both in the architectural structures the British built as well as the attention they gave to Crusader archaeological sites. The Old City of Akko is another example of the ideological monumentalizing of fortifications.

The State of Israel kept the general approach established by the British Mandate and designated The Old City of Akko as a tourist city with uniquely built heritage values and monuments.[46] Other than establishing unique building legislations, restrictions, and guidelines, the newly established state sought to create new tourist sites, and in Akko the emphasis focused on the remnants of the Crusader city. Israeli archaeologists conducted large-scale excavations underneath the British Prison and the former Ottoman Palace. Much of the underground Crusader Hospitaller compound was revealed along with streets east and south of the compound, as well as remnants of the Church of Saint John. The castrum and the fortifications were regarded as national assets and monuments with unique values,[47] and were defined as one of the most important historical assets in the country.[48] Tourism was designated as the means of preserving this material culture, with emphasis placed on the discovery, exposure, cleaning, and restoration of the Frankish castrum. In 2001, the Old City of Akko was nominated as a World Heritage Site and has since developed, attracting tourists from all over the world.

THE CASE OF RHODES

Without going into details of the earlier periods in Rhodes, I will stress that the town of Rhodes became the Hospitaller stronghold and the order's main center after the fall of the Kingdom of Jerusalem.[49] The order invested in building, developing, and fortifying the city of Rhodes, strengthening the Grand Master's castle and other castles assigned to the different administrative divisions of the Knights Hospitaller that settled on the Island. It was during this period that the city received its current form and size. The Hospitallers enhanced the harbor with a wall, fortified the city, built a hospital, and constructed inns for the different districts. On the north-west side of the city, they constructed the castrum of the Grand Master, similar in its shape, size, and functions to the one they had left in Akko.

The Crusader narrative well-suited Italian colonial authorities after occupying the Island during the Italian-Turkish War of 1911. As the rulers of the Island, the Italians curated and shaped the character of the Historic Urban, castles, and fortifications as monuments of Crusader Hospitaller legacy.[50] Led by the Italian architect Florestano di Fausto, the Italian authorities began a process of "Italianization" on the islands by drawing ideological links between its medieval and contemporary colonization. This stated policy of ideological and cultural assimilation was attempted through grandiose public works and ambitious projects (targeted at transforming the urban environment), establishing important industrial units, enhancing archeological sites and landscapes of particular beauty, and forging decisive intervention in urban planning.[51] The areas affected by the Italian intervention included, among others, the Arsenal Gates and the Palace of the Grand Master, with the opening of new gates through the walls and the reconstruction of the palace. To ensure that the restoration of the historic city focused on the remains of the Knights Hospitaller's rule, the Italians placed emphasis on the repair and restoration of important medieval monuments such as the Street of the Knights, the Great Hospital of the Knights, the Grand Master's Palace, and the Arsenal compound.

THE PLACE OF CRUSADER FORTIFICATIONS IN MODERN CITIES AND RURAL AREAS

Although far apart, and spread over several countries, many of these iconic rural and urban fortifications are touristic destinations and protected heritage spaces. In these sites, historical cultural heritage (tangible and intangible), collective memories, local patriotism, and identity are still present. Therefore, fortifications and castles are not only iconic historic attributes of the past but constitute in the present an important duty of preserving cultural heritage, civic pride, and identity.

The best-known Crusader castles today lie within the boundaries of Jordan, Israel, Syria, and Lebanon. Kerak, Beaufort, Saone, Crac des Chevaliers, Monfort, and others conjure up the romantic nineteenth-century prints of ruined Crusader bastions and are today major tourist sites that house museums or other attractions. They retain the aura of a ruin, ripe for ruminations on the once absolute dominion held by its masters, and tourists that visit these castles feel a sense of discovery. Visitors to present-day remains encounter the momentousness of the world history sites that were once linked by a circuit of bastions, towered walls, fortified gates, and a citadel. Inside the castle walls one can see the outlines of stone chapels, the tumbled masonry, overgrown buildings, and fine cut ashlar stones, and, while wandering along well-preserved ramparts and bastions, one can read practically the entire history of a castle. These fortifications are ample evidence of what made the medieval settlements so redoubtable, fearsome, and mighty.

Although these fortifications and castles have lost their original protective function, they have obtained a new task. They are the physical means to safeguard and preserve aspects of cultural heritage as mentioned in the UNESCO Recommendations on the Historic Urban Landscape, or, as UNESCO terms, "rural landscapes." With no specific frontiers, fromthis perspective, UNESCO is a strong player and is instrumental in preserving Crusader-built heritage, and, specifically, the fortification systems all over the Eastern Mediterranean as many of these Crusader fortifications have been declared World Heritage Sites or listed on the tentative list.

CONCLUSION

Examples presented in this chapter show that although Crusader fortifications are spread over several countries in the Eastern Mediterranean, they share many similarities, common features, and architectural characteristics. In many cases, currently, due to politics and national borders, there are no physical connections between these monuments and the way they are managed. Even so, the examples presented in this chapter show that these monuments are part of one heritage. Without actual connection, most countries regard these structures as monumental heritage that are worthy of preservation and have listed these structures as World Heritage Sites or as components on the World Heritage Tentative List. Although far apart they have commonly created a heritage space and in many cases have become tourist destinations, and demonstrate how a period from the past still has an impact over a vast area. The sites show that although physically separated, in heritage there were no actual borders in the past, and even in the present these borders have no meaning to the way we regard these monuments.

These Crusader heritages are case studies for understanding heritage without borders. They are not only a significant heritage for one nation but are also representative of a broader interest—an interest which manifested itself in explorations, restorations, and acquisitions and has a thriving presence in popular culture. This interest emerged when the territories once conquered by Crusaders and their successors again came under the rule of the expanding European powers during the colonization of the Mediterranean in modern times.

Rich literature on the preservation of Crusader heritage has drawn attention to the relationship between nationalism and heritage, especially in national and colonial projects. In a region of competing claims, sites connected to the history of the Crusades attracted the attention of all the major European powers, and the French, British, and Italians that had established formal empires in the Mediterranean showed great interest in these sites. These cross-cutting linkages allow us to use the Crusader sites as a prism for understanding the connection between heritage and transnationalism. Imperial actors are not the only ones interested in these sites; Greek, Arab, and Israeli nationalists also pursue agendas for preserving this heritage.

Highlighting the Crusader fortifications helps to understand how built heritage is created. By focusing on their similarities, I have presented this heritage as transnational. By presenting colonial or national preservation policies and procedures, I showed both trans-imperial and transnational entwinements over a span of time and space. The consideration of the local contexts in Cyprus, Israel, Greece, and Syria underscores the substantial similarities in preservation and development procedures of heritage. Sites that encounter the past and continue to serve the present are continuously altered by various interests. They can be seen as a national or colonial legacy and reveal how notions of lineage create a common heritage. Finally, Crusader vestiges are also a particularly intriguing case for reflecting on the construction of heritage across borders given that, for all the participants involved, they represented a unique category between a heritage of the self and a heritage of the other.

NOTES

1. Adrian J. Boas, *Crusader Archaeology—The Material Culture of the Latin East*, London and New York: Routledge, 1999, 3–4.

2. Maria Georgopoulou, "The Material Culture of the Crusades," in: Nicholson Helen J. (ed.), *Palgrave Advances in the Crusades*, Houndmills and New York: Springer, 2005, 84.

3. Joshua Prawer, הצלבנים, Jerusalem: Bialik Institute, 1975, 24–25.

4. Boas, *Crusader Archaeology*, 6.

5. Ronnie Ellenblum, *Crusader Castles and Modern Histories*, Cambridge: Cambridge University Press, 2007, 68–69.

6. Prawer, הצלבנים, 75–107.

7. Prawer, הצלבנים, 772.

8. Nicolle David, *Crusader Castles in the Holy Land 1192–1302*, New York: Ospery Publishing, 2005, 15.

9. Prawer, הצלבנים, 358.

10. Alessandro Camiz, *Gothic, Frankish or Crusader? Reconsidering the Origins of Gothic Architecture*, in: Seppänen Liisa, Verdiani Giorgio and Cornell Per (eds.), *Proceedings from the Scholarship Workshop on Architecture, Archaeology and Contemporary City Planning—Reformation, Regeneration and Revitalization*, Turku: Turku University, 2018, 149.

11. Letty Ten Harkel and Michael T. Fisher, "The EAMENA Database and its Potential Impact on Research and Heritage Management: A Case Study of Crusader Heritage in Lebanon," in: *Levant* 53, no. 3 (2021): 282–301.

12. Boas, *Crusader Archaeology*, 88–90.

13. Nikolas Bakirtzis, "The Visual Language of Fortification Facades: The Walls of Thessaloniki," *Monument and Environment* 9 (2005): 16.

14. Prawer, הצלבנים, 358.

15. Boas, *Crusader Archaeology*, 89.

16. Boas, *Crusader Archaeology*, 41–51.

17. Prawer, הצלבנים, 372.

18. Boas, *Crusader Archaeology*, 90.

19. Boas, *Crusader Archaeology*, 92–97.

20. Boas, *Crusader Archaeology*, 90.

21. David, *Crusader Castles in the Holy Land*, 14–15.

22. Boas, *Crusader Archaeology*, 98.

23. Boas, *Crusader Archaeology*, 99.

24. Boas, *Crusader* Archaeology, 103–105.

25. Boas, *Crusader* Archaeology, 105–113.

26. Prawer, הצלבנים, 390–395.

27. Ellenblum, *Crusader Castles and Modern Histories*, 29–30.

28. Ellenblum, *Crusader Castles and Modern Histories*, 43–49.

29. Ellenblum, *Crusader Castles and Modern Histories*, 32–39.

30. Ellenblum, *Crusader Castles and Modern Histories*, 18–23.

31. Ellenblum, *Crusader Castles and Modern Histories*, 49.

32. Nikolas Bakirtzis, "Fortifications as Urban Heritage: The Case of Nicosia in Cyprus and a Glance at the City of Rhodes," *National Narratives and the Medieval Mediterranean* 62 (2017): 173.

33. Bakirtzis, "Fortifications as Urban Heritage," 174.

34. Bakirtzis, "Fortifications as Urban Heritage," 176.
35. Bakirtzis, "Fortifications as Urban Heritage," 171.
36. Bakirtzis, "Fortifications as Urban Heritage," 178.
37. Anita Bakshi, "A Shell of Memory: The Cyprus Conflict and Nicosia's Walled City," *Memories Studies* 5, no. 4 (2012): 3.
38. Nathan Shur, תולדות עכו, Tel Aviv: Dvir Publishing House, 1990, 81.
39. Shur, תולדות עכו, 132–135.
40. Shur, תולדות עכו, 150–156.
41. Arie Ytzhaki, "מצודת עכו," in: Eli Schiller (ed.), עכו אותריה, Jerusalem: Ariel Publications, 1983, 81.
42. Shelley-Anne Peleg, *The Interaction and Relationship between the Local Population of Historical Cities in Israel and the Development and Conservation Procedures that Take Place Within Them*, Haifa: University of Haifa, 2017, 133–135.
43. Naim Makhouly and Cedric Norman Johns, *A Guide to Acre*, Jerusalem: Government of Palestine–Department of Antiquities, 1946, 68–73.
44. Percy H. Winter, *Acre Report: Preservation and Restoration of Acre Survey and Report*, Palestine: Government of Palestine Public Works Department, 1944.
45. Ron Fuchs and Gilbert Herbert, "Representing Mandatory Palestine: Austin St. Barbe Harrison and the Representational Buildings of British Mandate Palestine 1922–1937," *Architectural History* 43 (2000): 283.
46. Shelley-Anne Peleg, *The Interaction and Relationship between the Local Population of Historical Cities in Israel and the Development and Conservation Procedures that Take Place Within Them,* University of Haifa, 2017, 138–141.
47. Alex Kesten, *Old Acre*, The Old Acre Development Company (1993), 8–10.
48. Peleg, *The Interaction and Relationship*, 138–141.
49. Anthony Luttrell, "The Hospitallers of Rhodes: Prospectives, Problems, Possibilities," *Varioum Collected Studies* 158 (1982): 243–246.
50. Elias Kollias, *The Medieval Town of Rhodes—Restoration Works 1985–2000*, Rhodes: Ministry of Culture, 2001, 35.
51. Kollias, *The Medieval Town of Rhodes*, 36.

BIBLIOGRAPHY

Primary Sources

UNESCO. *Convention for the Safeguarding of the Intangible Cultural Heritage*, 2003. https://ich.unesco.org/en/convention (accessed August 22, 2021).

———. *Operational Guidelines for the Implementation of the World Heritage Convention,* 2019. https://whc.unesco.org/en/guidelines/ (accessed August 28, 2021).

———. *State Parties.* https://whc.unesco.org/en/statesparties (accessed August 28, 2021).

———. *Tentative List.* https://whc.unesco.org/en/tentativelists/ (accessed August 28, 2021).

———. *The UNESCO World Heritage List*. https://whc.unesco.org/en/list/ (accessed August 28, 2021).

———. *UNESCO World Heritage Convention*, 1972. https://whc.unesco.org/en/convention/ (accessed August 28, 2021).

Secondary Sources

Bakirtzis, Nikolas. "Fortifications as Urban Heritage: The Case of Nicosia in Cyprus and a Glance at the City of Rhodes." *National Narratives and the Medieval Mediterranean* 62 (2017): 171–192.

———. "From Fortification to Monument: The Walls of Nicosia, in: Hybrid Heritage Scapes as Urban Commons." In *Mediterranean Cities: Essays on Accessing the Deep-Rooted Spatial Interfaces of Cities*, edited by Georgios Artopoulo. Nicosia: The Cyprus Institute, 2018, 29–36.

———. "The Visual Language of Fortification Facades: The Walls of Thessaloniki." *Monument and Environment* 9 (2005): 15–34.

Bakshi, Anita. "A Shell of Memory: The Cyprus Conflict and Nicosia's Walled City." *Memories Studies* 5, no. 4 (2012): 479–496.

Boas, Adrian J. *Archaeology of the Military Orders*. London and New York: Routledge, 2006.

———. *Crusader Archaeology: The Material Culture of the Latin East*. London and New York: Routledge, 1999.

———. "Crusader Fortifications: Between Tradition and Innovation." In *The Crusader World*, edited by Adrian J. Boaz. London: Routledge, 2015, 437–459.

Camiz, Alessandro. "Gothic, Frankish or Crusader? Reconsidering the Origins of Gothic Architecture." In *Proceedings From the Scholarship Workshop on Architecture, Archaeology and Contemporary City Planning: Reformation, Regeneration and Revitalization—Abstract Collections*, edited by Liisa Seppänen, Giorgio Verdiani, and Per Cornell Per. Turku: Turku University, 2018, 31–32.

David, Nicolle. *Crusader Castles in the Holy Land 1192–1302*. New York: Ospery Publishing, 2005.

Duff, Douglas Valder. *Palestine Unveiled*. Glasgow: Blackie & Son, 1938.

Ellenblum, Ronnie. *Crusader Castles and Modern Histories*. Cambridge: Cambridge University Press, 2009.

Fuchs, Ron, and Gilbert Herbert. "Representing Mandatory Palestine: Austin St. Barbe Harrison and the Representational Buildings of British Mandate Palestine 1922–1937." *Architectural History* 43 (2000): 281–333.

Georgopoulou, Maria. "The Material Culture of the Crusades." In *Palgrave Advances in the Crusades*, edited by Helen J. Nicholson. Houndmills and New York: Springer, 2005, 88–108.

Harkel, Letty, and Michael T. Fisher. "The EAMENA Database and its Potential Impact on Research and Heritage Management: A Case Study of Crusader Heritage in Lebanon." *Levant* 53, no. 3 (2021): 282–301.

Kesten, Alex. *The Old City of Akko: Re-Examination and Conclusions*. Akko: The Old Akko Development Company, 1993.

Killebrew, Ann, DiPietro Dana, Peleg Shelley-Anne, Scham Sandra, and Taylor Evan. "Archaeology, Shared Heritage and Community at Akko Israel." *Journal of Eastern Mediterranean Archaeology and Heritage Studies* 5, nos. 3–4 (2017): 365–392.

Kollias, Elias. *The Medieval Town of Rhodes: Restoration Works 1985–2000*. Rhodes: Ministry of Culture, 2001.

Luttrell, Anthony. "The Hospitallers of Rhodes: Prospectives, Problems, Possibilities." *Varioum Collected Studies* 158 (1982): 243–246.

Magalio, Emma. "The Role of Historic Town of Rhodes in the Scenario of Ottoman and Italian Rules to the Light of Iconographic Sources." In *Città Mediterranee in Trasformazione Identità e Immagine del Paesaggio Urbano tra Sette e Novecento*, edited by Alfredo Buccaro and Cesare de-Seta. Napoli: Università di Napoli, 2014.

Makhouly, Naim, and Cedric Norman Johns. *A Guide to Acre*. Jerusalem: Government of Palestine–Department of Antiquities, 1946.

Manaousou, Netella Katerina. *Medieval Town of Rhodes: Restoration Works 1985–2000*. Rhodes: Ministry of Culture, 2001.

Meron, Benbenishti. *ערי ארץ ישראל ואתריה בתקופה הצבלנית ואתריה בתקופה*. Jerusalem: Ariel Publications, 1984.

Peleg, Shelley-Anne. "Built Heritage and Intangible Heritage in Historical Urban Landscapes." In *Sharing Cultures: Proceedings of the 6th International Conference on Intangible Heritage*, edited by Sergio Lira, Cristina Pinheiro, Rogerio Amoêda, Alison McCleery, and Alister McCleery. Guimares, 2019.

———. *The Interaction and Relationship Between the Local Population of Historical Cities in Israel and the Development and Conservation Procedures That Take Place Within Them*. Haifa: University of Haifa, 2017.

———. "היבטים חברתיים וקהילתיים ותפקידם בתהליך השימור של נכסי תרבות מוחשיים בנוף עירוני היסטורי." *Sites: The Magazine* 10 (2018): The Council for Conservation of Heritage Sites, Mikve Israel, 105–114.

Pluskowski, Aleks. "The Archaeology of the Military Orders: The Material Culture of Holy War." *Medieval Archaeology* 62, no. 1 (2018): 105–134.

Prawer, Joshua. הצלבנים. Jerusalem: Bialik Institute, 1975.

Prawer, Joshua. הצלבנים: דיוקנה של חברה קולוניאלית. Jerusalem: Bialik Institute, 1975.

Shur, Nathan. תולדות עכו. Tel Aviv: Dvir Publishing House, 1990.

Stern, Eliezer. "Acre During the Crusader Period and its Maritime Aspects in the Light of Archaeological and Recent Historical Research." PhD Thesis, University of Haifa, 2014.

Swenson, Astrid. "Crusader Heritages and Imperial Preservation." *Past and Present* 226, no. 10 (2015): 27–56.

Winter, Percy H. *Acre Report: Preservation and Restoration of Acre Survey and Report*. Palestine: Government of Palestine Public Works Department, 1944.

Ytzhaki, Arie. "מצודת עכו." In עכו ואתריה, edited by Eli Schiller. Jerusalem: Ariel Publications, 1983, 81–87.

Chapter 3

YU-NESCO

The Role of World Heritage in Making and Breaking Boundaries in Yugoslavia and Its Successor States: Croatia, Montenegro, and North Macedonia

Josef Djordjevski

Yugoslavia was a socialist federation of six republics and two autonomous provinces that existed from 1945 to 1991. It was also home to a patchwork of Slavic- and non-Slavic-speaking ethnic groups and people of different religious backgrounds, mainly Catholic, Orthodox Christian, and Islamic. Along with its impressive multicultural composition, Yugoslavia also boasted having a large concentration of natural and built heritage, with seven sites officially inducted into the UNESCO list of World Heritage Sites (WHS) by 1980, and nine sites included in the list by 1989. The well-preserved medieval towns of Dubrovnik and Kotor on the Adriatic coast, and the town and lake of Ohrid situated on the Yugoslav-Albanian border, unique for its natural features and built medieval and Ottoman-era heritage, were all inducted in 1979 and 1980 while also serving as the most important tourist destinations in the Socialist Republics of Croatia, Montenegro, and Macedonia. As I will show in this chapter, each of these sites was used to attract tourists while also providing national narratives and projecting Yugoslavia's beauty and the success of its socialist experiment. These three specific sites, therefore, best highlight the multifaceted and complex nature of Yugoslavia's relationship with its world heritage.

After the collapse of Yugoslavia in 1991, this heritage was quite suddenly and dramatically stripped of its multiethnic and transnational framework and seemingly became used to highlight national differences, with each site suddenly divided between—and confined within—the borders of three separate newly independent states. Since Yugoslavia's collapse, Dubrovnik has gone from being shelled during wartime to becoming second only to Venice in terms of most-visited Mediterranean cruise ship destinations.[1] Kotor has become the most important tourist destination in a Montenegro trying desperately, often with autocratic means, to assert its independence.[2] Ohrid has experienced mass tourism, has a lack of transparency in development, and has been warned multiple times by UNESCO of becoming labeled as "endangered."[3]

While there are some important pieces of literature on tourism and heritage in Dubrovnik, Kotor, and Ohrid, there is a surprising lack of studies putting these sites that were once part of the same country into a comparative perspective. There is also little attention given to the roles these sites played as part of Yugoslavia's cherished heritage, how they became recognized by UNESCO, and how their roles shifted in the context of post-socialist nation building and re-branding. This chapter will explore the reinterpretation of these sites from symbols of Yugoslavian to Croatian, Montenegrin, and North Macedonian identities.

I argue that by examining the interconnections and interdependencies between tourism and the process of making heritage in each of these sites, we can see how they have transcended boundaries by coproducing cultural, economic, and environmental bridges between political, local, transnational, interethnic, and global dimensions. This narrative will demonstrate how, as part of socialist Yugoslavia, Dubrovnik, Kotor, and Ohrid were meant to transcend internal and external boundaries in three major ways: through showcasing Yugoslavia's connections and importance on the global stage, by fostering interethnic unity among the different ethnic groups among the Yugoslav working class, and to attract both domestic and foreign tourists. I also argue that the post-Yugoslav nations drew on these same conditions for which these sites were used by Yugoslavia to emphasize their own internal boundaries, while continuing to draw external connections. Therefore, a major contribution of this study is to expose a broader paradox in how world heritage can be used to both make and break political, national, and ethnic boundaries.

CONNECTING HERITAGE BETWEEN YUGOSLAVIA AND ITS SUCCESSOR STATES

The existing literature on heritage in Southeastern Europe tends to focus on national tourism branding and the effects of tourism on heritage, local culture, and memory. Few studies synthesize analyses on sites from the former Yugoslavia and go into deeper discussions about their roles from a transnational and historical perspective. When it comes to the relationship between tourism, heritage, and branding in the former Yugoslav republics, Patrick Naef and Josef Ploner offer a great deal of insight by looking at how national tourism branding and heritage management intersect regarding the memory of war and conflict. According to them, building on the concept of "dissonant heritage" reveals an important role for tourism in influencing memory politics through the re-negotiation of heritage.[4] While insightful regarding sites of conflict, we are left wondering about the broader historical roles of heritage sites in the former Yugoslavia as well as in Yugoslavia itself, since conflict is only one part of their history.

It is also essential to examine the coproduction of physical heritage sites—which goes beyond the concept of *patrimonialization*, or the process of heritage-making—through the lens of tourism management and marketing. As Rodney Harrison suggests, heritage making is "fundamentally an economic activity,"[5] especially due to the fact that "tourism is required to pay for the promotion and maintenance of heritage, while heritage is required to bring in the tourism that buys services and promotes a state, region, or locality's 'brand.'"[6] Therefore, heritage and tourism are often codependent, which is especially the case for the three sites examined here. They also draw on and are shaped by the physical environments into which they are placed.

While the intertwined relationship between heritage and tourism has often been acknowledged, there are few studies that historicize the transformations of the roles of these heritage sites as they dramatically shifted from Yugoslavia to post-socialist states, especially by dedicating little attention to the period of Yugoslav socialism when these sites officially became part of the UNESCO World Heritage List. Those that do historicize these processes tend to avoid questions of tourism and the environment and instead focus on issues of memory. Vladana Putnik successfully shows how memorial parks dedicated to the heroes and victims of World War II shifted from a place of special significance in Yugoslavia to neglect and reinterpretation after the collapse of socialism.[7] While doing a great job examining the shifting nature of these memorials, due to their scale and lack of significance beyond the socialist state project, it is difficult to use these case studies to reach broader conclusions about heritage in Yugoslavia and its successor states.

Other studies examining the relationship between tourism and heritage fail to historicize them in ways that would help expose some of the important contingencies. For example, Fanny Arnaud and Lauren Rivera both discuss how Croatia's official approach to developing a national tourism brand seeks to distance itself from war and its Slavic, Byzantine, and socialist history while emphasizing its "Europeanness." But neither of these studies look at how this approach was developed earlier when Croatia was still part of Yugoslavia and how it, therefore, presents an important case of continuity.

While Arnaud sheds light on Croatia's recovery of its "touristicity" after war and post-socialist transformation,[8] and Rivera highlights some of the differences in touristic publications evident between the periods during and after socialism,[9] my research shows that there are some strong similarities in the ways in which Dubrovnik, Kotor, and Ohrid were presented by Yugoslav and post-Yugoslav tourism stakeholders and leaders. Rather than radically breaking with tradition and being used for a "national reinvention,"[10] Croatian, Montenegrin, and North Macedonian leaders and stakeholders drew on pre-existing representations of heritage to maintain some connections with tradition, while also reframing them to create internal national boundaries. These more exclusionary developments, however, did not come about ex nihilo.

I build on the existing literature by examining how three specific sites of constructed heritage in the former Yugoslavia have been negotiated, created, recreated, and utilized at the intersections of tourism, environmental management, and nation-branding. Nation-branding is a broader category of study that includes the commodification of heritage for tourist consumption purposes among other processes such as public diplomacy and commerce.[11] Most existing studies of nation-branding in Yugoslavia and its successor states focus solely on the touristic aspects of nation-branding and how local cultures and histories become a part of the tourism. The process of designating and projecting world heritage sites, however, offers insight into how heritage functions in broader nation-branding efforts of a given nation.[12] Through this examination we can see why certain world heritage sites were selected as part of a nation's self-image. While acknowledging the importance of the role of heritage in the branding of Yugoslavia and its successor's identities, I show how the projection of heritage as a major part of the process of branding in a multicultural and multiethnic society such as Yugoslavia has served the dual purpose of both promoting connections and creating boundaries. In doing so, I take seriously the concept that such sites are part of hybrid landscapes, both materially constructed and culturally or socially constructed.[13] The negotiation of these sites in the conceptual realm are part of a process that includes conflict and competition, and what makes world heritage sites all the more complicated is that by becoming world heritage, there is a notion that the heritage site belongs not only to the local population or nation but to the world as well.[14] We must also pay attention to the material, physical environments of the heritage sites and how they are read or interpreted. By taking these conditions seriously, we can see how environments, including heritage sites, are coproduced by a multitude of different subjects and actors including governments, tourists, interest groups, and material nature itself.[15]

To shed light on the roles of Dubrovnik, Kotor, and Ohrid as sites of World Heritage and how they functioned in making symbolic bridges and divisions, I draw on an array of sources that help us better understand this coproduction. Sources from the Archive of Yugoslavia in Belgrade, the UN Archives, the UNESCO digital archive, and the Croatian State Archive in Zagreb are combined with popular publications to show the multiple societal perspectives regarding the role of heritage. I also draw on tourism literature from collections at the Croatian Tourism Museum in Opatija and the National and University Library in Zagreb, which include tourist guidebooks and brochures. These sources, which are both visual and textual, are excellent sources for examining how heritage is presented.[16] Promotional materials like travel brochures that create destination images are therefore significant in projecting certain features, while "the inclusion or exclusion of certain dimensions determines what kind of image the destination is attempting to create in the minds of potential markets."[17] Therefore, it can be said that while tourism marketing materials are meant to convey certain attractions welcoming audiences, they can just as easily be used to exclude others. With this element of promotional materials in mind, I now turn to a discussion of how tourism and heritage intersected in Yugoslavia, creating conditions for which symbolic bridges and boundaries were applied to the presentation of the three World Heritage Sites.

THE IMPORTANCE OF HERITAGE AND TOURISM IN YUGOSLAVIA

By 1980—the same year that lifelong president of Yugoslavia Josip Broz Tito died without any clear successors—the country had seven sites that were given UNESCO protection. By the time these sites were inducted, Yugoslavia was a socialist country pursuing a path to communism independent of the Soviet Union, it had relatively good relations with its neighbors on either side of the Iron Curtain, and it was heavily decentralized after changes in the country's 1974 constitution bestowed greater executive power to each republic of Yugoslavia.[18] Of the seven sites selected by Yugoslavia and approved by UNESCO, three were located within the Socialist Republic of Croatia, with the Plitvice Lakes National Park, the Palace of Diocletian in Split, and the old town of Dubrovnik on the southern Adriatic coast all inducted in 1979. Also included in 1979 was the Adriatic town of Kotor located within the Socialist Republic of Montenegro, followed by the lake and town of Ohrid within the Socialist Republic of Macedonia, which were inducted together in 1980. While all these heritage sites were selected due to their perceived universal value, Dubrovnik, Kotor, and Ohrid were also the most significant tourist destinations in each respective republic.

Since the inception of the Socialist Federation of Yugoslavia in 1945, heritage was an important part of the communist-led state's path to modernization.[19] According to Lenka Nahodilova, socialist modernity "heralds a changing semantics of historical time, when the past stops accounting for the present and the future, and constant change and recurring crises become the dominant mode of experience."[20] While the Yugoslav communist emphasis on rapid industrialization was indeed part of this "changing semantics of historical time," the past and its official uses were still essential to the Yugoslav statist project of securing a brighter, better future for its working class.

As early as 1945, Yugoslavia passed a law on the protection of cultural heritage, placing all sites of artistic and scientific value under state protection, including historical buildings and monuments.[21] Shortly after the passing of this law, Croatian Art Historian Cvito Fisković, who saw many of the damages to the Dalmatia region's coastal heritage firsthand as a resistance fighter during World War II, declared that if cultural monuments were a natural product of their local environments, then they were of crucial value to the local population's heritage.[22] Therefore, rather than seeing the ancient and medieval cultural heritage of Dalmatia as superfluous, or as a pesky reminder of a time before communism as one might imagine, Fisković declared that since cultural heritage and monuments in Dalmatia were created under local circumstances they had special significance to the identities of the people currently living there.[23] He also highlighted that cultural heritage was nationally significant by testifying that the fascist occupiers demolished local monuments because they represented the nationality of the local population.[24] Contemporaneously, a new law was passed in 1946 on the protection of "natural rarities," which environmental historian Hrvoje Petrić suggests led directly to a series of nature protection laws being adopted in the republics between 1947 and 1949.[25] All this goes to show that from the beginning, cultural and natural heritage were significant at the national level in Yugoslavia.

Heritage, while significant for public memory and national cohesion, had its importance catapulted by the introduction of tourism as a major component of the Yugoslav economy.[26] While tourism on the Adriatic coast and in Ohrid existed during the interwar period, it was in the 1950s, especially after the split between Josip Broz Tito and Joseph Stalin in 1948, that tourism really became significant as Yugoslavia sought alternative economic connections in the West and displayed its "willingness to be integrated in the overall development trend of tourism in Europe and the wider world."[27]

The significance of heritage to tourism and its role in promoting Yugoslavia's image was bolstered even further in the 1960s as tourism reached incredible new heights. According to one figure, the number of international tourists in Yugoslavia marked a staggering 500 percent increase between 1960 and 1971, from just under 900,000 to over 5 million.[28] Many of these tourists came from Western Europe, especially from Austria.[29] This upsurge in the number of tourists accelerated throughout the 1970s until it peaked in the mid-1980s, and cemented the place of Yugoslavia's coast among the most visited of all Mediterranean destinations, just behind the more traditionally established hotspots of Italy, France, and Spain—yet far ahead of Greece and Turkey.[30] While the majority of these visits were to the Adriatic coast, Ohrid also saw significant increases in tourist visits as its total number of guests increased from just under 35,000 in 1960 to over 100,000 by 1975.[31]

Amid this dramatic growth in tourism to places such as Dubrovnik, Kotor, and Ohrid, which were also fragile environments, the Yugoslav government initiated measures to protect them. From the mid-1960s to 1972, the state engaged in two major spatial planning projects sponsored by the UN to rationally plan tourism and development on the Adriatic coast. Known as the Adriatic Projects, teams of Yugoslav experts supported by UN-appointed consultants from the United Kingdom, Sweden, France, Italy, the United States, and Poland declared that many parts of the coast, especially those with natural and cultural heritage, should be designated for the development of tourism rather than industry. For example, one of the basic assumptions and aims for the plans was that "the climatic advantages, landscapes and environmental riches of the area should be protected and used to the greatest possible extent for the physical and mental recreation of the inhabitants of Yugoslavia, and the people of Europe and the world as a whole."[32]

This transnational approach to equating the protection of heritage and the development of tourism reflects Scott Moranda's characterization of top-down, consumer-based, statist environmentalism, which occurred on a global scale and saw states assuming that "planning and proper zoning could appease all users of the land, contribute to a blossoming consumer society, and protect wild places."[33] Additionally, for coastal places such as Dubrovnik and Kotor with outstanding cultural heritage, the planners viewed them as sites in need of not only further tourisim growth and expansion but also further protection. During a seminar held in Dubrovnik in 1970 in which the Adriatic Projects were discussed and reflected upon by Yugoslav and international experts, the participants agreed that in drawing up plans for tourism growth in Dubrovnik and the Montenegrin coast, "particular attention was given to the protection of natural resources and the conservation of cultural and historical monuments, as they are basic raw material of tourism."[34] Unfortunately, while the emphasis on protection and conservation was a positive step in terms of the language of sustainable development, the equal emphasis on exploitation left a gleaming ambiguity in these projects, with little mention or discussion on how places such as Dubrovnik could withstand hordes of tourists while still protecting its heritage resources.

While the Adriatic seaside of Yugoslavia received the most attention, a similar approach to developing tourism based on heritage resources, along with its dual language of exploitation and conservation, could be found in plans to develop Ohrid. Based on an evaluation that recognized the town and lake of Ohrid along with its neighboring Lake Prespa as being a region of both important economic and natural-cultural elements, the Parliament of the Socialist Republic of Macedonia decided to adopt a spatial plan for developing tourism in the region.[35] Some of the planners involved mentioned that it had a similar approach to that of the Adriatic Projects, and like them, it involved foreign experts.[36] Despite the planners hoping for rapid development in the Ohrid region, especially in terms of touristic infrastructure, a later reflection by a tourism expert, going by the abbreviation "SMS" in the popular tourism magazine *Turizam*, claimed that while tourism was rising significantly in Ohrid, the preservation of the lake and its cultural heritage needed to be taken seriously.[37] These cases show that both heritage and tourism were intertwined and received a significant deal of attention in Yugoslavia. It was in this setting that Dubrovnik, Kotor, and Ohrid were made UNESCO World Heritage Sites.

THE ROLE OF WORLD HERITAGE IN TRANSCENDING BOUNDARIES IN YUGOSLAVIA

At 7:20 a.m. on April 15, 1979, an earthquake of 9.5 on the Mercalli Scale struck the coast of Montenegro. This earthquake left over hundreds of thousands homeless, killed hundreds and injured thousands, and devastated many parts of the coastline, including many hotels and numerous cherished cultural monuments.[38] About one month later after aftershocks had caused even further damage, director general of UNESCO, Amadou Mahtar M'Bow, issued a plea for an international effort to assist Yugoslavia by claiming that the earthquake damaged "the glorious Montenegrin cultural heritage, which bears witness to the many influences—Roman, Byzantine, Slav, Turkish, Venetian and Austrian—that have succeeded one another in the area down the centuries."[39] M'Bow specifically referenced Kotor and its monuments as being one of the worst affected, and ended his plea by hoping that his "appeal to international solidarity will be heard by everyone who knows or feels deep down that a nation's cultural heritage, wherever that nation may be, is an irreplaceable part of the common heritage of mankind."[40]

Partially due to the damages incurred, Kotor and Dubrovnik (which also received small damages from the earthquake due to its proximity) were inducted into the UNESCO World Heritage List the same year, after Yugoslavia nominated them in October of 1979. Ohrid was also nominated, for which its natural heritage was inducted, but its cultural heritage had to wait for further assessment and was included in 1980. Initially, the induction of these sites into the UNESCO World Heritage List received a surprisingly small amount of attention in the Yugoslav media. For example, in a 1979 issue of *Turizam* the decision by the Yugoslav Authorities in the Federal Executive Council (SIV) to nominate Dubrovnik, Kotor, and Ohrid, along with Diocletian's Palace in Split, Plitvice Lakes National Park, Durmitor National Park, and Stari Ras, was only briefly mentioned.[41] The economic newspaper *Privredni Vjesnik*, which often published articles concerned with tourism, also did not mention the induction of Dubrovnik and Kotor into the UNESCO World Heritage List in any of its 1979 issues.

Despite the lack of attention in the media, the significance of the UNESCO World Heritage Sites designation can be seen in the touristic literature and promotional materials, which can also be used to reveal how these sites were then used by the Yugoslav leadership and tourism stakeholders to brand the country as a whole. As Michael A. di Giovine argues, UNESCO designation, and its subsequent creation of heritage-scapes, is "more than merely a change in nomenclature or an empty titular reward, but rather the key element in a more ambitious placemaking strategy designed to rearrange the geopolitical landscape into a reconceptualization of the world."[42] But this "reconceptualization of the world" depends on who is doing the conceptualizing. For Yugoslavia (and its successor states), this also included the state defining and projecting itself both inwardly and outwardly. While much of the traditional literature on tourism and heritage focuses on how the consumer, tourist, or observer makes meaning out of the heritage being "gazed" upon, my discussion in this chapter focuses instead on how the interests of the state and local populations are projected in the promotion of the "heritage-scape" as a tourist destination.[43]

Despite the lack of media coverage on the induction of the sites into the UNESCO list, Yugoslav publications still promoted them to both domestic and foreign audiences as proof of Yugoslavia's ability to cultivate heritage, to unite its multiethnic people, and to connect itself to the rest of the world, especially to Europe. One such publication specifically dedicated to world heritage in Yugoslavia, published in Ljubljana and Zagreb in 1990 and written mainly by Slovenian contributors, told its domestic audience that Yugoslavia is a mix of Balkan, Central European, and Mediterranean culture, which is reflected in its heritage from the dramatic historical transformations that took place in its territory.[44] The book also displays a quote by its editor Marjan Krušič, author of several guidebooks, telling readers that Yugoslavia's heritage sites cover a specific and unique part of Europe, characterized by its different South-Slavic (mostly Orthodox and Catholic) influences.[45] By promoting the geographical and national labels of the heritage sites, the book highlights each culture and region's uniqueness while framing them as part of the same country and clearly as a part of Europe. It is interesting that, aside from the mention of Yugoslavia being "Balkan," there is no attempt to draw connections to Eastern Europe. This could be due to the writers' backgrounds as Slovenians, but other publications on these sites from elsewhere in Yugoslavia followed the same approach by framing the natural and cultural sites of Yugoslavia as integral parts of Europe.

Yugoslav Macedonia's lake and town of Ohrid were unique in both Yugoslavia and the UNESCO World Heritage List. While the natural heritage of Ohrid was accepted into the list by UNESCO in 1979, in the fourth session of the World Heritage Committee in 1980 the historical and cultural parts of Ohrid were added.[46] Ohrid is one of the oldest lakes in the world and is the deepest in Europe. Due to the rare endemic species of flora and fauna not found anywhere else, Ohrid can also be considered as "probably the most diverse lake in the world."[47] In addition to its unique biodiversity, Ohrid is oligotrophic, with low nutrient counts and a bright, clear blue complexion. This is coupled with medieval churches and fortress walls and unique Ottoman-era constructions that straddle the lake's shoreline. This combination of uniquely and beautifully built and natural features caused journalist Stoyan Pribichevich to declare that Ohrid "looks like a piece of the Dalmatian Adriatic transplanted into high wooded hills."[48] Yugoslav stakeholders in the development of tourism used these features to define national characteristics, especially the medieval Orthodox influence on its history, as well as to reach out beyond the borders of Yugoslav Macedonia.

A Yugoslav-published guidebook for Ohrid in 1987 drew on the region's unique features to make connections between the heritage site and the rest of Yugoslavia, and the world, especially Europe. The book gives a historical account of Ohrid, but rather than framing its history as a part of the struggle of the working class (as one might expect from a book published in a socialist country), it focused mainly on its religious history, including the construction of basilicas, artworks, churches, its role in the development of the Cyrillic alphabet, and how saints like Climent of Ohrid made connections with the rest of the Slavic world.[49] While the account points out the mixing of Hellenic, Roman, and Serbian influences on the local Macedonian character of the town, it quite egregiously leaves out mentions of Bulgarian, Turkish, and Albanian influences. The historical account is followed up by images of antiquities, some natural settings, modern constructions, ancient churches, and religious iconography. This attempts to demonstrate Ohrid's uniqueness simultaneously with its Europeanness and worldliness, presenting it as a center of the Orthodox and Slavic world and housing one of Europe's most pristine environments, while distancing itself from the Islamic traces of Ottoman rule.

It could be argued that since this publication came a bit later in 1987 during a time when nationalism was rising in Yugoslavia, this cannot be considered reflective of general patterns in the Socialist Federation of Yugoslavia.[50] However, the way this manuscript was framed is directly reflective of previous publications about Ohrid, including ones published before it became recognized by UNESCO. For example, a 1969 tourist guidebook translated into English for Yugoslav Macedonia similarly historicizes Ohrid as both a tourist destination and center of Slavic culture in general by claiming that "whenever the magnitude and importance of cultural heritage of Slavs and their influence on world culture is mentioned one cannot bypass their first centre of culture—Ohrid."[51] The guidebook then goes on to tell its readers about exciting new hotels alongside Orthodox churches. In other touristic literature promoting Ohrid and Macedonia, Turkish and Ottoman influence is sometimes mentioned but usually only in passing.[52] Bulgarian influence, on the other hand, is usually limited to quick summaries of the Bulgarian occupation of Macedonia during World War II.[53] Despite the leaving out of certain aspects of the region's culture and history, as we can see, literature promoting Ohrid's heritage simultaneously pointed out its uniqueness, ascribed it a nationality, and clearly tied it to both Yugoslavia and European Slavdom.

Like Ohrid, Kotor was considered both a cultural and natural World Heritage Site by UNESCO. Also, like Ohrid, its Orthodox and Slavic features were emphasized in publications promoting it as a heritage site and tourist destination while pointing out its uniqueness. However, more attention was given to its ties with Western and Mediterranean Europe than Ohrid. Kotor also presented a unique blend of built and natural environments, with one of the only fjord-like gulfs in Southern Europe and its dramatic hills jutting down into the bright blue Adriatic Sea, dotted with medieval and early modern Venetian architecture. UNESCO's decision to include Kotor's historical and cultural heritage along with its natural heritage was partially due to the damages incurred during the earthquake of 1979, putting it both on the World Heritage List as well as the list of World Heritage in Danger.[54] Despite the incentive caused by earthquake damages, in September of 1979, Kotor's inclusion into the list was due to its "outstanding universal value by the quality of its architecture, the successful integration of its cities to the gulf of Kotor and by its unique testimony of the exceptionally important role that it played in the radiance of the Mediterranean culture on the Balkan territory."[55]

The old town of Dubrovnik within its fortress walls was also added due to its contribution to Mediterranean heritage, while the Montenegro earthquake's damage to Dubrovnik's architectural treasures was also taken into account by UNESCO when placing it on the World Heritage List.[56] Considering it "one of the most important properties within the borders of Yugoslavia," Dubrovnik was selected by UNESCO due to its well-preserved medieval features as a European city, which had "considerable influence not only within a small area but on the greater area of the Adriatic Coast and the Balkans."[57]

Aside from their heritage, by the time of their induction into the list both Dubrovnik and Kotor were heavily reliant on tourism. Just to highlight the significance of tourism, almost immediately after the earthquake in Montenegro the Yugoslav federal government established a working committee to deal with the destruction of the earthquake and to raise money from each Yugoslav Republic for relief. At the first meeting of the committee during a discussion about which immediate measures should be taken to deal with the effects of the earthquake, one of the members, Ismail Bajra from the Albanian-majority southern coastal town of Ulcinj, argued that immediate action was needed in terms of bringing back tourists. He argued that promotion and information for foreigners were essential and should not be postponed to ensure that Montenegro's tourist season would be salvaged.[58] The other members of the committee agreed with him and planned to allocate funds to repair tourism facilities, which demonstrates the magnitude of the importance of tourism to coastal Montenegro's overall economy, for which Kotor was its greatest resource.

With tourism's importance already in place in Dubrovnik and Kotor in 1979, touristic publications from Yugoslavia, after their induction into the UNESCO World Heritage Sites List, further highlighted their connections with Mediterranean Europe. Dubrovnik's Catholic Croat heritage was emphasized while Montenegro's association with Orthodoxy was highlighted. Regarding Dubrovnik, one 1986 touristic guidebook for the Elafiti islands just off the Dubrovnik coast presents the islands as being tied to Dubrovnik's Golden Age by pointing out its Greco-Roman history, as well as its Catholic Croat character.[59] The guidebook *Svjetska Baština u Jugoslaviji* also emphasized Dubrovnik's Christian character along with Slavic settlers in the Middle Ages, who were identified as Croats (rather than Yugoslavs).[60] Without specifically mentioning that Dubrovnik belongs to Yugoslavia and Europe, the lines being drawn are quite clear. According to such presentations, Dubrovnik is part of European and Mediterranean culture while it has clearly Slavic and Croatian national features. The European character presented also reflects earlier portrayals of Dubrovnik, including a 1964 travel guide celebrating Dubrovnik as a site of both naturally and culturally pristine heritage.[61]

Kotor is presented as unique due to the blend of cultures in its history, from the ancient Illyrians to the Romans, while its later history is characterized by Venetian influence, Christianity, and Slavic culture. All of this put together portrays Kotor as being at the crossroads of the Catholic and Orthodox worlds, which have coproduced its unique character.[62] Montenegro's uniqueness as being at the threshold of the Balkans and the Mediterranean is accompanied by a national character that is neither Croat nor Serb, but a tough warlike people who have fought bravely to retain independence. As one earlier guide to Montenegro from 1969 put it, after the Slavs had settled and after they had shed their blood in defending the region on multiple occasions, the Montenegrins of Kotor perennially resisted all invaders, whether Christian or Islamic, throughout their history.[63]

With the blend of Slavic, Mediterranean, and Balkan characteristics of each World Heritage Site being displayed in the tourism literature, we can see how they were meant to simultaneously draw ties between Yugoslavs, highlight bridges with the rest of Europe, and engage in national branding. Rather than being used for exclusion, the national specificities were used to show each heritage site as being a unique part of Europe. The leaving out of Islamic culture in presentations of Ohrid can be considered exclusionary, though it is clear that materials promoting the region were used to make connections with the rest of Europe and the Slavic world by focusing on its Orthodox heritage. The unique qualities of Dubrovnik, Kotor, and Ohrid were projected as being integral parts of Yugoslavia, which was itself a significant part of a more broadly defined Europe.

MAINTAINING BRIDGES AND CREATING BOUNDARIES IN YUGOSLAVIA'S SUCCESSOR STATES

In October of 1991, right at the end of yet another successful summer tourist season, war came to Dubrovnik. By the end of the month the first shells began to fall on the well-preserved medieval core of town, by now Croatia's most-visited tourist destination, a UNESCO World Heritage Site, and the unofficial Jewel of the Adriatic. Only four months after Croatia's declaration of independence from Yugoslavia and the subsequent outbreak of hostilities between Croatian defenders and Serbian separatists, the Serbian-dominated Yugoslav Peoples' Army (JNA) and the Yugoslav Navy surrounded Dubrovnik and began a bombardment that destroyed several important cultural artifacts and virtually wiped out its tourist economy for the next several years.[64] Since Dubrovnik and its surrounding coastal municipalities had already become entirely dependent on tourism by the turn of the decade, this was a huge psychological and material blow. In what would become known as the Wars of Yugoslav Succession or the Yugoslav Civil Wars, the shelling of Dubrovnik was symbolic in its indiscriminate nature, with no real strategic aims other than to damage the morale of the civilian population and the country's economy.[65]

Serbia and Montenegro, through their domination of the JNA, were painted as uncivilized barbarians for their role in the siege. In a publication meant to attract attention to the plight of Dubrovnik, one contributor wrote that the shelling of the city was a result of "barbarian monomania, a demonic lack of history, a right to everything, founded on a substitution of Christ's love by the sacrament of hate conceived in the devotion to Saint Sava" (the patron saint of Orthodox Serbs).[66] Another Croatian writer put it in a way that would seem to give support to the idea that Dubrovnik was being radically reinvented from its Yugoslav past. He claimed that in socialist Yugoslavia, Dubrovnik had been neglected and even unknown by its own people due to Yugoslavism, and only after the wars of the 1990s, in the ashes of JNA shells were its specifically Croatian and European core finally becoming visible.[67]

Similarly, a tourist guidebook for Dalmatia published by the state-owned company *Turistkomerc* in Zagreb in 1991 used poetic language and a wealth of images to present the Dalmatian region as a sort of mythic, fantastical land. The book came out as the war in Croatia was at its height, and yet still sought to attract visitors by evoking the harmony between nature and the built environment, personifying the landscape and pointing out that all its different features culminate in the "call of Dalmatia to be an exception, but also a model for the whole Mediterranean."[68] In addition to the emphasis on nature, the authors also made sure to emphasize to their audience that the Serbian presence in parts of Dalmatia like Knin—which were under heavy combat and incorporated into the Serbian breakaway state of Serbian Krajina—represented a sort of usurpation under "a newer Orthodox gown,"[69] while the whole region of Dalmatia, the authors argued, "nevertheless renews the heritage of Croatian kings."[70]

Despite the clear references to the war, much of the same type of language is used as in previous Yugoslav depictions of Dubrovnik, including common themes such as the primordial environment, modern accommodations, Catholic religious relics, and Croatian nationality. A guidebook for Dubrovnik, published in 1964 by the *Jugoslavija* publishing house in Belgrade, opens up by giving details of Dubrovnik's physical environment, and how all the factors from the warm climate to clear waters "makes Dubrovnik a wondrous blend of the beauty of nature and the miracle of man's existence."[71] The guidebook then went on to provide a detailed history of the city, emphasizing the blend of Latin and Slavic cultures, their unity under Catholicism, and how the "Slavic element finally prevailed"[72] while "although the people of Dubrovnik were proud of being natives of their republic, they were keenly aware of their Slavic origin."[73]

The emphasis on *Slavic* rather than *Croat* in this guidebook could be suggestive that the ethnic specificity of branding after the independence of Croatia was indeed a far cry from the more Yugoslav-friendly publications of earlier periods. However, if the argument is that after socialism Croatian branding sought to distance its heritage from the Balkan and Yugoslav past by associating itself with Europe, this earlier guidebook already did so by emphasizing Western European heritage, especially through religion.

Political scientist Derek Hall states that since gaining independence, Croatia "as a destination brand is familiar, safe, pious, trustworthy. Its portrayal is of a country comfortably European and a component of successful Mediterranean tourism."[74] Fanny Arnaud and Lauren Rivera both follow up on this argument by arguing that Croatia sought to distance itself from its neighbors by adopting a Mediterranean identity, with Arnaud arguing that in order to de-balkanize itself Croatia has instead promoted its sea, sun, and coastal landscape to self-ascribe a "valued cultural ensemble, making visible its Mediterranean characteristics."[75] While this is a tempting conclusion when one focuses only on sources from after the breakup of Yugoslavia, we can see by looking at representations of Dubrovnik and Kotor before the collapse of Yugoslavia that "Mediterranean-ness" had already been a common trope before. As for Ohrid, its environment and cultural heritage were all presented in ways that ascribed it a Slavic and unique natural character which was used to make cultural bridges with Europe and the world, but also with other Yugoslavs. As Hall puts it, "under the communists . . . such heritage was employed to overcome or subdue ethnic rivalries and as a means to inculcate a unified sense of Yugoslav identity and pride."[76] I would add, however, that this heritage was also employed to create external bridges, especially through tourism. And while national and cultural uniqueness were highlighted in the literature, the highlighting of national, religious, and ethnic specificities was quite compatible with Yugoslavia's project of making connections on the world stage.

The collections of tourism brochures and guides at the National and University Library in Zagreb and the Croatian Museum of Tourism in Opatija have numerous pieces of touristic literature from the 1990s, while many of the more recent publications, especially by the Croatian Tourism Board, are available online. In looking through these, one sees the persistence of a common theme: *the Eastern Adriatic is Croatian, and therefore Mediterranean and European, and unique in its pristine natural and built settings*. Similar themes can be extracted from Montenegrin and North Macedonian tourism literature as well, though the Croatian tourism literature is a bit more prominent due to the maturity of its industry, even during wartime.

Despite direct references to the war and "Serbian aggression" in some tourist pamphlets,[77] the goal of Croatian tourism after independence was to continue on the path it was on before the breakup of Yugoslavia. Croatia's newly instituted Ministry of Tourism for its part also drew on previous policies and official views as it made sure to usher in a new era of the privatization of coastal tourism. In the 1992 Tourism Master Plan for Croatia, the Croatian Democratic Union (HDZ)-led Ministry intended to reexamine the tourism potential of the Croatian coast in the light of war damages and the transition to private capital. It argued that Croatia would need to intensively prepare for an inflow of international capital, along with the implementation of European standards. Considering these transitions, the Ministry saw the coast in a prime position since Croatia was a part of European civilization and still had untouched natural and cultural heritage.[78]

Montenegro, as it remained in a union with Serbia during and after the Wars of Yugoslav Succession until 2006, also sought to rebuild bridges it had lost with Europe and the world. During a seminar of Montenegrin tourism experts in 1998, the president of Montenegro Filip Vujanović told his audience that because of tourism some of the negative impacts of the Yugoslav Wars had already been lessened and that Montenegro was reentering the European and global economy.[79] He went further by specifying countries, mainly Russia, Norway, Italy, and Serbia, as potential sources of tourists. Part of this "return" was due to Kotor's brand as a tourist and world heritage destination. A 2013 travel guide published by the Montenegrin Tourism Board reflects the sentiment in the 1998 seminar as it mentions the connection between Kotor and the rest of Europe. It briefly discusses Kotor as part of the Serbian Monarchy but presents it as just another foreign ruler along with the Venetians, French, Ottomans, and Austrians. It highlights Kotor's Europeanness and Mediterranean-ness by describing the Christian heritage of Kotor and its surroundings.[80]

Ohrid continued to be presented by the independent Republic of Macedonia (since 2018 officially named North Macedonia) as a heritage site of both natural and cultural treasures, while mainly emphasizing Roman and early Christian influence, again with little reference to Ottoman heritage.[81] While North Macedonia avoided much of the war and conflict that Croatia and Montenegro felt, protests by neighboring Greece and Bulgaria over its use of the adjective "Macedonian" has been met with mixed reaction by the different governments in the country. A partial response to the perceived attack on its identity under the government of Nikola Gruevski was for it to distance itself from its Slavic roots and instead emphasize a nationalistically-tinged interpretation of Antiquity.[82] Recently, however, Ohrid has reopened itself to interpretations as a center of Slavic culture.[83] In addition to struggles over identity, Ohrid has also been subjected to unplanned development, with UNESCO threatening as recently as June 2021 to classify Ohrid as an endangered site.[84]

CONCLUSION

During and after the collapse of Yugoslavia, Dubrovnik, Kotor, and Ohrid retained much of the same characterizations that were ascribed to them before. However, by employing the same descriptions that they were given before, the tourism boards of now-independent Croatia, Montenegro, and North Macedonia have been able to reframe them in ways showing their differences more than before. Therefore, the erasing of boundaries between Dubrovnik, Kotor, Ohrid, Europe, and the rest of the world was not new after the collapse of Yugoslav socialism. What was new was the distancing between other cultures and peoples in the former Yugoslavia.

In the twenty-first century, Croatia's official tourism campaign adopted the slogan "The Mediterranean as it Once Was," while Montenegro adopted "Wild Beauty," and North Macedonia became "Timeless." Scholars of tourism and place branding have generally understood the late twentieth- and early twenty-first-century adoption of such slogans as reflecting attempts by post-socialist states to *re*-brand themselves in a more conspicuous way that they hoped would distance them from the troubled pasts of communism, the pejorative label of being Balkan, and the Yugoslav Wars. While there is perhaps a degree of validity to this, such arguments are problematic in that they ignore important continuities in the marketing of heritage under socialism and after.

By looking at the ways in which heritage sites such as Dubrovnik, Kotor, and Ohrid were presented and used to make and break boundaries, it becomes evident that heritage can be used to highlight similarities and divisions between cultures. By making connections between Dubrovnik and Europe during the existence of socialist Yugoslavia and later Croatia, for example, the same factors could also be read as bridging potential cultural gaps, while in different circumstances they could be read as creating divisions. By emphasizing the Croatian and Catholic character of Dubrovnik, stakeholders could make the statement that this meant it was an integral part of Yugoslavia, while just as easily making the claim that this meant it was separate from other Yugoslav cultures, especially the Orthodox and Islamic. All this goes to show that the interpretation and process of making heritage are rather fluid and do not need to go quite as far as reinvention.

NOTES

1. Barbara Matejcic, "Croatia's Drowning Dubrovnik 'Not Just an ATM'," *BIRN* Balkan Insight, July 18, 2018 (https://balkaninsight.com/2018/07/18/dubrovnik-dethroned-07-10-2018/ , accessed October 1, 2021).

2. Jelena Dragičević, "Balkan Spring: Two Studies of Autocratic States," *Harvard International Review* 41, no. 2 (2020): 53.

3. Sinisa Jakov Marusic, "UNESCO Warns North Macedonia Again on Heritage City's Status," *BIRN* Balkan Insight, January 11, 2021 (https://balkaninsight

.com/2021/01/11/unesco-warns-north-macedonia-again-on-heritage-citys-status/, accessed September 30, 2021).

4. Patrick Naef and Josef Ploner, "Tourism, Conflict and Contested Heritage in Former Yugoslavia," *Journal of Tourism and Cultural Change* 14, no. 2 (2016): 184.

5. Rodney Harrison, *Understanding the Politics of Heritage*, Manchester: Manchester University Press, 2010, 12.

6. Harrison, *Politics of Heritage*, 21.

7. Vladana Putnik, "Second World War Monuments in Yugoslavia as Witness of the Past and the Future," *Journal of Tourism and Cultural Change* 14, no. 3 (2016): 211.

8. Fanny Arnaud, "Memorial Policies and Restoration of Croatian Tourism Two Decades after the War in Former Yugoslavia," *Journal of Tourism and Cultural Change* 14, no. 3 (2016): 281.

9. Lauren Rivera, "Managing 'Spoiled' National Identity: War, Tourism, and Memory in Croatia," *American Sociological Review* 73, no. 4 (2008): 621.

10. Naef and Ploner, "Contested Heritage," 187.

11. Nadia Kaneva, "Nation Branding: Toward an Agenda for Critical Research," *International Journal of Communication* 5, no. 25 (2011): 118.

12. Florian Bieber, "Tourism, Nation Branding and the Commercial Hegemony of Nation Building in the Post-Yugoslav States," in: Ulrich Ermann and Klaus-Jürgen Hermanik (eds.), *Branding the Nation, the Place, the Product*, London: Routledge, 2017, 126.

13. Tom Selwyn and Jeremy Boissevain, "Introduction," in: Tom Selwyn and Jeremy Boissevain (eds.), *Contesting the Foreshore: Tourism, Society, and Politics on the Coast*, Amsterdam: Amsterdam University Press, 2004, 12.

14. Harrison, "What is Heritage?" 8.

15. Scott Moranda, "The Emergence of an Environmental History of Tourism," *Journal of Tourism History* 7, no. 3 (2015): 270.

16. John Urry, "The Tourist Gaze and the Environment," *Theory, Culture, and Society* 9, no. 3 (1992): 1.

17. Asli D. A. Tasci and William C. Gartner, "Destination Image and its Functional Relationships," *Journal of Travel Research* 45, no. 4 (2007): 415.

18. For example, in the 1980s Yugoslavia had close relations with Italy and Austria regarding environmental matters, see: OECD, *Environmental Policies in Yugoslavia: A Review by the OECD and its Environment Committee Undertaken in 1985 at the Request of the Government of Yugoslavia*, Paris: OECD, 1986.

19. In the early years of state-socialism, this meant rapid industrialization. By the 1960s, however, the emphasis shifted to socialist consumerism. See: Patrick Hyder Patterson, *Bought and Sold: Living and Losing the Good Life in Socialist Yugoslavia*, Ithaca: Cornell University Press, 2011, 6.

20. Lenka Nahodilova, "Rural Decline as the Epilogue to Communist Modernization: The Case of a Socialist Model Village," in: Ger Duijzings (ed.), *Global Villages: Rural and Urban Transformations in Contemporary Bulgaria*, London, New York, New Delhi: Anthem Press, 2014, 90.

21. *Službeni List Demokratske Federativne Jugoslavije* br. 10 god. 1. March 6, 1945.
22. Cvito Fisković, *Dalmatinski Spomenici i Okupator*, Split: Slobodna Dalmacija, 1946, 6.
23. Fisković, *Dalmatinski Spomenici*, 6.
24. Fisković, *Dalmatinski Spomenici*, 13.
25. Hrovje Petrić, "About Environmental Policy in Socialist Yugoslavia," in: Astrid Mignon Kirchoff and John R. McNeill (eds.), *Nature and the Iron Curtain: Environmental Policy and Social Movements in Communist and Capitalist Countries, 1945–1990*, Pittsburgh: University of Pittsburgh Press, 2019, 170.
26. Joel Palhegyi, "Tito under Glass: Museum and Myth in the Making of Croat Yugoslavism," PhD Dissertation, University of California San Diego, 2019.
27. Igor Tchoukarine, "The Yugoslav Road to International Tourism: Opening, Decentralization, and Propaganda in the Early 1950s," in: Karin Taylor and Hannes Grandits (eds.), *Yugoslavia's Sunny Side: A History of Tourism in Socialism*, Budapest and New York: Central European University Press, 2010, 107–108.
28. Mohamed Tangi, "Tourism and the Environment," *Ambio* 6, no. 6 (1977): 340.
29. HR-HDA. Glavna uprava za turizam i ugostiteljstvo vlade NRH, BOX 8, Folder "1951." *Uprava sluzbeni put, 7.VI.-30.VI.1951: Izvještaj*, 2.
30. Tangi, "Tourism," 340.
31. S.M.S, "Promet turista u Ohridu," *Turizam* 32, no. 1 (1984): 22.
32. UNDP, *South Adriatic Project: Physical Development Plan for the South Adriatic Region of Yugoslavia, Final Report*, Dubrovnik, September 1968, February 1969, 18.
33. Moranda, "The Emergence of an Environmental History," 275.
34. UN, "Report of the Interregional Seminar on Physical Planning for Tourism Development," Dubrovnik: UN, 1970, 28.
35. M. Barjaktarević, D. Bundovski, and J. Vekić, "Regionalno prostorni plan Ohridsko-Prespanske regije," *Turizam* 18, no. 5 (1971): 17.
36. Barjaktarevi, Bundovski, & Veki, "Ohridsko-Prespanske," 18.
37. S.M.S., "Ohrid sve posećeniji," *Turizam* 31, no. 1 (1983): 24.
38. UNESCO, *Montenegro Earthquake: The Conservation of the Historic Monuments and Art Tresures*, Italy: UNESCO, 1984, 5.
39. Amadou-Mahtar M'Bow, *Appeal: For Safeguarding the Cultural Heritage of Montenegro Devastated by an Earthquake*, Paris: UNESCO, 1979, 1.
40. M'Bow, *Appeal*, 3.
41. Doleum Galea L., "Informacija o prijedlogu za upis u spisak svjetske kulturne baštine kulturnih i prirodnih dobara jugoslavije," *Turizam* 27, no. 2 (1979): 29.
42. Michael A. Di Giovine, *The Heritage-Scape: UNESCO, World Heritage, and Tourism*, Lanham: Lexington Books, 2009, 6.
43. See for example: John Urry, *The Tourist Gaze: Leisure and Travel in Contemporary Societies*, Newbury Park: Sage Publications, 1990, and Wiendu Nuryanti, "Heritage and Postmodern Tourism," *Annals of Tourism Research* 23, no. 2 (1996): 249–260.
44. Janez Höfler, Ignacij Voje, and Matjaž Poc, *Svjetska Baština u Jugoslaviji*, Ljubljana-Zagreb: Založba Mladinska Knjiga, 1990, i.

45. Hoffler, Voje, & Poc, *Baština*, i.
46. UNESCO cc-80/conf.016/10, "Convention Concerning the Protection of the World Cultural and Natural Heritage, World Heritage Committee Fourth Session," Paris, September 1980, 4 (UNESCO digital archive, https://whc.unesco.org/archive/1980/cc-80-conf016-10e.pdf, accessed September 30, 2021).
47. Christian Albrecht and Thomas Wilke, "Ancient Lake Ohrid: Biodiversity and Evolution," *Hydrobiologia* 615 (2008): 103.
48. Stoyan Pribichevich, *Macedonia: Its People and History*, University Park: The Pennsylvania State University Press, 1982, 17.
49. Kosta Balabanov, *Ohrid: Cultural-Historical and Natural Region in the Catalogue of World's Heritage*, Zagreb: Grafički Zavod Hrvatske, 1987, 9.
50. Sabrina P. Ramet, *Nationalism and Federalism in Yugoslavia, 1962–1991*, Bloomington: Indiana University Press, 1992.
51. Jovan Popovski, *Macedonia*, Beograd: Turistički Štampa, 1969, 9.
52. See: Vera Branžanska et al. *Македонија од Распаката кон иднината—25 годинин развој на социјалистичка република македонија*, Beograd: Revija, 1969–1970, 121.
53. Balabanov, *Ohrid*, 19.
54. UNESCO, Decision: Conf 015 XI. 19, "Nomination Submitted by Yugoslavia of the Kotor Natural and Historical Region to the World Heritage List and the List of World Heritage in Danger," 1979 (UNESCO digital archive, https://whc.unesco.org/en/decisions/2769, accessed October 1, 2021).
55. UNESCO, Decision: 125-ICOMOS-137, "Natural and Culturo-Historical Region of Kotor," 1979, 1.
56. UNESCO Yugoslavia implementation report, 1985, 8.
57. UNESCO, PR-C1-S2-95, "State of Conservation of World Heritage Properties in Europe: Statement of Significance," Section II, 2.
58. AY 130. Folder 30/1979. Savezno Izvršno Veće. Sednice. *Stenografske Beleške: sa I sednice Koordinacionog radnog tela za otklanjanje posledica zamljotresa u SR Crnoj Gori*. 18. April, 1979. 5/4.
59. Ilija Živanović, *Elafiti—Dubrovnik*, Zagreb: Stvarnost, 7.
60. Hoffler, Voje, & Poc, *Baština*, 63.
61. Bariša Krekić, *Photoguides "Jugoslavija." Dubrovnik. 68 Plates. City Plan. Guide*. Beograd: Jugoslavija, 1964, 5.
62. Hoffler, Voje, & Poc, *Baština*, 90.
63. Brana Vucković, *Montenegro*, Titograd: Borba and Montenegroturist, 1969, 16.
64. Nicholas A. Wise and Ivo Mulec, "Headlining Dubrovnik's Tourism Image: Transitioning Representation/Narratives of War and Heritage Preservation 1991–2000," *Tourism Recreation Research* 37, no. 1 (2012): 58.
65. Wise & Mulec, "Headlining Dubrovnik's Tourism Image," 59.
66. Vlado Gotovac, "The Defence of Dubrovnik," in: Miljenko Foretić (ed.), *Dubrovnik in War*, Dubrovnik: Matica Hrvatsk, Ogranak Dubrovnik, 1994, 9.
67. Božidar Violić, "Harshness vs. Harmony," in: Miljenko Foretić (ed.), *Dubrovnik in War*, Dubrovnik: Matica Hrvatsk, Ogranak Dubrovnik, 1994, 16.

68. Veljko Barbieri, *Dalmatia—Legenda o Svijetlu, a Legend of Light*, Zagreb: Turistkomerc, 1991, Introduction.
69. Orthodox in this case refers to the Serbian Orthodox Church, which is contrasted by the Catholic Croatian heritage.
70. Barbieri, *Legenda o Svijetlu*, Introduction.
71. Krekić, *Photoguides*, 9.
72. Krekić, *Photoguides*, 9.
73. Krekić, *Photoguides,* 17.
74. Derek Hall, "Brand Development, Tourism and National Identity: The Re-Imaging of Former Yugoslavia," *Brand Management* 9, no. 4–5 (2002): 330.
75. Arnaud, "Memorial Policies," 283.
76. Hall, "Brand Development," 325.
77. Croatian National Tourist Board "Welcome to Dalmatia," *Slobodna Dalmacija*, 2004, 14. Nacionalna i Sveučilišna Knjižica u Zagrebu, Turistički Vodiči Hrvatska, 1972–2004, 1. HST-2/4, 98.
78. Ministarstvo Turizma Hrvatske, *Generalni Plan Razvoja Turizma Hrvatske*, Zagreb, 1992, 2.
79. Filip Vujanović, "Vraćanje Izgubljenih Pozicija," in: Lazar Seferović (ed.), *Kuda ide turistička Crna Gora, Ciklus seminara Crnogorski turizam na pragu 21. Vijeka. Prvi okrugli stol*, Ministarstvo Turizma Crna Gora, 1998, 3.
80. Visit-montenegro.com, *All About Kotor—Tourist Guide*, Visit-Montenegro.com, 2013.
81. БДС, Скопје и Сусткулт, предлог за измена на планот за управување со природното и културното наследство на Охридскиот регион, 2011, 13 (https://ohrid.gov.mk/wp-content/uploads/2017/08/Predlog_plan_izmeni_plan_upravuvanje_Plan_Upravuvanje_podracje_svetsko_nasledstvo_prirodno_kultuno_nasledstvo_Ohridski_region.pdf, accessed September 28, 2021).
82. Leonora Grcheva, "The Birth of a Nationalistic Planning Doctrine: The 'Skopje 2014' Project," *International Planning Studies* 24, no. 2 (2019): 143.
83. See for example the home page for Ohrid on the Macedonia timeless website: https://macedonia-timeless.com/eng/cities_and_regions/cities/ohrid/ (accessed September 30, 2021), which mentions that in the Middle Ages Ohrid became a "Slavic cultural centre."
84. Sinisa Jakov Marusic, "UNESCO Warns North Macedonia to Protect Lakeside Heritage Site," *BIRN* Balkan Insight, June 1, 2021 (https://balkaninsight.com/2021/06/01/unesco-warns-north-macedonia-to-protect-lakeside-heritage-site/, accessed October 1, 2021).

BIBLIOGRAPHY

Primary Sources

Archives of Yugoslavia (Arhiv Jugoslavije). 30/1979. Savezno Izvršno Veće. Sednice.

Hrvatski Državni Arhiv. Glavna uprava za turizam i ugostiteljstvo vlade NRH.
Ministarstvo Turizma Crna Gora.
Nacionalna i Sveučilišna Knjižica u Zagrebu. Turistički Vodiči—Hrvatska.
Službeni List Demokratske Federativne Jugoslavije.
Turizam: časopis za turistička pitanja.
UNESCO Archives. World Heritage Convention. "Documents."
United Nations Development Program. Physical Development Plans for the South and Upper Adriatic Regions of Yugoslavia.
visitmontenegro.com

Secondary Sources

Albrecht, Christian, and Thomas Wilke. "Ancient Lake Ohrid: Biodiversity and Evolution." *Hydrobiologia* 615 (2008): 103–140.
Arnaud, Fanny. "Memorial Policies and Restoration of Croatian Tourism Two Decades After the War in Former Yugoslavia." *Journal of Tourism and Cultural Change* 14, no. 3 (2016): 270–290.
Balabanov, Kosta. *Ohrid: Cultural-Historical and Natural Region in the Catalogue of World's Heritage*. Zagreb: Grafički Zavod Hrvatske, 1987.
Barbieri, Veljko. *Dalmatia—Legenda o Svijetlu, a Legend of Light*. Zagreb: Turistkomerc, 1991.
Barjaktarević, M., D. Bundovski, and J. Vekić. "Regionalno prostorni plan Ohridsko-Prespanske regije." *Turizam* 18, no. 5 (1971): 17–19.
BDS. Скопје и Сусткулт. предлог за измена на планот за управување со природното и културното наследство на Охридскиот регион. Skopje 2011. https://ohrid.gov.mk/wp-content/uploads/2017/08/Predlog_plan_izmeni_plan_upravuvanje_Plan_Upravuvanje_podracje_svetsko_nasledstvo_prirodno_kultuno_nasledstvo_Ohridski_region.pdf (accessed September 28, 2021).
Bieber, Florian. "Tourism, Nation Branding and the Commercial Hegemony of Nation Building in the Post-Yugoslav States." In *Branding the Nation, the Place, the Product*, edited by Ulrich Ermann and Klaus-Jürgen Hermanik. London: Routledge, 2017, 125–141.
Branžanska, Vera. *Македонија од Распаката кон иднината—25 годинин развој на социјалистичка република македонија*. Beograd: Revija, 1969–1970.
Di Giovine, Michael A. *The Heritage-Scape: UNESCO, World Heritage, and Tourism*. Lanham: Lexington Books, 2009.
Dragičević, Jelena. "Balkan Spring: Two Studies of Autocratic States." *Harvard International Review* 41, no. 2 (2020): 49–53.
Fisković, Cvito. *Dalmatinski Spomenici i Okupator*. Split: Slobodna Dalmacija, 1946.
Galea, Doleum L. "Informacija o prijedlogu za upis u spisak svjetske kulturne baštine kulturnih i prirodnih dobara Jugoslavije." *Turizam* 27, no. 2 (1979): 29.
Gotovac, Vlado. "The Defence of Dubrovnik." In *Dubrovnik in War*, edited by Miljenko Foretić. Dubrovnik: Matica Hrvatska, 1994, 7–11.

Grcheva, Leonora. "The Birth of a Nationalistic Planning Doctrine: The 'Skopje 2014' Project." *International Planning Studies* 24, no. 2 (2019): 140–155.

Hall, Derek. "Brand Development, Tourism and National Identity: The Re-Imaging of Former Yugoslavia." *Brand Management* 9, nos. 4–5 (2002): 323–334.

Harrison, Rodney. *Understanding the Politics of Heritage*. Manchester: Manchester University Press, 2010.

Höfler, Janez, Ignacij Voje, and Matjaž Poc. *Svjetska Baština u Jugoslaviji*. Ljubljana-Zagreb: Založba Mladinska Knjiga, 1990.

Kaneva, Nadia. "Nation Branding: Toward an Agenda for Critical Research." *International Journal of Communication* 5, no. 25 (2011): 117–141.

Krekić, Bariša. *Photoguides "Jugoslavija." "Dubrovnik." 68 Plates. City Plan. Guide*. Beograd: Jugoslavija, 1964.

M'Bow, Amadou–Mahtar. *Appeal: For Safeguarding the Cultural Heritage of Montenegro Devastated by an Earthquake*. Paris: UNESCO, 1979.

Marusic, Sinisa Jakov. "UNESCO Warns North Macedonia Again on Heritage City's Status." *BIRN Balkan Insight*, January 11, 2021. https://balkaninsight.com/2021/01/11/unesco-warns-north-macedonia-again-on-heritage-citys-status/ (accessed September 30, 2021).

Matejcic, Barbara. "Croatia's Drowning Dubrovnik 'Not Just an ATM'." *BIRN Balkan Insight*, July 18, 2018. https://balkaninsight.com/2018/07/18/dubrovnik-dethroned-07-10-2018/ (accessed October 1, 2021).

Ministarstvo Turizma Hrvatske. *Generalni Plan Razvoja Turizma Hrvatske*. Zagreb, 1992.

Moranda, Scott. "The Emergence of an Environmental History of Tourism." *Journal of Tourism History* 7, no. 3 (2015): 268–289.

Naef, Patrick, and Josef Ploner. "Tourism, Conflict and Contested Heritage in Former Yugoslavia." *Journal of Tourism and Cultural Change* 14, no. 2 (2016): 181–188.

Nahodilova, Lenka. "Rural Decline as the Epilogue to Communist Modernization: The Case of a Socialist Model Village." In *Global Villages: Rural and Urban Transformations in Contemporary Bulgaria*, edited by Ger Duijzings. London, New York, Delhi: Anthem Press, 2014, 89–104.

Nuryanti, Wiendu. "Heritage and Postmodern Tourism." *Annals of Tourism Research* 23, no. 2 (1996): 249–260.

OECD. *Environmental Policies in Yugoslavia: A Review by the OECD and Its Environment Committee Undertaken in 1985 at the Request of the Government of Yugoslavia*. Paris: OECD, 1986.

Palhegyi, Joel. "Tito Under Glass: Museum and Myth in the Making of Croat Yugoslavism." PhD Dissertation, University of California San Diego, 2019.

Patterson, Patrick Hyder. *Bought and Sold: Living and Losing the Good Life in Socialist Yugoslavia*. Ithaca: Cornell University Press, 2011.

Petrić, Hrovje. "About Environmental Policy in Socialist Yugoslavia." In *Nature and the Iron Curtain: Environmental Policy and Social Movements in Communist and*

Capitalist Countries, 1945–1990, edited by Astrid Mignon Kirchoff and John R. McNeill. Pittsburgh: University of Pittsburgh Press, 2019.

Popovski, Jovan. *Macedonia*. Beograd: Turistički Štampa, 1969.

Pribichevich, Stoyan. *Macedonia: Its People and History*. University Park: The Pennsylvania State University Press, 1982.

Putnik, Vladana. "Second World War Monuments in Yugoslavia as Witness of the Past and the Future." *Journal of Tourism and Cultural Change* 14, no. 3 (2016): 206–221.

Ramet, Sabrina P. *Nationalism and Federalism in Yugoslavia, 1962–1991*. Bloomington: Indiana University Press, 1992.

Rivera, Lauren. "Managing 'Spoiled' National Identity: War, Tourism, and Memory in Croatia." *American Sociological Review* 73, no. 4 (2008): 613–634.

Selwyn, Tom, and Jeremy Boissevain. "Introduction." In *Contesting the Foreshore: Tourism, Society, and Politics on the Coast*, edited by Tom Selwyn and Jeremy Boissevain. Amsterdam: Amsterdam University Press, 2004.

Tangi, Mohamed. "Tourism and the Environment." *Ambio* 6, no. 6 (1977): 336–341.

Tasci, Asli D. A., and William C. Gartner. "Destination Image and Its Functional Relationships." *Journal of Travel Research* 45, no. 4 (2007): 413–425.

Tchoukarine, Igor. "The Yugoslav Road to International Tourism: Opening, Decentralization, and Propaganda in the Early 1950s." In *Yugoslavia's Sunny Side: A History of Tourism in Socialism*, edited by Karin Taylor and Hannes Grandits. Budapest and New York: Central European University Press, 2010.

UNESCO. *Montenegro Earthquake: The Conservation of the Historic Monuments and Art Tresures*. Italy: UNESCO, 1984.

United Nations. *Report of the Interregional Seminar on Physical Planning for Tourism Development*. Dubrovnik: United Nations, 1970.

Urry, John. "The Tourist Gaze and the Environment." *Theory, Culture, and Society* 9, no. 3 (1992): 1–26.

———. *The Tourist Gaze: Leisure and Travel in Contemporary Societies*, Newbury Park: Sage Publications, 1990.

Violić, Božidar. "Harshness vs. Harmony." In *The Defence of Dubrovnik: Dubrovnik in War*, edited by Miljenko Foretić. Dubrovnik: Matica Hrvatsk, Ogranak Dubrovnik, 1994, 15–20.

Vucković, Brana. *Montenegro*. Titograd: Borba and Montenegroturist, 1969.

Wise, Nicholas A., and Ivo Mulec. "Headlining Dubrovnik's Tourism Image: Transitioning Representation/Narratives of War and Heritage Preservation 1991–2000." *Tourism Recreation Research* 37, no. 1 (2012): 57–69.

Živanović, Ilija. *Elafiti–Dubrovnik*. Zagreb: Stvarnost, 1986.

Chapter 4

The Labor Movement as UNESCO World Heritage

Claiming a Seat for Workers through Assembly Halls

Marie Brøndgaard

During the industrialization of the nineteenth century the working class grew as did their poor living conditions.[1] Workers around the world started to fight inequality by demanding spaces in which to assemble and organize themselves into unions. Many of these groups succeeded in establishing, building, or acquiring workers' assembly halls. These buildings were established across the globe over decades and are witness to the labor movement as a multigenerational effort.

Aiming to fill a gap on the UNESCO World Heritage List, the *Danish Workers Museum* embarked upon a venture in 2009 that was to take more than a decade.[2] The *Victorian Trades Hall* in Melbourne, the *Broken Hill Trades Hall* in Broken Hill, *Paasitorni* in Helsinki, *Vooruit* (now Viernulvier) in Ghent, and *The Workers Museum* (located in the *Workers' Union & Association Hall*) in Denmark worked jointly to locate assembly halls of the labor movement worldwide to develop a transnational serial nomination for the UNESCO World Heritage List. The list includes modern heritage as well as industrial sites, and there are properties inscribed onto the World Heritage List, where gathering spaces are a part of that property such as Blaenavon Industrial Landscape and Þingvellir (it's the Icelandic Þ called Thorn) National Park. However, where industrial inscriptions bear witness to the technical advances of industrialization, a representation of workers' assembly halls celebrates a global cultural phenomenon of the labor movement that puts emphasis on *workers*, the people on the factory floors. The workers' assembly halls encompass the intangible values of the labor movement such as freedom and equality. These buildings are remnants of a transnational labor history and witness to how ordinary people achieved the extraordinary.

There is a lack of literature on transnational serial nominations for world heritage, hence this chapter aims to add to the existing body of knowledge with a case study underlining the process behind a nomination as well as an analysis of how the monuments of the workers' movement are of universal value combining immaterial values with material structures. This chapter elucidates why it is important to add the labor movement to the UNESCO World Heritage List and highlights heritage as a transnational matter.

A list of all identified workers' assembly halls will not be provided, because the nomination project is in an identification phase at the time of writing (2022), but examples will be provided. Although workers' assembly halls are known by many names (house of the people, union hall, labor lyceum, trades hall, etc.), this chapter adopts the term *workers' assembly halls* to mean buildings acquired by the labor movement as instruments of organization and a platform for education, debate, cultural events, and social networks. These buildings were used by workers from various political standpoints, trades, and unions.

THE SPACES OF THE LABOR MOVEMENT

The democratic labor movement is inherently transnational, and disregarding of nation-states as coined by the common motto: "workers of the world unite." Workers' assembly halls have been instrumental in the organization of workers in most sections of the labor movement, often founded in trade unionism. The fact that the labor movement has manifested itself differently in different countries speaks to its diversity. At a time when industrialization meant progress to many, it also meant a decrease in acceptable living conditions and rights to many more. Industrialization, population increase, and urbanization in the nineteenth century were among the most dramatic changes in human history, creating large-scale migration from rural to urban areas, causing people to lose their communities and to create new ones and new common identities. Many workers lacked a sense of belonging and a sense of place, which the workers' assembly halls provided. Urban and rural workers had similar issues yet different realities in which to fight them, and many still existing assembly halls are urban. They are buildings established by the movement for the purpose of bringing workers together for political, social, cultural, and educational purposes. They bear testimony to the daily work and organization of the labor movement as a major force in shaping democracy and welfare states in many parts of the world. The labor movements, whether bearing different political, religious, or secular connotations, all start from a universal longing for emancipation and the acceptable conditions of workers' lives.

Tied together through common ideological values and organizational practicalities, these buildings bear witness to the labor movement as a global cultural practice. Because the labor movement sought to influence both political decision-making as well as provide social and cultural content in people's lives, the political and the cultural spheres became intermeshed.[3] This fluidity in which the movement worked was translated into the physical spaces of the workers' assembly halls. The labor movement has always had an international focus promoting international solidarity. Developing a UNESCO nomination of workers' assembly halls, therefore, must be an international effort because these gathering spaces and the intangible significance of being allowed to assemble in them is shared world heritage.

The heritage of the labor movement is found in a shared international ideology that espouses equality and that can be found in these buildings sharing purpose albeit in differing layouts. This transnational serial nomination highlights the interconnected cultural phenomenon of the labor movement around the world. Although the labor movement is less represented in some regions of the world or took different shapes, it is represented in some form across most of the world. Instead of nominating just one assembly hall in one country to represent the global migration of ideas, a series of buildings from around the world will make clear that the struggle for workers' rights cannot be contained within just one national setting. The labor movement and the insistence on establishing spaces for its members is not the heritage of one country, but of a universal longing for emancipation, democracy, and equality—a struggle in the past that continues today, hence a living tradition. This project is concerned with the spaces used by the labor movement to organize societal change and because "space is crucial to democracy,"[4] the workers' assembly halls can justify the labor movement as transnational history. Workers' assembly halls were the platforms, the epicenters for the planning and organization of workers, and the results of their endeavors were implemented in the workspace and therefore not connected with the assembly halls.[5] By adding workers' assembly halls to the World Heritage List, the spaces in which many social rights movements were made possible are celebrated rightly as the whole world's heritage.

But what is it that makes the labor movement worthy of being recognized as world heritage? And does the workers' assembly hall encapsulate the movement? The workers' assembly hall is the space, in which the mass organization of workers occurred, and they are the tangible testimony to the intangible values of the labor movement, the intangible values being dignity of workers, political inclusion, organized labor rights, emancipation, equality, citizenship, and democracy. The labor movement is a still living tradition and this series of diverse buildings shows how the labor movement manifested differently at different times in various countries adapting to local conditions. Space and *sense of place* matters and, therefore, this nomination is also a celebration of workers in countries that are not part of the series or where the democratic labor movement did not settle. The term "people's house" encapsulates the essence of the significance of workers' assembly halls; they were *houses* and to a certain extent *homes* not merely *buildings*. Margaret Kohn argues that "stone and mortar are particular potent symbols" that inspire action and change.[6]

The Democratic Labor Movement

International solidarity is a fundamental characteristic of the labor movement, a notion which speaks to a transnational nature. Despite cultural differences, the labor movement was always based on intercultural dialogue and the values of the movement migrated through the world. The tradition of constructing workers' assembly halls may have started in Europe and spread from here across the globe, but later buildings in Europe might also have been inspired by buildings further away.

This case is concerned with *democratic labor movements only.* In this nomination project the labor movement is embraced as a broad working-class movement that sought to bring together workers "engaged in social and political struggles beyond the shop floor"[7] and the union of workers was more important than individual identity or private interests. Here, the labor movement is not considered one political entity but instead a multilayered movement fighting for fundamentally better working and living conditions, emancipation, and equality, for the right to assemble and organize, and to unionize. It is the labor movement with all its facets —not focused on communism, temperance, secularism, or religion, but workers in general, skilled and unskilled, men and women, the people behind the machines, those fighting for "acceptable conditions for the working-class."[8] Although sections of the labor movements evolved from different origins, they shared a culture. It is a shared culture but within a *"constitutive diversity* of individuals and groups in the making of socio-spatial collective."[9]

Arguably, workers' assembly halls are not the only reason for why the labor movement and unions still work today,[10] but they were instrumental in the formal organization during early stages of the movement. The Danish newspaper *The Socialist* wrote in 1872 that a workers' assembly place was essential for the labor movement to prosper.

What Are Workers' Assembly Halls?

This section is concerned with how a workers' assembly hall can be defined and how it constitutes transnational heritage. It can be considered a buildings' movement, a movement within the labor movement as the phenomenon of workers' assembly halls can be documented globally. The individual halls have often had strong local attachment as for instance Broken Hill Trades Hall, which was built in a town that sprung up when mining activity commenced. A model example to describe what a workers' assembly hall looks like is Victor Horta's *Maison du Peuple* in Brussels inaugurated in 1899, which was demolished in the 1960s. This building is often highlighted as a prime example of an early workers' assembly hall, built to exude air and light with open congregational spaces. There are publications about workers' assembly halls and people's houses that focus on regions or specific countries.[11] These are valuable sources in piecing together what the phenomenon is and how widespread it was, and we hope this nomination will elucidate the transnational nature of the buildings' movement rather than focusing on one country.

Numerous names have been given to workers' gathering places: *trade union hall, labor union hall, labor temple, labor lyceum, casa del pueblo, Gewerkschaftshaus, folkets hus, Volkshaus, liberty hall, casa del popolo, maison du peuple, bourse du travail, workers' assembly hall*, and *people's palace*. This multiplicity of names complicates the search for workers' assembly halls. Arguably, the best documentation of the importance of these buildings are the buildings themselves:[12] their outline, their use, and their attendees. The type of workers' assembly hall with offices, a big main hall, and eating facilities or a co-op can be argued to be a Western model. It is easier to create an inventory of buildings in the United States, Australia, New Zealand, and Europe as many are still in existence. However, workers' assembly halls were not a Western tradition but developed in different parts of the world. If rooted in a European tradition, it traveled with migrants and became part of local settings across the globe. It is likely that the II International—an international organization of labor parties formed in 1889—provided a space to share ideas and ways of organizing including the building of workers' assembly halls among labor functionaries from a variety of countries. It is also difficult to speak of a European or Western type of workers' assembly halls as they varied in many ways. The French buildings were often built on land owned by the municipality, the German buildings were transformed into administrative centers after World War II leaving behind the idea of providing a space for social and cultural events for workers, the Spanish workers often met in rented spaces or their spaces were confiscated during Franco's dictatorship, many Belgian buildings included a co-op, and the buildings in the United Kingdom and New Zealand were often associated with solely one union whereas most North American, Scandinavian, and Australian buildings were built for workers of all affiliations.

Some workers' assembly halls in postcolonial countries were built much later because of colonial rule, which prevented the creation of an organized labor movement before independence. Some early examples of workers' assembly halls outside of Western countries date from the early 1900s including the Johannesburg Trades Hall. Others were built after World War II including those in St. Louis, Senegal (1946), and the *Hall of Trade Unions* in Accra, Ghana (1960).

Despite the abundance of names, the challenge of defining the workers' assembly halls in terms of usage and origin complicates the search further. In certain places the buildings were used primarily as political entities or as trade union offices (*Gewerkschaftshaus* in Frankfurt am Main, Germany, and the *Hall of Trade Unions* in Accra), others functioned as community centers solely for recreational activities (the 1912 *Nelson Independent Labour Party Clarion House*, United Kingdom), and some had been used mainly by men or women (*The Women Workers' Institute* from 1912, Cradley Heath, United Kingdom). Others were used by migrant groups as was the case with the *Casa Garibaldi* in Istanbul, Turkey, and the 1919 *Ukrainian Labour Temple* in Winnipeg, Canada. This nomination is concerned with gathering places that were multifunctional, social, and open to all, independent from the state, established out of necessity, and permanent.

Multifunctional Instruments of Organization

Workers' assembly halls were multifunctional spaces that included a main hall for political debates or cultural events such as concerts or dances, smaller rooms for trade union meetings, reading societies or study groups, and facilities to support such activities.[13] A large gathering hall is a common trait and one that Kohn emphasized when she explained the outline of the houses of the people as the opposite of a *panopticon*.[14] The heart of a panopticon is a space in which a guard could oversee the whole building like a prison. Instead, workers' assembly halls were built to evoke solidarity with a gathering hall in the middle for parties, education, debates, and large meetings. Central to all components in the series is that they were instruments of the organization of workers, where unions and associations were founded, political meetings were held for improving working conditions, and where mass mobilization of the working class occurred. In the floorplan shown in figure 4.1, it is shown how each room is designed for meetings or gatherings visible in the fact that each room is drawn to show specific table settings, a symbol that these rooms were for organizing people through meetings and assemblies.

1. sal

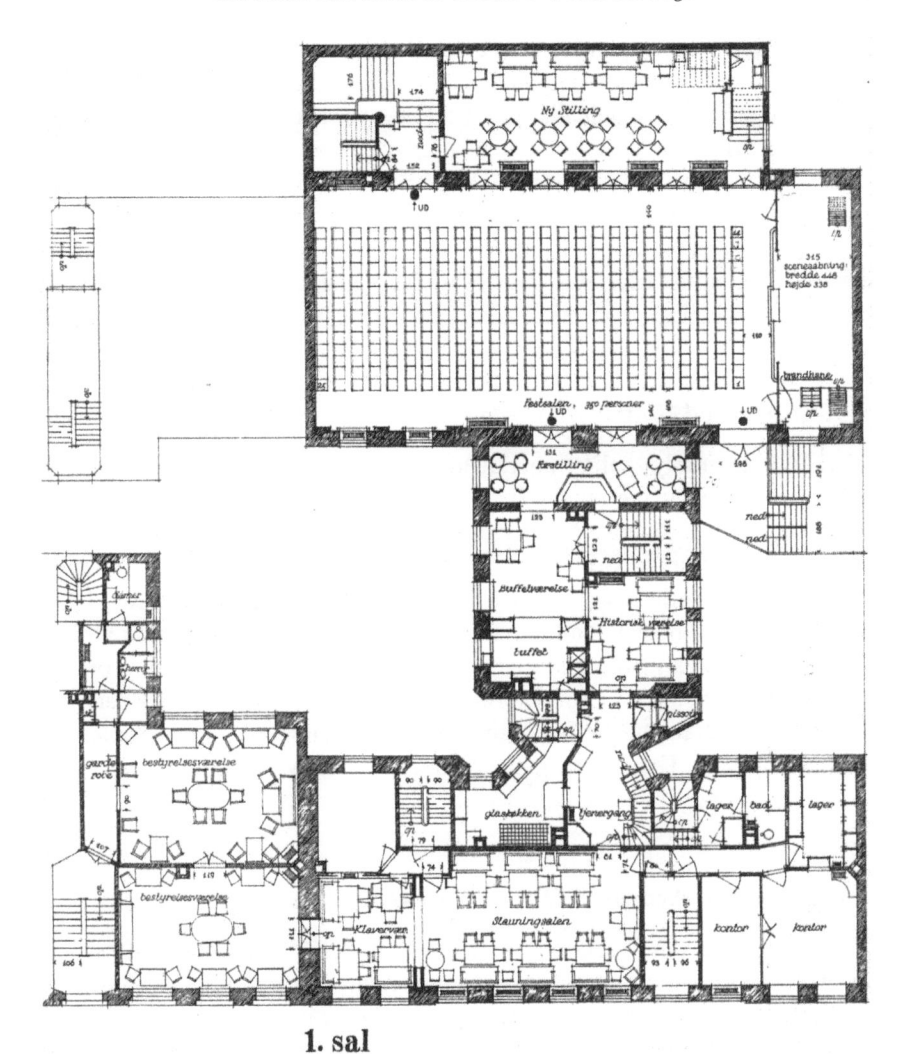

Figure 4.1. Plan of the Workers' Union & Association Hall, Now the Workers Museum in Copenhagen, 1943. *Source*: By courtesy of the Workers Museum, Library & Archive.

Sociability

Workers' assembly halls stood in contrast to the small, unsanitary workers' homes, crowded spaces that were considered yet another symbol of the need for workers' emancipation.[15] The collective spaces in the assembly halls served as safe spaces, in which like-minded people were given a sense of belonging and a place from which to organize change—providing spaces for workers from various political associations: "even though organizations such as the reformist cooperatives, mutual aid societies, the inter-classist popular university program, syndicalist producer co-ops, and the Marxist-influenced socialist parties were often ideological adversaries, they were united under one roof."[16] The workers' assembly halls offered activities of cultural, social, educational, and political nature and were inspired by the aim to democratize education, recreation, and entertainment to the masses. The assembly halls played a role in the everyday lives of workers just as they still play a role in the minds of people in their local area today even if their function has changed.

Self-Organized Entity

Workers' assembly halls functioned independently from the state and employers. Even if the land was allotted to the workers by the state,[17] the halls themselves operated by labor organizations independently of the state. Construction was often accomplished with money raised by workers themselves, but others are situated in repurposed buildings post-conflict or post-colonially where assembly halls might have been established in already existing structures or on land given to them. After World War II, workers' assembly halls in West Germany were returned to trade unions (they had been seized by the Nazis).[18] Self-containment was intended to build "social and cultural unity."[19] They were managed democratically and inclusively where trade unions or political activities with various visions coexisted.

Established or Acquired Out of Necessity

These buildings were acquired or built out of necessity to create safe spaces for workers to gather and were often not situated at the most prominent or regular-shaped lots as in the case of the *Paasitorni* in Helsinki or the *Maison du Peuple* in Brussels as no one wanted to sell land to a labor organization.[20] Sometimes a strawman was used as an intermediate buyer as with *The Workers Museum* in Copenhagen.[21] Even though the freedom of assembly became a constitutional right in many countries in the nineteenth century, in practice it was made impossible for workers to meet in restaurants as these establishments were threatened with losing their alcohol licenses if they hosted worker meeting. The physical buildings symbolize the necessity of workers to have a space they were previously denied and witness of the relationship between people and their built environment.[22] Once the right to assemble was constitutionalized in many countries, religious and political agents of left- and right-wing groupings started building community structures.

Long-Lasting, Time-Typical Structures

Workers' assembly halls were built in the hope of being long-lasting structures equal to the buildings owned by the factory proprietors. They were expected to stand out as landmarks equal to cathedrals and government buildings.[23] In some cases, workers referred to these buildings as their churches drawing parallel to other, at the time, more accepted and recognized forms of socialization.[24] They were built with ambition to mimic bourgeois culture and to claim a seat in society equal to others. They were built in recognizable architecture typical of its time to fit in. Figure 4.2 shows The Workers' Union & Association Hall built in a style similar to those in the neighborhood, many of which still exist, attesting to the longevity. Because the buildings in the series are from different times, they also represent different architectural styles, although their layout remained very similar. Early workers' gathering spaces from the 1800s in the United Kingdom differ much in style from the 1950 *Edificio de la Confederación General del Trabajo de la República de Argentina* in Buenos Aires, Argentina, but they share common functional designs.

Figure 4.2. The Workers' Union & Association Hall, Now the Workers Museum in Copenhagen, 1909. *Source*: By courtesy of the Workers Museum, Library & Archive.

These embedded architectural elements constitute a transnational serial nomination by being a platform from which the labor movement evolved, spread, and continues to develop. The attributes of multifunctionality, openness, independence, necessity, and permanence help identify a transnational tradition and the following sections will explain the nomination as UNESCO World Heritage as well as the processes around developing a nomination.

UNESCO WORLD HERITAGE

Heritage is often transnational, transcending time and space. The UNESCO World Heritage List offers a platform for heritage that represents all humankind explaining our common past. The meaning of workers' assembly halls impact society today, both the movement and the buildings, and one might not be here without the other. These buildings provided space, in which workers could think the thoughts that made way for the ideology applied in many current societies. These ideas were operationalized in workers' assembly halls, resulting in the introduction of suffrage, 8-8-8 (8 hours work, 8 hours freedom, 8 hours rest), social welfare systems, health insurance, and paid vacation. This is transnational heritage. After World War II, UNESCO was formed aiming for international cooperation to help bring peace to the minds of men and women. Although many wars have passed since, UNESCO's mandate remains valid in the ongoing fight for freedom of expression, the fight against intolerance, discrimination, and for acceptance of cultural diversity.[25]

The World Heritage Convention is essentially a conservation convention, a formalized contract in which state parties agree to preserve inscribed material heritage. Critics state that UNESCO is influenced by Western academic approaches to preservation.[26] To remedy this, *The International Convention for the Safeguarding of the Intangible Cultural Heritage* includes heritage practices outside Western heritage management.[27] Although this nomination has an intangible element, it is the tangible sites that are the bearing argument for inscription. The *Global Strategy for a Representative, Balanced and Credible World Heritage List* emphasizes UNESCO's effort to bring diverse inscriptions to the List to depict the world's shared heritage.[28] It encourages international cooperation and nudges more affluent states to take responsibility for an actual shared world heritage. The report prepared for the International Council on Monuments and Sites (ICOMOS), *Filling in the Gaps,* highlights gaps within the World Heritage List. It encourages international collaboration achieved through, among other things, transnational nominations.[29] Serial transnational properties are testimonies to the fact that political borders are not always cultural borders. Global phenomena such as the labor movement is just one example. The list has an overrepresentation of European sites from the times before the twentieth century.[30] This nomination fills a gap with its geographical range, its anti-elitist architecture, and its focus on the twentieth century.

Transnational Serial Nominations

The World Heritage List has forty-three transboundary sites at the time of writing and not all of these are serial. The transboundary and transnational sites as well as serial sites are witnesses to the true nature of world heritage. They defy assignment to a single modern nation and cross political borders. Ownership falls beyond that of the communities responsible for stewardship. Serial properties are a collection of sites physically unconnected but within the same state party, as for instance the Australian Convict Sites spread across Australia, which have no physical connection but share a common history and culture.[31] A transboundary property is a singular site that expands beyond the political borders of one state party, as for instance *The Wadden Sea*, a natural property that extends from Denmark through Germany to the Netherlands.[32] Other examples are the *Qhapaq Ñan, Andean Road System*, a cultural route through Argentina, Chile, Bolivia, Ecuador, Colombia, and Peru, and the *Colonies of Benevolence* in the Netherlands and Belgium inscribed in 2021.[33] Transnational series are categorized by multiple sites that are physically unconnected and that reach beyond the national borders of two or more countries.[34] Transnational series encompass an ideal of world heritage because they underline how heritage transcends time and geopolitical limitations. A transnational serial site example is *The Architectural Work of Le Corbusier*[35] that includes structures designed by the architect in Argentina, Belgium, France, Germany, India, Switzerland, and Japan. Conversely, transboundary inscriptions have obvious components because the geography binds the sites together, for instance with cultural routes like *The Silk Route*.[36] Workers' assembly halls, equally share similar meanings and functions based on a set of ideological notions, yet neither time period, geography, nor style are combining traits alone.

Transnational serial nominations risk growing too big and include too many components, and hence become: "unworkable in terms of delivering effective protection and management and meeting the requirements of integrity, or, in extreme cases, might challenge the credibility of the Convention."[37] The process behind any transnational serial nomination is a challenging, diplomatic, and rewarding journey, an exercise of navigating language barriers, different governing systems, and various preservation approaches as well as carrying the responsibility of creating a sound selection format on which to base the grouping of components. Consensus is that challenges with transnational serial nominations are plentiful;[38] consequently, the UNESCO Expert Meetings on this topic contribute to a greater understanding for those in the nomination process and for those who coordinate transboundary management plans.

When world heritage such as *The Maritime Mercantile City of Liverpool*, inscribed for its role as a merchant center and modern dock industry, was removed due to modernization of the dock compromising the integrity of the site,[39] it raises the question of how we manage still living traditions in modern heritage. The workers' assembly halls will, inscribed or not, still evolve to suit the changing needs of the labor movement as they have for decades, adding new styles, features, or up- or downscaling as it happened in the early twentieth century for halls that, for instance, incorporated cooperatives[40] or evolved into conference facilities. This is a constant focal point in this project and why the series must not be overwhelmingly large. The series does not need to represent every single country or every single branch of the labor movement to illustrate the overall cultural plurality of the workers' assembly halls.

Fundamental UNESCO values are cultural exchange and international cooperation and because transnational serial nominations have the potential to support this notion, this nomination type is increasingly more popular. However, "the enormous enthusiasm for serial properties must therefore not distract us from alternative ways of achieving transnational cooperation in the field of World Heritage."[41] One of the benefits of transnational nominations is that only one state party sends the combined nomination dossier, which means that participating state parties get a free pass, since only one nomination is permitted per annum per country.[42] In the case of workers' assembly halls Denmark will be the nominating party.

The Labor Movement as World Heritage

But how does this nomination contribute to the values of UNESCO? UNESCO's vision is to promote "cultural heritage and the equal dignity of all cultures"[43] and in so doing, strengthen the bonds among nations and foster international cooperation and cultural awareness. Furthermore, UNESCO marks the importance of "freedom of expression, as a fundamental right and a key condition for democracy and development."[44] These intangible values are characteristic for the democratic labor movement and, therefore, it is important to preserve the physical testimony of the organization of workers for the future. Many assembly places have been demolished or repurposed, and their function and central meaning for lives of the working class have diminished. Social structures have changed but the workers' assembly halls are remnants of time periods when the working class took charge and created the first "autonomous sites of popular mobilization."[45] This should be celebrated, and remaining buildings preserved for future generations. This nomination project suits the definition of world heritage. The *Operational Guidelines for the Implementation of the World Heritage Convention* state: "The cultural and natural heritage is among the priceless and irreplaceable assets, not only of each nation, but of humanity as a whole. The loss, through deterioration or disappearance, of any of these most prized assets constitutes an impoverishment of the heritage of all the peoples of the world."[46]

While the process of industrialization has long been included into the World Heritage List, those who have made it possible—workers—are still absent. The *Erzgebirge/Krušnohoří Mining Region* in Germany and Czechia and the *Blaenavon Industrial Landscape* in Wales celebrate and preserve the important industrial endeavors of many generations who gained technical skills and enhanced international trade and development. The *Blaenavon Industrial Landscape* in Wales even includes a *workmen's hall and institute*. New Lanark in Scotland is a built environment that pays tribute to the socialist experiments of Robert Owen with industrial production, workers' housing, and an educational institute and school.[47] These sites showcase working-class heritage but the workers' assembly halls will add knowledge about the organizing of the working class and democratic labor movement to the List.

THE NOMINATION PROJECT

Why do workers' assembly halls exist in certain places and not others? Various approaches to the labor movement and heritage legislation means that governments have either preserved these buildings, repurposed them, and ensured their destruction or foundation in the first place. Armed conflict, fiscal challenges, or visions of urban renewal provide some of the explanations for why the physical structures are absent in some cityscapes and can explain why architectural preservation has not been prioritized. In Japan most workers' assembly halls have been demolished, in United States many have been repurposed for commercial use causing loss of integrity to the interior, and many rural buildings have not survived. Workers' assembly halls are endangered, and it seems urgent to establish means for preserving the remaining buildings. The changing role of the labor movement and decreased trade unionization accentuate the preservation urgency further.

The Initial Research

The Workers Museum started researching workers' assembly halls in 2009. Our aim was to locate those still existing. The work included a comparative study of fifty-eight workers' assembly halls in twenty-three countries.[48] The final suggestion for a series included the following buildings:

- *Vooruit* in Ghent, Belgium, 1913
- *Paasitorni*, Helsinki, Finland, 1908
- *The Victorian Trades Hall*, Melbourne, Australia, founded 1859
- *The Broken Hill Trades Hall*, Broken Hill, Australia, 1905
- *The Workers Museum*, Copenhagen, Denmark, 1879
- *Gewerkschaftshaus*, Frankfurt am Main, Germany, 1929
- *The Socialist Labour Hall*, Barre, United States, 1900
- *Bourse du Travail*, Bordeaux, France, 1938
- *Folkets Hus*, Motala, Sweden, 1907

The initial research revealed a concentration of workers' assembly halls in Europe, North America, and Australia. During the first phase of research an effort was made to establish contact with people around the world who could contribute to finding buildings suitable for a transnational series of workers' assembly halls. Although the 2009 research gained much interest from the international labor movement and scholars in the field of social history, it also concluded that the tradition of workers' assembly halls as a focal point in the daily lives of the working class was a European tradition spanning from the late nineteenth to the early twentieth century. As it happens with many UNESCO nominations, this initial research came to a temporary halt but luckily not before findings were published in 2013.[49] Being the coordinating organization for this UNESCO bid, it functioned as a project reboot when *The Workers Museum* was accepted onto the Danish tentative list in 2018.[50] Developing the initial project, a sound foundation was in place for further investigation before settling on an all-encompassing serial grouping. Following the national tentative list inscription, a phase of fundraising began to ensure stability and possibility for concentrated resources on developing the series and writing the nomination dossier. Hence, the project was resumed at the end of 2020, this time to investigate areas outside of Europe in more depth.[51] At the time of writing, the nomination dossier and collection of the series are under development. In 2020 a project group was formed including a team from five representatives from the *Vooruit* (Viernulvier), *Paasitorni*, *Broken Hill Trades Hall*, *The Victorian Trades Hall*, and *The Workers Museum*.

The Method

After the assembling of a steering group of experts in UNESCO work, people from trade union organizations, and politicians, a smaller group of labor historians was charged with evaluating the suggested buildings. An essential aim of workers' assembly halls has always been inclusivity. Therefore, the 2020 project team removed a limitation to the 2009 collection design—not only to base the final series on those buildings found during the initial research but also to introduce a bottom-up approach appealing to people internationally to assist in the localization of workers' assembly halls. This was done through an elaborate collection campaign where a *call for buildings* was sent out through heritage, labor history, museum, university, trade union, and political networks and to individuals as well as through social media efforts to reach the public. The call was translated into several languages and launched internationally to make the selection of workers' assembly halls as democratic and inclusive as possible. Furthermore, members of the project and steering group conducted research and outreach to gather information and mobilize people around the world to help locate appropriate buildings to ensure a worldwide reach.

To ensure that the series be diverse both geographically and architecturally, the campaign goals were twofold: workers' assembly halls that suited the criteria could partake in the nomination. Workers' assembly halls that did not fit all criteria could join an international network of workers assembly places, a network that would reach beyond the nomination project and include outdoor spaces too. This will provide a forum in which managers of similar buildings can exchange knowledge and promote cultural and international diversity.

Challenges

One of the challenges of the project is an (assumed) impossibility of locating all still existing workers' assembly halls. Ideally, the project would reveal all that still stand and those that once did. At the time of writing, workers' assembly halls have been located in several countries: most European countries, Australia, New Zealand, Canada, Argentina, Tunisia, Ukraine, Turkey, Ghana, Russia, South Africa, Senegal, and the United States. They will not all partake in the nomination but will hopefully be part of the network. The Australian, American, and European buildings have in many cases been through initial stages of research, an effort conducted by the international project group supported by the Finnish Labor Museum and Amsab-ISH (Amsab—Institute of Social History) in Ghent. The campaign has reached far but challenges arise if suggested buildings cannot obtain inscription on national tentative lists or if a management plan cannot be established for the individual buildings. Despite the wide reach, a high risk remains that all relevant buildings may not be found in time, which is why the nomination is likely to consist of more than one nomination cycle. The project group is made of representatives from Europe and Australia and there is a risk of being too Western-centric in approaching this project. Ensuring ownership everywhere is also a challenge. Furthermore, workers have assembled and continue to do so in a variety of ways, whereas this project is solely concerned with workers' assembly halls.

CONCLUSION

The transnational serial nominations add to transnational history research as a category of world heritage that truly attempts to encompass transnationality, global phenomena, and shared heritage regardless of political borders. Transnational serial nominations for the UNESCO World Heritage List can bring people together across borders in commemorating shared heritage. Founded in the values of UNESCO this transnational series will promote equality, diversity, and international cultural tolerance. This chapter sought to give an outline of the project on developing a transnational serial nomination of still existing workers' assembly halls worldwide and shed light on the nomination process as an aid for heritage practitioners. By presenting a case study of a nomination, this chapter adds to the existing body of literature on transnational serial nominations in the hope of assisting others in their pursuit to develop nominations.

Why is it important to focus on a transnational serial nomination for the UNESCO World Heritage List that is not even inscribed? It is to explain the process of developing this nomination and the collaboration between state parties and between the organizations now managing the still existing workers' assembly halls. Furthermore, it illustrates the continuous transnational history of the labor movement. This chapter has presented a mid-way report of a nomination that even if not inscribed, will still have promoted cultural diversity, shared heritage, living traditions, and inclusivity through a collection campaign. The workers' assembly halls were the instruments of the organization of workers, a living tradition found in many places across the globe. It will be a nomination of *the people*, of transnational history, and intangible values manifested in tangible monuments witnessing the importance of claiming a seat for workers in society and on the UNESCO World Heritage List.

NOTES

1. A great thanks to the teams at Paasitorni, especially Osku Pajamäki, Vooruit (Viernulvier), especially Franky Devos, Broken Hill Trades Hall, especially Diana and Rosslyn Ferry, The Victorian Trades Hall, especially Colin Long, Andrew Reeves and Keir Reeves, The Finish Labor Museum, especially Kalle Kallio, Amsab-ISH (Amsab-Institute for Social History), especially Donald Weber, Piet Geleyns, all colleagues at The Workers Museum, especially museum director Søren Bak-Jensen, and everyone

who has helped with the collection campaign. Thank you to Cæcilie Brøndgaard and Caspar Thorup for editorial assistance.

2. Peter Ludvigsen, "Workers' Assembly Halls as a Proposition for UNESCO's World Heritage," *International Journal of Heritage Studies* 19, no. 5 (2013): 408–438.

3. Margaret Kohn, "The Power of Place: The House of the People as Counterpublic," *Polity* 33, no. 4 (2001): 518.

4. Kohn, "The Power of Place," 505.

5. Ludvigsen, "Workers' Assembly Halls," 410.

6. Margaret Kohn, *Radical Space*, New York: Cornell University Press, 2003, 23.

7. Stephen McFarland, "'With the Class-Conscious Workers Under One Roof': Union Halls and Labor Temples in American Working-Class Formation, 1880–1970," PhD Thesis, City University of New York, 2014, 16.

8. Ludvigsen, "Workers' Assembly Halls," 411.

9. Bernard Debarbieux, Chiara Bortolotto, Hervé Munz, and Cecilia Raziano, "Sharing Heritage? Politics and Territoriality in UNESCO's Heritage List," *Territory, Politics, Governance* XX, no. X (2021): 3 (pre-published online February 15, 2021, https://doi.org/10.1080/21622671.2020.1854112).

10. Holger Gorr, "Volkhäuser (houses of the people) in Germany: A Historical Overview from 1900 until Today," *International Journal of Heritage Studies* 19, no. 5 (2013): 469.

11. Kohn, *Radical Space*, 15; Margareta Ståhl, *Folkets Hus*, Stockholm: Bokförlaget Atlas, 2005; McFarland, "'With the Class-Conscious Workers Under One Roof'"; Nick Mansfield, *Buildings of the Labor Movement*, Swindon: English Heritage, 2003.

12. Kohn, "The Power of Place," 516.

13. Gorr, "Volkhäuser," 459.

14. Kohn, "The Power of Place," 519.

15. Kohn, "The Power of Place," 511.

16. Kohn, "The Power of Place," 509.

17. Ludvigsen, "Workers' Assembly Halls," 432.

18. Gorr, "Volkhäuser," 466.

19. Adele Lindenmeyr, "Building Civil Society One Brick at a Time: People's Houses and Worker Enlightenment in Late Imperial Russia," *The Journal of Modern History* 84, no. 1 (2012): 1.

20. Kohn, "The Power of Place," 523.

21. Nynne Helge, Jan Ingemann Sørensen, and Henning Grelle, *Velkommen til Forsamlingsbygningen*, Copenhagen: Arbejdermuseet Arbejderbevægelsens Bibliotek og Arkiv 2005, 23.

22. Kohn, *Radical Space*, 15.

23. Kohn, "The Power of Place," 514.

24. McFarland, "'With the Class-Conscious Workers Under One Roof,'" 28.

25. UNESCO, *UNESCO in Brief—Mission and Mandate* (https://en.unesco.org/about-us/introducing-unesco, accessed September 1, 2021).

26. Rodney Harrison, *Understanding the Politics of Heritage*. Manchester: Manchester University Press, 2010.

27. UNESCO, *Convention for the Safeguarding of the Intangible Cultural Heritage*, 2003 (https://ich.unesco.org/en/convention, accessed September 22, 2021).

28. UNESCO, *Global Strategy for a Representative, Balanced and Credible World Heritage List*, 1994 (https://whc.unesco.org/en/globalstrategy/, accessed September 1, 2021).

29. ICOMOS International, "The World Heritage List: Filling the Gaps—an Action Plan for the Future." *ICOMOS Open Archive*, 2004 (http://openarchive.icomos.org/id/eprint/433/, accessed August 20, 2021).

30. ICOMOS International, "The World Heritage List: Filling the Gaps—an Action Plan for the Future." *ICOMOS Open Archive*, 2004 (http://openarchive.icomos.org/id/eprint/433/, accessed August 20, 2021), 39.

31. UNESCO World Heritage List, Australian Convict Sites (https://whc.unesco.org/en/list/1306, accessed September 19, 2021).

32. The Wadden Sea World Heritage Site. *Our World Heritage* (https://www.waddensea-worldheritage.org/our-world-heritage, accessed September 19, 2021).

33. The UNESCO World Heritage List (https://whc.unesco.org/en/list/, accessed September 19, 2021).

34. *Operational Guidelines for the Implementation of the World Heritage Convention, 2019* (https://whc.unesco.org/en/guidelines/, Chapter III.C, 134–137, accessed September 7, 2021).

35. UNESCO, The World Heritage List, *The Architectural Work of Le Corbusier* (https://whc.unesco.org/en/list/1321, accessed September 7, 2021).

36. UNESCO, The Silk Road, The World Heritage List (https://whc.unesco.org/en/list/1442/, accessed September 1, 2021).

37. Swiss Federal Office of Culture, *UNESCO World Heritage: Serial Properties and Nominations*, 2010 (https://portals.iucn.org/library/node/48561, accessed August 19, 2021).

38. Swiss Federal Office of Culture, *UNESCO World Heritage: Serial Properties and Nominations*, 2010 (https://portals.iucn.org/library/node/48561, accessed August 19, 2021).

39. Josh Halliday, "UNESCO Strips Liverpool of Its World Heritage Status," *The Guardian*, July 21, 2021 (https://www.theguardian.com/uk-news/2021/jul/21/unesco-strips-liverpool-waterfront-world-heritage-status, accessed July 25, 2021).

40. Kohn, "The Power of Place," 515.

41. Swiss Federal Office of Culture, *UNESCO World Heritage: Serial Properties and Nominations*, 2010 (https://portals.iucn.org/library/node/48561, accessed August 19, 2021).

42. *Operational Guidelines for the Implementation of the World Heritage Convention, 2019* (https://whc.unesco.org/en/guidelines/, Chapter II.B, 61, accessed September 7, 2021).

43. UNESCO, *UNESCO in Brief—Mission and Mandate* (https://en.unesco.org/about-us/introducing-unesco, accessed September 1, 2021).

44. UNESCO, *UNESCO in Brief—Mission and Mandate* (https://en.unesco.org/about-us/introducing-unesco, accessed September 1, 2021).

45. Kohn, "The Power of Place," 513.

46. *Operational Guidelines for the Implementation of the World Heritage Convention, 2019* (https://whc.unesco.org/en/guidelines/, Chapter I.B, 4, accessed September 7, 2021).

47. The UNESCO World Heritage List, New Lanark (https://whc.unesco.org/en/list/429, accessed September 7, 2021).

48. Ludvigsen, "Workers' Assembly Halls," 410.

49. Ludvigsen, "Workers' Assembly Halls," 408–438.

50. Danish Agency for Culture and Palaces. *The Danish tentative list* (https://slks.dk/omraader/kulturarv/verdensarv/tentativlisten/arbejderbevaegelsens-forenings-og-forsamlingsbygninger/, accessed September 6, 2021).

51. https://www.arbejdermuseet.dk/en/unesco/the-history-of-the-unesco-project/.

BIBLIOGRAPHY

Primary Sources

Danish Agency for Culture & Palaces. *Arbejderbevægelsens forenings-og forsamlingsbygninger,* 2020. https://slks.dk/omraader/kulturarv/verdensarv/tentativlisten/arbejderbevaegelsens-forenings-og-forsamlingsbygninger/ (accessed July 28, 2021).

Halliday, Josh. "UNESCO Strips Liverpool of Its World Heritage Status." *The Guardian.* https://www.theguardian.com/uk-news/2021/jul/21/unesco-strips-liverpool-waterfront-world-heritage-status (accessed July 25, 2021).

ICOMOS International. "The World Heritage List: Filling the Gaps—An Action Plan for the Future." *ICOMOS Open Archive,* 2004. http://openarchive.icomos.org/id/eprint/433/ (accessed August 20, 2021).

National Trust. "The Tolpuddle Martyrs' Tree." https://www.nationaltrust.org.uk/max-gate/features/the-tolpuddle-martyrs-tree (accessed September 13, 2021).

Swiss Federal Office of Culture. *UNESCO World Heritage: Serial Properties and Nominations—Patrimoine mondial de l'UNESCO: biens et propositions d'inscriptions sériels,* 2010. https://portals.iucn.org/library/node/48561 (accessed August 15, 2021).

UNESCO. "Convention for the Safeguarding of the Intangible Cultural Heritage, 2003." https://ich.unesco.org/en/convention (accessed September 22, 2021).

UNESCO. "Global Strategy for a Representative, Balanced and Credible World Heritage List, 1994." https://whc.unesco.org/en/globalstrategy/ (accessed September 1, 2021).

UNESCO. "Operational Guidelines for the Implementation of the World Heritage Convention, 2019." https://whc.unesco.org/en/guidelines/ (accessed September 1, 2021).

UNESCO. "Tentative List." https://whc.unesco.org/en/tentativelists/ (accessed September 1, 2021).
UNESCO. "UNESCO in Brief—Mission and Mandate." https://en.unesco.org/about-us/introducing-unesco (accessed September 1, 2021).
UNESCO. "UNESCO World Heritage Convention, 1972." https://whc.unesco.org/en/convention/ (accessed September 1, 2021).
UNESCO. "The UNESCO World Heritage List." https://whc.unesco.org/en/list/ (accessed September 1, 2021).
The Wadden Sea World Heritage Site. "Our World Heritage." https://www.waddensea-worldheritage.org/our-world-heritage (accessed September 19, 2021).
The Workers Museum. "The History of the UNESCO Project, 2021." https://www.arbejdermuseet.dk/en/unesco/the-history-of-the-unesco-project/ (accessed August 3, 2021).

Secondary Sources

Debarbieux, Bernard, Chiara Bortolotto, Hervé Munz, and Cecilia Raziano. "Sharing Heritage? Politics and Territoriality in UNESCO's Heritage List." *Territory, Politics, Governance* (Pre-Published Online February 15, 2021). https://doi.org/10.1080/21622671.2020.1854112.
Gorr, Holger. "Volkhäuser (Houses of the People) in Germany: A Historical Overview From 1900 Until Today." *International Journal of Heritage Studies* 19, no. 5 (2013): 457–473.
Harrison, Rodney. *Understanding the Politics of Heritage*. Manchester: Manchester University Press, 2010.
Helge, Nynne, Jan Ingemann Sørensen, and Henning Grelle. *Velkommen til Forsamlingsbygningen*. Copenhagen: Arbejdermuseet Arbejderbevægelsens Bibliotek og Arkiv, 2005.
Kohn, Margaret. "The Power of Place: The House of the People as Counterpublic." *Polity* 33, no. 4 (2001): 503–526.
Kohn, Margaret. *Radical Space*. Ithaca: Cornell University Press, 2003.
Lindenmeyr, Adele. "Building Civil Society One Brick at a Time: People's Houses and Worker Enlightenment in Late Imperial Russia." *The Journal of Modern History* 84, no. 1 (2012): 1–39.
Ludvigsen, Peter. "WAHs as a Proposition for UNESCO's World Heritage." *International Journal of Heritage Studies* 19, no. 5 (2013): 408–438.
Mansfield, Nick. *Buildings of the Labour Movement*. Swindon: English Heritage, 2003.
McFarland, Stephen. "'With the Class-Conscious Workers Under One Roof': Union Halls and Labor Temples in American Working-Class Formation, 1880–1970." PhD Thesis, City University of New York, 2014.
Ståhl, Margareta. *Folkets Hus*. Stockholm: Bokförlaget Atlas, 2005.

Chapter 5

Approaching Balkan Dark/ Dissonant Cultural Heritage Places through Visual Arts

The Case of the ECHO Project

Nikos Pasamitros

Cultural heritage is subject to political use. State and intergovernmental actors that shape dominant heritage narratives interpret and attribute meaning to it in ways that build or reshape the identities of the in-groups. Often, in the Balkan context, heritage is subject to management by the national framework that (re)interprets it as ethnocentric and national as well as by a universalist framework, controlled by national authorities, that inscribes places of heritage in the UNESCO List, as objects of universal value. This chapter tries to discuss the ECHO (European Cultural Heritage Onstage)[1] project using theories on heritage perceptions, dark/dissonant heritage, and trauma. ECHO was a project in the fields of arts, culture, and heritage that aimed to enhance cultural production and reinforce the European sense of belonging by connecting contemporary artistic creation with Dark Cultural Heritage of local communities in Europe that ran from 2018 to 2019.[2]

The aim of the ECHO project was to approach dark heritage in an alternative manner and reflect upon collective trauma experiences of specific Balkan communities through artistic, visual creation. ECHO had an impact on local communities and involved artists. At the same time, it faced restrictions due to the political priorities of the funding institution, its short-term duration, and its limited implementation range. These restrictions were related to the very nature of the project. Specifically, ECHO could constitute a guide of alternative approaches that promoted a multilevel view of heritage as local, Balkan, and European at the same time. Despite restrictions, such creative projects could form alternative approaches based on local ownership and non-ethnocentric perception and use of heritage. This chapter examines the ECHO creative project that was managed by the Inter Alia nongovernmental organization based in Athens, Greece, with co-funding from the Creative Europe program of the European Commission and the Greek Ministry of Culture and Sports, within the framework of the European Year of Cultural Heritage 2018. Moreover, this chapter sets the theoretical framework in relation to heritage ownership and use, defines dark cultural heritage, cultural trauma, and the trauma-art relationship. Then, it presents an introduction to the intervention programs and projects in the Balkans and related criticism. Subsequently, it presents the conceptual background and the activities of the ECHO project, as well as its impact based on the quantitative and qualitative data of the partner organizations that implemented it and the artists that participated in it.

Overall, the ECHO project put forward an alternative conception and approach to dark/dissonant heritage through artistic creation for community rapprochement and the exploration of traumatic experiences inside a universalist heritage framework. In this framework, heritage is perceived as a means for intergroup reconciliation, which is based on a cosmopolitan perception of heritage. This view is evident in the strategies of the United Nations Educational, Scientific, and Cultural Organization (UNESCO), the International Council on Monuments and Sites (ICOMOS), the Council of Europe, and the European Union (EU). It is tied to the notion that certain aspects of heritage are seen and practiced as transnational, cosmopolitan, or world heritage without necessarily being decoupled from local, national, or ethnic understandings.[3]

THE THEORETICAL FRAMEWORK

Heritage: Perceptions and Ownership

Based on conventions, UNESCO defines and categorizes heritage as tangible and intangible, movable and immovable, and cultural and natural.[4] UNESCO inscribes positions of heritage in its World Heritage List based on criteria that prove their exceptional and universal value.[5] The definitions of UNESCO were not the first ones that tried to offer an international character to cultural monuments. Before them, there existed articles 27 and 56 of The Hague Convention of 1907 that referred to the protection of historical monuments and buildings,[6] the seven-point Athens Charter for the Restoration of Historic Monuments of 1931 that refers to the protection of historical monuments,[7] and articles 1 and 2 of the Roerich Pact of 1935 that concern the respect and protection of cultural treasures in times of war.[8]

Universalist perception and recording of monuments, objects, and practices was preceded by the national perception of heritage. This perception/

narrative is called Authorized Heritage Discourse (AHD), a term introduced by the Australian archaeologist Laurajane Smith. AHD focuses on aesthetically pleasing material objects, sites, places, and landscapes that current generations must protect in order to be passed on to future generations for their education and to forge a sense of common identity based on the past.[9] This professional discourse is often involved in the legitimatization and regulation of historical and cultural narratives, and the work that these narratives do in maintaining or negotiating certain societal values and the hierarchies that these underpin.[10] AHD has its roots in the rise of nineteenth-century nationalism and liberal modernism,[11] and favors large-scale, old places related to the aristocracy, the church, and the constructions and myths of the nation.[12] This means that even when international actors try to implement interventionist, conciliatory practices and processes, and setting international inscription standards, there in fact exists deep-rooted, authorized narratives that directly relate to ethnic and national identities.[13] In practice, the decision on what is worthy of protection and preservation is up to the national authorities that identify and nominate potential heritage objects to international organizations.[14] Therefore, the characterization and use of cultural heritage are highly political.

The AHD and universalist discourses have been criticized on several levels. Universalist approaches are criticized for promoting assimilationist policies[15] and for being restrictive in the sense that they require operation through state parties, a function that downplays communities and other sub-national groups.[16] The AHD is criticized for excluding and marginalizing subaltern groups and sub-groups. Both the AHD and the universalist discourses favor the grandiose and the imposing, constituting heritage as an object that attracts passive, popular gaze and encourages the audience to consume the message of heritage constructed by heritage experts.[17]

In contrast, critical approaches to heritage emphasize the need to examine alternative perceptions and definitions of heritage while criticizing the exclusion and alienation of nondominant groups. For example, the American public memory and patriotic views of the past serve the dominant cultural discourse by preserving the existing social inequalities. At the same time, it is common for non-dominant groups to directly or indirectly challenge dominant public memory and create new memories that serve their needs.[18] Therefore, in order to meet local and Indigenous needs, they call for the involvement of communities in the management of heritage and the expansion of perceptions of intangible heritage.[19] Similarly, in Queensland, northern Australia prominent female figures belonging to the groups of Aborigines and the Torres Strait Islanders undertook the protection and preservation of their heritage by being collectors and curators themselves. Thus, they created a female environment that empowered Indigenous women to express their cultural identity and their gender perceptions through art and exhibitions and, thereby, affirmed the ownership of cultural heritage beyond the dominant national approach.[20]

Heritage ownership emerges as a main issue of heritage use. Based on the AHD and universalist discourses of heritage, its ownership has a dual and contradictory meaning. On the one hand, international treaties consider world heritage to belong to humanity as a natural consequence of the universality of places and practices. International treaties, on the other hand, attach national or ethnic ownership to these same sites and practices designated as world heritage objects. Therefore, although heritage is considered to be of universal value, ownership is transferred to the sovereign states. David Lowenthal called our attention to the incompatibility of the different levels of heritage (global, national, local, community) that international treaties seek to reconcile.[21] Given this incompatibility, the attribution of identity ownership, and consequently the interpretation and use at the national level and the marginalization of sub-national groups and subgroups, critical approaches call for alternative practices. These alternative practices should, according to critical approaches, not only attempt to meet local and Indigenous needs but also consider the perceptions of non-dominant groups. In that way, they accentuate that on the one hand, the use of heritage itself creates and consolidates perceptions and, on the other hand, that AHD creates and perpetuates exclusions that prevent the cultivation of a culture of rapprochement and coexistence due to their ethnocentric character that promotes exclusion, in-group superiority, and out-group inferiority.

Dark Cultural Heritage, Cultural Trauma, and the Trauma-Art Relation

There is a kind of tangible and intangible heritage that, irrespectively of its registration on the national or universal level, is related to death and atrocity and is characterized as dissonant heritage, heritage that hurts, or difficult or dark heritage.[22] This dark heritage can be categorized based on its subject as well as according to the emotional burden and tension it holds, in entertainment and commercial places, and in places of death and distinct political and ideological influence that offer an educational experience.[23] Thus, dark heritage, like the rest of cultural and natural heritage, is indissolubly connected to the visitor. Dark heritage bears an important political and cultural importance and is related to the identity of imagined groups and collectives.[24] In most cases, dark heritage, based on the AHD, is integrated into the national framework of perception. Oftentimes, like in the case of places of death with political and cultural importance, heritage is connected to cultural traumas of related groups.

Cultural trauma refers to the permanent scars a tragic event can leave on the collective consciousness of a group, thus, significantly shaping its identity.[25] Cultural trauma is a concept related to historical trauma. It is a term that describes the long-term impact of colonialism, cultural oppression, and historical oppression of Indigenous people as for instance in the case of the United States and Canada,[26] as well as to the intergenerational trauma, namely the impact of traumatic experiences across generations, on children and grandchildren of those who were initially victimized.[27] Such collective traumas are also found in other groups where traumatic experiences are directly linked to war, such as the Holocaust,[28] the Greek Civil War,[29] or the Katyn Massacre.[30] Another kind of trauma associated with the subversion of the dominant culture is the trauma of social change, such as the one associated with the societies of the former socialist states. Sociologist Piotr Sztompka holds that change is traumatic when it is (1) sudden and rapid, (2) complete and wide, (3) radical, deep, and fundamental, and (4) unexpected.[31] Cultural trauma is often the subject of use, reuse, examination, and reexamination by arts. Research on intergenerational trauma of the Inuit people in Canada's Nunavut area related to colonialism shows that the fields of visual arts and filmmaking deal with the effects of colonial history and approach them in an alternative way, having in mind that the dominant narratives on trauma influence long-term perceptions about it.[32]

Numerous works of art have emerged from the influence of traumatic memory. This fact is sometimes obvious in the artwork, or it is subtle, mixed with imaginary elements, and expressed through an affective dynamic within the artwork.[33] Art is sometimes used as a therapeutic tool at the individual level.[34] In other cases, it is a way of expressing collective trauma or individual pain expressed as collective tragedy and heritage.[35]

Intervention Programs in the Balkans

In the Balkans, several programs by international and intergovernmental organizations sought to create supranational narratives on heritage and cultivate cultures of reconciliation at the interstate and intrastate level. Based on the universalist discourse, programs such as the Promotion of Cultural Diversity in Kosovo (PCDK) program[36] and several actions in the framework of the Cultural Cooperation Projects in the Western Balkans 2019 of the Creative Europe program[37] promoted cultural heritage as a means of contact, tolerance, diversity, and reconciliation.[38] UNESCO, the United Nations Development Program (UNDP), the Council of Europe, the EU, and ICOMOS are some of the organizations operating in the Balkans, and especially in the so-called Western Balkans region, trying to create transnational narratives and cultivate cultures of reconciliation. In particular, the EU, through the Creative Europe program and the European Year of Cultural Heritage 2018 and its successor programs, promotes an inclusive approach to culture and heritage in the context of cohesion policies for the Balkan member-states and in the framework of the political approach and convergence for potential member states.

These interventions have often been criticized, on the one hand, for their incompatibility with real needs in the field, and, on the other hand, for the inevitable interference of national perspectives. This criticism is part of the challenge to the Liberal Peace Framework for peace and democratization.[39] According to this framework, exogenous, regulatory involvement in the social, political, economic, and cultural systems of countries that are considered insufficiently developed, promotes liberal proposals without substantial involvement and ownership of domestic actors in the processes.[40] At the level of culture and heritage, in order for intervention practices to be effective and inclusive, they should try to meet local and Indigenous needs and take into account the perceptions of nondominant, sub-ethnic groups, and subgroups. Practices that follow the universalist discourse bear the risk of being nonfunctional and incompatible with local cultural realities. Accordingly, practices that promote the AHD degrade the role and discourse of non-dominant groups.

A typical example of simultaneous intervention by programs of universalist and AHD perception is Kosovo. In this case, on the one hand, the programs of the EU Office and the Council of Europe create a sense of external interference in the political leadership of Kosovo. On the other hand, the international framework for UNESCO registration is used for political purposes as it seeks to degrade non-dominant groups from the Kosovo-Albanian dominant ethnic group. This political use provokes reactions from the largest minority, the Kosovo Serbs, and feeds the existing ethnic conflict.

The ECHO project, which is examined in this chapter, is a typical example of an effort to overcome the contradictions of these interventions as it was implemented, with European and national funding, with the aim of promoting alternative cultural heritage perceptions and strengthening the involvement and ownership of local people in the process. Thus, ECHO, as a de facto intervention within the universalist discourse of heritage, tried to grasp and consider the needs of non-dominant groups and at the same time bring an external perspective on issues of dark heritage through visual creation.

ECHO PROJECT OVERVIEW

The ECHO pilot project was implemented from June 2018 to June 2019 within the framework of the European Year of Cultural Heritage 2018. Being an international project in the field of heritage, culture, and arts, ECHO aimed to enhance cultural creation and the European sense of belonging, namely, to contribute to building a common European identity by exploring dark heritage of local communities in Europe.[41] The program focused on the role of dark heritage in shaping identities on the local level, and used the medium of artistic creation for rethinking and reflecting on collective traumatic experiences. ECHO's specific goal was for artwork created during the program to remain in the local communities. The main target areas of ECHO were Bitola in North Macedonia and Novi Sad in Serbia, as well as their surrounding areas. On a second level, the program approached the border areas of Western Macedonia and the town of Veliki Preslav in Bulgaria. The project was managed and supervised by Inter Alia, while local actions were implemented by the partner organizations (Open Space Foundation in Bulgaria, Sfera International in North Macedonia, and the Vojvodina Civic Center in Serbia).

The project included the following activities: two art residencies for visual artists in Bitola and Novi Sad, four local engagement activities involving the local community and artists, two local exhibitions, the filming of a creative documentary (Western Macedonia, Bitola, and Novi Sad), a final overall exhibition at the Hotel Balkan in Veliki Preslav, and a final presentation of the Program at TWIXTlab in Athens, Greece.

Based on the technical report of the project application form submitted to the Education, Audiovisual and Culture Executive Agency (EACEA) of the European Commission, the methodology for the evaluation of results and impact was based on specifications jointly set by the partners of the consortium. For the hosting of artists in residency, three-member committees were set up consisting of one member of each organization (coordinator) and two external members (one community representative and one artist), who evaluated the compatibility of the activities with their own prerequisites and needs throughout the residencies. At the same time, the committees referred to the leading organization of the consortium, which was responsible for compliance with the program specifications as set out in the funding application. The feedback from the local community during the engagement actions and the internal, reciprocal evaluation between artists and locals in co-creation was used as a qualitative indicator for the collaborative creative process. Feedback from domestic audiences was used as a qualitative indicator for local exhibitions. The reviews of the audience, professionals from the cultural and creative sectors (CCS), and artists were used as a qualitative indicator for the creative documentary. An account/impact analysis was used as a qualitative indicator for the overall impact of the project activities. In addition, there were also minimum quantitative indicators set as evaluation measures. These indicators concerned the number and outreach of artworks created, the engagement of people the co-creation process, and the understanding of dark heritage.

Art Residencies

Local partners in Bitola and Novi Sad selected specific historical events and related heritage to provide the theoretical framework and inspiration to the visual artists in residency that stayed in the local communities for the duration of one month. In the case of Bitola, the Macedonian front of World War I was chosen and, specifically, the battles of 1916 and 1917 between Serbian and French forces on the one side and Bulgarian and German troops on the other side. The places of reference were (1) Mount Baba and the Pelister Peak in the north of Bitola and the surrounding villages where, during the battles, more than 1,000 bombs were dropped, (2) the city of Bitola which was successively occupied by the warring parties, (3) Mount Nidze and the Peak of Kaimaktsalan where the main battlefront was located, and (4) the Serbian, French, and German cemeteries of Bitola. In the case of Novi Sad, the Novi Sad Raid (or Novi Sad massacre) was chosen, where, in January of 1942, in retaliation for resistance fighter action in the Vojvodina area, Hungarian troops invaded the city and executed 3,000 Serbs and 1,300 Jews. Victims were thrown into the frozen Danube either dead or alive. Thus, the reference point was the Danube River.[42] The four project partners conducted four separate open calls for artists in Bulgaria, Greece, North Macedonia, and Serbia. Each committee, consisting of the program manager and the quality assurance manager in each organization, selected two artists, one for each residency, based on their portfolios and cover letters. During the art residencies, four artists from the four different countries explored local heritage in each location, visited sites, searched archives, met local experts and non-experts, and created artworks (paintings, sculptures, performances, and installations) inspired by local dark heritage.[43]

Community Engagement Activities, Local and Final Exhibitions, Creative Documentary, and Presentation of the Project in Greece

During the art residencies, two community engagement activities per community were organized. These meetings between the artists and the locals aimed at bringing them together in interacting and discussing perceptions on heritage and at achieving the dynamic involvement of the local community in the ongoing work of the artists.[44] The project also aimed to involve people from local communities in the creative process. At the end of each residency, local art shows exhibited the produced artworks. In the case of Novi Sad, due to the increased interest of the locals, an additional exhibition was organized in collaboration with the School of Fine Arts of the city titled EHO77—marking the seventy-seventh anniversary of the Novi Sad Raid.[45] Respectively, in

Figure 5.1. Depy Antoniou, "Mračno Nasleđe"/"Dark Heritage," from the Recorded Performance Documented by Andreas Agrafiotis, 5:21 Minutes, 2018. *Source*: By courtesy of Depy Antoniou.

Bitola, the artists of the program participated in the annual two-day SFEST music festival of the city.[46]

While the artists where attending the art residency, a two-member team from the Caravan Project organization traveled from Greece to Bitola, Novi Sad, and Western Macedonia and produced a creative documentary titled *Dark Vein*.[47] The aim of *Dark Vein* was to track landscape trauma from the effects of armed conflict and human impact on the environment.[48] The creative documentary was screened at the final exhibition in Veliki Preslav, Bulgaria, at the "A Field Guide to Getting Lost Vol.2" group exhibition in Aegina, Greece, in September 2019,[49] in the "Tradition Anew" event of the Biennale of Western Balkans in Ioannina, Greece, in May 2019,[50] in the local activity at the TWIXTlab, in Athens, Greece, in June 2019,[51] and finally at the Thessaloniki Documentary Festival in June 2021.[52] The *Dark Vein* creative documentary, by using lethargic images and natural soundscapes, made a poetic statement on the scars and traumas human activity leaves on earth. Its screening in Athens coincided with the first anniversary of the Prespa Agreement signing that settled the name dispute between Greece and North Macedonia. This occasion sparked a lively dialogue on Balkan identity and cultural proximity between the two peoples among the audience and the creators.

The four-day final exhibition of the artworks of the project was organized and implemented in the abandoned building of the Hotel Balkan in Veliki Preslav, Bulgaria, in April 2019. Beyond all artworks created in the residencies and the presence of all participating artists, the exhibition included artworks by students of the Varna Vocational School of Textile and Fashion

Design and of the Smolyan School of Fine Arts, as well as the first official screening of the *Dark Vein* creative documentary.

Engagement of Artists and Audiences

According to the official project report/impact analysis, the organizations that participated in the consortium reported that ninety-four artworks were created during the lifetime of the project attracting 1,030 people. Seventy-two of these artworks remained in the local communities (Figures 5.2, 5.3, and 5.4). In addition, the residency process gave artists an understanding of the needs of the local community and boosted the involvement of the local art scene and the community as a whole in the creative process. Regarding awareness on dark heritage by the communities, the Sfera International organization in Bitola reported that it received feedback from people who were interested in learning and researching more about the dark heritage of their community. Vojvodina Civic Center in Novi Sad noted the demand of the locals for participation and the lively dialogues that took place during the EHO77 exhibition. The Open Space Foundation in Veliki Preslav reported that older people came to the final exhibition to commemorate the past and at the same time, many young people approached the subject with curiosity and studiousness.[53]

Talking about their experience, project artists reported that they gained awareness of dark heritage they did not have the opportunity to learn about during their studies. In addition, some of the artists explored new dimensions of topics they already knew about, and some of them reported that the knowledge they acquired had a significant impact on their life. Regarding the involvement of the locals in the creative process, the artists identified the existence of a core of people who participated with their knowledge (theoretical discussions and transmission of historical knowledge) but also in practical terms (technical support and providing materials). In relation to the perception and understanding of dark heritage by the communities, the artists stated that the locals had the opportunity to acquire different perspectives on dark heritage of which they were already aware. For those coming from other communities, the international audience, and the people unfamiliar with domestic history and heritage, the fact that there was a constant dialogue on similar experiences encouraged these groups to explore dark heritage and search for commonalities and differences with the dark heritage of their own communities, creating conditions for reflection. What further attracted their interest was the artistic freedom of the exploration process and the feedback to the artists. Emotional mobilization was also important, as people were often moved and inspired by the artworks. Emotion was at the forefront with heritage and history in the background, making it easier for audiences to access artistic creation. For example, the

Figure 5.2. Ljubica Meshkova Solak. Untitled, collage, 725 x 535 cm, 2018, installed at the Bitola National Library. *Source*: By courtesy of the Association for sustainable development SFERA International.

sculpture of Aristaios Tsousis, titled "Xenos" (Figure 5.4), depicts the word "stranger" combining letters from the Greek and the Cyrillic alphabet. The accompanying text of the artwork is a fictional letter of a Greek soldier in the Macedonian front, writing to his family about the linguistic similarities of Greeks and Macedonians:

> *The inhabitants of this old, famous city, Bitola, which in the old times, the Ottomans named it Manastir due to its many monasteries, are very likeable and hospitable. We are so similar in so many things. Even their language sounds familiar. Same melody and many common words. Turkish, Greek, Slavic, Latin, Albanian, even Jewish. And a similar alphabet, too! It is easy to read with a minor effort. I almost managed it already.*[54]

108   Chapter 5

Figure 5.3.   Ljubica Meshkova Solak. Untitled, collage, 725 × 535 cm, 2018, installed at the Bitola National Library. *Source*: By courtesy of the Association for sustainable development SFERA International.

Figure 5.4.   Aristaios Tsousis, "Xenos." Metal sheets, 50 × 70 × 15 cm, 2018, installed at the Bitola Technical School. *Source*: By courtesy of the Association for sustainable development SFERA International.

In this way, Tsousis underlines the local heritage of the Macedonians, Greeks, and trilingual Vlachs, by emphasizing linguistic proximity, cultural similarity, and the cross-border legacy of the Ottoman times. In Tsousis' approach, there is an underlying comment about the human-made partition state borders produce, reminding the audience that the Greek and Vlach cultures are part of the past and present of Bitola as well as the Macedonian culture is a part of the prefecture of Western Macedonia in Greece.

In the case of Depy Antoniou's "Mračno Nasleđe"/"Dark Heritage" (figure 5.1) performance, the artist blasts a balloon in a bucket with water, which represents her symbolized view of the way Hungarian soldiers killed their victims in the Danube. Antoniou, by holding a knife, comments on the large number of women who participated in the Yugoslav National Liberation Army.[55] Antoniou chose to focus on the little-known massive engagement of women in the anti-Nazi resistance. She used the means of performance to comment on the underrated female contribution in wartime, which is stereotypically considered a male affair.

Kiril T. Konstantin, with his work "Scream 1&2," presents the horror and scream of war, the human madness, the inhumanity, the pain and ashes that it leaves behind and, at the same time, shows the strength of humanity that, despite all the suffering and pain, is born again from the ashes.[56] Konstantin conveys a touching, optimistic message through the shocking image of the screaming human, with a clear reference to "The Scream" by Edward Munch. His work is a depiction of the desperate human condition in which people struggle to avoid repeating the same mistakes.

In addition to the creative part, the artists considered that experiential learning opportunities were also presented to the audience. The artwork *Surface* by Bojan Josic is a typical example of experiential art. The installation was made of Plexiglas and salt. In its center, a video of water is projected in a hole. The artwork aims to depict the holes opened in the frozen Danube by the Hungarian troops to throw their victims into the river. The installation invited the audience to walk on the salty surface, resembling walking on ice, and feel the experience of the event.[57] The visual similarity of salt with ice, its creaking sound, and the view of the water in the hole offered the audience a sensory experience of the final moments of thousands of Serbs and Jews.

THE IMPACT ON THE MAKING OF IDENTITIES

The ECHO project approached dark heritage at the local level through artistic creation. Its pilot application brought people from different Balkan countries together in a process of reflecting on the traumatic past. In this way, it encouraged local communities to reflect on intergenerational trauma and enabled locals to speak about it through the process of co-creation and the artistic expression of people who did not belong to the local communities. Using the local level of analysis, it attempted to bypass national narratives that overshadowed local perceptions of heritage and identity. In the case of Bitola, the approach of the project moved away from the official state policy effort (from 2006 to 2017) to build the Macedonian national identity. In Novi Sad, the artists approached dark heritage through the prism of the multiculturalism of the Vojvodina region. The result was a multicultural approach to heritage and traumatic experience beyond the exclusive, ethnocentric narrative and perception. The artworks and the creative process helped in the direction of a sensory, emotional approach to the dark past that moved away from divisive views of direct political analysis. In this way, ECHO moved into a critical direction, against the AHD framework. At the same time, given the presupposition that heritage is highly political, ECHO tried to create a perception of dark heritage beyond the in-group—out-group cleavage. To this end, it did not focus on the national level where usually the dominant group appropriates heritage in ways that creates polarizing narratives and images toward the "other" in order to cultivate national cohesion.

On the contrary, the project undertook a transnational, pan-European approach, giving priority to organizations and, through them, to local communities to avoid the trap of the universalist approach, thus, increasing local involvement and ownership, and trying to incorporate the perceptions of non-dominant, sub-ethnic groups, and subgroups. Starting from the common European and Balkan identity of the communities, it projected an image of a common heritage through similar traumatic experiences, and quantitative and qualitative results showed a significant contribution of the program to an alternative approach to heritage. The issue of local ownership of actions and proposed solutions was raised during the residencies, local engagement activities, and exhibitions, involving the communities in the process of creation and reflection. The artists were inspired by the microhistory of the places and the members of the local community who participated in the co-creation or came to contribute to the artists' work shared their oral, family, and local stories, and related objects and documents for study. This dialogue on dark heritage between locals and outsiders has brought to the surface local readings that are often overshadowed by national narratives and uses. External perceptions of foreign artists on local dark heritage provided new perspectives to the local communities and created a ground for dialogue on similar experiences. The fact that some of the artworks remained in the places of creation offer opportunities for further dissemination of the ideas and views of the project on dark heritage.

It is necessary to mention that there are significant limitations to the impact of the ECHO project. Most importantly, it was implemented with major funding from the Creative Europe program. This means, on the one hand, flexibility in the development of the objectives of the project, but on the other hand, it means that it has worked within the framework and the political priorities of the EU. Therefore, despite the freedom of action and implementation offered by the Creative Europe program, at least compared to other EU programs, ECHO came under the universalist, conciliatory context governing EU partner countries. Thus, based on the sponsor-donor relationship defined by the EACEA, these programs place constraints on consortia resulting from the dominant cultural and heritage management models as reflected in the political priorities of the European Union. In addition, the short duration of such projects (twelve months in the case of ECHO) raises significant limitations to the continuation and impact of the interventions. Moreover, ECHO's vision depended entirely on the perceptions of the consortium partners/organizations. Their stance against ethnocentric narratives and their embracing of cosmopolitanism determined the approach and implementation. In this sense, ECHO's concepts and objectives could not constitute a widely applicable framework for heritage.

Overall, the ECHO project promoted an alternative perception and approach to dark heritage using as its means artistic creation to approach and visit traumatic experiences, allowing local communities to respond and participate in the (re)exploration of their dark heritage. Given the limitations, the small scale, and the short duration of the project, its impact is significant for communities and artists. Its focus on the local level shows that it contributed to the involved communities and could constitute a good practice (it was selected and presented as a good practice by the Greek Creative Europe Desk) and starting point for similar projects. Finally, an important element that supports the effectiveness of ECHO is that, in the framework of the Creative Europe—Cooperation Projects program for 2020, the EACEA and the Greek Ministry of Culture decided to finance the implementation of "ECHO II: Traditions in Transition," which explores local community traditions and practices across Europe.[58] Moreover, under Creative Europe—Cooperation Projects 2021, the EACEA approved the implementation of "ECHO III: For Memory's Sake" that approaches cultures of forced marriage in the Balkans. Both follow-up projects demonstrate the willingness of the EU to offer space to alternative approaches and the pertinence of interventions that reflect on identities on a Balkan level.

CONCLUSIONS: WHAT DO THE BALKANS NEED? WHAT DID ECHO DO?

In conclusion, past experience in Europe and the Balkans shows that rapprochement and coexistence, either between neighboring people or between different ethnic groups within states, cannot be based on ethnocentric notions that promote exclusion, supremacy of the in-group, and inferiority of the "other." The AHD cannot adequately respond to such issues given the unbreakable link between national heritage and national identity. What is more, universalist, reconciliatory interventions in the Balkans often fail for a variety of reasons. They do not enforce appropriate local ownership of solutions to interested groups, they are often incompatible with or insensitive to local needs and cultural realities in the field, and they are blind to nondominant, sub-ethnic, local, and Indigenous perceptions.

Specifically, in the Balkans, since the time of the Balkan Wars of the 1910s, the image of the region has been stereotypically linked to violence and nationalism in Western European perceptions. Western Europeans have adopted stereotypical depictions of a mythologized tradition of violence between solid ethno-religious groups. Nonetheless, interventions should consider syncretism and the coexistence of small communities often based on habits and beliefs shaped by religion. Balkan identities are full of ambiguities, they tiptoe between conflict and coexistence, and they often rely on religion(s) to (re)construct themselves. Lastly, in the field of cultural heritage, Balkan states' decision makers, despite external pressure for the implementation of policies of multiculturalism and diversity, are reluctant to endorse them and continue to promote ethnocentric policies.[59] All these perceptions and practices balance between established ethnocentrism of local actors and externally imposed cosmopolitanism.

The ECHO project tried to reflect on the past and reexamine dark heritage at the local level through artistic creation. Its aim was to bring out local perspectives on heritage in an attempt to avoid ethnocentric heritage perceptions and imposed interventions. It provided an alternative perspective based on the local level of analysis, the involvement of communities, and the engagement of artists. In its attempt to interpret dark heritage on the local level, the project involved local organizations in setting the framework of analysis. Then, it involved members of the local community in the artistic research by making them transmitters of local heritage and in the artistic process by engaging them in creation. Lastly, it provided the artistic output based on the sensory, emotional approach of the artists. These methods do not render ECHO a depoliticized project. On the contrary, its intervention is a very political process against ethnocentrism, which has proved disastrous for the Balkans in the past, and against universalist, cosmopolitan intervention practices, which are widely hated or disdained among Balkan people. By bringing the study of dark heritage to the local level, ECHO managed to bring to the fore local identities and, in combination with visual arts' approaches, boost dialogue. In this context, intercultural reflection on dark heritage is less bound to ethnocentric perspectives and identities. When it comes to the contribution of visual arts, dark heritage was approached and mixed with imaginary elements through the affective dynamic of artworks. Thus, it provided the opportunity to reflect on dark heritage based on emotional and sensory stimuli. One should note that ECHO was implemented within the framework and political priorities of the EU. This means that it was given a significant degree of flexibility and that it functioned under the universalist, conciliatory context of EU funding programs. In total, the ECHO pilot project, due to its innovative nature, and despite its limitations and disadvantages, is a successful practice and a guide for exploring local dark heritage and strengthening local ownership of domestic communities through artistic creation.

NOTES

1. For an overview of the ECHO: European Cultural Heritage Onstage project (see: https://echo-ii.eu/the-project/background/, accessed September 20, 2022).

2. Inter Alia, "European Cultural Heritage Onstage (ECHO) Application." Athens: Inter Alia, 2017.

3. Mads Daugbjerg and Thomas Fibiger, "Introduction: Heritage Gone Global. Investigating the Production and Problematics of Globalized Pasts," *History and Anthropology* 22, no. 2 (2011): 135–147.

4. UNESCO, *UNESCO Web Site: Convention for the Protection of Cultural Property in the Event of Armed Conflict with Regulations for the Execution of the Convention 1954.* May 14 (http://portal.unesco.org/en/ev.php-URL_ID=13637&URL_DO=DO_TOPIC&URL_SECTION=201.html, accessed August 11, 2021); UNESCO, "Convention Concerning the Protection of the World Cultural and Natural Heritage," Paris: UNESCO, November 16, 1972 (http://whc.unesco.org/archive/convention-en.pdf, accessed September 20, 2022). UNESCO, "Convention for the Safeguarding of the Intangible Cultural Heritage," Paris: UNESCO, October 17, 2003 (http://unesdoc.unesco.org/images//0013/001325/132540e.pdf, accessed August 11, 2021).

5. UNESCO, The Criteria for Selection: UNESCO (https://whc.unesco.org/en/criteria/, accessed May 16, 2021).

6. ICRC, "International Committee of the Red Cross Website: Treaties, States Parties and Commentaries: Convention (IV) respecting the Laws and Customs of War on Land and its Annex: Regulations concerning the Laws and Customs of War on Land," International Committee of the Red Cross Website. October 18, 1907 (https://ihl-databases.icrc.org/applic/ihl/ihl.nsf/Treaty.xsp?action=openDocument&documentId=4D47F92DF3966A7EC12563CD002D6788, accessed August 19, 2021).

7. ICOMOS, ICOMOS Website: Charters and Other Doctrinal Texts: Catégories en français: Ressources Charters and Other Standards: The Athens Charter for the Restoration of Historic Monuments—1931 (http://www.icomos.org/en/charters-and-texts/179-articles-en-francais/ressources/charters-and-standards/167-the-athens-charter-for-the-restoration-of-historic-monuments, accessed August 11, 2021).

8. Roerich Pact. 1935. "Treaty on the Protection of Artistic and Scientific Institutions and Historic Monuments (Roerich Pact)." (https://ihl-databases.icrc.org/ihl/INTRO/325?OpenDocument, accessed September 15, 2022).

9. Laurajane Smith, "Class, Heritage and the Negotiation of Place," *Missing Out on Heritage: Socio-Economic Status and Heritage Participation* (http://www.english-heritage.org.uk/about/who-we-are/how-we-are-run/heritage-for-all/missing-out-conference/, accessed September 15, 2022).

10. Laurajane Smith, "Discourses of Heritage: Implications for Archaeological Community Practice," *Nuevo Mundo Mundos Nuevos* 2012 (https://doi.org/10.4000/nuevomundo.64148, accessed September 15, 2022).

11. Laurajane Smith, *Uses of Heritage*. London: Routledge, 2006.

12. Laurajane Smith, "Class, Heritage and the Negotiation of Place."

13. Nikolaos Pasamitros, "Cultural Heritage: Contested Perspectives and Strategies in Kosovo," in Ioannis Armakolas, Agon Demjaha, Arolda Elbasani, Stephanie Schwandner-Sievers, Elton Skendaj and Nikolaos Tzifakis (eds.), *State-Building in Post-Independence Kosovo: Policy Challenges and Societal Considerations*, Pristina: Kosovo Foundation for Open Society, 291–310.

14. Janet Blake, "On Defining the Cultural Heritage," *International and Comparative Law Quarterly* 49, no. 1 (2000): 61–85.

15. Smith, *Class, Heritage and the Negotiation of Place*.

16. Laurajane Smith, "Intangible Heritage: A Challenge to the Authorised Heritage Discourse," *Revista D'Etnologia de Catalunya* 40 (2015): 133–142.

17. Smith, *Uses of Heritage*.

18. Paul Shackel, "Public Memory and the Search for Power in American Historical Archaeology," *American Anthropologist* 103, no. 3 (2001): 655.

19. Kathryn Lafrenz Samuels, *Academia Website: What is Cultural Heritage? Mapping a Concept, Integrating Fields.* March 31, 2014 (https://www.academia.edu/6638341/What_is_Cultural_Heritage_Mapping_a_Concept_Integrating_Fields, accessed August 22, 2021).

20. Olivia Robinson and Trish Barnard, "'Thanks, But We'll Take It from Here': Australian Aboriginal and Torres Strait Islander Women Influencing the Collection of Tangible and Intangible Heritage," *Museum International* 59, no. 4 (2007): 34–45.

21. David Lowenthal, *The Heritage Crusade and the Spoils of History*, Cambridge: Cambridge University Press, 1998.

22. Rudi Hartmann, "Dark Tourism, Thanatourism, and Dissonance in Heritage," *Journal of Heritage Tourism* 9, no. 2 (2014): 166–182; Suzie Thomas, Oula Seitsonen Vesa-Pekka Herva, and Eerika Koskinen-Koivisto, "Dark Heritage," in: Claire Smith (ed.), *Encyclopedia of Global Archaeology*, Cham: Springer, 2019, 1–11.

23. Avital Biran, Yaniv Poria, and Oren Gila, "Sought Experiences at (Dark) Heritage Sites," *Annals of Tourism Research* 38, no. 3 (2011): 820–841.

24. Paul Connerton, *How Societies Remember*, Cambridge: Cambridge University Press, 1989.

25. Jeffrey C. Alexander, "Culture Trauma, Morality and Solidarity: The Social Construction of 'Holocaust' and Other Mass Murders," *Thesis Eleven* 132, no. 1 (2016): 3–16.

26. Laurence J. Kirmayer, Joseph P. Gone, and Joshua Moses, "Rethinking Historical Trauma," *Transcultural Psychiatry* 51, no. 3 (2014): 299–319.

27. Peter Menzies, "Intergenerational Trauma from a Mental Health Perspective," *Native Social Work Journal* 7 (2010): 63–85.
28. Natan P. F. Kellerman, "Epigenetic transmission of Holocaust Trauma: Can Nightmares Be Inherited?" *Israel Journal of Psychiatry and Related Sciences* 50, no. 1 (2013): 1–9.
29. Nikos Demertzis, "The Greek Civil War as Cultural Trauma" ["Ο ελληνικός Εμφύλιος ως πολιτισμικό τραύμα."], in: Nikos Demertzis, Eleni Paschaloudi, and Giorgos Antoniou (eds.), *Επιστήμη και Κοινωνία: Επιθεώρηση Πολιτικής και Ηθικής Θεωρίας* 28 (2011): 81–109.
30. Ron Eyerman and Dominik Bartmanski, "The Worst Was the Silence: The Unfinished Drama of the Katyn Massacre," in: Ron Eyerman (ed.), *Memory, Trauma and Identity*, Cham: Palgrave Macmillan, 2019, 111–142.
31. Piotr Sztompka, "Trauma of Social Change: A Case of Postcommunist Societies," in: Jeffrey C. Alexander, Ron Eyerman, Bernhard Giesen and Neil J. Smelser (eds.), *Cultural Trauma and Collective Identity*, Berkeley: University of California Press, 2004, 155–195.
32. Allison Crawford, "'The Trauma Experienced by Generations Past Having an Effect in their Descendants': Narrative and Historical Trauma among Inuit in Nunavut, Canada," *Transcultural Psychiatry* 51, no. 3 (2014): 339–369.
33. Jill Bennett, *Empathic Vision: Affect, Trauma, and Contemporary Art*, Stanford: Stanford University Press, 2005.
34. Barbara Ann Baker, "Art Speaks in Healing Survivors of War," *Journal of Aggression* 12, no. 1–2 (2006): 183–198; Arpad Barath, "Cultural Art Therapy in the Treatment of War Trauma in Children and Youth: Projects in the Former Yugoslavia," in: Stanley Krippner and Teresa M. McIntyre (eds.), *The Psychological Impact of War Trauma on Civilians: An International Perspective*, Westport: Praeger, 2003, 155–170; Jane Edwards, "Humanity, Human Rights, and the Creative Arts Therapies," *The Arts in Psychotherapy* 49 (2016): A1–A2; Debra Kalmanowitz and T. H. Ho. Rainbow, "Out of Our Mind. Art Therapy and Mindfulness with Refugees, Political Violence and Trauma," *The Arts in Psychotherapy* 49, no. X (2016): 57–65.
35. Rachel Dinitto, "Narrating the Cultural Trauma of 3/11: The Debris of Post-Fukushima Literature and Film," *Japan Forum* 26, no. 3 (2014): 340–360; Anne Fuchs, *Phantoms of War in Contemporary German Literature, Films and Discourse: The Politics of Memory*, Hampshire: Palgrave Macmillan, 2008; Maryam Khosroshahibonab and Mansour Hessami Kermani, "A Study of the Representation of Individual and Collective Trauma Resulting from Two World Wars in Art with a Look at the Works of Two German Painters," *The Scientific Journal of NAZAR Research Center (Nrc) for Art, Architecture & Urbanism* 14, no. 52 (2017): 5–18.
36. Council of Europe, *EU/CoE support to the promotion of cultural diversity in Kosovo*: Council of Europe*, 2020 (https://www.coe.int/en/web/culture-and-heritage/kosovo, accessed November 17, 2020).
37. EACEA, *Cultural Cooperation Projects in the Western Balkans 2019: EACEA*, 2019 (https://eacea.ec.europa.eu/sites/ipa/funding/coopwb_en, accessed November 17, 2020).

38. Nikolaos Pasamitros, "Cultural Heritage: Contested Perspectives and Strategies in Kosovo."

39. Ullrich Kockel, *Re-Visioning Europe: Frontiers, Place Identities and Journeys in Debatable Lands*, Hampshire: Palgrave Macmillan, 2010.

40. Nicolas Lemay-Hébert, "Critical Debates on Liberal Peacebuilding," *Civil Wars* 15, no. 2 (2013): 242–252; K. Van Brabant, *Peacebuilding How? Broad Local Ownership*, Geneva: International Peace Alliance, 2010.

41. Inter Alia, "European Cultural Heritage Onstage (ECHO) Application," Athens: Inter Alia, 2017.

42. Inter Alia, *ECHO: InterAliaProject.com* (https://www.interaliaproject.com/news.php?id=213, accessed May 29, 2021).

43. Inter Alia, "ECHO: InterAliaProject.com," June 20, 2019 (https://drive.google.com/file/d/1AFG7WUk4CvLr8obmud-83owwfshE5nPX/view, accessed May 29, 2021).

44. Sfera International, *Coffee with Artists: SferaInternational.org* (https://sferainternational.org/coffee-with-artists/, accessed May 30, 2021); Sfera International, *Intercultural evening at atelier SOLAK: SferaInternational.org* (https://sferainternational.org/intercultural-evening-at-atelier-solak/, accessed May 30, 2021).

45. NSUZIVO, *Multimedijalna izložba EHO 77 u Kulturnoj stanici Svilara: NSUZIVO.rs* (https://nsuzivo.rs/novi-sad/multimedijalna-izlozba-eho-77-u-kulturnoj-stanici-svilara, accessed May 30, 2021).

46. Sfera International, *SFEST festival: SferaInternational.org* (https://sferainternational.org/sfest-festival/, accessed May 29, 2021).

47. *Dark Vein*. Directed by Stratis Vogiatzis and Giorgos Samantas. Produced by Inter Alia and Caravan Project (https://vimeo.com/356574424).

48. Inter Alia, *ECHO: InterAliaProject.com*.

49. CultureNow.gr., *A Field Guide to Getting Lost Vol.2: Ομαδική έκθεση στην Αίγινα: CultureNow.gr* (https://www.culturenow.gr/a-field-guide-to-getting-lost-vol-2-omadiki-ekthesi-stin-aigina/, accessed Novemebr 17, 2020).

50. Biennale of Western Balkans, *International Museum Day ICOM · The future of tradition: bowb.org* (https://bowb.org/icombowb-2019-en/, accessed May 30, 2021).

51. Inter Alia, *ECHO: InterAliaProject.com*.

52. Thessaloniki Documentary Festival, *Dark Vein: Thessaloniki Documentary Festival* (https://www.filmfestival.gr/en/section-tdf/movie/13540, accessed September 2021).

53. Inter Alia, *Impact Analysis ECHO*. Athens: Inter Alia, 2019.

54. https://echo-ii.eu/staff/aristaios-tsousis/.

55. https://echo-ii.eu/staff/depy-antoniou/.

56. https://echo-ii.eu/staff/kiril-konstantin/.

57. Inter Alia, *Impact Analysis ECHO*, 2019.

58. ECHO II: Traditions in Transition (https://echo-ii.eu/, accessed August 11, 2021); Inter Alia, *ECHO II: Traditions in Transition: Projects: Inter Alia* (https://interaliaproject.com/project/echo-ii-traditions-in-transition/, accessed 17, 2020).

59. Stephanie Schwandner-Sievers and Isabel Ströhle, "An Ethnography of 'Political Will': Towards a Thick Description of Internal Scripts in Post-War Kosovo," *Südosteuropa* 60, no. X (2012): 497–513.

BIBLIOGRAPHY

Primary Sources

Biennale of Western Balkans. 2019. *International Museum Day ICOM: The Future of Tradition: bowb.org*, available online: https://bowb.org/icombowb-2019-en/ (accessed May 30, 2021).

Council of Europe. 2020. *EU/CoE Support to the Promotion of Cultural Diversity in Kosovo*: Council of Europe*, available online: https://www.coe.int/en/web/culture-and-heritage/kosovo (accessed November 17, 2020).

CultureNow.gr. 2019. *A Field Guide to Getting Lost Vol.2: Ομαδική έκθεση στην Αίγινα: CultureNow.gr*, available online: https://www.culturenow.gr/a-field-guide-to-getting-lost-vol-2-omadiki-ekthesi-stin-aigina/ (accessed November 17, 2020).

EACEA. 2019. *Cultural Cooperation Projects in the Western Balkans 2019: EACEA*, available online: https://eacea.ec.europa.eu/sites/ipa/funding/coopwb_en (accessed November 17, 2020).

ECHO II. 2021. *ECHO II: Traditions in Transition*, available online: https://echo-ii.eu/ (accessed August 11, 2021).

———. 2021. *ECHO II: Traditions in Transition. Aristaios Tsousis*, available online: https://echo-ii.eu/staff/aristaios-tsousis/ (accessed May 11, 2022).

———. 2021. *ECHO II: Traditions in Transition. Depy Antoniou*, available online: https://echo-ii.eu/staff/depy-antoniou/ (accessed May 11, 2022).

———. 2021. *ECHO II: Traditions in Transition. Kiril T. Konstantin*, available online: https://echo-ii.eu/staff/kiril-konstantin/ (accessed May 13, 2022).

ESDIAPOK. 2020. *Report for the 5th Conference of ESDIAPOK* [Απολογισμός για το 5ο συνέδριο της ΕΣΔΙΑΠΟΚ]: *esdiapok.blogspot.com*, available online: http://esdiapok.blogspot.com/2020/05/5.html (accessed May 30, 2021).

ICOMOS. 2011–2015. *ICOMOS Website: Charters and Other Doctrinal Texts: Catégories en français: Ressources Charters and Other Standards: The Athens Charter for the Restoration of Historic Monuments—1931*, available online: http://www.icomos.org/en/charters-and-texts/179-articles-en-francais/ressources/charters-and-standards/167-the-athens-charter-for-the-restoration-of-historic-monuments (accessed August 11, 2021).

ICRC. 1907. "International Committee of the Red Cross Website: Treaties, States Parties and Commentaries: Convention (IV) Respecting the Laws and Customs of War on Land and its Annex: Regulations Concerning the Laws and Customs of War on Land." *International Committee of the Red Cross Website*, available online: https://ihl-databases.icrc.org/applic/ihl/ihl.nsf/Treaty.xsp?action=openDocument&documentId=4D47F92DF3966A7EC12563CD002D6788 (accessed August 19, 2021).

Inter Alia. 2017. *European Cultural Heritage Onstage (ECHO) Application*. Athens: Inter Alia.

———. 2019. "ECHO: InterAliaProject.com." June 20, available online: https://drive.google.com/file/d/1AFG7WUk4CvLr8obmud-83owwfshE5nPX/view (accessed May 29, 2021).

———. 2019. *Impact Analysis ECHO*. Athens: Inter Alia.

———. 2019. *ECHO: InterAliaProject.com*, available online: https://www.interaliaproject.com/news.php?id=213 (accessed May 29, 2021).

———. 2020. *ECHO II: Traditions in Transition: Projects: Inter Alia*, available online: https://interaliaproject.com/project/echo-ii-traditions-in-transition/ (accessed November 17, 2020).

NSUZIVO. 2019. *Multimedijalna izložba EHO 77 u Kulturnoj stanici Svilara: NSUZIVO.rs*, available online: https://nsuzivo.rs/novi-sad/multimedijalna-izlozba-eho-77-u-kulturnoj-stanici-svilara (accessed May 30, 2021).

Roerich Pact. 1935. "Treaty on the Protection of Artistic and Scientific Institutions and Historic Monuments (Roerich Pact)," available online: https://ihl-databases.icrc.org/ihl/INTRO/325?OpenDocument (accessed Sepetmber 15, 2022).

Sfera International. 2018. *Coffee With Artists: SferaInternational.org*, available online: https://sferainternational.org/coffee-with-artists/ (accessed May 30, 2021).

———. 2018. *Intercultural Evening at atelier SOLAK: SferaInternational.org*, available online: https://sferainternational.org/intercultural-evening-at-atelier-solak/ (accessed May 20, 2021).

———. 2018. *SFEST Festival: SferaInternational.org*, available online: https://sferainternational.org/sfest-festival/ (accessed May 29, 2021).

Thessaloniki Documentary Festival. 2021. *Dark Vein: Thessaloniki Documentary Festival*, available online: https://www.filmfestival.gr/en/section-tdf/movie/13540 (accessed September 5, 2021).

UNESCO. 1954. *UNESCO Web Site: Convention for the Protection of Cultural Property in the Event of Armed Conflict With Regulations for the Execution of the Convention 1954*, available online: http://portal.unesco.org/en/ev.php-URL_ID=13637&URL_DO=DO_TOPIC&URL_SECTION=201.html (accessed August 11, 2021).

———. 1972. *Convention Concerning the Protection of the World Cultural and Natural Heritage*. Paris: UNESCO, available online: http://whc.unesco.org/archive/convention-en.pdf (accessed August 11, 2021).

———. 1992–2016. *UNESCO Website: Culture: World Heritage Centre: The List: Global Strategy: Criteria*, available online: http://whc.unesco.org/en/criteria/ (accessed August 18, 2021).

———. 1992–2020. *The Criteria for Selection: UNESCO*, available online: https://whc.unesco.org/en/criteria/ (accessed May 16, 2021).

———. 2003. *Convention for the Safeguarding of the Intangible Cultural Heritage*. Paris: UNESCO, available online: http://unesdoc.unesco.org/images//0013/001325/132540e.pdf (accessed August 11, 2021).

———. 2019. *Dark Vein*. Directed by Stratis Vogiatzis and Giorgos Samantas. Produced by Inter Alia and Caravan Project, available online: https://vimeo.com/356574424 (accessed August 18, 2021).

Secondary Sources

Alexander, Jeffrey C. "Culture Trauma, Morality and Solidarity: The Social Construction of 'Holocaust' and Other Mass Murders." *Thesis Eleven* 132, no. 1 (2016): 3–16.

Baker, Barbara Ann. "Art Speaks in Healing Survivors of War." *Journal of Aggression* 12, nos. 1–2 (2006): 183–198.
Barath, Arpad. "Cultural Art Therapy in the Treatment of War Trauma in Children and Youth: Projects in the Former Yugoslavia." In *The Psychological Impact of War Trauma on Civilians: An International Perspective*, edited by Stanley Krippner and Teresa M. McIntyre. Westport: Praeger, 2003, 155–170.
Bennett, Jill. *Empathic Vision: Affect, Trauma, and Contemporary Art*. Stanford: Stanford University Press, 2005.
Biran, Avital, Yaniv Poria, and Oren Gila. "Sought Experiences at (Dark) Heritage Sites." *Annals of Tourism Research* 38, no. 3 (2011): 820–841.
Blake, Janet. "On Defining the Cultural Heritage." *International and Comparative Law Quarterly* 49, no. 1 (2000): 61–85.
Connerton, Paul. *How Societies Remember*. Cambridge: Cambridge University Press, 1989.
Crawford, Allison. "The Trauma Experienced by Generations Past Having an Effect in Their Descendants: Narrative and Historical Trauma Among Inuit in Nunavut, Canada." *Transcultural Psychiatry* 51, no. 3 (2014): 339–369.
Daugbjerg, Mads, and Thomas Fibiger. "Introduction: Heritage Gone Global. Investigating the Production and Problematics of Globalized Pasts." *History and Anthropology* 22, no. 2 (2011): 135–147.
Demertzis, Nikos. "The Greek Civil War as Cultural Trauma" ["Ο ελληνικός Εμφύλιος ως πολιτισμικό τραύμα."], edited by Nikos Demertzis, Eleni Paschaloudi, and Giorgos Antoniou. *Επιστήμη και Κοινωνία: Επιθεώρηση Πολιτικής και Ηθικής Θεωρίας* 28 (2011): 81–109.
Dinitto, Rachel. "Narrating the Cultural Trauma of 3/11: The Debris of Post-Fukushima Literature and Film." *Japan Forum* 26, no. 3 (2014): 340–360.
Edwards, Jane. "Humanity, Human Rights, and the Creative Arts Therapies." *The Arts in Psychotherapy* 49 (2016): A1–A2.
Eyerman, Ron, and Dominik Bartmanski. "The Worst Was the Silence: The Unfinished Drama of the Katyn Massacre." In *Memory, Trauma and Identity*, edited by Ron Eyerman. Cham: Palgrave Macmillan, 2019, 111–142.
Fuchs, Anne. *Phantoms of War in Contemporary German Literature, Films and Discourse: The Politics of Memory*. Hampshire: Palgrave Macmillan, 2008.
Hartmann, Rudi. "Dark Tourism, Thanatourism, and Dissonance in Heritage." *Journal of Heritage Tourism* 9, no. 2 (2014): 166–182.
ICOMOS UK. n.d. *ICOMOS UK Webiste: World Heritage*, available online: http://www.icomos-uk.org/world-heritage/ (accessed August 18, 2021).
Kalmanowitz, Debra, and Rainbow T. H. Ho. "Out of Our Mind. Art Therapy and Mindfulness With Refugees, Political Violence and Trauma." *The Arts in Psychotherapy* 49 (2016): 57–65.
Kellerman, Natan P. F. "Epigenetic Transmission of Holocaust Trauma: Can Nightmares Be Inherited?" *Israel Journal of Psychiatry and Related Sciences* 50, no. 1 (2013): 1–9.
Khosroshahibonab, Maryam, and Mansour Hessami Kermani. "A Study of the Representation of Individual and Collective Trauma Resulting From Two World

Wars in Art With a Look at the Works of Two German Painters." *The Scientific Journal of NAZAR Research Center (NRC) for Art, Architecture & Urbanism* 14 (2017): 5–18.

Kirmayer, Laurence J., Joseph P. Gone, and Joshua Moses. "Rethinking Historical Trauma." *Transcultural Psychiatry* 51, no. 3 (2014): 299–319.

Kockel, Ullrich. *Re-Visioning Europe: Frontiers, Place Identities and Journeys in Debatable Lands.* Hampshire: Palgrave Macmillan, 2010.

Lemay-Hébert, Nicolas. "Critical Debates on Liberal Peacebuilding." *Civil Wars* 15, no. 2 (2013): 242–252.

Lowenthal, David. *The Heritage Crusade and the Spoils of History.* Cambridge: Cambridge University Press, 1998.

Menzies, Peter. "Intergenerational Trauma From a Mental Health Perspective." *Native Social Work Journal* 7 (2010): 63–85.

Meskell, Lynn. "UNESCO's World Heritage Concention at 40: Challenging the Economic and Political Order of International Heritage Conservation." *Current Anthropology* 5, no. 4 (2013): 483–494.

Pasamitros, Nikolaos. "Cultural Heritage: Contested Perspectives and Strategies in Kosovo." In *State-Building in Post-Independence Kosovo: Policy Challenges and Societal Considerations*, edited by Ioannis Armakolas, Agon Demjaha, Arolda Elbasani, Stephanie Schwandner-Sievers, Elton Skendaj, and Nikolaos Tzifakis. Pristina: Kosovo Foundation for Open Society, 2018, 291–310.

Robinson, Olivia, and Trish Barnard. "'Thanks, But We'll Take It From Here': Australian Aboriginal and Torres Strait Islander Women Influencing the Collection of Tangible and Intangible Heritage." *Museum International* 59, no. 4 (2007): 34–45.

Samuels, Kathryn Lafrenz. *Academia Website: What is Cultural Heritage? Mapping a Concept, Integrating Fields*, available online: https://www.academia.edu/6638341/What_is_Cultural_Heritage_Mapping_a_Concept_Integrating_Fields (accessed August 11, 2021).

Schwandner-Sievers, Stephanie, and Isabel Ströhle. "An Ethnography of 'Political Will': Towards a Thick Description of Internal Scripts in Post-War Kosovo." *Südosteuropa* 60, no. 1 (2012): 497–513.

Shackel, Paul A. "Public Memory and the Search for Power in American Historical Archaeology." *American Anthropologist* 103, no. 3 (2001): 655–670.

Smith, Laurajane. "Class, Heritage and the Negotiation of Place." In *Missing Out on Heritage: Socio-Economic Status and Heritage Participation*, available online: http://www.english-heritage.org.uk/about/who-we-are/how-we-are-run/heritage-for-all/missing-out-conference/ (accessed September 15, 2022).

———. "Discourses of Heritage: Implications for Archaeological Community Practice." *Nuevo Mundo Mundos Nuevos* 2012, available online: https://doi.org/10.4000/nuevomundo.64148 (accessed September 15, 2022).

———. "Intangible Heritage: A Challenge to the Authorised Heritage Discourse." *Revista D'Etnologia de Catalunya* 40 (2015): 133–142.

———. *Uses of Heritage.* London: Routledge, 2006.

Stone, Philip R. "A Dark Tourism Spectrum: Towards a Typology of Death and Macabre Related Tourist Sites, Attractions and Exhibitions." *Tourism: An Interdisciplinary International Journal* 54, no. 2 (2006): 145–160.

Sztompka, Piotr. "Trauma of Social Change: A Case of Postcommunist Societies." In *Cultural Trauma and Collective Identity*, edited by Jeffrey C. Alexander, Ron Eyerman, Bernhard Giesen, and Neil J. Smelser. Berkeley: University of California Press, 2004, 155–195.

Thomas, Suzie, Vesa-Pekka Herva, Oula Seitsonen, and Eerika Koskinen-Koivisto. "Dark Heritage." In *Encyclopedia of Global Archaeology*, edited by Claire Smith. Cham: Springer, 2019, 1–11.

Van Brabant, K. *Peacebuilding How? Broad Local Ownership*. Geneva: International Peace Alliance, available online: http://www.dmeforpeace.org/sites/default/files/2010_IP_Peacebuilding_How_Broad_Local_Ownership.pdf (accessed September 15, 2022).

Chapter 6

The Champlain Quadricentennial
Celebrating 400 years of...?
Anastasia L. Pratt

At first glance, the list of activities designed to celebrate the Champlain Quadricentennial in 2009 seems very much like those of the Champlain Tercentenary in 1909: parades, speeches, concerts, and reenactments—activities to bring out community members and to bring in tourists. Press releases and advertisements were quick to connect Samuel de Champlain to every kind of event, adopting commemorative themes for Burlington, Vermont's First Night festivities (on December 31, 2008), Plattsburgh, New York's Fourth of July Parade, and Quebec City's year-long birthday party. Hundreds of other events—from bike tours to museum exhibits, cultural festivals to boat races—planned throughout the Champlain Valley, north and south of the border between the United States and Canada, similarly brought the history of the seventeenth century into the present by offering playful and serious opportunities to consider the importance of the anniversary. Making the connection to Champlain seemed as easy as snapping one's fingers. Much harder was agreeing on what, exactly, was being celebrated. For some, this anniversary was a chance to celebrate the history of the Champlain Valley as a whole, an opportunity to honor 400 years of life in the region and, especially, to commemorate the lives of Indigenous peoples who were often left out of the history of the area. For others, the anniversary was the chance of a lifetime, the moment to celebrate an iconic hero, Samuel de Champlain.

The lack of a clear and unified focus for the celebrations was endemic. The US Congress, with H.R. 1520 and S. 1148, sponsored by Representatives Maurice D. Hinchey [D-NY-22] and thirty-one of his Republican and Democrat colleagues (mostly representing New York and Vermont), and Senators Hillary Rodham Clinton [D-NY], Charles E. Schumer [D-NY], Patrick J. Leahy [D-VT], and Bernard Sanders [Ind-VT], respectively, called on the Champlain Commission to include, among other things, the planning, developing, and executing of "programs and activities appropriate to commemorate the 400th anniversary of the voyage of Samuel de Champlain, the first European to discover and explore Lake Champlain"; encouraging "civic, patriotic, historical, educational, artistic, religious, economic, and other organizations throughout the United States to organize and participate in anniversary activities to expand the understanding and appreciation of the significance of the voyage of Samuel de Champlain"; and helping to "ensure that the observances of the voyage of Samuel de Champlain are inclusive and appropriately recognize the experiences and heritage of all people present when Samuel de Champlain arrived in the Champlain Valley."[1] While the national focus was very much centered on Champlain as founder and explorer, Vermont's focus was on placing "an international spotlight on the lake and its history and culture," creating the Lake Champlain Quadricentennial Commission "to advise the governor on the direction, planning, promotion and implementation of heritage tourism activities and programs in the Lake Champlain region, in coordination with similar efforts on the part of the State of New York and the Province of Quebec, in order to commemorate the arrival of Samuel de Champlain in 1609 and to celebrate the natural and cultural history of the lake."[2] Canadian celebrations focused mostly on Quebec City, celebrating its 400th birthday. And Indigenous peoples took the opportunity to remind the rest of the world of their much longer history in the New World. Almost the only thing the celebrations shared was the idea that the past still matters in the present and the reality that, for those who settled and live in the northeastern portion of North America, history is, at its core, transnational.

WHO WAS SAMUEL DE CHAMPLAIN?

Samuel de Champlain, the person, is, at the least, illusive. Journalist John Allemang writes:

> Anniversary celebrations need their icons, of course, but this is still a lot to live up to. And when you start to look for the real Champlain beneath all the statuesque gilding, the story of our history becomes much more challenging. The reason we can say so much about Champlain, it seems, is because we know so little—an odd thing to discover about a man whose collected writings fill six volumes in the Champlain Society edition published in the 1920s and 1930s.[3]

Champlain was born somewhere in the neighborhood of 1567, most likely in Brouage, on the Bay of Biscay, in southwestern France. From this town overlooking the Atlantic Ocean, he grew into the man who, as Quebec historian

Patrice Groulx explains, has been variously named as founder of Canada and of French Canada, mainstay of Christianity in Canada, leading colonizer of Quebec (city and province) and Acadia, creator of good France-United States relations, cartographer of the New World, and father of both European civilization in Ontario and agricultural colonization.[4]

As a matter of fact, Champlain was not the first European to explore the Atlantic coastline. Beginning in 1534, Jacques Cartier undertook a series of voyages on behalf of France, seeking a trade route to China and, upon finding various Indigenous peoples, looking to bring God to the Natives, Gold back to the King, and, always, to bring Glory to France. Cartier's efforts gave his country the strategic advantage of a settlement in Acadia, a system of *voyageurs* and *coureur du bois* living and working as fur traders in the areas now known as Canada and the northern United States, a series of outposts and routes for Jesuit efforts to convert the masses, and clear maps of the area. When Samuel de Champlain began his travels, he was heading to a land that was a known entity and, to his credit, he did not rest on Cartier's laurels. During his first trip, in 1604, Champlain, with François Gravé Du Pont, established the city of Quebec. He started his second trip by sorting out a territorial dispute between Captain Darache,[5] who was the master of a Basque ship, and Pont Gravé, who was in the service of the Pierre Dugua, the Sieur du Mons who had the fur trade monopoly for Acadia. It was a small venture into diplomacy, but his political savvy became a trademark celebrated by future generations.

His descriptions of the Indigenous people he encountered, people he was later credited with befriending and protecting, began after this meeting. "In this place," Champlain wrote, "were a number of savages who had come for traffic in furs, several of whom came to our vessel with their canoes, . . . From Choüacoet along the coast as far as the harbor of Tadoussac, they are all alike."[6] By June 3, 1608, he had chosen the point of Quebec as the place of settlement, setting workmen to cutting down the nut-trees that populated the land, sawing boards, making a cellar, and digging ditches. He found the place where Cartier wintered and noted the remains of the explorer's efforts and continued to notice the Indigenous people surrounding him.[7] Of them he wrote:

> Meanwhile, a large number of savages were encamped in cabins near us, engaged in fishing for eels. . . . I paid especial attention to their customs . . . I am of the opinion that, if one were to show them how to live, and teach them the cultivation of the soil and other things, they would learn very aptly. For many of them possess good sense, and answer properly questions put to them. They have a bad habit of taking vengeance, and are great liars, and you must not put much reliance on them, except judiciously, and with force at hand. They make

promises readily, but keep their word poorly. . . . The most of them observe no law at all, so far as I have been able to see, and are, besides, full of superstitions.[8]

Whatever else he might have been, "there is no doubt that de Champlain was, literally, a colonizer."[9] The purposes of his voyage were to stake a land claim for France, establish a place in the fur trade, and find a faster trade route to Asia before any other Europeans could do so. That reality makes commemoration exceedingly difficult. For some, like David Hackett Fischer, Champlain was a truly admirable and heroic figure, arguing that, unlike other European leaders, who slaughtered the Indigenous people that they encountered, Champlain treated them with dignity and respect and got on very well with them. He was much more interested in learning from them and cooperating with them than exploiting them. The result was a bonding of several Indian nations with the early French settlers that made the lucrative fur trade possible.[10]

Many others, though, see a sham, a politician who was putting one over on the Cardinal Richelieu and all the other important and otherwise-engaged decision makers in far-away France. As a colony and a nation-in-training, Quebec was little short of a disaster. Several decades after the colony's scurvy-ravaged founding, despite all of Champlain's self-promoting propaganda and frequent trips back to France to reassure anxious investors, barely 200 people called Quebec home.[11]

Perhaps the nature of the history is difficult to pin down because it crosses many borders and is with us still, in the Wendat in Quebec and the Wyandotte in Oklahoma, in the Haudenosaunee, whose Great Law of Peace was used as a model for the US Constitution, and in Samuel de Champlain, who "will live on in monuments and in history books, in street and college names."[12]

REMEMBERING CHAMPLAIN

Monuments are particularly important in this transnational history. During the Tercentenary in 1909, monuments to Champlain were erected throughout New England, Quebec, and Ontario. Often those statues portrayed Champlain as the erstwhile soldier, bringing commerce and culture to the New World, helped on his journeys by obviously subservient Indigenous people. One hundred years later, in 2009, commemorative activities sought to address concerns over that one-sided representation.

In Orillia, Ontario, the Quadricentennial in 2009 offered a chance to reconsider the 100-year-old monument to Champlain, its interpretation, and its role in crossing the borders not just between English- and French-speaking Canadians but also between the Indigenous people of North America and European-descended people. Sculptor Vernon March's design was selected after a call for entries open to British subjects, who included any citizen of a British colony or protectorate, and French citizens. Charles Harold Hale, one person from the community of local, civic-minded businessmen behind the commission, hoped that unveiling this "noble national monument" would promote "the historical links between Ontario and Quebec" and would "give distinction to the occasion and a flavour that could not be imparted elsewhere." True to the sentiments of the time, he personally invited Rodolphe Lemieux, Speaker of the House of Commons, to deliver the keynote speech at the unveiling of the monument, commenting that Lemieux was qualified for this honor by his "office, lineage, and record to exemplify and give expression to the unity of purpose and of a sentiment which should characterize the two great races [British and French] that form the basis of Canadian nationality."[13]

Measuring twelve feet tall, the statue shows Champlain dressed for court, with cloak, long boots, spurs, plumed hat, and sword. A group of Indigenous people is shown at the bottom of the statue, leaning against one side of the plinth made of Benedict stone; a fur trader and missionary are on the other side of the plinth. Champlain's prominence on the monument, as was common in all these early twentieth-century statues honoring the explorer, when combined with the stated "desire to strengthen ties between English and French Canada trumped any possible intention to portray Champlain's complex interaction with Huronia's Indigenous population in an equitable and historically accurate manner."[14] A plaque embedded in the plinth of the monument makes the intentions clear:

1615–1915

Erected to commemorate the advent into Ontario of the white race, under the leadership of Samuel de Champlain, the intrepid French explorer and colonizer, who, with fifteen companions, arrived in these parts in the summer of 1615, and spent the following winter with the Indians, making his headquarters at Cahiagué, the chief fillable of the Hurons, which was near this place.

A symbol of the good will between the French- and English-speaking people of Canada.[15]

Neither the monument nor the unveiling ceremonies honored "Champlain's reciprocal and mutually beneficial relationship with his Huron hosts in 1615–16 . . . , and the Orillia committee made no attempt to include First Nations participation with the exception of inviting several Indigenous chiefs, including Lorenzo Big Canoe of the Chippewas at Georgina Island Ovide Sioui of the Hurons at Lorette."[16] After the 1969 White Paper, "Statement of the Government of Canada on Indian Policy," portrayals of history across Canada were reconsidered and a group led by John Wesley Oldham, a minister in Orillia, sought corrections to this monument. His Unity Advisory Committee, which consisted of local Aboriginal and municipal officials, drafted the text for a new descriptive plaque, to be completed when the monument was rededicated:

> With the arrival of the French in North America, both they and the Huron Confederacy recognized and welcomed the benefits of equal trade and cultural alliances between the two nations based on mutual trust and respect. Because of this historic partnership the French gained strategic access and a warm welcome to the vast territories of Turtle Island beyond the lands of the Wendat, while the Hurons became a significant partner in what was to become a worldwide trading network based upon the fur trade in beaver pelts. This monument, originally designed in 1915 but not completed until 1925, was re-dedicated on _____ 199_ to commemorate that historical alliance.[17]

Parks Canada did not follow up on this proposal, but, when they again discussed the Champlain monument in 2000, "emphasized that drafting a sensitively-worded plaque would be a 'delicate undertaking' and that any new plaque 'should be respectful of the monument itself.'"[18] Left as it was, the monument was vandalized repeatedly. That vandalism, along with the normal effects of weathering on stone monuments, led to a 2015 Parks Canada condition assessment and the subsequent removal of the monument for restoration. With the Orillia City Council, the federal agency established the Samuel de Champlain Monument Working Group, a group composed of key stakeholders from Parks Canada, the City of Orillia, the Chippewas of Rama First Nation, the Huron-Wendat Nation, the Elementary Teachers' Federation of Ontario, and citizens-at-large, and charged it with developing "a plan for the monument and surrounding park lands that presents a balanced and respectful representation of both Indigenous and non-Indigenous perspectives."[19] The working group's key recommendations, developed after months of discussion, consultation, and research, included reinstalling the monument with only the central figure of Champlain atop the plinth, consulting further with Indigenous groups regarding the remaining figures with the hope of "re-imagining their presence in the immediate vicinity of the original Monument," updating the monument's in-set plaque "so that it will honour the original intent within the context of contemporary knowledge and wisdom," and developing additional interpretive signs and materials—created with the participation of Indigenous peoples—"to tell a historically accurate story of Samuel de Champlain and his relationship with First Nations."[20] Parks Canada accepted all of the working group's recommendations in 2019, issuing a statement reaffirming the government's commitment to "reconciliation and renewed relationships with Indigenous Peoples, based on a recognition of rights, respect, co-operation, and partnership."[21] Neither Parks Canada nor the Samuel de Champlain Monument Working Group addressed the similarly-thorny issue of whether a work of art should be altered.

The first two phases of the restoration proceeded as expected, but, by 2018, Parks Canada, the agency charged with protecting and presenting "nationally significant examples of Canada's natural and cultural heritage,"[22] placed the project on hold, citing concerns over the representations of Indigenous people. Amanda Dale, director of Bear Waters Gathering in Muskoka, called the monument "Insulting . . . harmful. It promotes one narrative. It memorializes someone who shouldn't necessarily take the front stage."[23] A "change.org" petition created by Luana Shirt called for the Rama First Nations, Parks Canada, the City of Orillia, and the Elementary Teachers Federation of Ontario, to halt the reinstallation on traditional Wendat-Huron territory of a statue that is "racist and derogatory to Indigenous Peoples; depicting Champlain as 'savour [sic] and lord' over the people." The petition cites Huron-Wendat Grand Chief Konrad Sioui's 2018 letter to Orillia mayor Steve Clarke, which described the monument as "degrading and preposterous" and expressed concern that "it might additionally perpetuate a disgraceful notion of our Peoples as being submissive, subservient and obedient to the French Crown, whereas portraying them as an inferior class of residents."[24]

In September 2021, Parks Canada confirmed that reinstallation of the statue would be deferred indefinitely. The discovery of children's remains in unmarked graves at sites that once housed the 140 federally run Indian Residential Schools led the Huron-Wendat Nation and the Chippewas of Rama First Nation to resign from the working group and its deliberations of the site. With work on the monument stalled indefinitely, Parks Canada has made the park safe and accessible by removing screening and fencing.[25] And the story of the Indigenous People of Huronia and their interactions with European-descended people—the complex and very human story of those interactions, which has evolved over time—has been left for other venues. The Truth and Reconciliation Commission, created as part of the Indian Residential Schools Settlement Agreement, will help tell the story well, especially as it calls for "a sincere indication and acknowledgement of the injustices and harms experienced by Aboriginal people and the need for continued healing."[26]

The shared history of life in North America has come under similar attack in Burlington, Vermont, where the Samuel de Champlain Monument in the Rozendaal Courtyard of Champlain College has attracted criticism. James Sardonis, a Vermont sculptor, created a monument to Champlain that depicts the man crouched down, spyglass to his eye, a visual metaphor for exploring.[27] Commissioned by Trustee Emeritus John W. Heisse Jr., MD, the statue was unveiled during the summer of 2009 as part of Vermont's year-long celebrations of the Quadricentennial. But, by 2019, the continued elevation of Champlain to hero status and the absence of Indigenous people in the monument had become a major point of contention. Jay Covert, student and Champlain Student Government Association director of diversity and engagement, proposed a resolution calling for the statue to be turned over to an unnamed local museum. The resolution "labels de Champlain a colonizer and recognizes the 'pain inflicted' on Indigenous people by placing the statue on campus." Continuing, the resolution explains that "they created a new society, but through that they erased the history of many people who lived before them."[28] Not everyone on campus agreed with this resolution, though. Student and president of the Champlain College Republican Club, Nicholas Chace, for example, argued: "Those who are demanding the removal of the statue are not well informed on the history of Samuel de Champlain and the Abenaki people. The demand . . . is based on a mistaken belief that Samuel de Champlain represents white colonialism and the atrocities committed against Native American tribes by early American settlers. While in actuality he was an ally of the Native American people that he met."[29] Inserting a very different viewpoint, Don Stevens, alumnus and chief of the Nulhegan band of the Coosuc Abenaki nation, asked: "Why wouldn't we have an Abenaki statue that would be of equal value? You don't always have to tear things down in order to build things up. . . . De Champlain allied with the Abenaki. . . . We don't really have that big of an issue with Champlain himself." That new statue, Stevens argued, would reintegrate Native Americans with the story of the lake. Stevens continued: "It was here, it was ours, and we actually worked with the French. . . . They helped us; we helped them."[30] Melody Walker Brook, of the Elnu Abenaki Tribe, agreed, writing, "what would be most appropriate is actually to add a statue for Indigenous people next to the one of Champlain. This is how people learn. Understanding the connections that are possible between people and acknowledging the Indigenous voice is essential."[31]

Ultimately, Sardonis's statue was left in place, but the discussions will no doubt continue as each new generation of college students comes to terms with a history that is too real and complex to be fully covered by a single monument. Indeed, many of the memorials to Champlain—monuments, statues, and other commemorative installations that span three states, three provinces, and two continents—include, in the 2020s, interpretive panels and signs to help contextualize the history of the colonial era and of the commemorations of Champlain's journeys in North America. In Plattsburgh, New York, for example, locals, concerned about the portrayal of crouching Native Americans at the base of the plinth holding a bronze Champlain, worried that the monument might be damaged by those eager to correct the historical record in the 2020s (Figure 6.1). While the statue was apparently intended to pay tribute to Champlain's Native guide and includes a birchbark canoe to emphasize that connection, the position of the Indigenous man, and the incorrect headdress were quite problematic. Also problematic were the words engraved on the base of the statue: "Navigator; Discoverer; Colonizer." Rather than remove the statue, the group of locals led by Penelope Clute, a former Plattsburgh City Court judge and local historian, and Pastor Gregory Huth, developed a panel, unveiled in the summer of 2020, called "Who Discovered Lake Champlain?" to better explain the history of the region and of the statue. In addition to describing the region before Champlain's arrival, the panel attempted to correct the errors in depiction acknowledged by Hugh McLellan, who designed the monument, and Carl Heber, who sculpted it, in 1914.

Offering both French and English text, the 250-word panel "describes the region before Champlain came across it, the monument's features and briefly recaps the claimed ownership of the New World. . . . It also addresses the headdress mishap, stating, 'the sculpture mistakenly gave the Native guide a headdress worn by the peoples of the western plains, not the northeast.'"[32]

EXPANDING BORDERS: WHAT ARE WE CELEBRATING?

Indeed, it is education that will allow us to expand the borders of our shared history to include all the people who lived and worked here. Many of the Quadricentennial celebrations held throughout Canada and the United States attempted to begin that work by paying homage to Champlain but decentering him. While, at times, that created a sense of disorientation—What, exactly, are we celebrating here?—it made good sense in that it let other voices, other histories, other perceptions enter our collective memory. Whether a monument or exhibit focused on Champlain's map-making skills, or a publication such as *Lake Champlain Voyages of Discovery: Bringing History Home*, the Quadricentennial offered a different point of entry to the past.

One of the best examples of this changed focus was the Vermont Indigenous Celebration, developed to showcase "the fact that Vermont has and has always had a vibrant Native American community."[33] With presentations of citizens of the Missisquoi, Koasek of the Koas, Nulhegan Band of Abenakis, the Elnu Abenaki Tribe of the Koasek, and the Koasek Traditional Band—all Abenaki bands—and guest appearances by "our Mohawk cousins from the other side of Bitabagw,"[34] this was the Vermont Indigenous Celebration Signature Event, and it focused on Indigenous life. Presentations focused on 11,000 years of Abenaki fashion, the creation and reading of wampum, conservation, storytelling, and sovereignty, while demonstrations and exhibitions honored traditional arts such as quillwork, beadwork, leatherwork, and basketmaking. Rounding out the festivities were screenings of

Figure 6.1. Samuel de Champlain Monument, Plattsburgh, New York. Source: Photograph by the author.

films that offered a different vision of the encounters between Champlain and the local Indigenous people as well as the history of the Abenaki post encounter and an Abenaki encampment, a seventeenth-century cultural village.

Being remembered is, indeed, the point. Local groups strove to establish many ways to recognize and remember local Native heritage and history. The development of a curriculum that drew "on a diverse array of primary documents, journals, images, and prints" to "help students examine the multiple and varied perspective involved in our shared history, including examination of implications and repercussions of the alliances and conflicts generated by the meeting of cultures" offered a new way to integrate a more nuanced version of history into classrooms on both sides of Lake Champlain.[35]

Likewise, the Ontario Heritage Trust, the organization charged with conserving, interpreting, and sharing Ontario's heritage,[36] sought to offer different perspectives on Champlain, arguing that the wide variety of approaches to Champlain and his various identities and activities

> contribute to our understanding of Champlain and his role in the history of Ontario and North America more broadly. They also contribute to our understanding of what it means to be Canadian and how this identity is formed and considered over time.[37]

True to that purpose, the Trust considers Champlain as explorer, map maker, founder of Quebec, father of New France, sailor, soldier, builder of relationships with other nations, and leader; it also questions Champlain's exploration and colonization, recognizing that "facing up to the past means owning all of our history, rather than perpetuating the myth of white settlers creating civilization in uncharted wilderness."[38]

Similar curricular projects led to the creation of a 13' x 9' ceramic tile mosaic in northern New York. Titled *Clinton County History Through the Eyes of Its Children* (Figure 6.2), this mosaic brought local Indigenous people and their perspectives on pre-Champlain history together with seventh-grade Social Studies and Art teachers throughout Clinton County. Indigenous people helped to contextualize local history and offer representations of their ancestors so that the students and artists could design and create tiles for the mosaic, allowing the project to cross boundaries of nation and generation. Commemorative activities across Canada, the United States, and the local Indigenous nations in 2008 and 2009 also helped to fuel the Newspapers in Education curriculum that allowed local teachers to tie historic events to current news stories through their ten-part educational series that included "Samuel de Champlain and Lake Champlain," "Native People of New York," and "Celebrations: 1909 to Today."[39]

Exhibitions like *Alnobak: Wearing Our Heritage*, at the Flynn in Burlington, Vermont, and *Uncommon Threads* at the Maine State Museum offered a more detailed view of the way that Native identity changes over time, evolving with each generation.[40] On the face of it, the exhibitions are important, showing Indigenous art and artifacts. Their significance is even greater, though, protecting the Wobanaki textiles that Bruce Borque calls "one of North America's most dynamic Indigenous textile traditions," whose "'scattered, scarce and fragile' historical examples are slipping away."[41]

Vermont's formal recognition of four Abenaki tribes, the Elnu, Nulhegan, Koasek, and Missisquoi, in 2011 and 2012, was, arguably, the most public way "to reclaim [their] place in New England history, to make connections between [their] shared past and the present, and for [their] art to be accepted

Figure 6.2. One Portion of the *Clinton County History through the Eyes of Its Children* Mosaic in Clinton County, New York. Source: Photograph by the author.

on the same terms as art from other cultures of the world."[42] Recognition, which had, ironically, not occurred before "because they had never entered into a treaty that surrendered their territory to the United States" allowed the Abenaki, who had "continued to live in their homelands, and maintain strong oral histories and traditions from earlier times," to bring their own stories to the larger histories of the Champlain Valley.[43] The creation of the Vermont Indigenous Heritage Center (VIHC) in Burlington, then, was a fitting legacy project for the Vermont Lake Champlain Quadricentennial Commission. Developed after the Vermont Abenakis secured state recognition as "Indian tribes," the VIHC partnered with Alnôbaiwi, "another grass roots cultural revitalization society focused on preserving Vermont Abenaki history and culture," to organize programs that honored and highlighted Indigenous Vermont activity. The Heritage Center works to teach Abenaki history, archaeology, and spirituality, through formal courses and workshops and through community events ranging from a Forgiveness Day ceremony to a Harvest Celebration.[44] The ongoing preservation of all of these sources in the form of websites and digital archives—including those created by the Samuel de Champlain History Center in Champlain, New York, to memorialize Quadricentennial events throughout New York, New England, and Canada—guarantees that they are accessible and helps to ensure that a more nuanced and representative history will continue to be told.

We are left with the question, though, of what we were really celebrating during the Quadricentennial. Was it really about Samuel de Champlain, the man and legend? Or was it more a celebration of life along the rivers he explored and the lake that was renamed after him? Was it about Champlain's arrival on the banks of the Bitabagw after traveling up the Richelieu River? Or was it about the settlement of Quebec? Hundreds of events were planned and attended by people from all around the world. Great pomp and circumstance accompanied many of those events, though a lot of them avoided all mention of history, they were still branded with Champlain's name. In fact, it became a "Top 100 Event in the United States," with "something for everybody."[45]

In describing the Tercentenary celebrations, Sylvie Beaudreau argued that the commemoration allowed for

> a well-developed image of the region as a historical entity worthy of global attention [to] first [emerge]. In essence, then, what the citizens of the valley were doing in 1909 was not merely celebrating the life of the discoverer of the lake; they were also commemorating the rich history of the lake itself, . . . The tercentenary events allowed for a historical "production" of the region, bringing to the foreground the extent to which the valley was steeped in history. . . . what the commissioners planned and what ordinary citizens witnessed was the "invention" of a historic region: the Champlain Valley.[46]

While Canadians could point to Champlain as the "Father of New France" or "Founder of Quebec," Americans have a slightly more complicated relationship with the Frenchman. To honor him as the person who explored the network of rivers and lakes that provided a pathway from what we now know as Quebec to present-day New York City means we must accept that "he was the real leader of the colonization process" and that "much of the success that the French had in forming a viable French society here—one that thrives to this day—is due in large measure to Champlain himself."[47] To honor him at all means to recognize the disproportionate power relationship between

Indigenous people and the Europeans whose colonizing efforts forever changed North America. In the United States, Champlain remains a colonizer.

With commemorations rife with so much difficulty, perhaps it makes sense that, really, more than anything, the Quadricentennial celebrations throughout the northeastern United States and Canada and on Indigenous lands focused far more on the future than on the past. The University of Vermont's Forums on the Future asked students and community members to think about life in the near and far future, and to consider what they wanted Vermont to become. The birch-bark canoe flotilla, organized by boatbuilder and amateur historian Douglas Brooks, recalled "the significance of birch-bark canoes during the 1909 and 1959 celebrations across Lake Champlain,"[48] and called attention to the possibility of an artisanal and craft culture well into the future. Kevin Dann, then a lecturer at SUNY Plattsburgh, offered his own take on this joint remembrance of the past and expression of hope for the future through the "Corridor of Amity," his "pilgrimage of peace from Montreal to Manhattan to promote peace and friendship, talking to local residents about historical instances of conflict resolution rather than famous battles"—a pilgrimage enacted with the goal of creating a historic map to "serve as an alternative to those indicating battle locations. It will mark where courageous and creative acts of dissent against economic, racial, social and political violence took place."[49]

Similarly, a new monument built in Orillia to celebrate the Quadricentennial offered a materially different representation of Indigenous people in Canadian history. Unveiled on August 1, 2015, in Penetanguishene, *The Meeting* portrays Chief Aenon of the Huron-Wendat's Bear tribe receiving Champlain in "a summit of two equals, breaking the tradition, according to sculptor Timothy Schmalz, of depicting Indigenous peoples as 'gargoyles or in animal filigree.'"[50]

And, of course, there was the lake. From their declaration that the "Quadricentennial is an opportunity to learn some history, recreate, and explore. It's also a time to think about the lake's future and how we can ensure it's a healthy one," the Lake Champlain Committee (LCC) naturally moved to a request to take "the LCC's Lake Protection Pledge and committing to steps that will reduce your personal impact on water quality."[51] A multitude of local activities looked to the lake, its health, its history as a political and economic corridor, its role in the battles of Valcour (1776) and Plattsburgh (1814), its presence in the daily lives of those who live along its shores, its basin offering water to the many farms of the region, and to its very existence. At the heart of all those activities was the Lake Champlain Basin Program (LCBP).

Congressionally designated "to restore and protect Lake Champlain and its surrounding watershed," the LCBP works across borders, partnering with agencies in New York, Vermont, and Quebec "to coordinate and fund efforts to address challenges in the areas of phosphorus pollution, toxic substances, biodiversity, aquatic invasive species, and climate change" and to administer "the Champlain Valley National Heritage Partnership, which builds appreciation and improves stewardship of the region's rich cultural resources by interpreting and promoting its history."[52] This program, with its mission of stewardship, helped to guide Quadricentennial activities through administering grant funds, developing interpretive panels, and bringing partners together wherever possible.

When the next anniversary comes, perhaps that spirit of partnership and amity will prevail. Perhaps, instead of celebrating Samuel de Champlain, we will remember the friendships made possible because of his travels and the subsequent generations of life along Lake Champlain, once known as Bitabagw, "the lake in between."

CONCLUSION

What are we celebrating when we commemorate Samuel de Champlain's explorations? The tenor of the commemorative events has changed over the more than 400 years since Champlain traveled along the Atlantic coast and inland via the rivers of North America, moving from those that honor a European hero to those that contextualize the man, his journeys, and his mission to determine whether this land was ripe for French colonization. Quadricentennial commemorations throughout Canada and the northeastern United States were careful to note the complicated relationships between Indigenous Peoples and Champlain, hopefully leading the way for future anniversaries.

NOTES

1. S. Rept. 110-179—Hudson-Fulton-Champlain Quadricentennial Commemoration Commission Act of 2007. 110th Congress. Section 4, c.

2. Lake Champlain Quadricentennial Commission, "Lake Champlain 2009 Strategic Plan," February 2006 Version 1, 4.

3. John Allemang, "Sam the Sham: The Myth of Champlain," *The Globe and Mail*, March 14, 2008 (https://www.theglobeandmail.com/news/national/sam-the-sham-the-myth-of-champlain/article22501155/, accessed September 14, 2021).

4. Allemang, "Sam the Sham."

5. Captain Darache's first name is unknown.

6. Samuel de Champlain, *Voyages of Samuel de Champlain, 1604–1618* (reprint). New York: Charles Scribner's Sons, 1907, 127.

7. Champlain, *Voyages,* 131 and 137.
8. Champlain, *Voyages,* 141.
9. Molly Walsh, "The College Named After Samuel de Champlain Debates Whether to Keep His Statue," *Seven Days,* November 6, 2019 (https://www.sevendaysvt.com/vermont/the-college-named-after-samuel-de-champlain-debates-whether-to-keep-his-statue/Content?oid=28860398, accessed September 14, 2021).
10. David Hackett Fisher, *Champlain's Dream.* New York: Simon & Schuster, 2008.
11. Allemang, "Sam the Sham."
12. Joseph Boyden, "Don-de-Dieu," *CottageLife.com* (Summer 2015), 83.
13. Michael D. Stevenson, "'Free From All Possibility of Historical Error': Orillia's Champlain Monument, French-English Relations, and Indigenous (Mis) Representations in Commemorative Sculpture," *Ontario History*, 109, no. 2 (2017): 213–237.
14. Stevenson, "Free From All Possibility of Historical Error," 216.
15. Stevenson, "Free From All Possibility of Historical Error," 228.
16. Stevenson, "Free From All Possibility of Historical Error," 230.
17. Stevenson, "Free From All Possibility of Historical Error," 234.
18. Stevenson, "Free From All Possibility of Historical Error," 235.
19. "Monument to Champlain in Orillia" (https://routechamplain.ca/en/listings/monument-to-samuel-de-champlain-in-orillia/, accessed October 3, 2021).
20. "Monument to Champlain in Orillia" (https://routechamplain.ca/en/listings/monument-to-samuel-de-champlain-in-orillia/, accessed October 3, 2021).
21. "Parks Canada Announces Decision Regarding the Future of the Samuel de Champlain Monument," News Release, July 24, 2019.
22. "Parks Canada" (https://www.pc.gc.ca/en/agence-agency/mandat-mandate, accessed March 15, 2022).
23. Lexy Benedict, "Renewed Opposition to Orillia's Samuel de Champlain Monument," CTV News, June 28, 2020 (https://barrie.ctvnews.ca/renewed-opposition-to-orillia-s-samuel-de-champlain-monument-1.5003777, accessed October 3, 2021).
24. "Do Not Reinstall Racist Samuel de Champlain Statute in Orillia" (https://www.change.org/p/parks-canada-city-of-orillia-do-not-reinstall-racist-samuel-de-champlain-statue-in-orillia, accessed October 3, 2021).
25. "Champlain Monument Working Group" (https://www.orillia.ca/en/living-here/champlain-monument-working-group.aspx#, accessed October 3, 2021); Rachel Treisman, "This New Canadian Holiday Reflects On The Legacy of Indigenous Residential Schools," NPR, September 30, 2021 (https://www.npr.org/2021/09/30/1041836090/canada-indigenous-residential-schools-national-day-for-truth-and-reconciliation, accessed October 3, 2021).
26. "Schedule N: Mandate for the Truth and Reconciliation Commission" (http://www.residentialschoolsettlement.ca/SCHEDULE_N.pdf, accessed October 3, 2021).
27. "History of the Samuel de Champlain Statue" (https://docs.google.com/document/d/1w3Tz0zrQQT8vE6jGD-5xm1shpohaFE6pCNdJ5OS0HGE/edit, accessed October 3, 2021).

28. Walsh, "The College."
29. Walsh, "The College."
30. Walsh, "The College."
31. Cat Gullotta, "Community Discusses Removal of de Champlain Statue," *The Crossover*, November 8, 2019 (https://champlaincrossover.org/1312/news/community-discusses-removal-of-de-champlain-statue/, accessed October 3, 2021).
32. McKenzie Delisle, "Correcting History: Educational Panel Installed at Historic City Monument," *Press-Republican*, July 22, 2020 (https://www.pressrepublican.com/news/local_news/correcting-history-educational-panel-installed-at-historic-city-monument/article_dd5d9a54-04e2-56af-861f-4d141d503426.html, accessed October 3, 2021).
33. "The Vermont Indigenous Celebration" (http://www.vtindigenous.com/Celebrating11000Years.html, accessed October 3, 2021).
34. "Vermont Indigenous Celebration" (http://vtindigenous.com/, accessed October 3, 2021).
35. "Navigating the Champlain Valley 1609: Quadricentennial Curriculum" (https://www.google.com/url?sa=t&rct=j&q=&esrc=s&source=web&cd=&ved=2ahUKEwid9KCFxa_zAhVtEFkFHbmuBugQFnoECAYQAQ&url=http%3A%2F%2Fwww.lcmm.org%2Fnavigating%2FQuadCurriculum_Introduction.pdf&usg=AOvVaw2o65PcQpQmTBFg-AZKc4AN, accessed October 3, 2022).
36. "Mandate of the Ontario Heritage Trust" (https://www.heritagetrust.on.ca/en/index.php/pages/about-us/our-mandate, accessed March 15, 2022).
37. "Champlain through the eyes of North Americans" (https://www.heritagetrust.on.ca/en/pages/our-stories/exhibits/samuel-de-champlain/champlain-through-the-eyes-of-north-americans, accessed October 3, 2021).
38. "Champlain through the eyes of North Americans" (https://www.heritagetrust.on.ca/en/pages/our-stories/exhibits/samuel-de-champlain/champlain-through-the-eyes-of-north-americans, accessed October 3, 2021).
39. "Hudson-Fulton-Champlain Quadricentennial Newspaper in Education (NIE)" (https://www.google.com/url?sa=t&rct=j&q=&esrc=s&source=web&cd=&ved=2ahUKEwiqr6L2p6_zAhU2M1kFHZ7SD8AQFnoECAIQAQ&url=http%3A%2F%2Fwww.nynpa.com%2Fdocs%2Fnie%2Fniequad%2FTeachersGuide.pdf&usg=AOvVaw0qwhVaFehmgjN13KjGUwy1, accessed October 3, 2021).
40. "*Alnobak: Wearing Our Heritage*" (https://www.flynnvt.org/Your-Visit/Venues/Amy-E-Tarrant-Gallery/Exhibit-Archives/Alnobak, accessed September 14, 2021).
41. "*Alnobak: Wearing Our Heritage*" (https://www.flynnvt.org/Your-Visit/Venues/Amy-E-Tarrant-Gallery/Exhibit-Archives/Alnobak, accessed September 14, 2021).
42. Vera Longtoe Sheehan and Eloise Bell, "History Space: Celebrating Abenaki Culture," *Burlington Free Press*, June 23, 2018 (https://www.burlingtonfreepress.com/story/news/2018/06/23/history-space-celebrating-abenaki-culture/36315955/, accessed September 14, 2021).
43. Sheehan and Bell, "History Space."

44. "VIHC History–Alnobaiwi.org" (https://www.alnobaiwi.org/vihc-history, accessed September 14, 2021).

45. "Vermont Quadricentennial Named a Top 100 Event in US," Press Release (https://vermontbiz.com/news/2008/october/01/vermont-celebrates-champlain-named-top-100-event-us, accessed September 14, 2021).

46. Sylvie Beaudreau, "Commemorating a Transnational Hero: the 1909 Celebration of the Tercentenary of the Discovery of Lake Champlain," *Vermont History* 77, no. 2 (2009): 101.

47. Bruce Hyde, "Countdown to Lake Champlain Quadricentennial," *Times Argus*, December 20, 2008 (https://www.timesargus.com/articles/countdown-to-lake-champlain-quadricentennial/, accessed September 14, 2021).

48. "Lake Champlain Quadricentennial Celebration Wraps Up," The Associated Press, July 15, 2009 (https://www.reformer.com/local-news/lake-champlain-quadricentennial-celebration-wraps-up/article_6444a71d-d353-521d-8344-536d6a7a83a5.html, accessed September 14, 2021).

49. "Lecture Features Pilgrimage of Peace," *Times Herald-Record*, June 25, 2009 (https://www.recordonline.com/article/20090625/COMM/306259978?template=ampart, accessed October 3, 2021).

50. Stevenson, "Free From All Possibility of Historical Error," 235.

51. "Celebrate the Quadricentennial!" (https://www.lakechamplaincommittee.org/learn/news/item/celebrate-the-quadricentennial, accessed September 14, 2021).

52. "What We Do" (https://www.lcbp.org/about-us/what-we-do/, accessed October 3, 2021).

BIBLIOGRAPHY

Primary Sources

Allemang, John. "Sam the Sham: The Myth of Champlain." *The Globe and Mail*, March 14, 2008, available online: https://www.theglobeandmail.com/news/national/sam-the-sham-the-myth-of-champlain/article22501155/ (accessed September 14, 2021).

"*Alnobak: Wearing Our Heritage*," available online: https://www.flynnvt.org/Your-Visit/Venues/Amy-E-Tarrant-Gallery/Exhibit-Archives/Alnobak (accessed September 14, 2021).

Benedict, Lexy. "Renewed opposition to Orillia's Samuel de Champlain Monument." *CTV News*, June 28, 2020, available online: https://barrie.ctvnews.ca/renewed-opposition-to-orillia-s-samuel-de-champlain-monument-1.5003777 (accessed October 3, 2021).

Boyden, Joseph. "Don-de-Dieu." *CottageLife.com* (Summer 2015), 83.

"Celebrate the Quadricentennial!" available online: https://www.lakechamplaincommittee.org/learn/news/item/celebrate-the-quadricentennial (accessed September 14, 2021).

"Champlain Monument Working Group," available online: https://www.orillia.ca/en/living-here/champlain-monument-working-group.aspx# (accessed October 3, 2021).

"Champlain Through the Eyes of North Americans," available online: https://www.heritagetrust.on.ca/en/pages/our-stories/exhibits/samuel-de-champlain/champlain-through-the-eyes-of-north-americans (accessed October 3, 2021).

Delisle, McKenzie. "Correcting History: Educational Panel Installed at Historic City Monument." *Press-Republican*, July 22, 2020, available online: https://www.pressrepublican.com/news/local_news/correcting-history-educational-panel-installed-at-historic-city-monument/article_dd5d9a54-04e2-56af-861f-4d141d503426.html (accessed October 3, 2021).

"Do Not Reinstall Racist Samuel de Champlain Statute in Orillia," available online: https://www.change.org/p/parks-canada-city-of-orillia-do-not-reinstall-racist-samuel-de-champlain-statue-in-orillia (accessed October 3, 2021).

Gullotta, Cat. "Community Discusses Removal of de Champlain Statue." *The Crossover*, November 8, 2019, available online: https://champlaincrossover.org/1312/news/community-discusses-removal-of-de-champlain-statue/ (accessed October 3, 2021).

"Hudson-Fulton-Champlain Quadricentennial Newspaper in Education (NIE)," available online: https://www.google.com/url?sa=t&rct=j&q=&esrc=s&source=web&cd=&ved=2ahUKEwiqr6L2p6_zAhU2M1kFHZ7SD8AQFnoECAIQAQ&url=http%3A%2F%2Fwww.nynpa.com%2Fdocs%2Fnie%2Fniequad%2FTeachersGuide.pdf&usg=AOvVaw0qwhVaFehmgjN13KjGUwy1 (accessed October 3, 2021).

Hyde, Bruce. "Countdown to Lake Champlain Quadricentennial," *Times Argus*, December 20, 2008, available online: https://www.timesargus.com/articles/countdown-to-lake-champlain-quadricentennial/ (accessed September 14, 2021).

"Lake Champlain Quadricentennial Celebration Wraps Up," *The Associated Press*, July 15, 2009, available online: https://www.reformer.com/local-news/lake-champlain-quadricentennial-celebration-wraps-up/article_6444a71d-d353-521d-8344-536d6a7a83a5.html (accessed September 14, 2021).

Lake Champlain Quadricentennial Commission, "Lake Champlain 2009 Strategic Plan," February 2006 Version 1, available online: https://www.google.com/url?sa=t&rct=j&q=&esrc=s&source=web&cd=&ved=2ahUKEwibwJi2x6_zAhUEGFkFHZIpDqoQFnoECAMQAQ&url=http%3A%2F%2Fwww.lcbp.org%2FPDFs%2FLCQCStrategicPlan_Draft2006.pdf&usg=AOvVaw2fEZ0SFqlrq0EVO-Dwbain (accessed September 14, 2021).

Lake Champlain Tercentenary July 4–10, 1909, State of New York Education Department, 1909.

"Lecture Features Pilgrimage of Peace," *Times Herald-Record*, June 25, 2009, available online: https://www.recordonline.com/article/20090625/COMM/306259978?template=ampart (accessed October 3, 2021).

"Monument to Champlain in Orillia," available online: https://routechamplain.ca/en/listings/monument-to-samuel-de-champlain-in-orillia/ (accessed October 3, 2021).

"Navigating the Champlain Valley 1609: Quadricentennial Curriculum," available online: https://www.google.com/url?sa=t&rct=j&q=&esrc=s&source=web&cd=&ved=2ahUKEwid9KCFxa_zAhVtEFkFHbmuBugQFnoECAYQAQ&url=http%3A%2F%2Fwww.lcmm.org%2Fnavigating%2FQuadCurriculum_Introduction.pdf&usg=AOvVaw2o65PcQpQmTBFg-AZKc4AN (accessed October 3, 2021).

"Parks Canada Announces Decision Regarding the Future of the Samuel de Champlain Monument." *News Release*, July 24, 2019, available online: https://www.canada.ca/en/parks-canada/news/2019/07/parks-canada-announces-decision-regarding-the-future-of-the-samuel-de-champlain-monument.html (accessed September 14, 2021).

S. Rept. 110-179 – Hudson-Fulton-Champlain Quadricentennial Commemoration Commission Act of 2007. 110th Congress. Section 4, c, available online: https://www.congress.gov/congressional-report/110th-congress/senate-report/179 (accessed September 14, 2021).

"Schedule N: Mandate for the Truth and Reconciliation Commission," available online: http://www.residentialschoolsettlement.ca/SCHEDULE_N.pdf (accessed October 3, 2021).

Sheehan, Vera Longtoe, and Eloise Bell. "History Space: Celebrating Abenaki Culture." *Burlington Free Press*, June 23, 2018, available online: https://www.burlingtonfreepress.com/story/news/2018/06/23/history-space-celebrating-abenaki-culture/36315955/ (accessed September 14, 2021).

Treisman, Rachel. "This New Canadian Holiday Reflects on the Legacy of Indigenous Residential Schools." *NPR*, September 30, 2021, available online: https://www.npr.org/2021/09/30/1041836090/canada-indigenous-residential-schools-national-day-for-truth-and-reconciliation (accessed October 3, 2021).

"Vermont Indigenous Celebration," available online: http://vtindigenous.com/Encampment.html (accessed October 3, 2021).

"Vermont Quadricentennial Named a Top 100 Event in US" Press Release, available online: https://vermontbiz.com/news/2008/october/01/vermont-celebrates-champlain-named-top-100-event-us (accessed September 14, 2021).

"VIHC History – Alnobaiwi.org," available online: https://www.alnobaiwi.org/vihc-history (accessed September 14, 2021).

Walsh, Molly. "The College Named After Samuel de Champlain Debates Whether to Keep His Statue." *Seven Days,* November 6, 2019, available online: https://www.sevendaysvt.com/vermont/the-college-named-after-samuel-de-champlain-debates-whether-to-keep-his-statue/Content?oid=28860398, (accessed September 14, 2021).

"What We Do," available online: https://www.lcbp.org/about-us/what-we-do/ (accessed October 3, 2021).

Wiseman, Frederick M. "Evolutionary Decolonization of the Vermont Indigenous Heritage Center," available online: https://wwww.alnobaiwi.org/decolonization-statement (accessed October 3, 2021).

Secondary Sources

Beaudreau, Sylvie. "Commemorating a Transnational Hero: The 1909 Celebration of the Tercentenary of the Discovery of Lake Champlain." *Vermont History* 77, no. 2 (2009): 99–118.

Bishop, Morris. *Champlain: The Life of Fortitude*. New York: Alfred A. Knopf, 1948.

Dann, Kevin. "Pageants, Parades, and Patriotism: Celebrating Champlain in 1909." *Vermont History* 77, no. 2 (2009): 87–98.

de Champlain, Samuel. *Voyages of Samuel de Champlain, 1604–1618*. Reprint. New York: Charles Scribner's Sons, 1907.

Fisher, David Hackett. *Champlain's Dream*. New York: Simon & Schuster, 2008.

"History of the Samuel de Champlain Statue," available online: https://docs.google.com/document/d/1w3Tz0zrQQT8vE6jGD-5xm1shpohaFE6pCNdJ5OS0HGE/edit (accessed October 3, 2021).

Kammen, Michael. *Mystic Chords of Memory: The Transformation of Tradition in America Culture*. New York: Vintage Books, 1991.

Lowenthal, David. "Archives, Heritage, and History." *University of Michigan Advanced Study Center Seminar Paper*, October 18, 2000, 1–18.

Lowenthal, David. *The Past is a Foreign Country*. Cambridge: Cambridge University Press, 1985.

Nora, Pierre. "Between Memory and History: Les Lieux de Memoire." *Representations* 26 (1989): 7–24.

Stevenson, Michael D. "'Free From All Possibility of Historical Error': Orillia's Champlain Monument, French-English Relations, and Indigenous (Mis) Representations in Commemorative Sculpture." *Ontario History* 109, no. 2 (2017): 213–237.

Chapter 7

Fugitives No More

A Multinational Comparative Study of Maroon Heritage Preservation

Barry L. Stiefel

Maroons, as well their descendants, were enslaved people who escaped from slavery in the Americas and Oceania who unilaterally liberated themselves between the sixteenth and nineteenth centuries by finding refuge in isolated locations and were, thus, able to express their own agency. In these instances, they are African or of African descent. Because of maroons' escaped enslavement for self-liberation they had to quickly learn how to survive in their local environments. Sometimes maroons encountered native peoples who shared subsistence knowledge with them and formed new Indigenous communities. In some circumstances, maroons developed built environments and cultural landscapes that are now subjects of preservation, interventions, and cultural heritage conservation.

Maroons in the Americas and some of the Indian Ocean islands were forcibly displaced from their place of origin in Africa; yet they are often considered a different form of Indigenous people because they belong nowhere else due to their creolization. Indeed, according to the Inter-American Court on Human Rights ruling in *Saramaka People v. Suriname* (2007), the United Nations Declaration on the Rights of Indigenous Peoples also applies to maroons.[1] The Court found that Suriname's government failed to implement effectual procedures to acknowledge the Saramaka people's right to the use and enjoyment of their traditional lands. Yet, at the same time, maroon people are diasporic (dispersed through the slave trade), migratory (due to their ancestors' escape from bondage), and are found in several countries (making them transnational). Multiple maroon groups can also coexist within close proximity to one another and maintain distinct cultural identities from each other. This chapter covers four sites that are significant to transnational maroon heritage: Central Suriname Nature Reserve, a UNESCO World Heritage nature preserve that is maintained in coordination with contemporary maroon people in northeastern South America; Fort Gadsden/Prospect Bluff Historic Sites National Historic Landmark, the only identifiable site pertaining to maroon history in the United States of high national level distinction; Le Morne Cultural Landscape of Mauritius, the first site on UNESCO's World Heritage List where the cultural significance is maroon heritage; and Blue and John Crow Mountains World Heritage Site and the Maroon Heritage of Moore Town, Jamaica, on UNESCO's List of Intangible Cultural Heritage of Humanity.

The Moore Town site is one of the few identifiable instances of an intersectional tangible heritage site and an intangible heritage tradition listed on two separate UNESCO heritage registers. The preservation and interpretation of Fort Gadsden/Prospect Bluff Historic Sites (Florida) has occurred under the larger umbrella of African American historic sites, instead of a distinct and separate maroon heritage. Though maroon communities of escaped slaves were also established in Louisiana, North Carolina, Virginia, Texas, and even Canada, the Black Seminole of Florida were the only group in North America to establish a lasting maroon society.[2] The tendency of maroon assimilation into the larger African American presence does threaten the existence of this minority-within-a-minority identity in the United States.[3]

In addition to providing an overview of each heritage site, this chapter examines how maroon heritage is perceived and treated in each country. For example, maroon heritage is often considered a phenomenon of the Americas because of the prolific scholarship of anthropologist and historian Richard Price who has published extensively on the subject.[4] Yet, we see some of the most robust preservation endeavors occurs in Mauritius, an island nation in the Indian Ocean, which has not traditionally been considered part of the transatlantic slave trade sphere. Maroon heritage is a fundamental aspect of Mauritian identity. Suriname and Jamaica are also countries where maroon heritage has made valuable contributions to the formation of national identity. In Suriname, the maroons have a similar position to Indigenous peoples and have been invited by Suriname's Ministry of Natural Resources to be part of the management of nature preserves, such as negotiating locations for mining and logging concessions.[5] In Jamaica, the focus was first on documenting and educating its people on the intangible aspects of maroon culture as a means of preservation (instead of a physical place or material object), and then later on initiatives focused on preservation efforts pertaining to material culture and historic landscapes. Assessing the differences in approach and treatment of maroon heritage preservation between countries is important to understand where and what accomplishments are occurring.

Bringing together this constellation of maroon heritage sites, this chapter provides new insights into the management of maroon culture and the reasons its preservation is more visible in some places than in others—a comprehensive approach to maroon heritage preservation that has not been taken before. Assessing the differences in approach and treatment of maroon heritage preservation between countries is important to understand where and why successes and failures are occurring. From these findings an exchange of knowledge can lead to improvements in practice regarding maroon heritage preservation among cultures that could learn from these approaches.

MAROON HERITAGE PRESERVATION IS NOT ALONE: A LITERATURE REVIEW ON MANAGEMENT

The study of preserving maroon culture emerged in the 1990s, beginning with Emmanuel K. Agorsah's edited book, *Maroon Heritage: Archaeological, Ethnographic, and Historic Perspectives*. According to B. W. Higman, author of the book's Foreword,

> Maroons have never been marooned in the sense of being lost, cast up in some isolated, desolate place, without networks to the wider world. They have always been in the world and of the world. An acceptance of this past and present interactive relationship is essential for the future preservation of Maroon heritage as well as the study of Maroon peoples and their history.[6]

Higman's observations are important to keep in mind because of the unique circumstances that maroons are a diasporic people that transcend national borders, but at the same time, they have a sense of indigeneity to the lands to which they have escaped and in which they made their homes. From the perspective of preservation, *Maroon Heritage* was an important first step for discussing preservation issues of various maroon heritage case studies, most significantly from Jamaica, Mexico, and Suriname. In a subsequent publication, Agorsah also provides a geographically far-reaching survey of where archaeology has been done on maroon-associated sites around the coastal areas of the Caribbean and the Gulf of Mexico.[7] According to Higman, Agorsah, and other scholars, preservationists should be able to learn from one another regarding common issues related to best practices. Since the publication of *Maroon Heritage* other publications on this preservation topic have been produced, but these are individualized case studies rather than comparative studies. Examples include Sulatānā Āpharoja's *Invisible Yet Invincible*; Vijaya Teelock and Julie Cornec's *Maroonage and the Maroon Heritage in Mauritius;* and Terrance Weik's "Allies, Adversaries, and Kin in the African Seminole Communities of Florida."[8] Herbert Aptheker, Sylviane A. Diouf, and Daniel O. Sayers have also done extensive research on various maroon communities in the United States, occasionally assessing archaeological resources for information, but they do not address the preservation of maroon heritage(s) in the present or the conservation of cultural landscapes or specific sites, such as found at the Negro Fort.[9] In these respects, achievements have been made by policy makers and practitioners in the preservation of maroon heritage, particularly related to their civil, cultural, and property rights, but always in isolation of the actors from each other. While there is a foundational historical literature on maroon heritage within a diasporic context, little has been done by scholars to tie together the experiences of maroon heritage sites within a preservation practice assessment to ascertain what actions are taking place collectively.

CASE STUDY I: MAROONS FORGOTTEN IN THE WILDERNESS: THE CENTRAL SURINAME NATURE RESERVE

Maroon culture and communities emerged in Suriname during the early eighteenth century as escaped African slaves formed communities in areas of the Dutch colony uninhabited by European settlers. They often interacted with the Indigenous Amerindian tribes. They also had to contend with maintaining their self-emancipation from European colonial authorities. In 1863, slavery was abolished in Suriname, but by this time many of Suriname's maroon communities had been living on their own for multiple generations, outside of colonial society. Suriname's maroons have many similarities with the Indigenous Amerindian tribes, with a long tradition of autonomy and the preservation of cultural heritage, and so relations between the government—independent from the Netherlands since 1975—and maroons also evolved in a parallel way.[10]

In 1998, President Jules Albert Wijdenbosch proclaimed a resolution that the proposed Central Suriname Nature Reserve should be listed on the World Heritage List in order to protect the region's very important ecology. This decision was also made to foster Suriname's ecotourism-based industry. Both maroons and Amerindians (collectively called bushland inhabitants) were removed to form the Central Suriname Nature Reserve. Removal of human inhabitants—even of Indigenous peoples who resided on the land for many generations—was a common practice during the twentieth century in the formation of natural parks and wildlife preserves.[11] Only recently has the continued habitation of Indigenous people in preserved wild areas become accepted.

The Presidential Resolution only provided protections for bushland inhabitant villages and settlements, which adversely affected the maroon Kwinti communities of Kaimanston and Witagron because agricultural areas for food sustenance where not included.[12] Some Kwinti have benefited from the creation of the Central Suriname Nature Reserve by working as tour guides, which were the only ways that allowed maroons to participate in the management of the nature preserve. However, the economic opportunities for maroons and collaborations between them and the Ministry of Natural Resources fell short of what was hoped for in the original nomination and management for the Central Suriname Nature Reserve.[13]

While the maroons were documented as living on the land since the eighteenth century and the Amerindians even earlier, the World Heritage Committee was unable to do anything, not even sanction the Central Suriname Nature Reserve as a site in danger for purposes of delisting, because the nature reserve was strictly on the World Heritage List as a natural site, which by itself was not being threatened.[14] In this example, the Central Suriname Nature Reserve is a property that should perhaps be reevaluated and reconsidered as a mixed natural-cultural heritage site in order to address the problem of maroons not being considered part of the heritage of the place. Delisting is the only form of punishment that UNESCO can impose on countries that mistreat their World Heritage Sites, which comes with significant negative international publicity.[15] A lesson can be learned from this experience regarding the delicate relationship between maroons and their environment, which exhibits some very similar parallels between Indigenous peoples and their native environments. According to legal scholars Ellen Rose Kambel and Fergus MacKay, Suriname has not been fulfilling its fiduciary obligations to its bushland inhabitants from the perspective of the UN International Convention on Biological Diversity: evaluation of Indigenous and maroon cultural property rights needs to be part of environmental impact studies prior to development projects in order to provide some protections and mitigation.[16] Thus, in Suriname, government policies seem to reflect the prioritization of nature conservation and foreign bio-tourism over cultural heritage preservation. Maroon and Indigenous inhabitants are only part of the policy implementation if their employment serves this purpose, leaving little consideration for their cultural well-being as well as preservation of this aspect of the past.

CASE STUDY II: MAROON AMNESIA AND REMEMBERING AT FORT GADSDEN/ PROSPECT BLUFF HISTORIC SITES NATIONAL HISTORIC LANDMARK, FLORIDA

Fort Gadsden and the Negro Fort were built under the auspices of the British in Spanish Florida during the War of 1812 (1812–1815). During the war the

British were offering freedom and asylum to enslaved Africans who fled their American masters, many from North Carolina, South Carolina, and Georgia. They subsequently formed a community of maroons with the Indigenous Seminole tribe around the fort. This refuge became a base for maroons to attack and raid American settlers along the border with Spanish Florida. The maroon vengeance/violence along the border was one of several factors that prompted the forces of General Andrew Jackson to invade Florida during the War of 1812 and again during the First Seminole War (1817–1818). Jackson's invasions of Florida led to the eventual American purchase of the territory from Spain in 1821.[17] After the Florida Purchase, Fort Gadsden and the Negro Fort were abandoned by military forces until they were briefly occupied again by the Confederate Army during the American Civil War. From 1819 to 1861, the Negro Fort was the largest settlement of free African Americans in the United States. After slavery ended in the United States, the African American community near Negro Fort dissolved and the fort was abandoned.

After nearly a century of neglect, the recognition of Fort Gadsden as a historic site began in 1961 as a state park, covering a 78-acre area, eventually becoming part of Apalachicola National Forest managed by the US National Forest Service.[18] Fort Gadsden National Historic Landmark was officially listed as a historic site in 1974 and was renamed Prospect Bluff Historic Sites National Historic Landmark in 2016 to better reflect the multiple historic aspects of the landmark, which are known as Fort Gadsden and the Negro Fort. However, on the National Historic Landmark nomination form from 1972 the word "maroon" is not even mentioned once. Today, the earth work foundations are all that remain for both forts in an outdoor archaeological park with self-guided tours.

According to historian Marcia M. Greenlee, who authored the National Historic Landmark nomination, the "Negro Fort is also important because it is symbolic of a forgotten aspect of African American history—the cooperation and friendship that often existed between blacks and Indians."[19] Greenlee was a prolific historian and proponent of the preservation of African American heritage in the United States during the 1970s and 1980s, when she was involved with the Black Women Oral History Project and the Afro-American Bicentennial Corporation (AABC). She served as director of Historical Projects for AABC from 1972 to 1975.[20] Between 1972 and 1976 the objective of the AABC was to begin a nationwide study of potential historical landmarks associated with African American heritage in coordination with the National Park Service.[21] AABC came about from an initiative started by the Afro-American Institute for Historic Preservation and Community Development. Between 1970 and 1988 more than sixty historic sites located across twenty-two states and Washington D.C. with African American heritage were studied and successfully nominated to the National Historic Landmarks program, the most preeminent historical registry program in the United States.[22]

African American history and heritage has also been applied broadly to sites and places of interest without distinction between subcultures, in contrast to that of maroons found in the other countries of this study. This explains the omission of the term "maroon" from the original National Historic Landmark nomination of Fort Gadsden.[23] For example, as of 2007, Fort Gadsden National Historic Landmark was simply listed as another stopping point on the Florida Black Heritage Trail by the government's Division of Historical Resources. Within the brief description of the historic site, it is only mentioned in passing that this was a destination of escaped enslaved Africans from Georgia and the Carolinas, with no attention on the significance of the maroon past.[24]

After the initial interests by the Florida state government and the AABC during the 1960s and 1970s Fort Gadsden National Historic Landmark was largely ignored for decades. Between 2015 and 2016 the US Forest Service spent nearly $60,000 "to make the remote historic site safer and more user friendly" in preparations for its two hundredth anniversary.[25] Improvements to the user experience at the historic landmark included the

> removal of encroaching plants from the parking area, installing interpretive signage, upgrading paths to make the most accessed areas compliant with the Americans with Disabilities Act (ADA), and refurbishing the structure and exhibits in the interpretive kiosk, constructed in 1980 as the centerpiece of the historic site.[26]

During this project archaeological studies and workshops were also conducted to better understand the maroon past at the historic landmark with public presentations, supported by grants given to the Florida Public Archaeology Network by the Florida Humanities Council and the National Endowment for the Humanities.[27]

When the historic landmark's official name changed in 2016 to Prospect Bluff Historic Sites the maroon past became more readily recognizable in the interpretation of its historic significance. The renaming of the historic landmark coincided with the fort's 200th anniversary. The reason for the name change was to have Negro Fort on an equal footing of significance with Fort Gadsden following reflection on the significance of the Prospect Bluff Historic Sites by historians and the public.

At another historic site excavated at approximately the same time in Virginia, Dan Sayers, an archaeologist reported that "until recently, the idea that maroons also existed in North America has been rejected by most historians"; by "downplaying American marronage, and valorizing white involvement in the Underground Railroad, historians have shown a racial bias" and "a reluctance to acknowledge the strength of black resistance and initiative."[28] Sayers's critical reconsideration for maroon heritage in the United States is likely the impetus for why we see more action taking place in recent years and the reevaluation of the Negro Fort as equally important in history as Fort Gadsden. The redeveloped interpretation of the Negro Fort and Fort Gadsden also occurred in response to the programmatic activities of the Florida Public Archaeology Network, which showed a special interest in African American history.

The activities of the AABC and the Afro-American Institute for Historic Preservation and Community Development are also reflective of a more monolithic perspective of African-(North) American culture, in contrast to Jamaica, Mauritius, or Suriname where in the twenty-first-century maroons and their descendants are viewed as culturally distinct. As a matter of comparison there is a maroon site in Canada of the Cole Harbour Meeting House, a historic church built in 1830/31 for Jamaican maroons (primarily from Trelawny Town) who had come to Dartmouth, Nova Scotia Colony, following their expulsion from the island in 1796 due to the Second Maroon War (1795–1796).[29] This church was listed on the Canadian Register of Historic Places in 2007, but its significance is not identified as being related to a distinct Canadian maroon culture. Instead, the heritage interpretation of Cole Harbour Meeting House is that of transplanted Jamaican maroons who became part of Canada, following the perspective of a homogenous African-(North) American culture, similar to the United States.[30] Even after the American Revolution, the history of Africans and their descendants in the United States and Canada are intrinsically tied to each other. During the War of 1812, and again from 1834 (when the British Slavery Abolition Act came into effect) to 1865, the British colonies that would become Canada served as asylum for escaped enslaved Africans from the United States. This demographic of people is considered part of the African Canadian milieu and not uniquely maroon. We see this heritage interpretation at the Victoria Road United Baptist Church, built in Dartmouth, Nova Scotia in 1853 and listed on the Canadian Register of Historic Places in 2005 among other historic sites.[31]

The redeveloped interpretation of the Negro Fort occurred in response to the programmatic activities of the Florida Public Archaeology Network, which also had a special interest in African American history. While the undertakings supported by the Florida government at the Negro Fort are exceptional for the United States, there has been more striking public interest by government initiatives in the preservation of maroon heritage elsewhere, particularly in Mauritius and Jamaica.

CASE STUDY III: THE STRUGGLE FOR THE LE MORNE CULTURAL LANDSCAPE

Prior to the seventeenth century, Mauritius was an uninhabited island in the Indian Ocean, which was visited occasionally by Arab and Portuguese adventurers. In 1638, the Dutch made the first of multiple unsuccessful colonization efforts. In 1715, the French successfully established a permanent colony on Mauritius and soon after founded sugarcane plantations based on a similar model established in the West Indies, which depended on labor performed by enslaved people imported from Africa. On occasion enslaved people fled captivity and hid in Mauritius' mountainous areas, such as Le Morne Brabant—a volcanic monolith on the southeast corner of the island that protrudes into the Indian Ocean. In 1810, the British seized the colony during the Napoleonic Wars. Slavery was abolished in 1835 and in 1968 Mauritius gained independence.[32]

The preservation story of maroon heritage begins in the 1970s when Mauritius' pro-black movement began lobbying for a memorial to slavery. Until then the history of Mauritian slavery had been a taboo topic of discussion outside of small intellectual circles, and so it took many years for sufficient public support to build to sanction a memorial which was completed in 1985. During the 1990s, when the government developed a tourist-based economy, heritage preservation projects became more frequent in Mauritius. In 1995, the Mauritian government also ratified the World Heritage Convention of 1972, though its first site, Aapravasi Ghat (on the heritage of nineteenth-century indentured laborers from India), was added only in 2006.

By the end of the 1990s, plans were made to develop a hotel and tourist cable car facilities on Le Morne Brabant because of the spectacular view. The developer, Innovative Leisure Limited, became interested in real estate investment on Le Morne Brabant. A grassroots movement to protect Le Morne Brabant from tourist development began among Mauritians and then spread internationally. Advocates to protect the site included a diverse group of people, from heritage preservationists to Rastafarians. The public had been using Le Morne Brabant for outdoor recreation purposes, such as sightseeing, hiking, and coastal fishing for many years. The government's intervention was due to the findings from a consultation with UNESCO regarding how the proposed tourist development would adversely affect Le Morne Brabant, and protests were conducted by local villagers and members of the opposition party. Environmentalists also became involved in 2000 when the Mauritius Wildlife Fund sued in order to protect endangered Indigenous trees that were illegally logged to build a helipad for the tourist development. These projects attracted international attention when UNESCO declared that

2000 to 2010 would be the decade of socially responsible tourism, which showcased respect for cultural and natural heritage preservation.[33]

The Mauritian government began to intervene in the development of plans and preparations for Le Morne Brabant regulating what would be an acceptable balance between tourism facilities, preservation of cultural heritage activities, and the conservation of ecological resources. In quick succession the Environmental Protection Act, National Heritage Fund Act, and Le Morne Heritage Trust Fund Act were respectively passed in 2002, 2003, and 2004. A Planning and Policy Guidance document "to guide and transform a resort development with high negative impacts, to be respectful to and better sustain the values inherent to the cultural landscape while avoiding or mitigating negative impacts" was also created.[34] Mauritius's New Economic Agenda of 2003 also sought a balance between economic development in appropriate places, social cohesion, and environmental protection. That same year Le Morne Brabant became tentative to the World Heritage List.

In 2004, another development company, the Rogers Group, obtained permission to build bungalows and villas at the southern edge of Le Morne Brabant. However, at the same time, Mauritius ratified the Convention for the Safeguarding of Intangible Cultural Heritage, which had been adopted by UNESCO in the previous year. An international conference on "Slavery and its Aftermath: Memory and Life of Yesterday and Today," organized by UNESCO, was held on the island in 2002 to facilitate learning and dialogue.[35] A complex situation was evolving where various stakeholders in Mauritius saw a preservation opportunity regarding this special place on the island, which had first attracted maroons during the colonial period and sheltered their subsequent descendants. Pressure had risen because of the economically affluent developers attracted to the landscape's beauty and the relative seclusion from the bulk of the population. In 2007, the Le Morne Cultural Landscape was nominated by the Mauritius Ministry of Arts and Culture to the World Heritage List, which was accepted the following year. This cultural landscape listing from 2008 indicates that maroon heritage, once considered peripheral by many heritage managers, was now acceptable for mainstream preservation recognition and at an international level.[36]

With the listing of Le Morne Cultural Landscape, the World Heritage Committee of UNESCO also provided several caveats, recommending that the state party increase the organizational infrastructure of Le Morne Brabant with professionally trained staff, create sub-plans for managing the cultural resources and buffer zone, monitor terrestrial and maritime viewsheds, respect oral traditions, refrain from new property development, analyze the effects of building heights in the buffer zone in the neighboring villages, and monitor the integrity of the landscape's skyline.[37] These recommendations and requests clearly demonstrate that the UNESCO World Heritage

Committee acknowledged the importance of Le Morne Cultural Landscape. Therefore, a new Management Plan to better protect Le Morne Brabant was developed. After all, since Mauritius had been an uninhabited island prior to colonial settlement in the seventeenth and eighteenth centuries, the maroons were in a certain sense the closest thing the country had to an Indigenous heritage and was, thus, in need of protections due to its rarity and threats from encroaching tourism development. Therefore, the UNESCO World Heritage Committee wanted the Mauritian government to do more to ensure that the area would be sufficiently protected from tourist development, especially since sites on the World Heritage List tend to attract more tourists—particularly from abroad—than they did prior to listing.

CASE STUDY IV: PRESERVING MAROON HERITAGE OF JAMAICA: THE INTANGIBLE HERITAGE OF MOORE TOWN AND THE CULTURAL AND NATURAL HERITAGE OF THE BLUE AND JOHN CROW MOUNTAINS

African slavery was brought to Jamaica by the Spanish during the sixteenth century as a labor supplement to the enslaved Indigenous people and increased significantly after the English conquest of the island in 1655. Due to the island's size and unsettled interior wilderness, the island's center offered ample places for runaway slaves to hide and establish independent settlements. Organized communities of maroons with native Tainos formed in the wilderness by the late seventeenth century and worked together to maintain autonomy and freedom from the British, with whom peace treaties were negotiated in the eighteenth century. One of these successful communities was Moore Town, located in Jamaica's eastern interior in the Blue and John Crow Mountains.[38] Legal slavery ended in Jamaica with the Slavery Abolition Act of 1833 and the island became independent in 1962. With Jamaica's own sovereignty, maroon history and cultural traditions were taken seriously as a matter of pride and expression of black agency during colonialism, with historical figures like Nanny (c.1686—c.1733), an eighteenth-century leader of the Jamaican maroons, taking on legendary and national hero status. Thus, before 2000 there was already great public interest in maroon history and culture.[39] Therefore, in 2001 the Maroon Heritage of Moore Town was among the first to appear on the Masterpieces of the Oral and Intangible Heritage List, a special program instituted by UNESCO to bring awareness to the often-neglected subject of intangible heritage preservation. Due to the success of the Masterpieces program, which was created by director-general proclamation, the Convention on Intangible Cultural Heritage of 2003 was established to make intangible preservation a permanent UNESCO undertaking. Until 2018, Maroon Heritage was Jamaica's only representation on the Intangible Cultural Heritage List.[40]

The recognition of Moore Town's Maroon Heritage as a Masterpiece of Oral and Intangible Heritage galvanized preservation efforts in Jamaica and spurred the people and government to think more critically about Jamaica's cultural contributions to the world—especially when in 2004, UNESCO gave $900,000 (USD) to the Moore Town maroon community for purposes of funding community preservation initiatives of their culture. From this donation, $670,000 was allocated for establishing a museum and cabins for visitors in the remote Blue Mountains. The facilities were built using traditional maroon methods and vernacular architectural styles, so that visitors and guests could travel to Moore Town and learn about maroon heritage through personal experience.[41] Heritage tourism became an engine of economic development for the Moore Town maroons, but official recognition focused on intangible practices, such as social expressions, spiritual customs, and traditional music. In 2005, the Action Plan for Safeguarding the Maroon Heritage of Moore Town was created with the assistance of a $179,960 (USD) grant from the Norway Funds-in-Trust, the Norwegian government's means of extra-budgetary financial support for UNESCO activities. The Action Plan articulated several objectives and activities, including transmitting maroon heritage to the next generation, increasing appreciation of maroon culture among the young, research on maroon culture and knowledge, training technicians for field research and audio-visual documentation, and developing a database of the Maroon Heritage of Moore Town.[42]

Interest in acknowledging the physical landscape and environment of Moore Town grew subsequently, resulting in a desire by Jamaicans who were not even of maroon background and the government to place the area on the World Heritage List. Previously, in 1988, the interior region of the Blue and John Crow Mountains where Moore Town is located was established as a national park for purposes of preserving the native ecology. It is Jamaica's only national park.[43]

Over the centuries a unique, interdependent socio-biological relationship has developed between the regional environment and maroon peoples of the area because their ancestors had to adapt to survive in the wilderness. This area of Jamaica is also the most biodiverse on the island. Since 2006, the national park has been managed by the Jamaica Conservation and Development Trust, which began with the encouragement of the government to seek World Heritage List nomination for the region. In 2011, the World Heritage Committee officially recommended to Jamaica that the nomination should be expanded to include both cultural and natural heritage as a mixed property, highlighting the biodiversity and maroon heritage of the Blue and John Crow Mountains co-existing at this very special landscape.[44] Aspects of Moore Town Maroon Heritage functioned in ways similar to Indigenous Taino traditions by living with the environment through the cultural exchange that occurred during the seventeenth and eighteenth centuries when the two groups worked together toward autonomy from the British.

Jamaica was the first country to successfully balance and combine the tangible heritage of sites with intangible cultural heritage, between the Maroon Heritage of Moore Town inscribed in 2008 on the UNESCO Representative List of the Intangible Cultural Heritage of Humanity and the Blue and John Crow Mountains UNESCO World Heritage Site listing in 2015, which is also a mixed cultural-natural site. Therefore, it appears that the UNESCO-inspired ideal regarding the preservation of intangible cultural, tangible cultural, and natural heritage is pertinent to maroon heritage. This example is epitomic of how heritage conservation ought to be done within a best practice framework.

CONCLUSION

For white supremacy based in labor exploitation, maroons and their built environments on the cultural landscape represented a ruined economic opportunity. However, for the enslaved who escaped to freedom maroonage was a new lease of life through self-emancipation. The examples from Suriname, the United States, Mauritius, and Jamaica demonstrate that maroon heritage is diasporic across a vast geographic expanse, though with a common African root. All maroons share a common experience of multiple migrations: first, from Africa to a European colony far beyond their original homelands, and second, the ordeal of fleeing slavery into a wilderness for liberation and then having to contend with challenges of survival and the struggle for maintaining autonomy. In each setting maroonage was slightly different because of variations in location conditions, which resulted in maroon heritage becoming distinct in a particular place.

How maroons express their culture, language, and traditions in Suriname or Jamaica is different from the ways in which these things are expressed in the United States or Mauritius. An extension of this diversity between maroon communities is how their host societies perceive maroons within the larger social fabric. In Florida as well as other parts of North America, maroons are considered part of the larger African American milieu—not dissimilar from it. This contrasts with Suriname, Jamaica, and Mauritius where maroon people are recognized as a component of a heterogenous, multicultural society, but not necessarily appreciated in the same way. Within Jamaica, maroons and the natural environments surrounding their historical settlements have been at the forefront of conservation efforts. This is in contrast to Suriname where the government is exclusively focused on the protection of natural ecology without consideration for how the maroon inhabitants and their culture have become synthesized with ecosystem processes that highly mimic Indigenous ways of living. The example of Mauritius is intriguing because here the government is primarily concerned with maroon heritage cultural resources, and cares secondarily for the ecological well-being of the place, which is what traditionally provided sustenance and material resources for the maroons that lived on the island.

Interest in maroon history and its preservation emerged simultaneously in Mauritius and the United States in the 1970s, likely as an outgrowth of the Civil Rights, Black Power, and African independence movements. Maroon heritage, after all, represents Africans in places of oppression taking action through whatever means necessary for self-determination. Besides initial government efforts on site recognition at Fort Gadsden and Le Morne Brabant during the 1970s, little else materialized for nearly two decades. During the 1990s, UNESCO began encouraging its state parties to think beyond conventional architectural monuments and to reconceptualize the memory of living cultures and landscapes, which was codified in 1994 through the Global Strategy.[45] From this point forward, an improved diversity of cultural and natural heritages began to be reflected on the World Heritage List, as well as from unrepresented regions outside of Europe and North America. The early 2000s is when UNESCO began to formally recognize intangible heritage through its documentation programs, since these aspects of heritage were beyond the purview of the World Heritage Convention of 1972.

UNESCO's privileging of cultural landscapes and intangible heritage definitions had a positive effect on the recognition and public attention of migration diasporic heritage, especially in Jamaica and Mauritius. From these UNESCO initiatives at the turn of the twenty-first century, we see the emergence of policy responses in Mauritius and Jamaica for the preservation of maroon heritage, though with varying degrees of success. In 2008, Le Morne Cultural Landscape became a world heritage site and the Maroon Heritage of Moore Town, Jamaica, was also added to UNESCO's Representative List of Intangible Cultural Heritage of Humanity. Here the approach for preserving maroon heritage was not centered on buildings or landscape but on oral traditions, folklore, music, and rituals, and is, thus, the only representation of maroon heritage on the Intangible List. These preservation efforts led to the designation of the Blue and John Crow Mountains, as a mixed cultural and natural site on the World Heritage List, centered around Nanny Town.

The United States never adopted the Convention on Intangible Cultural Heritage of 2003, though the multinational progression of cultural landscape and intangible heritage preservation has influenced some American practitioners, as was observed from the archaeologists and historians involved in the reevaluation of Prospect Bluff Historic Sites National Historic Landmark in the 2010s. In the United States, the National Park Service began assessments on the need for preserving minority heritages during the early 2000s.[46] Combined with the renewed interests in Fort Gadsden/Prospect Bluff Historic Sites National Historic Landmark, the bicentennial anniversary (2016) certainly promoted public reflection and introspection on maroon determinism for freedom, which also simultaneously occurred with Jamaica's success of Moore Town's intangible heritage recognition. These events, while independent of one another, are signifiers of a growing interest in the preservation of maroon heritage on multiple fronts despite their isolation from one another. Dmitri Nikulin, a philosopher of history, has found that because

> history is never given as a whole and is always a construction, there can be *many different histories*. There may well be a history to which particular histories converge as its normative purpose. Such a history could be either actually reached at a certain point or else remains an ideal that is only partially realized by different histories. This sort of history may require the equal and just distribution of goods and the recognition of others as free and equal in their rights and dignity.[47]

The implications for conceptualizing the past in this way (such as within the context of maroons) is that histories of mobility, migration, and community settlement can become multiethnic, multicultural, and transnational. A culturally pluralistic understanding of the past will then impact the heritage preservation profession because it will necessitate the consideration and reevaluation of historic places, landscapes, and cultural expressions of people that had formerly been marginalized. Maroons and their heritage then cease to be overlooked or marginalized because they are no longer peripheral to preservation approaches or policy making. And, as the Jamaican case exemplifies, maroons can even set the standard for a multifaceted preservation approach that is inclusive of the tangible and intangible as well as the cultural and natural principles involved in best practice.

NOTES

1. Stuart Kirsch, "Judaification of Indigenous Politics," in: Julia M. Eckert, Brian Donahoe, and Christian Strümpell (eds.), *Law Against the State: Ethnographic Forays into Law's Transformations*, Cambridge: Cambridge University Press, 2014, 23–43.

2. See: Barry W. Higman, "Foreword," in: Emmanuel K. Agorsah (ed.), *Maroon Heritage: Archaeological, Ethnographic, and Historical Perspectives*, Kingston: Canoe Press, 1994, vii.

3. Terrance Weik, "Allies, Adversaries, and Kin in the African Seminole Communities of Florida: Archaeology at Pilaklikaha," in: Akinwumi Ogundiran and Toyin Falola (eds.), *Archaeology of Atlantic Africa and the African Diaspora*, Bloomington: Indiana University Press, 2007, 311–331.

4. Richard Price has published more than twenty books related to maroon history and culture in the Americas, including Richard Price, *Maroon Societies: Rebel Slave Communities in the Americas*, Baltimore: The John Hopkins University Press, 1996; Richard Price and Sally Price, *Maroon Arts: Cultural Vitality in the African Diaspora*, Boston: Beacon Press, 1999; and Richard Price, *Rainforest Warriors: Human Rights on Trial*, Philadelphia: University of Pennsylvania Press, 2012.

5. I. S. Redjosentono, "Nomination Dossier for the Central Suriname Natures Reserve for the World Heritage List," Paramaribo, Suriname: Minister of Natural Resources, 1999.

6. Higman, "Foreword," vii.

7. Emmanuel K. Agorsah, "Scars of Brutality: Archaeolgy of the Maroons in the Caribbean," in: Akinwumi Ogundiran and Toyin Falola (eds.), *Archaeology of Atlantic Africa and the African Diaspora*, Bloomington: Indiana University Press, 2007, 332–354.

8. Sulatānā Āpharoja, *Invisible yet Invincible: The Islamic Heritage of the Maroons and the Enslaved Africans in Jamaica*, London: Austin & Macauley, 2012; and Vijaya Teelock and Julie Cornec, *Maroonage and the Maroon Heritage in Mauritius*, Réduit: University of Mauritius, 2005; and Weik, "Allies, Adversaries, and Kin in the African Seminole Communities of Florida," 311–331.

9. Herbert Aptheker, *To Be Free: Studies in American Negro History*, New York: International Publishers, 1968; Sylviane A. Diouf, *Slavery's Exiles: The Story of the American Maroons*, New York: New York University Press, 2016; and Daniel O. Sayers, *Desolate Place for a Defiant People: The Archaeology of Maroons, Indigenous Americans, and Enslaved Laborers in the Great Dismal Swamp*, University Press of Florida, 2016.

10. Ellen-Rose Kambel and Fergus MacKaym, *The Rights of Indigenous Peoples and Maroons in Suriname*, Copenhagen: International Work Group for Indigenous Affairs, 1999, 112–117.

11. Stanley Stevens, *Conservation Through Cultural Survival: Indigenous Peoples And Protected Areas*, Washington, D.C.: Island Press, 1997; and Barry L. Stiefel, "A Tale of Two Plains: Natural Heritage Conservation in the United States and Canada," in: Anthony J. Amato (ed.), *Conservation on the Northern Plains: New Perspectives*, Sioux Falls: The Center for Western Studies Augustana University, 2017.

12. Kambel and MacKaym, *The Rights of Indigenous Peoples and Maroons in Suriname*, 112–117.

13. Andy Isaacson, "Visiting Maroon Village in the Suriname Jungle," *San Francisco Chronicle*, 2008 (https://www.sfgate.com/travel/article/Visiting-Maroon-village-in-the-Suriname-jungle-3259149.php, accessed October 19, 2018); and Redjosentono, "Nomination Dossier for the Central Suriname Natures Reserve for the World Heritage List."

14. Price, *Rainforest Warriors*, 136–137.

15. Barry L. Stiefel, "Rethinking and Revaluating UNESCO World Heritage Sites: Lessons Experimented within the USA," *Journal of Cultural Heritage Management and Sustainable Development* 8, no. 1 (2017): 47–61.

16. Kambel and MacKaym, *The Rights of Indigenous Peoples and Maroons in Suriname*, 112–117.

17. See: Nathaniel Millett, *Maroons of Prospect Bluff and Their Quest for Freedom in the Atlantic World*, Gainesville: University Press of Florida, 2015.

18. "Bloodshed Common at Fort Gadsden," *The Apalachicola Times*, 2017 (http://www.apalachtimes.com/news/20170330/bloodshed-common-at-fort-gadsden, accessed October 22, 2018).

19. Marcia M. Greenlee, "Fort Gadsden Historic Memorial," National Register of Historic Places Nomination Form—National Historic Landmark, Washington, D.C.: National Park Service, 1974, 5.

20. Ruth E. Hill (ed.), *The Black Women Oral History Project: Volume 1*, Boston: De Gruyter, 1991; and Sara K. Dykens. "Commemoration and Controversy: The Memorialization of Denmark Vesey in Charleston, South Carolina," MS Thesis, Clemson University/College of Charleston, 2015.

21. Fred Brown Jr., "Preserving America's Black Historical Landmarks," *The Washington Post*, February 20, 1989 (https://www.washingtonpost.com/archive/lifestyle/1989/02/20/preserving-americas-black-historic-landmarks/68a2c680-7abd-42a4-85c7-68d87f9a03f9/?noredirect=on&utm_term=.b0be7dccf314, accessed October 22, 2018).

22. Yvonne S. Lamb, "Robert DeForrest; Identified Black Landmarks," *The Washington Post*, March 6, 2007 (http://www.washingtonpost.com/wp-dyn/content/article/2007/03/05/AR2007030501528.html, accessed October 22, 2018).

23. "National Register of Historic Places: Digital Archive on NP Gallery," *National Park Service*, 2018 (https://npgallery.nps.gov/nrhp, accessed October 22, 2018); and "National Register of Historic Places," *National Archives Catalog*, 2018 (https://catalog.archives.gov/search?q=%22national%20register%20of%20historic%20places%22%2075000647, accessed October 22, 2018).

24. Florida Division of Historical Resources, *Florida Black Heritage Trail*, Tallahassee: Florida Department of States, 2007, 6.

25. Lois Swoboda, "A Facelift for Fort Gadsden," *The Apalachicola Times*, July 15, 2015 (https://www.apalachtimes.com/article/20150715/NEWS/307159945, accessed October 22, 2018).

26. Lois Swoboda, "Hundreds attend Fort Gadsden dedication," *The Apalachicola Times*, November 16, 2016 (http://www.apalachtimes.com/news/20161116/hundreds-attend-fort-gadsden-dedication, accessed October 22, 2018).

27. David Adlerstein, "Apalachicola River 'Maroons' A Tale of Survival," *The Apalachicola Times*, October 20, 2016 (http://www.apalachtimes.com/news/20161020/apalachicola-river-maroons-tale-of-survival, accessed October 22, 2018); "Aug. 13 Program to Discuss Negro Fort History," *The Apalachicola Times*, July 27, 2016 (http://www.apalachtimes.com/news/20160727/aug-13-program-to-discuss-negro-fort-history, accessed October, 22 2018); and "Current Archeological Prospection Advances for Non-destructive Investigations of Fort Gadsden, a War of 1812 Fort and

Fight," Workshop Application Form by the Midwest Archaeological Center and the National Park Service, Apalachicola National Forest, Franklin County, Florida, 2016.

28. Dan Sayers is quoted by Richard Grant, "Deep in the Swamps, Archaeologists Are Finding How Fugitive Slaves Kept Their Freedom," *Smithsonian Magazine*, September 2016 (https://www.smithsonianmag.com/history/deep-swamps-archaeologists-fugitive-slaves-kept-freedom-180960122/, accessed November 5, 2018).

29. John N. Grant, "Jamaican Maroons in Nova Scotia," *The Canadian Encyclopedia* (https://www.thecanadianencyclopedia.ca/en/article/maroons-of-nova-scotia, accessed March 29, 2018).

30. "Cole Harbour Meeting House," *Canadian Register of Historic Places*, 2018 (https://www.historicplaces.ca/en/rep-reg/place-lieu.aspx?id=6651&pid=0, accessed October 22, 2018).

31. "Victoria Road United Baptist Church," *Canadian Register of Historic Places*, 2018 (https://www.historicplaces.ca/en/rep-reg/place-lieu.aspx?id=3852&pid=0, accessed October 22, 2018).

32. See: Auguste Toussaint, *History of Mauritius*, London: Macmillan, 1977.

33. Rosabelle Boswell, *Le Malaise Créole: Ethnic Identity in Mauritius*, New York: Berghahn Books, 2006, 192–195.

34. Karel A. Bakker and Francois Odendaal, "Managing Heritage in a Contested Space: The Case of Le Morne Cultural Landscape in Mauritius," *South African Journal of Art History* 23, no. 1 (2008): 240.

35. Rosabelle Boswell, *Challenges to Identifying and Managing Intangible Cultural Heritage in Mauritius, Zanzibar and Seychelles*, Senegal: Counsel for the Development of Social Science Research in Africa [CODESRIA], 2008, 41–54.

36. World Heritage Committee, *World Heritage 32 COM: Decisions Adopted at the 32nd Session of the World Heritage Committee*, Quebec City: UNESCO, 2008 (Revised 2009), np. Criterion iii is "to bear a unique or at least exceptional testimony to a cultural tradition or to a civilization which is living, or which has disappeared"; and Criterion vi "to be directly or tangibly associated with events or living traditions, with ideas, or with beliefs, with artistic and literary works of outstanding universal significance. The World Heritage Committee considers that this criterion should preferably be used in conjunction with other criteria.

37. World Heritage Committee, *World Heritage 32 COM*.

38. Brooke N. Newman, *Dark Inheritance: Blood, Race, and Sex in Colonial Jamaica*, New Haven: Yale University Press, 2018.

39. Jenny Sharpe, *Ghosts of Slavery: A Literary Archaeology of Black Women's Lives*, Minneapolis: University of Minnesota Press, 2003, 1–43.

40. Jon Blistein, "Reggae Added to UNESCO's 'Intangible Cultural Heritage' List," *Rolling Stone*, 2018 (https://www.rollingstone.com/music/music-news/reggae-unesco-intangible-cultural-heritage-list-761286/, accessed November 29, 2018).

41. "UNESCO Giving US$900,000 to Moore Town Maroons," *Observer Reporter*, June 9, 2004 (http://www.jamaicaobserver.com/news/60961_UNESCO-giving-US-900-000-to-Moore-Town-Maroons, accessed January 14, 2016).

42. "Action Plan for Safeguarding the Maroon Heritage of Moore Town," *Projects and Activities*, January 8, 2005 (http://www.unesco.org/culture/ich/en/projects/action

-plan-for-safeguarding-the-maroon-heritage-of-moore-town-00058, accessed January 15, 2015).
43. See: Susan Iremonger, *A Guide to Plants in the Blue Mountains of Jamaica*, Kingston: University of the West Indies Press, 2002.
44. World Heritage Committee, *World Heritage 35 COM: Decisions Adopted at the 35th Session of the World Heritage Committee*, Paris: UNESCO, 2011.
45. Stiefel, "Rethinking and Revaluating UNESCO World Heritage Sites."
46. Ned Kaufman, "Cultural Needs Assessment: Phase I," National Park Service. Washington, D.C., 2002.
47. Dmitri Nikulin, *The Concept of History*, New York: Bloomsbury Publishing, 2017, 5.

BIBLIOGRAPHY

Primary Sources

"Action Plan for Safeguarding the Maroon Heritage of Moore Town." *Projects and Activities*, January 8, 2005, available online: http://www.unesco.org/culture/ich/en/projects/action-plan-for-safeguarding-the-maroon-heritage-of-moore-town-00058 (accessed January 15, 2015).

Adlerstein, David. "Apalachicola River 'Maroons' a Tale of Survival." *The Apalachicola Times*, October 20, 2016, available online: http://www.apalachtimes.com/news/20161020/apalachicola-river-maroons-tale-of-survival (accessed October 22, 2018).

"Aug. 13 Program to Discuss Negro Fort History." *The Apalachicola Times*, July 27, 2016, available online: http://www.apalachtimes.com/news/20160727/aug-13-program-to-discuss-negro-fort-history (accessed October 22, 2018).

Blistein, Jon. "Reggae Added to UNESCO's 'Intangible Cultural Heritage' List." *Rolling Stone*, 2018, available online: https://www.rollingstone.com/music/music-news/reggae-unesco-intangible-cultural-heritage-list-761286/ (accessed November 29, 2018).

"Bloodshed Common at Fort Gadsden." *The Apalachicola Times*, 2017, available online: http://www.apalachtimes.com/news/20170330/bloodshed-common-at-fort-gadsden (accessed October 22, 2018).

Brown, Fred, Jr. "Preserving America's Black Historical Landmarks." *The Washington Post*, February 20, 1989, available online: https://www.washingtonpost.com/archive/lifestyle/1989/02/20/preserving-americas-black-historic-landmarks/68a2c680-7abd-42a4-85c7-68d87f9a03f9/?noredirect=on&utm_term=.b0be7dccf314 (accessed October 22, 2018).

"Current Archeological Prospection Advances for Non-Destructive Investigations of Fort Gadsden, a War of 1812 Fort and Fight," Workshop application form by the Midwest Archaeological Center and the National Park Service, Apalachicola National Forest, Franklin County, Florida, 2016.

Florida Division of Historical Resources. *Florida Black Heritage Trail*. Tallahassee: Florida Department of States, 2007, 6.

Greenlee, Marcia M. "Fort Gadsden Historic Memorial." In *National Register of Historic Places Nomination Form—National Historic Landmark*. Washington, D.C.: National Park Service, 1974.

Hill, Ruth E., ed. *The Black Women Oral History Project: Volume 1*. Boston: De Gruyter, 1991.

Isaacson, Andy. "Visiting Maroon Village in the Suriname Jungle." *San Francisco Chronicle*, December 7, 2008, available online: https://www.sfgate.com/travel/article/Visiting-Maroon-village-in-the-Suriname-jungle-3259149.php (accessed October 19, 2018).

Lamb, Yvonne S. "Robert DeForrest; Identified Black Landmarks." *The Washington Post*, March 6, 2007, available online: http://www.washingtonpost.com/wp-dyn/content/article/2007/03/05/AR2007030501528.html (accessed October 22, 2018).

"National Register of Historic Places." *National Archives Catalog*, 2018, available online: https://catalog.archives.gov/search?q=%22national%20register%20of%20historic%20places%22%2075000647 (accessed October 22, 2018).

"National Register of Historic Places: Digital Archive on NP Gallery." *National Park Service*, 2018, available online: https://npgallery.nps.gov/nrhp (accessed October 22, 2018).

Redjosentono, I. S. *Nomination Dossier for the Central Suriname Natures Reserve for the World Heritage List*. Paramaribo, Suriname: Minister of Natural Resources, 1999.

Swoboda, Lois. "A Facelift for Fort Gadsden." *The Apalachicola Times*, July 15, 2015, available online: https://www.apalachtimes.com/article/20150715/NEWS/307159945 (accessed October 22, 2018).

Swoboda, Lois. "Hundreds Attend Fort Gadsden Dedication." *The Apalachicola Times*, November 16, 2016, available online: http://www.apalachtimes.com/news/20161116/hundreds-attend-fort-gadsden-dedication (accessed October 22, 2018).

"UNESCO Giving US$900,000 to Moore Town Maroons." *Observer Reporter*, June 9, 2004, available online: http://www.jamaicaobserver.com/news/60961_UNESCO-giving-US-900-000-to-Moore-Town-Maroons (accessed January 14, 2016).

World Heritage Committee. *World Heritage 32 COM: Decisions Adopted at the 32nd Session of the World Heritage Committee*. Quebec City, Canada: 2008 (Revised 2009), UNESCO.

World Heritage Committee. *World Heritage 35 COM: Decisions Adopted at the 35th Session of the World Heritage Committee*. Paris, France: UNESCO, 2011.

Secondary Sources

Agorsah, Emmanuel K. "Scars of Brutality: Archaeolgy of the Maroons in the Caribbean." In *Archaeology of Atlantic Africa and the African Diaspora*, edited by Akinwumi Ogundiran and Toyin Falola. Bloomington: Indiana University Press, 2007, 332–354.

Āpharoja, Sulatānā. *Invisible yet Invincible: The Islamic Heritage of the Maroons and the Enslaved Africans in Jamaica.* London: Austin & Macauley, 2012.

Aptheker, Herbert. *To Be Free: Studies in American Negro History.* New York: International Publishers, 1968.

Bakker, Karel A., and Francois Odendaal. "Managing Heritage in a Contested Space: The Case of Le Morne Cultural Landscape in Mauritius." *South African Journal of Art History* 23, no. 1 (2008): 225–244.

Boswell, Rosabelle. *Challenges to Identifying and Managing Intangible Cultural Heritage in Mauritius, Zanzibar and Seychelles.* Senegal: Counsel for the Development of Social Science Research in Africa [CODESRIA], 2008.

Boswell, Rosabelle. *Le Malaise Créole: Ethnic Identity in Mauritius.* New York: Berghahn Books, 2006.

"Cole Harbour Meeting House." *Canadian Register of Historic Places*, 2018, available online: https://www.historicplaces.ca/en/rep-reg/place-lieu.aspx?id=6651&pid=0 (accessed October 22, 2018).

Diouf, Sylviane A. *Slavery's Exiles: The Story of the American Maroons.* New York: New York University Press, 2016.

Dykens, Sara K. "Commemoration and Controversy: The Memorialization of Denmark Vesey in Charleston, South Carolina." MS Thesis, Clemson University, College of Charleston, 2015.

Grant, John N. "Jamaican Maroons in Nova Scotia." *The Canadian Encyclopedia*, available online: https://www.thecanadianencyclopedia.ca/en/article/maroons-of-nova-scotia (accessed March 29, 2018).

Grant, Richard. "Deep in the Swamps, Archaeologists Are Finding How Fugitive Slaves Kept Their Freedom." *Smithsonian Magazine*, September 2016, available online: https://www.smithsonianmag.com/history/deep-swamps-archaeologists-fugitive-slaves-kept-freedom-180960122/ (accessed November 5, 2018).

Higman, B. W. "Foreword." In *Maroon Heritage: Archaeological, Ethnographic, and Historical Perspectives,* edited by Emmanuel K. Agorsah. Kingston: Canoe Press, 1994, i–ii.

Iremonger, Susan. *A Guide to Plants in the Blue Mountains of Jamaica.* Kingston: University of the West Indies Press, 2002.

Kambel, Ellen-Rose, and Fergus MacKaym. *The Rights of Indigenous Peoples and Maroons in Suriname.* Copenhagen: International Work Group for Indigenous Affairs, 1999.

Kaufman, Ned. *Cultural Needs Assessment: Phase I.* Washington, D.C.: National Park Service, 2002.

Kirsch, Stuart. "Judaification of Indigenous Politics." In *Law Against the State: Ethnographic Forays into Law's Transformations,* edited by Julia M. Eckert, Brian Donahoe, and Christian Strümpell. Cambridge: Cambridge University Press, 2014, 23–43.

Millett, Nathaniel. *Maroons of Prospect Bluff and Their Quest for Freedom in the Atlantic World.* Gainesville: University Press of Florida, 2015.

Newman, Brooke N. *Dark Inheritance: Blood, Race, and Sex in Colonial Jamaica.* New Haven: Yale University Press, 2018.

Nikulin, Dmitri. *The Concept of History.* New York: Bloomsbury Publishing, 2017.
Price, Richard. *Maroon Societies: Rebel Slave Communities in the Americas.* Baltimore: The John Hopkins University Press, 1996.
Price, Richard. *Rainforest Warriors: Human Rights on Trial.* Philadelphia: University of Pennsylvania Press, 2012.
Price, Richard, and Sally Price. *Maroon Arts: Cultural Vitality in the African Diaspora.* Boston: Beacon Press, 1999.
Sayers, Daniel O. *Desolate Place for a Defiant People: The Archaeology of Maroons, Indigenous Americans, and Enslaved Laborers in the Great Dismal Swamp.* Gainesville: University Press of Florida, 2016.
Sharpe, Jenny. *Ghosts of Slavery: A Literary Archaeology of Black Women's Lives.* Minneapolis: University of Minnesota Press, 2003.
Stevens, Stanley. *Conservation Through Cultural Survival: Indigenous Peoples and Protected Areas.* Washington, D.C.: Island Press, 1997.
Stiefel, Barry L. "Rethinking and Revaluating UNESCO World Heritage Sites: Lessons Experimented Within the USA." *Journal of Cultural Heritage Management and Sustainable Development* 8, no. 1 (2018): 47–61.
Stiefel, Barry L. "A Tale of Two Plains: Natural Heritage Conservation in the United States and Canada." In *Conservation on the Northern Plains: New Perspectives*, edited by Anthony J. Amato. Sioux Falls: The Center for Western Studies Augustana University, 2017.
Teelock, Vijaya, and Julie Cornec. *Maroonage and the Maroon Heritage in Mauritius.* Réduit. Mauritius: University of Mauritius, 2005.
Toussaint, Auguste. *History of Mauritius.* London: Macmillan, 1977.
"Victoria Road United Baptist Church." *Canadian Register of Historic Places*, 2018, available online: https://www.historicplaces.ca/en/rep-reg/place-lieu.aspx?id=3852&pid=0 (accessed October 22, 2018).
Weik, Terrance. "Allies, Adversaries, and Kin in the African Seminole Communities of Florida: Archaeology at Pilaklikaha." In *Archaeology of Atlantic Africa and the African Diaspora*, edited by Akinwumi Ogundiran and Toyin Falola. Bloomington: Indiana University Press, 2007, 311–331.

Chapter 8

Rediscovering the Roots That Remained Abroad

Challenges and Methods in Teaching Transborder Genealogy

Izabella Parowicz

Simply put, genealogy is knowledge of one's lineage (from Greek: *γενεά*, geneá—"lineage" and *λόγος*, logos—"word," "knowledge"). It is the discipline that investigates the family ties and relationships between individuals based on the kinship and affinity between them. It is no coincidence that the words "genealogy" and "genetics" share the same root word "gene"— genealogical research is concerned primarily with individuals who are related biologically (genetically), through descent from common ancestors or from each other (Lat. *filiatio*). A second focus of genealogy are the relationships of men and women who join (Lat. *coitio*) to form new families through the generation of offspring.[1]

Knowledge of one's own lineage and one's own family history is also part of one's heritage, a very individual and unique part. Only full siblings have identical ancestors—with every other relative one shares only part of them. It is primarily an intangible heritage, although it is also the legal basis for inheriting photographs, documents, memorabilia, money, and even real estate. Without knowledge of family history, however, all these things will be merely mute objects without meaning or uncontextualized property. Only by deepening knowledge of family history is it possible to realize which ancestor was successful enough to secure the future of distant generations, what events allowed only a token fragment of former wealth to survive, or perhaps, why in a given family there was nothing at all to materially inherit. The individual who studies his family history begins to better understand or properly contextualize even the most fleeting memories or family anecdotes. He sometimes recognizes from whom he has inherited facial features, smiles, hair and skin color, gestures, behavior, and tendencies to make certain life decisions. In other words, students of genealogy find the whole of that elusive and very intimate set of attributes which form an integral part of a person's identity—the one that answers the question: "Where do I come from?"

Eviatar Zerubavel wrote that genealogy is "first and foremost a way of thinking." Indeed, thinking genealogically is one of the distinctive characteristics of human cognition. As the very objects of our genealogical imagination, ancestors and relatives, therefore, deserve a prominent place among the foundational pillars of the human condition.[2] As early as 1932, Adolf Bocheński, an eminent Polish publicist, lamented that the majority of educated people had no idea of what their father's grandfather did or where he lived, let alone of earlier generations.[3] Not much has changed since. Most people show either a mere superficial interest in their ancestry or none, focusing their attention on the here and now, on their personal aspirations and achievements, and attaching importance only to their current group affiliation.[4] However, a growing number of people, encouraged by technological advances and increasingly easy internet access to historical records, are beginning to research their family histories, with the average age of genealogists continuously decreasing.[5] They are willing to do this on their own rather than outsource their genealogical research to companies that offer such services on a commercial basis. This decision is motivated primarily not by financial considerations. Self-research, though tedious and time-consuming, is far more rewarding, as individuals can truly immerse themselves in their family history, engaging mentally and emotionally in the painstaking process of assembling salvaged fragments of information into a single, coherent, and above all, credible whole—their unique, familial heritage.

To become interested in one's own family history, one must develop what Eviatar Zerubavel called a "genealogical imagination," which consists of the realization that the "phenomenal world is socially inhabitable not only by our contemporaries, but also by our predecessors who remain present in our minds long after they die."[6] This genealogical imagination allows us to envision our distant ancestors no longer as, for example, our father's grandfather, but *our own* great-grandfather, thus transforming the indirect ancestral ties between non-successive generations into direct ties. Moreover, this concept of grandparenthood can be expanded indefinitely; as Zerubavel rightly points out, this awareness of ancestors who had died long before we were born is a feature that distinguishes humans from all other living creatures.[7]

Most genealogists are self-taught individuals who have spent years becoming proficient at finding the most veiled, forgotten, and hidden details of their ancestors' lives, piecing them together and reconstructing their family history step by step, verifying or debunking family legends, and re-personifying the dead who, through these efforts, stop being just names and become real persons.[8] However, not everyone has the determination, or perhaps the courage, to try to explore their own family history. Curiosity and good intentions are often inhibited by inner dilemmas: "I do not know how to go about it," "I no longer have anyone to ask," "No one has ever told me about our family history—maybe I should not touch the subject for some reason." Lack of time, preoccupation with other matters, or the loosening of ties with one's family, perhaps even its disintegration, cause the intention to investigate the family history to be postponed indefinitely. People with a migration background are additionally discouraged by the fact that genealogical research would require them to overcome external barriers—physical ones (national borders) as well as linguistic, and cultural ones. In other words, their family heritage is a transnational one. Thus, they are faced with the physical, mental, and perhaps emotional effort of returning to the land of their ancestors to research their family's roots. At the same time, it is among this group of people, who live with a certain, migration-induced sense of rupture or discontinuity, that the desire to reveal and explore the transnational ties that bind the present and the past of their own family is often greatest, stemming from the need to redefine or contextualize their own identity.[9]

These observations have prompted me to try to give young people a helping hand by offering a cross-border genealogy course at the Department of Cultural Studies of the European University Viadrina in Frankfurt (Oder), Germany. Specifically, I offer them the opportunity to research the history of their ancestors and to discover their familial heritage across the German-Polish border, located right next to my university. In this chapter, I shall present a rationale for conducting family history research in an academic context with a particular focus on the challenges to be met when teaching transborder genealogy. Subsequently, I outline the methods I use in working with students and the results of that work.

GENEALOGY AS AN ACADEMIC DISCIPLINE

The necessary prerequisite for genealogical research is its rigor and reliability, as only these factors can lead to documented and trustworthy findings. Thus, genealogy is increasingly considered not merely a hobby but a serious leisure.[10] Its uniqueness lies in the fact that, as Jill Lepore argues, genealogy focuses on microhistory, defined as "the history of hitherto obscure people" and concentrating "on the intensive study of particular lives."[11] While it is acknowledged as one of the many subfields of history,[12] Lepore's definition causes it to be treated as a peripheral discipline, providing history at large with details of the family relationships of the figures being studied. However, genealogy simultaneously brings together at least forty-five disciplines under its umbrella, among them social history, (historical) geography, anthropology, migration studies, computer science, and genetics, synergistically creating a new and integrative field of research.[13] This complexity leads more and more scholars to ask why genealogy has not yet become a recognized academic discipline.[14] After all, it teaches one to think historically by seeking to contextualize information about family life in the past, by being rigorous in collecting and evaluating historical evidence, by juxtaposing and critically analyzing one's sources in the hope of understanding how and why historical phenomena occurred, and by acquiring a sophisticated understanding of a variety of primary and secondary sources, along with a number of other skills that academics associate with advanced historical research.[15] Arnon Hershkovitz argues that, admittedly, genealogy meets most of the requirements to become an academic discipline: (1) it is characterized by unique research methods; (2) there is significant market demand for the discipline; (3) there is a growing number of professionals working substantively in the field worldwide; (4) the field uses a specific technical language; and (5) advances in the field are regularly published in journals. Yet two important prerequisites have still not been met: (1) a comprehensive and structured body of knowledge is lacking; and (2) an international community of scholars willing to put genealogy at the forefront of their research interests has not yet emerged.[16] Such a community would have to be inherently transdisciplinary to meet the challenges posed by genealogical research.[17] Nevertheless, degree courses in genealogy are already emerging at some universities around the world (for instance, at the University of Strathclyde, Glasgow, at the University of Dundee, at Brigham Young University in Provo, Utah, at Boston University, and at Cardinal Stefan Wyszyński University in Warsaw), responding to the growing demand for formalized educational offerings in the field.[18]

The (self-)didactic aspect of genealogical research cannot be overstated. Arnon Herskovitz and Sharon Hardof-Jaffe argue that genealogy, understood as a learning process, takes place on at least three levels: First, those who engage in such research naturally learn about their family history. Second, genealogists learn about themselves because genealogical research often helps people find a connection between their family history and their inner self. Third, people who engage in genealogical research usually gain knowledge about unknown historical resources and new research techniques, and, thereby, develop their research skills.[19] In order to better understand their ancestors, genealogists, furthermore, educate themselves in areas that made up the content of their lives. Genealogy serves to sharpen the detective's sense; the family historian learns to pay attention to seemingly insignificant details from the history of a region or country, which nevertheless had a significant impact on the daily life of the ancestors and their decisions.[20] Thus, genealogists often gain knowledge in other disciplines, for example, in the realm of historical uniforms by learning the history of the military unit in which their ancestor served or the battle in which he fought. When coming across a case of an epidemic that decimated a genealogist's family, they are inclined to learn more about smallpox, cholera, or any other disease that had such a great impact on their own family history. The genealogist investigates how and where their ancestors lived, what occupations they held, and how the latter placed them in the social hierarchy.[21] If it turns out that an ancestor lost his landed property through no fault of his own, the genealogist may gain historical legal knowledge by studying the statute that deprived a particular social group of land and privileges. As Diana Hart points out, they would have most likely had no interest in these topics, had it not been for genealogy.[22] It is noteworthy that the unique historical knowledge accumulated in this way has a tremendous impact on the identity of those engaged in genealogical research.[23]

In the case of genealogy, we find self-directed learning that is ignited by self-motivated people, usually adults.[24] This type of learning attitude is the most desired by teachers, because the individuals themselves diagnose their learning needs, formulate their learning goals, choose appropriate learning strategies, and evaluate the results of the educational process they have undergone.[25] Such self-direction is crucial for achieving meaningful educational outcomes and allows one to maintain enthusiasm and desire for further educational growth.[26]

For most genealogists, the beginning of their journey is the same—the realization that one did not know one's family history sets off a wave of questions and a burning need to find answers. This moment often comes after the death of a (senior) family member who was versed in genealogical matters and triggers a lasting sense of regret for unrequited conversations and missed opportunities.[27] An individual is afflicted by genealogical nostalgia stemming from the gap between personal memory and (unbequeathed) knowledge of one's genealogical heritage.[28] A need arises to unearth from the abyss of oblivion the smallest details of one's ancestors' lives, their attitudes, motivations, and all the cause-and-effect relationships that determined the fate of one's relatives and made one who one is and put them where they are. This need and the authentic interest in one's own family history become the best incentive to undertake and continue the learning process, and it is for this reason, as the following case will show, that genealogy is proving to be such a graceful subject to teach at the university. Although genealogical research is always tedious and often frustrating, it is also more student-centered than most other subjects taught. Because of this constant self-direction, students demonstrate a great passion for the subject of their research that is much less observed among conventional history students. Moreover, genealogical research, based largely on technology and communication, is an active, stimulating, and engaging process, constantly bringing not only new facts, but also new emotional experiences into the student's life.[29] Students increasingly realize that the more they delve into researching their family history, the more education becomes part of their discoveries since they are learning much more than just family history.[30]

MOTIVATION FOR GENEALOGY

A crucial challenge in teaching genealogy is to help students to recognize and define the motivation behind their decision to research family history. There are many motives that lead people to undertake genealogical research. Some want to demystify their family history and remove obscurities that have accumulated over time.[31] Some are driven by a duty to chronicle and pass on family history to future generations, while others seek to understand their own lives through the lens of the values and traits inherited from their ancestors and the decisions they made.[32] Still others wish to discover and define their ethnicity or enrich themselves by exploring the under-recognized past in the hope that it will allow them to reclaim their individual and transpersonal identity.[33] In the case of transborder genealogical research, three main, intertwined motivations come to the fore with particular intensity: the need to recover and preserve the memory of one's ancestors, the need to place one's ancestry in a foreign (and perhaps unfamiliar) geographical context, and the need to (re)define one's identity, with the means to meet all three types of needs located across administrative, linguistic, and historical borders.

Genealogy and Memory

As Maurice Halbwachs noted, a fundamental condition of memory is the communication of what is remembered.[34] The most natural starting point for genealogical research is the memory preserved and transmitted by family members. It depends largely on the longevity of family members and their living memories from direct contact with previous generations.[35] Jan Assmann suggests that personal memories can be communicated over about three to four generations, and that the so-called communicative memory passes with the death of its last carriers.[36] Within a family, communicative memory can span at least five generations. A person retains memories associated with their grandparent and passes them on to their grandchildren, for whom the grandparent in question is already a great-great-grandparent.

Although Harald Welzer, Sabine Moller, and Karoline Tschuggnall argue that family memory is a partial, albeit central, area of communicative memory,[37] it is difficult to accept this concept without reservation. Family memory need not and should not die with its last carrier. On the contrary, it can and should be re-remembered or brought back "to life."[38] It can be constructed and reconstructed by the next generation, even if there has been a rupture in the transmission of memories. Discovering letters, diaries, documents, or press reports (facilitated nowadays by common digitalization of collections in various archives) serves this purpose. Family memory progresses toward cultural memory, becoming a keystone between communicative memory and cultural memory, although it is possible that for a long time (or never) there will be no community interested in becoming familiar with and preserving this memory. It may or may not fulfil the main task of cultural memory, which is to convey to this community (a family) a collective, that is cultural, identity.[39] It may be that the family historian, due to his relatives' lack of interest, remains the sole seeker of truth and guardian of family secrets.[40]

What connects family memory and cultural memory is the fact that oral transmission is at one stage replaced, for instance, by documents. Cultural memory is based not only on what has been transmitted in memories, which can be fallible, but also on documents that make it possible to verify and consolidate the preserved oral message. Family memory, in order to last, must be based, on the one hand, on preserved memories and, on the other hand, on documents and photographs, which make it possible to preserve the image of the ancestors even when there are no more living witnesses of their character, personality, and emotions.[41] Besides, family histories, told or documented, are never isolated from national or local history; the latter gives context to the experiences of our ancestors.[42] For example, migrations were often triggered by either oppression in the place of origin, encouragement from the host country, or a combination of both. Therefore, oral memory often only makes sense when juxtaposed with an in-depth knowledge of what historical events influenced the fate of ancestors.

Family memory, thus, consists of oral memory and documentary memory. By combining these two types of memory, family history can be painstakingly reconstructed and inheritable knowledge about the family's past can be created.[43] Thus, genealogy is about reconstructing, documenting, and perpetuating family memory.

The challenge for the genealogist is to preserve family memory. Sometimes they must contend with their relatives' intentional or unconscious submersion of inconvenient or traumatic facts from the past. Particularly when family memories, confronted with either national memory or contemporary evaluation of history, reveal many discomforting facts in the life of a relative or ancestor, such can be passed over in silence, revised, or deliberately altered so that the next generation sees the ancestors as positive or neutral figures.[44] This applies, for instance, to perpetrators in dictatorships. Such non-memory is manifested in the attitude to which Welzer, Moller, and Tschuggnall dedicated their book *Opa war kein Nazi*.[45] In such instances, the genealogist often becomes an affirmation of Marcus L. Hansen's Law of the Third Generation, which states that "what the son wishes to forget, the grandson wishes to remember."[46] Their memory does not extend to uncomfortable or traumatic moments in their ancestors' lives, and even though they may have felt a family atmosphere filled with obscurities and understatements, they are emotionally ready to face them, and even feel the need to do so as part of their own work on their identity. In this case, the genealogist's motivation is not so much to preserve memory as to reconstruct it, to discover, and understand what has been silenced, to reveal what has been falsified and to work through the painful history of the family, to be able to construct one's own identity anew in truth.

Genealogy and (Hybrid) Identity

In trying to grasp the importance of genealogy for human identity, it is worth noting Assmann's distinction between *individual identity*, which refers to the contingency of a given life, with all its essential moments from birth to death, its corporeality, and all its basic needs, and *personal identity*, which refers to self-definition, social recognition, as well as affirmation and continuous negotiation of identity.[47] This self-definition is not merely limited to the discovery of one's individuality, but extends to that of one's communality.[48] It needs a context—a placement within a larger community with which we have something in common. In the process of discovering our very selves, we often intuitively discover that to provide meaning to who we are and to make sense of that self.[49] We need to reconstruct our family histories, because it was the unique combination of choices, attitudes, journeys, or illnesses of each and every of our most obscure ancestors, as well as the circumstances in which they lived, that have determined our existence and made us the persons we think we are.[50] Perceived personality traits may elicit a strong sense of identification with the collectivity that is the family, comprised of living relatives and deceased ancestors.[51] The importance of kinship and ancestry to one's identity becomes palpable when, in the course of a genealogical search, one recognizes that one's appearance, behavioral patterns, ailments, strengths and weaknesses were undeniably inherited from one's ancestors.[52] There comes the realization that personal identity is necessarily contained within, yet still shaped by, a collective, familial identity, and that personal ancestral traits, stories and choices continue to construct and reconstruct understandings of the self within one's broader social context.[53]

This realization is particularly poignant for people with a migration background. Even long established settlers or subsequent generations who were born in receiving countries cherish and pass on the memory of their past homeland.[54] They live with a sense of nostalgia at the thought of a time when "place, identity, culture, and ancestry coincided."[55] Regardless of what determined the migration of their ancestors and whether they belonged more to the category of the refugees, the "bearers of hope," or "the world players,"[56] ethnic interest is likely to resurrect[57] as subsequent generations living in the new country and separated from the old country are trying to find answers to the questions with which they struggle.[58] Therefore, the search for identity is often the same as the longing for the concept of one's home and homeland—no matter how vaguely grasped—to find and return to a locus of belonging and imagined community, as Paul Basu puts it.[59]

When conducting genealogical research, we find that we have more than one of these homelands. Even among people who would not categorize themselves as migrants, there is rarely a person whose ancestors all came from one region. Therefore, personal identity is impacted by a number of heritages associated with different places.[60] A person can easily identify with these different layers of heritage (the Matryoshka doll model, named after a traditional Russian toy consisting of a set of wooden, hollowed-out dolls, the smaller nested inside the larger) and see them as non-rivalrous and even mutually enriching.[61] As a result of the accumulation of cultural backgrounds, a *hybrid identity* is created, which involves a sense of belonging to more than one cultural or national group. This sense of multiple belonging is often not observed until the second generation of migrants, who— while maintaining emotional, cultural, linguistic, and memory ties to their homeland—successfully socialize in the host country and consider it theirs as well.[62] However, this sentiment may also be an incidental (while not necessarily secondary) effect of genealogical research. A third or subsequent generation may develop a sense of multiple belonging as a result of family history research that displaces the previously exclusive mono-affiliation with the host country in which not only they, but also their parents, and perhaps even grandparents were born.[63] The realization of this hybrid identity by the descendants of migrants may deepen their longing for the original homelands that remained outside the borders of the country, in which they were born and now inhabit.[64] Thus, Michel Foucault's words that through genealogical research one does not so much discover the roots of one's identity as commit oneself to its dissipation are particularly apt.[65]

Genealogy and Geography

Ancestry, like national and any other heritage, is intrinsically a spatial phenomenon.[66] It is tied to some area or place. The concept of place is central to a sense of identity, particularly collective identity, and is an essential factor in contextualizing, negotiating, and interpreting a sense of belonging.[67] Also, memory, to survive, needs anchor points; it needs a location that has witnessed past events and now epitomizes them.[68] However, Pierre Nora's argument that real environments of memory (*milieux de mémoire*) have been replaced by specific (and symbolic) sites or places (monuments) of memory (*lieux de mémoire*) does not seem to apply to our genealogical approach.[69] A family history researcher does not necessarily covet a symbolic landmark dedicated to an ancestor. They are rather interested in the land that still exists today on which the ancestor walked in a distant past. This necessarily involves coming to terms with the scenic differences between the past and the present, and in special cases, where there has been a shift of borders, migration, displacement, or extermination of an ethnic group, with the superseding of material traces of one culture by another. Although the landscape may have changed dramatically in the meantime, it can be experienced dynamically and can still inspire and create bonds with generations of ancestors.[70]

Genealogy is closely intertwined with geography. First, anthropogeography, particularly historical geography, provides the genealogist with vital information about historical patterns of migration, other demographic processes, and spatial networks of intra- and inter-familial relationships. Moreover, by providing a spatially situated sense of self,[71] it contributes to the construction of a personal identity associated with one's ethnic roots, family history, and ancestral home.[72] Paula Nicolson aptly speaks of "emotional geographies" because the genealogist usually creates a mental image of their ancestors' places of origin and connects with them emotionally even if they have never visited them.[73] Therefore, exploring and recreating the geography of family history plays such an important role in genealogical research.[74]

The orientation toward anthropogeography, especially historical, political, and denominational geography, is crucial for locating the parishes, offices, and archives in which sources about one's ancestor may be stored.[75] It presents a significant technical challenge for transborder genealogical research. Fortunately, advances in digital technology make genealogical research nearly unbounded by geography, as a wealth of information can be gleaned without moving from behind a desk.[76] It is undeniable that family history researchers need guidance and even concrete help in this area, but here, too, internet technologies, and social media come to the rescue. Genealogists doing research in a particular country find themselves in common interest groups and are happy to offer each other help.

MY FIVE YEARS OF TEACHING EXPERIENCE IN TRANSBORDER GENEALOGY

As a coordinator of the MA program "Strategies for European Cultural Heritage," specializing in the marketing and management of cultural heritage, I am also a genealogist with over thirty years of experience. Convinced of the rationale of elevating genealogy to an academic level, I have been running a one-semester course since 2018 at the School of Cultural Studies at the European University Viadrina entitled "Introduction to Genealogy in Poland." As I am keen to be able to support students individually throughout the course and to offer them the most targeted assistance possible, seats are limited and there are approximately ten students per semester taking the class. They are mostly female, which is consistent with the worldwide trend in genealogy.[77]

The Framework

The choice of Poland as a location for genealogical research is not accidental. The European University Viadrina sits right at the border between Germany and Poland. Its buildings are located both on the German bank of the Oder River (in Frankfurt (Oder)) and on its Polish bank (in Słubice). As a Polish national, I am well versed in the inner workings of the Polish archival landscape and its bureaucratic procedures. Having extensive practice in genealogical research, I can support students in their own efforts. In addition, there is an exceptionally large number of genealogical crowd-sourcing initiatives in Poland. A genealogist doing research in Poland has at his disposal not only the most popular, worldwide known databases (for instance, www.familysearch.org and www.ancestry.com) but also a huge and still growing number of thematic and regional genealogical search engines, which are continuously filled with information coming from the indexation of vital records carried out by hundreds of volunteers. Genealogical research is supported by the policy of Polish state archives, which under the Law on National Archival Holdings and Archives are obliged to make their holdings available free of charge.[78] In practice, this means that an increasing number of civil birth, marriage, and death certificates are being made available in digital form on the internet (on the State Archives' website, www.szukajwarchiwach.gov.pl). Additionally, visitors to the research reading rooms in the state archives may take photographs or make scans of the archival documents of interest to them without paying any fees.

Church archives are, by contrast, not as accessible as state archives. Each ecclesiastical (i.e., archdiocesan) archive has its own policy on accessibility: there is usually a fee for use, not every archive allows scans or photographs to be taken of its holdings, and in some cases the archives entrust the search to a selected commercial genealogical firm which must be contacted by an amateur genealogist to obtain the information of interest. However, in 2020, the library at the Collegium Polonicum in Słubice, where my genealogy classes are conducted, has been granted the status of a FamilySearch affiliated library, and thus has obtained privileges to limited-access FamilySearch databases containing microfilms of registry books from all over the world, including some of the Polish ecclesiastical archives.[79] These factors enable my students to conduct genealogical research in Poland either completely free of charge or at a relatively low cost, thus, not overburdening the budget of the average student.

Finally, Poland can be of genealogical interest to many students at the European University Viadrina. In recent years, the percentage of Poles among the student body has fluctuated between 6.3 and 7.7 percent.[80] However, among the students of German nationality, there are also many who, having a migration background, originate from present-day Poland. On the one hand, these are the children of Polish immigrants who moved to Germany in the 1980s and 1990s for economic reasons or after marrying a German partner. Students from this group at least have a passive, some even an excellent, command of the Polish language and maintain contact with their families in Poland. Another group is made up of the descendants of the indigenous Germans who, until 1945, inhabited, among others, the territories of Silesia, East Prussia, and West Prussia incorporated into Poland after World War II, and who under the terms of the Potsdam Conference were resettled west of the new border on the Oder and Lusatian Neisse. In the families of these students, the memory of the lost "country of childhood" left in the East is still cherished, prompting the students to discover the history of their ancestors. Finally, there are also students of other nationalities including Ukrainians, Belarusians, and Jews, whose family history has been more or less connected with the present Polish territory or with the so-called Polish Eastern Borderlands, which as a result of the Yalta Conference were incorporated into the USSR. Metric records from these eastern territories are also partly found in Polish archives and, therefore, are an object of genealogical research in Poland. The boundaries between these groups are not distinct, and often students whose ancestors belonged to different nationalities come to the course. However, the common denominator for the search remains the territory of Poland.

An undoubted advantage of students as adepts of genealogy is their age. Most of them are less than twenty-five years old, which means that in many cases they still have living grandparents and can make use of their memories, ideally going back two more generations to the person's great-great-grandparents. In addition, they are usually proficient in computer technology, allowing them to take full advantage of the growing genealogical resources available on the internet. Those who start their genealogical search at a later age, when all the relatives who remembered important details from the past have passed away, albeit having ample time for their research, have a much more difficult task, because they do not have the valuable support of the family transmission and communication memory of previous generations.[81]

Young age goes against the students in the sense that most of them have not yet acquired the necessary research skills. Moreover, descendants of Polish migrants or descendants of German families, especially the second and third generation, struggle with the language barrier. In the former case, their families have lost the necessary knowledge of the Polish language for communication with Polish registry offices and archives, while the latter families have never spoken the language. Young people also sometimes must deal with the reluctance of their parents and grandparents to dwell on the past. Although classes are conducted in a completely nonjudgmental and egalitarian atmosphere, students' enthusiasm for exploring family history is sometimes dampened by their relatives. While an ancestor's Nazi past may be one factor hindering genealogical research, another one is the complicated family relationships of some students, expressed in statements such as "My mother never met her biological father and my grandmother doesn't want to talk about him"; or "My father does not keep in touch with his parents and siblings"; or "My father abandoned our family when I was young. I don't know anything about the spear side of my family"; or "My great-grandmother is still alive, but to this day she does not want to tell my grandmother who her father is." Handling these factors requires great sensitivity. I gently encourage students to try to find creative ways to get the information they need without opening their relatives' old wounds, such as by trying to contact other family members who may have a less emotional attachment to a particular painful event and are willing to talk more openly about it.

The Overall Approach

Classes last for one semester and are divided into eight four-hour sessions held every fortnight. This allows each session to impart a good deal of theoretical knowledge and for learners to do the exercises that I will discuss in this section. The breaks between the sessions are long enough for the students to gather new knowledge about their ancestors. To begin with, they are asked to familiarize themselves with the family archives kept in their own homes and in the homes of their relatives. They are made aware of the types of documents they should look for in drawers, chests, and attics. They are instructed that the qualities they must arm themselves with are patience, perseverance, and inquisitiveness. Students are encouraged to involve their families in their genealogical research. They receive various forms and supporting materials from me for this purpose (e.g., ancestor charts and personal forms) which can help them in their discussions with relatives. It is particularly vital that their oldest relatives be involved in their genealogical research to obtain as much relevant information as possible from people who remember past events, can identify the place of origin of their ancestors, and above all, are able to identify the characters in surviving family photographs. Particularly in the case of personal memories and family photographs, genealogists are always running a race against time; when the last person who remembers a particular family event or who can recognize relatives in an old photograph dies, they take this knowledge or this ability with them to the grave. Therefore, students are constantly reminded that the acquisition of personal memories and the description of old photographs must always take priority over any search in archives. Archival collections are relatively safe and can be discovered and researched secondarily. This sequence of steps itself is also not without significance, because human memory can be unreliable, making it necessary to verify the memories of older relatives based on the vital records found.

During the first sessions, students are introduced to basic genealogical terms and a universal genealogical search methodology for any region of origin. They learn about the numbering systems for ancestors and descendants and how to graphically represent family relationships in the form of genealogical trees, tables, and charts. At the same time, I familiarize them with the exceptionally complicated historical developments within the present-day territory of Poland, the description of which goes far beyond the framework of this chapter. Suffice it to recall that for 123 years (1795–1918) Poland did not exist as a state, being partitioned by Prussia, Russia, and Austria, with the first two states conducting a brutal Germanisation and Russification policy on the territories they annexed. This territory was inhabited for hundreds of years by a multiethnic society. By 1945, the Jewish population of this area was almost completely exterminated in the German death camps and another political-ethnic reshuffle took place. The former Prussian territories became part of Poland, while the former Eastern Polish territories fell to the USSR. They became part of the Ukraine, Lithuania, and Belarus after the downfall of communism. When the Iron Curtain closed, many survivors of all faiths and nationalities who had been separated from their families because of the war, mass deportations, confinement in concentration camps and gulags, forced labor, and other random events were unable to find each other and reunite. They often lost all contact with each other for many decades or forever. Mass migrations and resettlements followed, making genealogical research a necessarily transborder endeavor for many of my students.

The Language Challenge

Given that students in my course are trying to explore their transnational heritage, a linguistic challenge arises. Due to the intricate history of Poland's territories, the vital records that genealogists must deal with were written in one of four languages: Polish, Latin, Russian, or German, depending on the period and partition in which they were established and on the religion of the person for which one is looking. In subsequent classes, we focus on vital records written in German, Latin, and Russian. Since Polish handwriting has not changed in the last two hundred years and, therefore, can be read by most modern Poles, it is easy to find a fellow student at the European University Viadrina who can help one read a manuscript. In contrast, old German-language manuscripts, which due to the almost complete disappearance of the ability to read the old German cursive (*Kurrentschrift*), commonly used in official writing in Germany until 1941, are virtually impossible to read even by most contemporary German native speakers.[82] Therefore, students are introduced to the letters in German cursive and then practice reading German-language metrics, gradually moving from easier and clearer notation to increasingly difficult ones. Despite the initial difficulties, students begin to read the metric documents with relative ease. They are helped by a very good, often native, knowledge of German, which allows them to guess the meaning of a word from its context, as well as by the repetitiveness of vocabulary in metric documents.

The next language that students must face is Latin. In this case, I take a slightly different approach. I first introduce the students to typical genealogical vocabulary in Latin, and then I show them nineteenth-century metrics in table form, as it is easier for them to find information in separate columns. Having practiced finding the information within the tables, we move on to older, usually eighteenth-century, metrics, written in the form of a continuous text with the order of information mostly depending on the preference and personal style of the priest. Therefore, with every new case, students must get used to the local form of writing to find and read the personal data of the persons appearing in the registry, dates, and other relevant information. Having tried several times, they begin to do well at this task.

Few of my students speak Russian. Apart from the language barrier, there is also a visual barrier due to unfamiliarity with the alphabet. Fortunately, there is a way to at least identify the metrics in which one is interested. As early as 1732, pursuant to a decree issued by Tsar Peter the Great, an all-Russian uniform method of producing birth, marriage, and death certificates was introduced, which was maintained until World War I in the Russian partition of Poland.[83] This means that each registry was compiled according to the same model, using almost identical phrases, and the individual information (dates, personal data, etc.) was placed in a fixed order, while the names of baptisms, marriages, and deaths were often written in brackets in Latin letters. In addition, most Russian-language books have an alphabetical index of names at the end of the calendar year, also often in Latin characters. With these tips, students who are not familiar with Russian can focus on finding and trying to read the names that interest them in a particular metric and then ask for help from their many colleagues of Russian, Ukrainian, or Belarusian origin studying at the European University Viadrina. As with metrics written in Polish, deciphering nineteenth-century Russian manuscripts is usually not a problem for most contemporary people fluent in Russian.[84]

Further Teaching Challenges and Methods

The multitude of online genealogical search engines in Poland have their advantages and disadvantages from the point of view of their potential users. On the one hand, numerous initiatives undertaken by genealogists in various regions of Poland, thanks to which more and more data is available, should be appreciated. On the other hand, users must first know all these search engines and then must learn how to use them, while these tools are not always completely intuitive. This can be an obstacle, especially for foreigners, and particularly in the case of those search engines that do not have an English or German-language interface. Therefore, students are taught to use the most high-ranking genealogical search engines. Moreover, the existence of search engines can often be deceptive to the younger generation of genealogists who are accustomed to finding everything on the internet. When students do not find scans of the genealogical records, they were looking for, they tend to conclude that their search is over and that these records simply do not exist. I make them aware that proper names were sometimes passed down only orally in the past, which led to their frequent defacement and alteration, thus making it necessary to look for similar sounding but differently spelled versions of the names.[85] I also make them aware that their genealogical research must extend beyond search engines. This means starting the painstaking search for their metrics of interest in the yet unindexed collections of state and church archives.

Hence, another important element of the course is teaching students how to use the primary resources of state and church archives. Terms such as archival collection name and archival unit number are introduced, and students learn how to formulate their queries to these institutions. Due to the long distances separating most Polish archives from the European University Viadrina, conducting archival research on one's own is usually not an option for students even during non-pandemic periods. Therefore, their archival searches must be commissioned by correspondence. Students receive a set of universal text modules in Polish and German for this purpose. These text modules can be combined with each other to compose an appropriate, and duly specific, query to a given archive. In addition, students are encouraged to make use of digital libraries (for instance, www.polona.pl), which are growing each year with many scanned archival newspapers. Browsing through them can reveal surprising facts about the daily lives of ancestors, or even their obituaries, which can also provide a wealth of information for one's genealogical research.

Usually, the fifth or sixth session takes the form of an individual consultation, allowing each student to approach me with their specific research problem. This enables me to give them more assistance and guidance for their research. During the penultimate session, I usually quiz students on their ability to use genealogical search engines and the archival resources available on the internet. I give them assignments to find, with small clues on my part, specific data on selected people living in the nineteenth and early twentieth centuries. The tasks are interrelated—finding the correct answer to the first question asked is a prerequisite for solving the next task. During this (ungraded) quiz, I gain definitive confirmation as to whether the person has a genealogical potential, or whether the student struggles to research and piece together the myriad of facts, circumstances, and premises.

I place great importance on accustoming students to conducting their research diligently and systematically and to documenting the results carefully. As a final credit, students are asked to maintain a family tree on any online platform of their choice (e.g., www.myheritage.com, www.ancestry.com) or in another format. In addition, they are required to keep a binder in which they carefully document their findings. The binder must include separate personal forms set up for each ancestor who receives their permanent number according to the Stephan Kekulé method also known as the Sosa-Stradonitz method.[86] These forms are to be constantly supplemented and enriched with photographs, birth/marriage/death certificates, and other documents, carefully noting the sources of the information obtained. The binder should also contain copies of correspondence with family members, archives, registry offices, and other institutions. It will serve as an invaluable reference point enabling the students to quickly identify gaps in their genealogical raw framework in the future, even if they have to abandon their research for a while.[87]

The last class is devoted to the presentation of research results. Students are asked to give a visual representation of the initial and current state of their research (by demonstrating how much they have expanded their family trees over the course of the semester). In addition, they are asked to discuss their most important discoveries and the biggest obstacles or brick walls they have encountered that may not have yet been overcome. I do not base the final grade on the number of ancestors found, as the students' chances are very unequal. Some are fortunate in that their ancestors lived in the same locality for several generations, and their vital records are easily available on the internet. Others have little family documentation and memories to sift through.[88] They have to struggle, for example, with the constant loss of traces due to the frequent migration of their ancestors, with the inaccessibility of vital records irretrievably lost to fire or warfare, or have to search painstakingly and creatively for information about a great-grandfather who was killed as a young man during World War I, and no one knows where he came from or who his parents were anymore. Some students have a long wait for the results of a commissioned archival search, on which the success and pace of further research depends. Therefore, my assessment is mainly governed by the commitment and diligence with which the students have conducted their research throughout the semester.

CONCLUSION

There is a reason why I introduce myself to the students in my first class in the manner adopted at Alcoholics Anonymous meetings (*My name is Izabella, and I am* an alcoholic *a genealogist.*). I warn them that genealogy is addictive, that many of them will not settle with just a one-semester course, but will develop an irrepressible passion that, as in treasure hunters, can only be satisfied temporarily by new discoveries and that this hunger to discover more and more pieces of family history will stay with them forever. This warning sticks with students, and by the second or third class I usually begin hearing admissions that it has already been fulfilled. The fact that precious moments of discovery are almost always preceded by wearisome hours of research does not discourage them.[89] In many cases, initial curiosity turns into determination to reconstruct as many details of one's own family's past as possible with all available means. Student evaluations often reflect that this is the first university course in which the participants have finally done (and learned) something for themselves. The effect of their efforts is truly sustainable, as they embark on a life-long, emotional, intellectual, and symbolic journey (for even if the genealogist must sometimes interrupt the search, they will inevitably return to it) that is also a life-long learning endeavor.[90] Students not only learn about their family history; nor do they only improve their research skills. The gradual discovery of discontinuous knowledge and focus on the past helps them understand their personal and familial present.[91] As they gain a better understanding of their personal and familial *heritage*, also in terms of spatial and transborder dimensions, they eventually realize that a clear answer to the question of identity is almost never possible.[92] Moreover, their genealogical research usually has an integrative effect: bridging between living and deceased family members, it also brings together living generations.[93] Many students succeed in overcoming the initial reserve or reluctance of their loved ones, infecting their families with their passion. Thus, they gain another skill, namely, collaborative learning.[94] Not insignificantly, genealogical research usually contributes to students and their families developing a positive emotional attitude toward their deceased family members, making them empathetic toward the difficult choices their ancestors made and the not-so-positive facts of the family history they discovered.[95] Often, I find that the entire extended family has become involved in the genealogical search, and many family secrets have been uncovered or verified. Some students manage to reestablish long-broken ties with distant relatives to the delight of both parties. The most recent example is that of a student who, through a genealogy platform, reached out to her late great-grandmother's ninety-six-year-old sister and, with the help of her children, was able to have a long, and very fruitful, conversation with her over the internet.

Because genealogy is by definition a very personal endeavor, teaching it as an academic discipline is challenging since the basic knowledge of each person's family history cannot be taught.[96] In fact, teaching transborder genealogy is as complex as genealogy itself. What I can give my students is universal methodological guidance, specific knowledge about genealogical research in Poland in the context of its complex history, a wealth of tools in the form of specimen metrics, alphabets, and historical maps, while remaining aware that genealogy continues to present family history researchers with new challenges, forcing them to seek additional tools and research aids. My course is not the place for judging the past. The focus of the class is solely on data acquisition; its interpretation and the possible need for coming to terms with the past is naturally left to the students and their families.[97] At the same time, I make sure to offer emotional support to students when they make unexpected and painful discoveries about difficult facts in family history. I continuously strive to provide a stimulating and supportive context for learning, to develop in students a vein of detective work, and to conquer their inner resistance resulting from prevailing against language, international, and historical barriers. In fact, the Polish-German border in the context of genealogical research appears as a twofold, but still traversable threshold. Behind it lies not only another country, but also the family past left behind.

Genealogical research can also inspire in-depth academic work. Those students who have more extant material on their ancestors may consider whether it can be used in writing a term paper or perhaps even an undergraduate or graduate thesis. In a recent course, there was a student who found the handwritten diaries of her great-grandfather, a German soldier, written for his wife from the Eastern Front and richly illustrated by him.

I encouraged the student to consider, in consultation with her study supervisor, how this unique material could be used if she considered the broader historical context and presented it, for example, in the form of a term paper or a website. There is no doubt that rigorous, scholarly work on a topic that is the subject of a student's personal passion will be far more exciting and rewarding than completing a task that does not evoke much emotion. It also provides a unique opportunity to restore marginalized or forgotten people to their place in history, to enrich universal history with previously unknown facts and aspects, knowledge of which is preserved only in family transmission or documentation, while contextualizing family memories in light of broader history.[98]

Genealogy is often treated rather condescendingly by some historians and cultural heritage specialists as a kind of harmless, not very serious hobby. This judgment is not only very unfair; its endurance greatly impoverishes the potential of the research carried out in both these fields. As a reader of history and biographies, I have more than once noticed in such serious works that there were omissions or misrepresentations of basic facts about the person studied, which were indicative of a failure on the part of the historian or biographer to carry out basic genealogical research. Occasionally I would try to establish these impossible to ascertain facts, and it turned out that the missing genealogical data was readily available. All it took was knowing how to look and where. Simultaneously, it often escapes the attention of heritage professionals that the "micro heritage" of individuals and families is an important (though not always realized) component of regional, national, and global heritage. Just as it is never fully known what treasures of material culture are still kept in private homes, carefully preserved from generation to generation as valued family heirlooms, the memories, stories, and traditions preserved by individual families—their unique intangible heritage—remain undiscovered as well. Yet this is a heritage that is by all means worthy of being saved from oblivion, preserved and passed on to future generations. This is why many research projects in history would greatly benefit from broadening their scope to include tasks in which genealogists specialize. In other words, the added value of genealogy to scholarship is virtually unlimited. This presents another compelling argument for genealogy to become a fully fledged academic discipline.

NOTES

1. While not everyone is raised by their biological parents, and a person may have very strong emotional ties to their adoptive parents (even stronger than to their birth parents), the essence of genealogical research is precisely to find information

about those people with whom that person has blood ties and who are their biological ancestors, that is, lineage and family in the genetic sense.

2. Eviatar Zerubavel, *Ancestors & Relatives. Genealogy, Identity, & Community*, New York: Oxford University Press, 2021, 131.

3. Adolf Bocheński, "Funkcje społeczne ruchu heraldycznego i rodzinoznawczego w Polsce," *Herold. Organ Kolegjum Heraldycznego* 2 (1932): 32–36.

4. Jeanne Kay Guelke and Dallen J. Timothy, "Locating Personal Pasts: An Introduction," in: Dallen J. Timothy and Jeanne Kay Guelke (eds.), *Geography and Genealogy: Locating Personal Pasts*, Aldershot: Ashgate, 2008, 1–20.

5. Arnon Hershkovitz, "A Suggested Taxonomy of Genealogy as a Multidisciplinary Academic Research Field," *Journal of Multidisciplinary Research* 4, no. 3 (2012): 5–21.

6. Zerubavel, *Ancestors & Relatives*, 16.

7. Zerubavel, *Ancestors & Relatives*, 16–19.

8. Anna Green, "Intergenerational Family Stories: Private, Parochial, Pathological?" *Journal of Family History* 38, no. 4 (2013): 387–402.

9. Gérôme Truc, "A Halbwachsian Socio-Ethnography of Collective Memory," *International Social Science Journal*, 62 (2011): 147–159.

10. Robert A. Stebbins, *Serious Leisure: A Perspective for Our Time*, New Brunswick: Transaction Publishers, 2007, 3.

11. Jill Lepore, "Historians Who Love Too Much: Reflections on Microhistory and Biography," *Journal of American History*, 88, no. 1 (2001): 129–144.

12. In continental European tradition, history is considered a science and genealogy an auxiliary science of history (in German: *historische Hilfswissenschaft*.)

13. Thomas W. Jones, *Postsecondary Study of Genealogy: Curriculum and its Context* (https://avotaynuonline.com/2007/10/postsecondary-study-of-genealogy-curriculum-and-its-contexts-by-thomas-w-jones-phd-cg-cgl-fasg/, accessed September 28, 2021); Hershkovitz, "A Suggested Taxonomy of Genealogy," 7.

14. Bruce Durie, "What Is Genealogy? Philosophy, Education, Motivations and Future Prospects," *Genealogy* 1, no. 4 (2017): 1–7; Hershkovitz, "A Suggested Taxonomy of Genealogy."

15. Tanya Evans, "The Emotions of Family History and the Development of Historical Knowledge," *The Journal of Theory and Practice*, 24, no. 3–4 (2020): 310–331.

16. Arnon Hershkovitz, *Leveraging Genealogy as an Academic Discipline* (https://avotaynuonline.com/2016/09/leveraging-genealogy-academic-discipline/, accessed September 28, 2021).

17. Bruce Durie, "What Is Genealogy?": 1–7.

18. Casey Daniel Hoeve, "Finding a Place for Genealogy and Family History in the Digital Humanities,"*Digital Library Perspectives* 34, no. 3 (2018): 215–226.

19. Arnon Hershkovitz and Sharon Hardof-Jaffe, "Genealogy as a Lifelong Learning Endeavor," *Leisure/Loisir* 41, no. 4 (2017): 535–560.

20. Werner Zurek, *Ahnen- und Familienforschung in Polen leicht gemacht. Ein praktischer Ratgeber, Leitfaden und Forschungshilfe für Deutsche und Polen*, Frankfurt am Main: R.G. Fischer Verlag, 2014, 11.

21. Zurek, *Ahnen- und Familienforschung in Polen leicht gemacht*, 13.

22. Diana Hart, "Other Ways of Knowing: The Intersection of Education when Researching Family Roots," *Genealogy* 2, no. 2 (2018): 1–19.

23. Catherine Nash, "'They're Family!': Cultural Geographies of Relatedness in Popular Genealogy," in: Sara Ahmed, Claudia Castada, Anne-Marie Fortier, and Mimi Sheller (eds.), *Uprootings/Regroundings: Questions of Home and Migration*, Oxford: Berg, 2003, 179–203.

24. Arnon Hershkovitz, "Genealogy and Learning Among Teenagers," *Proceedings of the Symposium on Genealogy and the Sciences* (2018): 37–46.

25. Malcolm S. Knowles, *Self-directed Learning. A Guide for Learners and Teachers*, New York: The Adult Education, 1975, 18.

26. D. Randy Garrison, "Self-directed learning: Toward a Comprehensive Model," *Adult Education Quarterly* 48, no. 1 (1997): 18–33.

27. Hershkovitz and Hardof-Jaffe, "Genealogy as a Lifelong Learning Endeavor," 542.

28. Jennifer Bowering Delisle, "'Genealogical Nostalgia': Second-Generation Memory and Return in Caterina Edwards' Finding Rosa," *Memory Studies* 5, no. 2 (2012): 131–44.

29. Evans, "The Emotions of Family History and the Development of Historical Knowledge," 322.

30. Hart, "Other Ways of Knowing," 1, 4.

31. Carla Almeida Santos and Grace Yan, "Genealogical Tourism: A Phenomenological Examination," *Journal of Travel Research* 49, no. 1 (2010): 56–67.

32. Roy Rosenzweig and David P. Thelen, *The Presence of the Past. Popular Uses of History in American Life*, New York: Columbia University Press, 1998, 45–52.

33. Julia Watson, "Ordering the Family: Genealogy as Autobiographical Pedigree," in: Sidonie Smith and Julia Watson (eds.), *Getting A Life, Everyday Uses of Autobiography*, Minneapolis: University of Minnesota Press, 1996, 297–326.

34. Maurice Halbwachs, *Das Gedächtnis und seine sozialen Bedingungen*, Frankfurt am Main: Suhrkamp, 1985, 163–202.

35. Green, "Intergenerational Family Stories," 391.

36. Jan Assmann, *Das kulturelle Gedächtnis. Schrift, Erinnerung und politische Identität in früheren Hochkulturen*, Munich: Verlag C. H. Beck, 1992, 50.

37. Harald Welzer, Sabine Moller, and Karoline Tschuggnall, *"Opa war kein Nazi." Nationalsozialismus und Holocaust im Familiengedächtnis*, Frankfurt am Main: Fischer Taschenbuch, 2021, 13.

38. Truc, "A Halbwachsian Socio-Ethnography of Collective Memory," 152.

39. Jan Assmann, "Communicative and Cultural Memory," in: Astrid Erll and Ansgar Nünning (eds.), *Cultural Memory Studies. An International and Interdisciplinary Handbook*, Berlin: De Gruyter, 2008, 109–118.

40. Matthew Stallard and Jerome de Groot, "'Things Are Coming Out That Are Questionable, We Never Knew About': DNA and the New Family History," *Journal of Family History* 45, no. 3 (2020): 274–94.

41. Green, "Intergenerational Family Stories," 391.

42. Katie Barclay and Nina Javette Koefoed, "Family, Memory, and Identity: An Introduction," *Journal of Family History* 46, no. 1 (2021): 3–12.
43. Hershkovitz and Hardof-Jaffe, "Genealogy as a Lifelong Learning Endeavor," 551.
44. Barclay and Koefoed, "Family, Memory, and Identity," 6.
45. Welzer, Moller, and Tschuggnall, *"Opa war kein Nazi."*
46. Marcus L. Hansen, *The Problem of the Third Generation Immigrant*, Rock Island, Illinois Augustana Historical Society, 1938.
47. Assmann, *Das kulturelle Gedächtnis*, 132, 142.
48. Michael Erben, "Genealogy and Sociology: A Preliminary Set of Statements and Speculations," *Sociology* 25, no. 2 (1991): 275–92.
49. Robert Ball, "Visualizing Genealogy through a Family-Centric Perspective," *Information Visualization* 16, no. 1 (2017): 74–89.
50. Paula Nicolson, *Genealogy, Psychology and Identity*, London/New York: Routledge, 2017, 102.
51. Green, "Intergenerational Family Stories," 395.
52. Anne-Marie Kramer, "Kinship, Affinity and Connectedness: Exploring the Role of Genealogy in Personal Lives," *Sociology* 45, no. 3 (2011): 379–395.
53. Rina Benmayor and Andor Skotnes, "Some Reflections on Migrations and Identity," in: Rina Benmayor and Andor Skotnes (eds.), *Migration and Identity*, New York/London: Routledge, 2017, 1–18.
54. Ralph Grillo, "The Family in Dispute: Insiders and Outsiders," in: Ralph Grillo (ed.), *The Family in Question, Immigrant and Ethnic Minorities in Multicultural Europe*, Amsterdam: Amsterdam University Press, 15–36.
55. Nash, "'They're Family!'" 179.
56. Verena Vordermayer, *Identitätsfalle oder Weltbürgertum? Zur praktischen Grundlegung der Migranten-Identität*, Wiesbaden: VS Verlag für Sozialwissenschaften/Springer Fachmedien, 2012, 43, 46.
57. Cardell K. Jacobson, "Social Dislocations and the Search for Genealogical Roots," *Human Relations* 39, no. 4 (1986): 347–57.
58. Ball, "Visualizing Genealogy through a Family-Centric Perspective," 75.
59. Paul Basu, "My Own Island Home: The Orkney Homecoming," *Journal of Material Culture* 9, no. 1 (2004): 27–42. See also: David Brett, *The Construction of Heritage*, Cork: Cork University Press, 1996, 8–9.
60. Gregory Ashworth, Brian Graham, and John Tunbridge, *Pluralising Pasts. Heritage, Identity and Place in Multicultural Societies*, London/Ann Arbor: Pluto Press, 2007, 4.
61. Gregory Ashworth and Peter Howard, *European Heritage: Planning and Management*, Exeter/Portland: Intellect Ltd, 1999, 60.
62. Consuela Wagner, "Migration and the Creation of Hybrid Identity: Chances and Challenges," *Research Association for Interdisciplinary Studies* 16 (2016): 237–255.
63. Wagner, "Migration and the Creation of Hybrid Identity: Chances and Challenges," 242.

64. Yaakov Bayer, "Memory and Belonging: The Social Construction of a Collective Memory During the Intercultural Transition of Immigrants from Argentina in Israel," *International Journal of Multidisciplinary Research Review* 8, no. 1 (2016): 5–27.

65. Michel Foucault, "Nietzsche, Genealogy, History," in: Donald F. Bouchard (ed.), *Language, Counter-memory, Practice: Selected Essays and Interviews*, Ithaca: Cornell University Press, 1977, 139–164.

66. Brian Graham, Gregory J. Ashworth, and John Tunbridge, *A Geography of Heritage. Power, Culture & Economy*, London: Arnold, 2000, 4–5.

67. Laurajane Smith, *Uses of Heritage*, London/New York: Routledge, 2006, 75, 77.

68. Assmann, *Das kulturelle Gedächtnis*, 39.

69. Pierre Nora, "Between Memory and History: Les Lieux de Memoire," *Representations* 26 (1989): 7–24.

70. Robert S. Nelson and Margaret Olin, *Monuments and Memory, Made and Unmade*, Chicago/London: The University of Chicago Press, 2003, 74.

71. Catherine Nash, "Genealogical Identities," *Environment and Planning D: Society and Space* 20, no. 1 (2002): 27–52.

72. Samuel M. Otterstrom and Brian E. Bunker, "Genealogy, Migration, and the Intertwined Geographies of Personal Pasts," *Annals of the Association of American Geographers* 103, no. 3 (2013): 544–569.

73. Nicolson, *Genealogy, Psychology and Identity*, 73; Truc, "A Halbwachsian Socio-Ethnography of Collective Memory," 151.

74. Graham, Ashworth, and Tunbridge, *A Geography of Heritage*, 4–5.

75. Rafał T. Prinke, "Genealogical Tourism: An Overlooked Niche," *Rodziny. The Journal of the Polish Genealogical Society of America* (2010): 16–23.

76. Anna Fenyvesi, "Digital Genealogy," *Hungarian Studies* 2, no. 1 (2020): 75–86.

77. Hershkovitz and Hardof-Jaffe, "Genealogy as a Lifelong Learning Endeavor," 538.

78. *The Law on National Archival Holdings and Archives,* Art. 16c (http://isap.sejm.gov.pl/isap.nsf/download.xsp/WDU20200000164/O/D20200164.pdf, accessed September 29, 2021).

79. *FamilySearch Affiliate Libraries* (https://www.familysearch.org/wiki/en/FamilySearch_Affiliate_Libraries, accessed September 29, 2021).

80. *Entwicklung der Gesamtstudierendenzahl und des Ausländeranteils* (https://www.europa-uni.de/de/struktur/verwaltung/dezernat_1/statistiken/Entwicklung-der-Gesamtstudierendenzahl.pdf, accessed September 29, 2021).

81. Jacobson, "Social Dislocations and the Search for Genealogical Roots," 347.

82. Joanna Drejer and Izabella Parowicz, *Kurrenta. Zeszyt ćwiczeń do nauki pisma neogotyckiego*, Słubice: Fundacja Dobro Kultury, 2021, 5.

83. Paweł Hałuszczak, *Niezbędnik Genealoga*, Mnichowo-Poznań: Wielkopolskie Towarzystwo Genealogiczne "Gniazdo", 2012, 41.

84. While Russian handwriting has not undergone any significant modifications in the last two hundred years, one ought to bear in mind that as a result of the 1917 spelling reform, three letters that had appeared in older manuscripts were eliminated from the Russian alphabet.

85. Helmut Ivo, *Familienforschung leicht gemacht. Anleitungen, Methoden, Tipps*, Munich/Zurich: Piper Verlag, 2010, 132.
86. Ivo, *Familienforschung leicht gemacht*, 39–40.
87. Ivo, *Familienforschung leicht gemacht*, 36.
88. Tanya Evans, "How Do Family Historians Work with Memory?" *Journal of Family History* 46, no. 1 (2021): 92–106.
89. Nash, "Genealogical Identities," 29.
90. Prinke, "Genealogical Tourism: An Overlooked Niche," 21; Hart, "Other Ways of Knowing," 13.
91. Kate Kearins and Keith Hooper, "Genealogical Method and Analysis," *Accounting, Auditing & Accountability Journal* 15, no. 5 (2002): 733–757.
92. Nash, "Genealogical Identities," 49.
93. Hershkovitz and Hardof-Jaffe, "Genealogy as a Lifelong Learning Endeavor," 550.
94. Hershkovitz, "Genealogy and Learning Among Teenagers," 39.
95. Hershkovitz, "Genealogy and Learning Among Teenagers," 39; Hart, "Other Ways of Knowing," 9.
96. Hershkovitz and Hardof-Jaffe, "Genealogy as a Lifelong Learning Endeavor," 552.
97. Gabriele Rosenthal and Claudia Gather, *Die Hitlerjugend-Generation: biographische Thematisierung als Vergangenheitsbewältigung*, Essen: Die Blaue Eule, 1986.
98. Barclay and Koefoed. "Family, Memory, and Identity," 7.

BIBLIOGRAPHY

Primary Sources

Entwicklung der Gesamtstudierendenzahl und des Ausländeranteils, available online: https://www.europa-uni.de/de/struktur/verwaltung/dezernat_1/statistiken/Entwicklung-der-Gesamtstudierendenzahl.pdf (accessed September 29, 2021).

FamilySearch Affiliate Libraries, available online: https://www.familysearch.org/wiki/en/FamilySearch_Affiliate_Libraries (accessed September 29, 2021).

Hershkovitz, Arnon. "Leveraging Genealogy as an Academic Discipline," available online: https://avotaynuonline.com/2016/09/leveraging-genealogy-academic-discipline/ (accessed September 28, 2021).

Jones, Thomas W. "Postsecondary Study of Genealogy: Curriculum and its Context," available online: https://avotaynuonline.com/2007/10/postsecondary-study-of-genealogy-curriculum-and-its-contexts-by-thomas-w-jones-phd-cg-cgl-fasg/ (accessed September 28, 2021).

"The Law on National Archival Holdings and Archives, Art. 16c." In Dziennik Ustaw Rzeczypospolitej Polskiej, Warszawa February 3rd 2020, 164, 9, available online: http://isap.sejm.gov.pl/isap.nsf/download.xsp/WDU20200000164/O/D20200164.pdf (accessed September 29, 2021).

Secondary Sources

Almeida Santos, Carla, and Grace Yan. "Genealogical Tourism: A Phenomenological Examination." *Journal of Travel Research* 49, 1 (2010): 56–67.
Ashworth, Gregory, Brian Graham, and John Tunbridge. *Pluralising Pasts: Heritage, Identity and Place in Multicultural Societies.* London and Ann Arbor: Pluto Press, 2007.
Ashworth, Gregory, and Peter Howard. *European Heritage. Planning and Management.* Exeter and Portland: Intellect Ltd, 1999.
Assmann, Jan. "Communicative and Cultural Memory." In *Cultural Memory Studies: An International and Interdisciplinary Handbook*, edited by Astrid Erll and Ansgar Nünning. Berlin: De Gruyter, 2008, 109–118.
Assmann, Jan. *Das kulturelle Gedächtnis. Schrift, Erinnerung und politische Identität in früheren Hochkulturen.* München: Verlag C. H. Beck, 1992.
Ball, Robert. "Visualizing Genealogy Through a Family-Centric Perspective." *Information Visualization* 16, no. 1 (2017): 74–89.
Barclay, Katie, and Nina Javette Koefoed. "Family, Memory, and Identity: An Introduction." *Journal of Family History* 46, no. 1 (2021): 3–12.
Basu, Paul. "My Own Island Home: The Orkney Homecoming." *Journal of Material Culture* 9, no. 1 (2004): 27–42.
Bayer, Yaakov. "Memory and Belonging: The Social Construction of a Collective Memory During the Intercultural Transition of Immigrants From Argentina in Israel." *International Journal of Multidisciplinary Research Review* 8 (2016): 5–27.
Benmayor, Rina, and Andor Skotnes. "Some Reflections on Migrations and Identity." In *Migration and Identity*, edited by Rina Benmayor and Andor Skotnes. New York and London: Routledge, 2017, 1–18.
Bocheński, Adolf. "Funkcje społeczne ruchu heraldycznego i rodzinoznawczego w Polsce." *Herold. Organ Kolegjum Heraldycznego* 2 (1932): 32–36.
Bowering Delisle, Jennifer. "'Genealogical Nostalgia': Second-Generation Memory and Return in Caterina Edwards' Finding Rosa." *Memory Studies* 5, no. 2 (2012): 131–144.
Brett, David. *The Construction of Heritage.* Cork: Cork University Press, 1996.
Drejer, Joanna, and Izabella Parowicz. *Kurrenta. Zeszyt ćwiczeń do nauki pisma neogotyckiego.* Słubice: Fundacja Dobro Kultury, 2021.
Durie, Bruce. "What Is Genealogy? Philosophy, Education, Motivations and Future Prospects." *Genealogy* 1, no. 4 (2017): 1–7.
Erben, Michael. "Genealogy and Sociology: A Preliminary Set of Statements and Speculations." *Sociology* 25, no. 2 (1991): 275–292.
Evans, Tanya. "The Emotions of Family History and the Development of Historical Knowledge." *The Journal of Theory and Practice* 24, nos. 3–4 (2020): 310–331.
Evans, Tanya. "How Do Family Historians Work with Memory?" *Journal of Family History* 46, no. 1 (2021): 92–106.
Fenyvesi, Anna. "Digital Genealogy." *Hungarian Studies* 2, no. 1 (2020): 75–86.
Foucault, Michel. "Nietzsche, Genealogy, History." In *Language, Counter-Memory, Practice: Selected Essays and Interviews*, edited by Donald F. Bouchard. Ithaca: Cornell University Press, 139–164.

Garrison, D. Randy. "Self-Directed Learning: Toward a Comprehensive Model." *Adult Education Quarterly* 48, no. 1 (1997): 18–33.
Graham, Brian, Gregory J. Ashworth, and John Tunbridge. *A Geography of Heritage: Power, Culture & Economy*. London: Routledge, 2000.
Green, Anna. "Intergenerational Family Stories: Private, Parochial, Pathological?" *Journal of Family History* 38, no. 4 (2013): 387–402.
Grillo, Ralph. "The Family in Dispute: Insiders and Outsiders." In *The Family in Question, Immigrant and Ethnic Minorities in Multicultural Europe*, edited by Ralph Grillo. Amsterdam: Amsterdam University Press, 2008, 15–36.
Guelke, Jeanne Kay, and Dallen J. Timothy. "Locating Personal Pasts: An Introduction." In *Geography and Genealogy. Locating Personal Past*, edited by Dallen J. Timothy and Jeanne Kay Guelke. Aldershot: Ashgate, 2008, 1–20.
Halbwachs, Maurice. *Das Gedächtnis und seine sozialen Bedingungen*. Frankfurt am Main: Suhrkamp, 1985.
Hałuszczak, Paweł. *Niezbędnik Genealoga*. Mnichowo-Poznań: Wielkopolskie Towarzystwo Genealogiczne "Gniazdo", 2012.
Hansen, Marcus L. *The Problem of the Third Generation Immigrant*. Rock Island: Illinois Augustana Historical Society, 1938.
Hart, Diana. "Other Ways of Knowing: The Intersection of Education When Researching Family Roots." *Genealogy* 2, no. 2 (2018): 1–19.
Herskowitz, Arnon. "A Suggested Taxonomy of Genealogy as a Multidisciplinary Academic Research Field." *Journal of Multidisciplinary Research* 4, no. 3 (2012): 5–21.
Hershkovitz, Arnon. "Genealogy and Learning Among Teenagers." *Proceedings of the Symposium on Genealogy and the Sciences* 2018: 37–46.
Hershkovitz, Arnon, and Hardof-Jaffe Sharon. "Genealogy as a Lifelong Learning Endeavor." *Leisure/Loisir* 41, no. 4 (2017): 535–560.
Hoeve, Casey Daniel. "Finding a Place for Genealogy and Family History in the Digital Humanities." *Digital Library Perspectives* 34, no. 3 (2018): 215–226.
Ivo, Helmut. *Familienforschung leicht gemacht. Anleitungen, Methoden, Tipps*. Munich and Zurich: Piper Verlag, 2010.
Jacobson, Cardell K. "Social Dislocations and the Search for Genealogical Roots." *Human Relations* 39, no. 4 (1986): 347–357.
Kearins, Kate, and Keith Hooper. "Genealogical Method and Analysis." *Accounting, Auditing & Accountability Journal* 15, no. 5 (2002): 733–757.
Knowles, Malcolm S. *Self-directed Learning: A Guide for Learners and Teachers*. New York: The Adult Education, 1975.
Kramer, Anne-Marie. "Kinship, Affinity and Connectedness: Exploring the Role of Genealogy in Personal Lives." *Sociology* 45, no. 3 (2011): 379–395.
Lepore, Jill. "Historians Who Love Too Much: Reflections on Microhistory and Biography." *Journal of American History* 88, no. 1 (2001): 129–144.
Nash, Catherine. "Genealogical Identities." *Environment and Planning D: Society and Space* 20, no. 1 (2002): 27–52.
Nash, Catherine. "'They're Family!': Cultural Geographies of Relatedness in Popular Genealogy." In *Uprootings/Regroundings: Questions of Home and Migration*,

edited by Sara Ahmed, Claudia Castada, Anne-Marie Fortier, and Mimi Sheller. Oxford: Berg, 2003, 179–203.

Nelson, Robert S., and Margaret Olin. *Monuments and Memory, Made and Unmade.* Chicago and London: The University of Chicago Press, 2003.

Nicolson, Paula. *Genealogy, Psychology and Identity.* London and New York: Routledge, 2017.

Nora, Pierre. "Between Memory and History: Les Lieux de Memoire." *Representations* 26 (1989): 7–24.

Otterstrom, Samuel M., and Brian E Bunker. "Genealogy, Migration, and the Intertwined Geographies of Personal Pasts." *Annals of the Association of American Geographers* 103, no. 3 (2013): 544–569.

Prinke, Rafał T. "Genealogical Tourism: An Overlooked Niche." *Rodziny. The Journal of the Polish Genealogical Society of America* (2010): 16–23.

Rosenthal, Gabriele, and Claudia Gather. *Die Hitlerjugend-Generation: biographische Thematisierung als Vergangenheitsbewältigung.* Essen: Die Blaue Eule, 1986.

Rosenzweig, Roy, and David P. Thelen. *The Presence of the Past. Popular Uses of History in American Life.* New York: Columbia University Press, 1998.

Smith, Laurajane. *Uses of Heritage.* London and New York: Routledge, 2006.

Stallard, Matthew, and Jerome de Groot. "'Things Are Coming Out That Are Questionable, We Never Knew About': DNA and the New Family History." *Journal of Family History* 45, no. 3 (2020): 274–294.

Stebbins, Robert A. *Serious Leisure: A Perspective for Our Time.* New Brunswick: Transaction Publishers, 2007.

Truc, Gérôme. "A Halbwachsian Socio-Ethnography of Collective Memory." *International Social Science Journal* 62 (2011): 147–159.

Vordermayer, Verena. *Identitätsfalle oder Weltbürgertum? Zur praktischen Grundlegung der Migranten-Identität.* Wiesbaden: VS Verlag für Sozialwissenschaften/Springer Fachmedien, 2012.

Wagner, Consuela. "Migration and the Creation of Hybrid Identity: Chances and Challenges." *Research Association for Interdisciplinary Studies* 16 (2016): 237–255.

Watson, Julia. "Ordering the Family: Genealogy as Autobiographical Pedigree." In *Getting a Life, Everyday Uses of Autobiography*, edited by Sidonie Smith and Julia Watson. Minneapolis: University of Minnesota Press, 1996, 297–326.

Welzer, Harald, Sabine Moller, and Karoline Tschuggnall. "Opa war kein Nazi." In *Nationalsozialismus und Holocaust im Familiengedächtnis.* Frankfurt am Main: Fischer Taschenbuch, 2021.

Zerubavel, Eviatar. *Ancestors & Relatives: Genealogy, Identity, & Community.* New York: Oxford University Press, 2021.

Zurek, Werner. *Ahnen- und Familienforschung in Polen leicht gemacht. Ein praktischer Ratgeber, Leitfaden und Forschungshilfe für Deutsche und Polen.* Frankfurt am Main: R.G. Fischer Verlag, 2014.

Chapter 9

Stateless Heritage

The Sealing Sites of the South Shetland Islands, Antarctica

Michael Pearson and Melisa A. Salerno

Antarctica is unique in the modern world as the only large land mass with no national government. Buildings, infrastructure, and scientific bases in Antarctica are only recognized as being the property of specific nations because they are owned by them as physical objects—the land on which they sit is not owned. In the case of sites of human occupation in the past, these are only identified as being cultural heritage if a nation claims them to be so, effectively stating ownership. The best-known heritage sites in Antarctica are the huts built by the explorers of the Heroic Era at the turn of the nineteenth to the twentieth centuries—those of Scott, Shackleton, Mawson, and Nordenskjöld. These are linked to well-known stories of nationalistic endeavor and human endurance and are treasured as national icons and conserved by their respective nations. The first sites of human occupation of the continent, some eighty years before the Heroic Era, are the early nineteenth-century sealing sites, and these sites are not claimed or managed as cultural heritage by any nation. They are stateless heritage with no protection or governance, and as such are under constant threat of deterioration or destruction. The lack of widespread knowledge of the sealing sites, and the asymmetrical valuing of them as heritage compared to heritage sites of the Heroic and later eras, is a result of the specific environmental constructs that surround Antarctica, and the governance and management systems that have been developed to support national activity there.

By the early nineteenth century, the sealing industry, like the closely associated whaling industry, had become a global enterprise.[1] In 1819 sealers discovered the South Shetland Islands, in the Antarctic Peninsular region, and triggered a sealing boom which saw vessels from the United Kingdom, the

United States, Australia, Chile, and Argentina landing sealing gangs to gather fur seal pelts and elephant seal oil. Over the following three summer seasons, during which seals were driven to near extinction, sealer camp sites were set up on most of the islands making up the South Shetland archipelago. These campsites, consisting of occupied caves and stone-walled shelters, are now being located by archaeological survey and studied through archaeological excavation and recordings. There are smaller numbers of sealing sites resulting from sporadic sealing activity in later years, mainly by American and Canadian sealers. Over fifty sealing campsites have been identified to date in the South Shetland Islands, and twenty-three of them have been studied through archaeological excavation.[2] Figure 9.1 shows the extent of the South Shetland Islands, and their relationship to the Antarctic Peninsula.

At the time of the sealing boom no nation claimed sovereignty over the region. Despite subsequent territorial claims to the South Shetland Islands by Argentina, the United Kingdom, and Chile, the implementation of the Antarctic Treaty in 1961 set aside existing sovereignty claims and prevented new ones from being made, ensuring that there is still no recognized national sovereignty in Antarctica. In this context it is necessary to look briefly at the history of commercial sealing and Antarctic sealing camps within the broader context of modernity. The concept of modernity is intrinsically associated with the forces of nationalism, imperialism, and capitalism.[3] Although these forces are sometimes part of the same equation, there are cases in which some of them can gain specific relevance.

The growth of international commercial sealing, like that of whaling, took place during the late eighteenth and early nineteenth centuries. At that

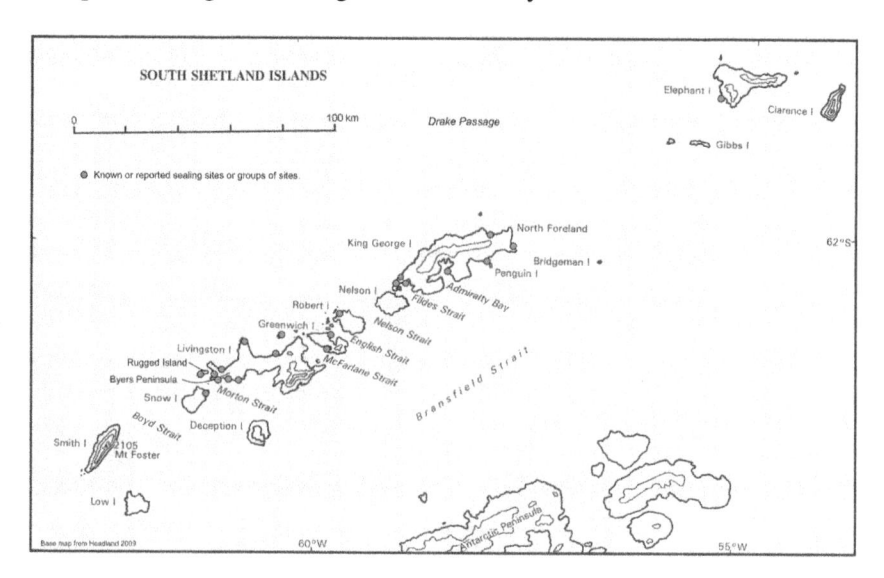

Figure 9.1. Map of the South Shetland Islands. *Source*: Map created by Melisa Salerno.

time, mercantilism was replaced by capitalism accompanied by the growth of industry. Mercantilism was based on the possibility of making a profit through trade; moving products from places where they could be obtained at lower costs to others where they could be sold at higher prices. It was also connected to absolutism, as it was seen as a way of increasing state powers by creating a positive economic balance.[4] Furthermore, trade dynamics were relevant to territorial expansion and associated colonial and imperialist aspirations. Within this framework, some territories could be considered as sources of raw materials, and in the case of inhabited areas as potential markets for manufactured goods. Industrialization gave the opportunity to increase productivity by the application of technology to resource acquirement, manufacturing, and distribution. The abundance of new manufactured goods eventually proved to be relevant for trade.

Commercial sealing was carried out by companies from different nations,[5] though companies from the United Kingdom and the United States played a prominent role in the industry on a global scale.[6] While sealing companies were private enterprises, national events and policies had a clear impact on their activity. For instance, between 1812 and 1815 (just before the discovery of the South Shetland Islands by William Smith) American companies suffered the loss of vessels and constraints in trading operations because of the conflicts between the United States and the United Kingdom.[7] Sealing companies varied greatly in size, from owners of a single ship to companies with sizeable fleets. Ships were sent to wherever a profitable trade could be had, and in some cases, ships owned by several companies, associated by family ties or commercial links, could be combined into a fleet heading to locations such as the South Seas or the South Shetland Islands. Although these vessels shared the same national origin, it was their company affiliation or shared home port that was of primary importance.

Within a mercantilist framework, sealers sought and sold their prey wherever they had a chance to maximize their profit. Exploitation was not limited by national boundaries. Fur seals and elephant seals were found in great numbers in some regions of the South Seas, where national controls were poor or did not exist. Commercial sealing was a highly exploitative activity, and animal colonies were usually taken to the edge of local extinction after a couple of hunting seasons.[8] When resources were abundant, a single vessel could take thousands of sealskins and seal elephant oil barrels after working one or two months at a given hunting ground. This led sealers to increasingly remote regions, including the South Shetland Islands in the 1820s. Sealing cycles fluctuated in line with the availability of resources and the demand for sealing products.[9] Industrialization was relevant in this expansion. Among other things, new technological processes diversified the manufacture of sealskin products, and elephant seal oil was widely used for lubricating industrial machines and for lighting.[10] Markets for sealskins were not just in the American and British homeports of the sealing companies, but, particularly in the early years of the industry, in Canton in China, involving global trade networks.[11]

Sealing companies hired their crews at home ports, but some men could also be hired at intermediate ports of call, so the crew of a single vessel may have included men of many nationalities, and languages. Just to give an example, the crew of an American sealing vessel could come from different areas of the United States (both from coastal and inland locations), from the United Kingdom and other European countries, or from the Pacific or Atlantic islands, including Portuguese from the Azores and Africans from the Cape Verde Islands.[12] There is also some evidence that indigenous people from Southern America were taken aboard as laborers, though the evidence other than in the Patagonian sealing context is as yet slight.[13] Although tensions among people from different origins could have existed, collaboration needed for work and the development of a working identity could have helped blur some of them.[14]

On the sealing grounds, geographical exploration was necessary to identify the location of resources. However, it also gathered wider knowledge of previously unexplored regions. Given the intense rivalry for the resources, much of this exploration was kept secret or only vaguely reported with generalized geographical references to regions visited. Despite this tendency, some sealing owners and captains were particularly interested in making explicit their addition to geographical knowledge and the accomplishments of their nations. For instance, the Enderby family of London, United Kingdom, included members of the Royal Geographical Society and of the Royal Society who were proud of their discoveries, and promoted them as contributions to science and geography.[15] Meanwhile, some American sealers such as Edmund Fanning, Nathaniel Palmer, and Benjamin Pendleton attempted to gain governmental support, and eventually conducted their own commercial and (unsuccessful) geographical expedition—sparking debate at the time about the contribution that a private enterprise could bring to national affairs.[16] Beyond all the above, it has been suggested that the mere presence of sealers in recently discovered regions served as an advance guard for their countries - contributing to their economy, and to their imperial or colonial aspirations, intentionally or not.[17]

In the case of the South Shetland Islands, while American sealers on the whole failed to undertake or record their geographical exploration unless it was directly related to known seal resources (e.g., the early exploration by Nathaniel Palmer to the Antarctic Peninsula looking for seals is not documented in a detailed journal or on maps), a number of British sealing captains compiled detailed maps of the archipelago and region (e.g., James Weddell's voyage into the dangerous waters of the sea subsequently named after him was as much for geographical fame as for the prospect of finding sealing grounds).[18] This probably reflects the global political positioning of the two countries. The United States was still focused on expanding and consolidating its national boundaries—the South Shetland Islands sealing boom occurred just six years after the end of the War of 1812 with the United Kingdom, and sixteen years after the Louisiana Purchase that had nearly doubled the size of the nation. An attempt by sealing entrepreneur James Byers in 1820 to get the American government to consider sending naval vessels to protect American sealers and establish a settlement on the South Shetland Islands was declined by the government.[19] The United Kingdom, by contrast, was in full swing in its development of an international empire, so the national sentiment shared by sealing owners and masters favored an extension of geographical knowledge and economic activity as symbols of national standing, and the various (mostly unratified) sovereignty claims that went with it.

On the South Shetland Islands, the great global sealing enterprise was reduced to the hard manual labor of gathering of seal products and ensuring personal survival in a very unforgiving environment. Sealing ships arrived, often with smaller tenders called shallops accompanying them or built ashore from prefabricated parts, and small whaleboats in which to get ashore. The first tasks were to find a safe anchorage for the large sealing ship, and to find beaches where seals could be hunted. Shallops and whaleboats were sent out searching for both, the whaleboat crews sleeping under their up-turned boats.[20] Depending on the number of seals on a particular beach, crews either camped under their boats while gathering furs, lived in their shallop offshore, or built stone shelters for longer stays. Gangs were made up of a varying number of ordinary sealers under the command of an officer. Rivalry was strong between different gangs and nationalities, with several confrontations being mentioned in the sources, especially between the British and American sealing gangs.[21] However, gangs sometimes collaborated to share ships, shallops, and crews, and this included agreements between gangs from different countries.[22] These various interactions between the gangs of the same and different countries were matters of on-the-spot pragmatic response to local circumstances, and did not and indeed could not call upon national jurisdictional controls or intercession.

Some fifty sealer shelter sites have been identified so far in the South Shetland Islands, most of them dating from 1820 to 1822, and the largest number being on the Byers Peninsula of Livingston Island (see Figure 9.2). In most cases it has not yet been possible to definitively distinguish British from American sites or those, far fewer, of other nations. Few of the surviving

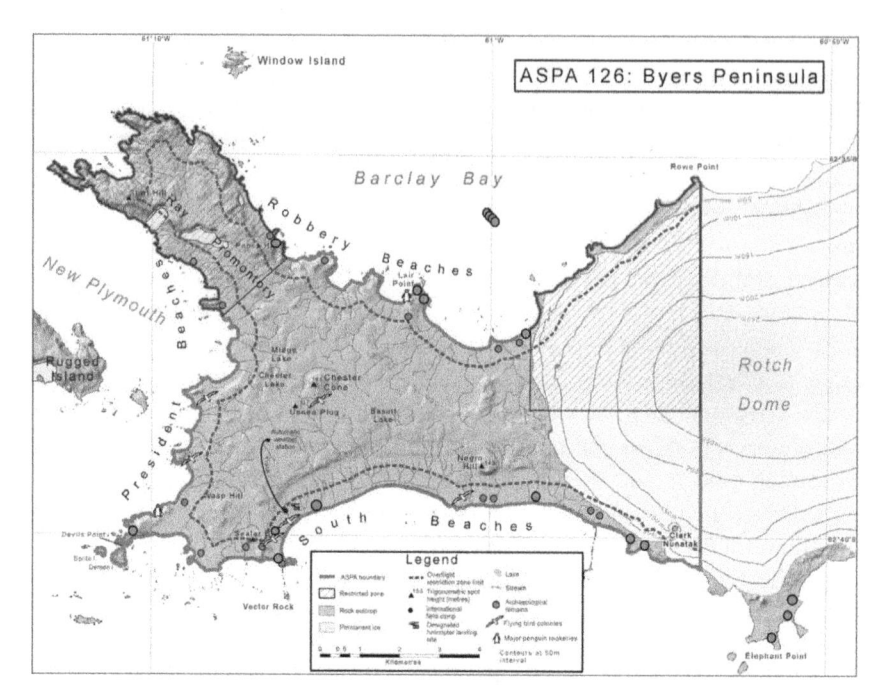

Figure 9.2. Map of Byers Peninsula. *Source*: By courtesy of the Antarctic Treaty Secretariat.

historical accounts provide detailed information about exact landing locations, and they also indicate that both American and British sealers competed for many beaches, meaning that except in a few cases the documentary evidence cannot be linked to specific sites. The sealing sites are to the uninitiated eye uninspiring collections of stone of low-visibility and ambiguous origin, and they only began to be revealed during surveys undertaken for other scientific studies since the 1950s. They have been studied in detail archaeologically since the 1980s, since which time many more have been identified (see example at Figure 9.3). Analysis has shown that material culture found at these sites was rather homogenous, making it difficult to distinguish national differences. These material traces inform us of a very basic lifestyle, the sealers being put ashore with only a few sealing tools and minimal food and clothing supplies. While the archaeological research has been carried out by universities and museums of a number of nations, supported by their respective government Antarctic Treaty Party (henceforth "state party" or "party"), the lack of definition of national origin of sealing sites in general has meant that none of them have been formally nominated for listing as Historic Sites and Monuments within the Antarctic Treaty System—they are, thus, not seen as being elements of historical national activity in Antarctica.

Figure 9.3. Elephant Point 2 Sealer Shelter, Livingston Island, South Shetland Islands, Being Excavated. Shows stone walls, whale rib roof beams, vertebra seats, and proximity to the beach. *Source*: Photograph by Michael Pearson.

THE ANTARCTIC TREATY MANAGEMENT SYSTEM AND NATIONAL STORYTELLING

Cultural heritage—those sites, structures, places, landscapes, objects, and associations that are valued as reflecting the human past—can be seen as a resource having multiple values.[23] This cultural heritage might be tangible, such as in the case of sealer and explorer's huts, or not based on human-created fabric, as in the case of places and landscapes with significant historical associations but little or no physical evidence of human presence. It can be used by different social actors for different purposes. Cultural heritage sites can help produce and reproduce stories about the past, which have an impact on the understanding of the present and the future. The definition of what is cultural heritage and what is not, and the stories that can be told through it can often be a matter of debate. The recognition and interpretation of cultural heritage is bound to power dynamics, including relationships of dominance and resistance. Nation states have long recognized the potential of cultural heritage to tell stories which are presented as both authentic and inevitable.[24] In this way, cultural heritage can be used to present specific versions of the antiquity of a certain nation in a given territory, helping assert ownership or territorial claims (especially in disputed areas). Furthermore, cultural heritage can be used to create an "imaginary community" that includes all citizens who are presented as sharing an identity based on a common past.[25] National discourses on cultural heritage frequently stress specific events and characters considered to be relevant for the destiny of a nation. Historical researchers have been traditionally called upon to support national discourses on cultural heritage, although many scholars have written counter to the nationally authorized story, and there is a growing critical perspective on the subject.[26]

These observations on the nature of heritage and its use can be observed globally, but in Antarctica there are other layers of environmental and cultural perspectives that further complicate the issue. The Antarctic Continent was untouched by human presence until the arrival of the sealers in 1819—although the atmospheric impacts of human induced burning in New Zealand has been detected in black carbon (soot) in ice cores dated to around 1300 AD, and carbon dioxide and methane concentrations in ice cores indicate the impacts of the industrial revolution from about 1800.[27] With no permanent population centers and no industrial development, it has been regarded as an untouched wilderness, and the Antarctic Treaty and its Environmental Protocol try to limit human pollution of the continent—even though the number of scientific stations is growing quickly, and tourist numbers now exceed 70,000 per year. In this context, states engage in scientific activities that establish their credentials as caretakers of the continent—protecting historic sites that originated in the commercial killing of seals, however, plays no part in that national agenda.

Outside Antarctica, states have the power to declare and protect valued sites and monuments within their territory as part of their own national heritage. Since 1972, the UNESCO World Heritage Convention (WHC) has sought to identify and protect cultural and natural sites considered to be of "outstanding universal value," not to a single country but to all humankind (although critical voices have been raised pointing to the dominance of a Western perspective in selection processes, and the use of World Heritage to promote national prestige and tourism).[28] The World Heritage approach aims at avoiding nationalist or particularistic perspectives (such as commemorating specific events or characters), by identifying sites that meet specific criteria, which are presented as reflecting a universal set of heritage values. These criteria include the potential of a site to represent a masterpiece of human creative genius, exhibit an important interchange of human values, be an outstanding example of a traditional human settlement, land-use, or sea-use which is representative of a culture (or cultures), or human interaction with the environment, and so forth. Furthermore, with the aim of not limiting heritage to the boundaries of a single country, sites can also be identified on a transboundary basis—such as the Rhaetian railway crossing from Switzerland to Italy—or a serial transnational basis—such as in cases where separate component parts of a serial listing occur in multiple countries as in the case of the Silk Road though Central Asia, the architectural works of Le Corbusier, the Limes of the Roman Empire in Europe and a number of other cases.

While World Heritage values are not limited by modern national boundaries, the system is totally dependent on individual states agreeing to both nominate and manage sites that are inscribed on the World Heritage List. The decision to list is in the hands of the World Heritage Committee made up of representatives from state parties to the Convention elected by their General Assembly, but no listing will happen within any state that has not itself made a nomination and has undertaken to manage that place for the values identified in the listing. State parties are expected to use their own resources to achieve this end. However, considering that these are the world's heritage, it is also the duty of the international community to collaborate in their protection. Therefore, the World Heritage Committee might provide international assistance to local management, including technical and financial support.

The Antarctic Treaty was agreed before the concept of the World Heritage Convention was developed. During and after World War II several nations with interests in Antarctica competed to establish and assert their territorial rights and to counter those of other nations. This led to disagreements that posed serious political and legal problems for Antarctica, heightened by the growing tensions of the Cold War. The Antarctic Treaty had its genesis in the International Geophysical Year of 1957/58, in which nations with previously uneasy relationships carried out research and exploratory programs in a peaceful and collaborative manner. The twelve countries involved in Antarctic research during the International Geophysical Year built on this collaborative approach and developed and signed the Antarctic Treaty in 1959. It came into force in 1961, and the countries subsequently becoming signatories now number fifty-four.[29] In this context the Treaty both put aside existing territorial claims and devised a system of governance based on national action to implement a consensually agreed upon set of policies. As a result, there is no sovereign control within the continent, and the World Heritage Convention, which relies on state control, cannot operate there. In this framework, the relationship between nation states and heritage follows a particular course in Antarctica.

Among the signatories of the Treaty were seven countries—Argentina, Australia, Chile, France, New Zealand, Norway, and the United Kingdom—with territorial claims, sometimes overlapping especially in the South Shetland Islands and Antarctic Peninsula region where three countries have overlapping claims. The United States and Russia maintain a "basis of claim"—reserving the right to claim in the future. Ecuador made a territorial claim in 1967 before becoming a treaty signatory in 1987, and this is treated in the same way as the other claims. All territorial positions are explicitly protected but not ratified in Article IV, which preserves the status quo:

> No acts or activities taking place while the present Treaty is in force shall constitute a basis for asserting, supporting or denying a claim to territorial sovereignty in Antarctica or create any rights of sovereignty in Antarctica. No new claim, or enlargement of an existing claim to territorial sovereignty in Antarctica shall be asserted while the present Treaty is in force.[30]

Antarctica is the only continent wholly governed through an international agreement, and the member nations established a governance approach based on collaborative policy decisions made at Consultative Meetings, to be implemented through national law and Antarctic operational management. It is supported by specialist scientific and management groups that help develop and advise on policy and implementation guidelines.[31] This became what is now called the Antarctic Treaty System.

At the first Antarctic Treaty Consultative Meeting in 1961 it was resolved that governments interested in "tombs, buildings or objects of historic interest" should consult together on their restoration and preservation and adopt all adequate measures to protect them from damage and destruction. In 1970 this was formalized by the proposal of a list of such items, but residual tensions based in national interests led to disagreement over the wording of place names and descriptions, resulting in an agreement in 1972 that described the list as to be the "List of Historic Monuments as identified and described by the proposing government or governments." The resulting list of forty-three sites sent to members to ratify carried a footnote stating that "The Consultative Meeting does not approve or disapprove the place names appearing in the texts of this List in the different languages."[32] Places were to be added to the Historic Sites and Monuments list through nomination by parties in an *ad hoc* process.

The listing as an Historic Site and Monument is the only formal mechanism for identifying sites of cultural heritage value in Antarctica. However, it is not based on a systematic assessment of the heritage values of sites, but it is a mechanism for individual nations or nations in combination to identify sites important to them. While the Treaty outlaws acts that assert or support a claim to territorial sovereignty, the Historic Sites and Monuments system could be interpreted as a mechanism that in a small way does exactly that—it allows nations to nominate not just historic sites and buildings but recent monuments to national presence, effectively marking their legitimacy as current or future claimants to rights on the continent. This has meant that no nominated Historic Site and Monument has ever been rejected by a Treaty meeting, and delisting has only occurred when sites were combined or boundaries changed and they required re-listing in their new form, or the physical focus of the listing has ceased to exist. Subsequent efforts have been made within the Antarctic Treaty System to tighten up the Historic Sites and Monuments list assessment process through the adoption of assessment criteria and the provision of more detailed information about each site, but given the consensus basis for decision making the process of reform is glacially slow with only small increments over the last thirty years.

In 1991 the Protocol on Environmental Protection stressed the need to protect the Antarctic environment and the intrinsic value of the region. Annex V to the Protocol made the Historic Sites and Monuments list the key mechanism for protecting historic values in Antarctica from damage, removal, and destruction. Furthermore, it broadly stated that the criterion for including a site on the Historic Sites and Monuments list should be its "recognised historic value." A Resolution in 2009 made specific recommendations for parties to assess the "historic significance" of sites for nomination.[33] Assessment criteria were adopted (but not made mandatory). These criteria included the association of specific sites with relevant events and people in the history of Antarctic science and exploration; feats of endurance or achievements; wide-ranging activities in the development and knowledge of the region; the specific value of its construction; the symbolic and commemorative value of the location for people of many nations; and the potential of the place for further study and education. Most of these criteria are difficult to apply to sealing sites without very free and generous interpretation.[34]

The potential usefulness of management plans, condition monitoring, and boundaries and buffer zones were identified, but these were not made necessary components of a nomination, though the nation or nations accepting responsibility for the protection of each site had to be identified. Subsequent decisions addressed the removal of significant material from Antarctica, and provision was made for more detailed information about each historic site and monument, incorporating new fields of information.[35]

Nominated sites to the Historic Sites and Monuments list include the obvious icons of Antarctic exploration such as the huts and other sites and monuments related to the Heroic Era explorers of the early twentieth century, the early scientific and exploratory sites of the later twentieth century and the Treaty era, graves associated with those, and monuments commemorating national activities. All these sites help produce and reproduce historical narratives in which national authorship is clear. These narratives bring to the fore events and characters that are presented as milestones for national history in Antarctica or are seen as proof of national commitment to the territory. These narratives frequently show respect to an ideal of nature conservation, making no reference to national interests surrounding the exploitation of resources (a subject that nonetheless keeps on arising within the system—the Protocol on Environmental Protection to the Antarctic Treaty being signed in 1991 was seen as a way to regulate human presence in the continent and to seek at least a transitory halt to national claims for the exploitation of mineral resources).

Because the nominations of sites to the Historic Sites and Monuments list rests entirely with state parties, sites that do not reflect specific national activity and do not seem to represent the values of the Antarctic Treaty System do not get nominated. Since sealing sites cannot be easily associated with one or another nation's activities, they are not able to produce or reproduce stories of singular personal or national achievement, but only a multi-authored historical narrative. As such, sealing sites are hard to link to specific events and characters, or national involvement in Treaty-related objectives, providing instead evidence of historical processes and the traces left behind by vessels of multiple nations and an almost anonymous workforce with even more varied origins. Although the sealers' presence was essential to the early exploration of Antarctica and the number and distribution of sealing sites on the South Shetland Islands prove the success of this activity, the materiality of camp sites only stresses a particular focus on exploitation. As a result, sealing sites do not sit comfortably with the values of peace and science underpinning the Antarctic Treaty System, and have difficult or embarrassing associations considering the System's emphasis on nature conservation. For all these reasons, sealing sites are both distasteful and not acknowledged as signifiers of responsible national involvement. The result is that there are no sealing sites on the Historic Sites and Monuments list despite their obvious international historical significance.

Though sealing camps are absent from the Historic Sites and Monuments list, it does include two monuments (not sites) commemorating events and characters of the sealing era. However, the reasons for their listing are not related to sealing as such, but to the contribution that specific nations made to geographical exploration. The first case is a replica of a plaque erected by Eduard Dallmann at Potter Cove, on King George Island, to commemorate the visit of his expedition to the Antarctic Seas on board the steam-driven whaling ship *Grönland*, in 1874, which while aimed at evaluating whale resources, ended up mainly charting geographical features.[36] Therefore the Historic Sites and Monuments plaque celebrates Dallmann's part in

Germany's contributions to Antarctic exploration. The second case is a commemorative plaque at Yankee Harbour to the memory of the British Captain Andrew McFarlane, who sailed a sealing vessel the *Dragon* from Valparaíso, Chile, to the Antarctic in 1820, and in the process made what was possibly the first landing on the Antarctic mainland.[37] Therefore, the memorial celebrates the United Kingdom and Chile's role in McFarlane's first Antarctic continental landing, not in his sealing activities.

Some other relevant listings on the Historic Sites and Monuments list commemorate the whaling industry at the turn of the nineteenth and early twentieth centuries. One comprises a message post left in 1895 by the Norwegian whaling expedition led by Henryk Bull and Captain Leonard Kristensen, of the ship *Antarctic*, on Svend Foyn Island, Possession Islands, during which the first confirmed landing was made on the Greater Antarctica mainland (on Victoria Land).[38]

The Historic Sites and Monuments commemorating the whaling site at Whalers Bay, Deception Island, includes the remains of early whaling operations (1906–1912) on the shore base operated by the Sociedad Ballenera de Magallanes, Chile; those of the Norwegian Hector Whaling Station (1912–1931); and the site of a cemetery and a memorial of men lost at sea, and the remains of a British scientific station operating between 1944 and 1969. Many of the physical remains of the site were swept away by a volcanic mudflow in 1969 (see Figure 9.4). While whaling in Antarctica represents another form of resource exploitation similar to sealing, it has strong national origins, resulted in much more substantial development, and whaling has already been woven into the Antarctic conservation ethos by the successful public and political campaign to end it in the late twentieth century. The remains of whaling consequently have attributes that give them relevance in the context of national storytelling, being clearly attributed to the activity of specific nations such as Chile and Norway. While there have been campaigns opposing sealing, these have been mainly in the northern hemisphere, while those against whaling had a direct impact in Antarctic Seas. Within this framework, public and then national actions to stop whaling have given rise to multiple stories of success. Finally, while the remains of sealing camps show a humble materiality, those of the whaling station are far more impressive, and account for national stories stressing the historical and technical value in its construction. Added to this, the Deception Island whaling sites were subsequently used as a British scientific base, bringing the site into the scientific orbit of the Treaty.

National interests are not limited to nominations to the Historic Sites and Monuments list, but impact on the broader production of historical narratives on Antarctica. The history of scientific and geographical exploration carried out by national parties from the late nineteenth century onwards has received much more attention than the history of resource exploitation in the

Figure 9.4. Whaling Station at Whaler's Bay, Deception Island, South Shetland Islands. The whaling factory digesters to the left, and the former whalers' barracks and subsequently British scientific station building to the right. Damage done by 1969 volcanic eruption and subsequent decay. *Source*: Photograph by Michael Pearson.

earlier sealing era. Where historical research on sealing has taken place, it has sometimes focused on the role that vessels and captains from specific nations played in the discovery and early exploration of the South Shetland Islands and the Antarctic continent. While research conducted to enhance national stories has often made relevant contributions to the Antarctic historical record, it has also led to the construction of fragmented and distorted narratives. Archaeological and historical research has, intentionally or not, challenged the constraints of national storytelling, shedding light on the complex process whereby national interests could be a formative factor in particular interpretations of the past. The ambiguous character of sealing—the exploitation of wildlife or the nursery for Antarctic explorers—and the propensity for evidence-based historical interpretation to be skewed by national interests have been driving forces behind the archaeological study of sealing sites.

STATELESS HERITAGE IN ANTARCTICA—HOW IT IS EITHER IGNORED OR PROTECTED AND MANAGED

Because of the lack of national interest and responsibility, and the uneasy fit with Antarctic Treaty political philosophies, the sealing sites have not received sufficient consideration in terms of their recognition, protection, and conservation. The work of studying the sealing sites has been carried out by university and museum-based archaeological teams (none of which were based in the United Kingdom or the United States, the two main sources of the sealing sites), and while these expeditions have had logistical support from their respective national Antarctic program managers, no state party has proposed that the sites be identified as Historic Sites and Monuments. Only one site of the over fifty sealing sites so far identified in the South Shetland Islands has been added to the Historic Sites and Monuments list, and that is a shipwreck site on the shore of Elephant Island that may be of a sealing vessel.[39]

The Environment Protocol specifies that any area may be designated as an Antarctic Specially Protected Area to protect not only environmental, scientific, aesthetic, and wilderness values but also outstanding historical values.[40] It also requires any sites or monuments that are found within Antarctic Specially Protected Areas to be listed as Historic Sites and Monuments. There is no reciprocal requirement that Historic Sites and Monuments be protected by being also listed as Antarctic Specially Protected Areas, though it was recommended that this should be considered if sites required protection and management.[41]

The sealing sites on the Byers Peninsula on Livingston Island, the largest collection of such sites in the South Shetland Islands, are protected because they lie within Antarctic Specially Protected Area No. 126. While the primary purpose of the Antarctic Specially Protected Area is to protect the terrestrial and lacustrine habitats of the area, the Management Plan for this area indicates that one of the "values to be protected" is that the "area contains one of the highest concentrations of historic sites and artifacts associated with the activities of sealers in the early 19th century, and is of outstanding value with regard to our knowledge of the earliest activities of humans in Antarctica."[42]

The Management Plan's aims and objectives include the aim to "allow archaeological research and measures for artefact protection, while protecting historic artefacts present within the Area from unnecessary destruction, disturbance or removal."[43] All proposed activities require a permit and must not jeopardize the ecological, geological, historic, and scientific values of the area. Movement across the area and the establishment of any camp sites should be undertaken so as not to disturb archaeological remains, and anthropogenic materials (i.e., artefacts) can only be removed in accordance with a permit.

The current (2022) edition of the Byers Peninsula Antarctic Specially Protected Area Management Plan was modified to include detailed information about the location and form of sealer sites, greatly enhancing it as a tool in the conservation of these cultural features. With that change, scientists from a range of disciplines received information necessary to avoid damaging the sealing sites while carrying out their own research. Previously, substantial damage occurred at one site by a geological party, not recognizing that the stones they used to build a base for a drill-stand were in fact the walls of a sealing hut.[44] After this, the Chilean government proposed the addition of an appendix providing more detailed locations and descriptive material including plans in 2007, and this suggestion was implemented in the 2022 edition.[45] While the Management Plan recognizes the historic values of the sites and the aim of protecting them, none of them have been designated as Historic Sites and Monuments as the Environment Protocol requires.

The lack of protection still exists in cases where the sealing sites do not lie within the boundaries of an Antarctic Specially Protected Area. While the Environment Protocol aims to limit the adverse impacts of human activities on the environment including its historic values, the lack of an explicit regulatory framework to control those activities as they might affect historical sites (including Historic Sites and Monuments) is problematic. Tourists have become a regular presence at some locations were sealing sites have been found and even more so in areas where no site surveys have been carried out.[46] While tourists are encouraged not to destroy or remove materials from the environment, the lack of systematic formal recognition of cultural heritage sites other than as Historic Sites and Monuments within the Antarctic Treaty System mechanisms makes it difficult to implement effective protection measures. This situation is made worse by the humble materiality of the sites which often makes them invisible to the untrained eye: the best-intentioned tourist party might trample on an unrecognized site.

There are several factors in this orphan status applying to sealing sites. In the case of the sealing sites the question of who owns this past and the sites that reflect it remains ambiguous. Nations such as Chile, Argentina, and Brazil, which have carried out the majority of research on the sites, have lobbied for better protection, but appear to be reluctant to themselves propose Historic Sites and Monuments status, possibly to avoid the diplomatic embarrassment of upsetting the nations originally responsible for the existence of the sites, the United Kingdom and the United States. Those nations in turn appear to be reluctant to claim ownership since they do not fit into the image of responsible Antarctic environmental management (as sites of seal exploitation) and do not enhance the national storytelling or presence on the continent. While the process of nominating Historic Sites and Monuments remains solely the voluntary prerogative of state parties to the Treaty, the effective recognition and protection of sealing sites seems to be a remote possibility.

WAYS FORWARD

Sealing sites on the South Shetland Islands provide the earliest examples of human presence in Antarctica and have the potential to reveal information and educate people about what was clearly the dominant activity in the region for a whole century after its discovery—half its human history. Sealing sites cannot be clearly related to identifiable characters and events, but to multiple actors and complex historical processes. These activities cannot be primarily associated with science, the dominant theme within the Antarctic Treaty System, but sealers' contributions to geographical knowledge through their exploratory voyages are worth considering and have been acknowledged in a few listings. Although the materiality of sealing sites might not have an outstanding technical or architectural value in a formal sense in their materials, design, or method of construction, they do have an undeniable historical or cultural value which could be also framed under revised Historic Sites and Monuments criteria. Their simplicity not only attests to the sealers' ability to make-do, but also to their endurance in Antarctic conditions.

In view of existing problems surrounding the orphan status of sealing sites, what possible ways might exist to achieve their recognition and protection as heritage sites? Some questions might guide further discussions: Could the Antarctic Treaty System be developed further to protect and conserve these places? Could this be through the expansion of the system of listing Historic Sites and Monuments that partly or totally decouples it from state party nomination (and would such a system, which diminishes party control be accepted)? Is the creation of another, parallel, category of site recognition and protection based on the systematic assessment of values needed or achievable? If an Historic Sites and Monuments list not based on state party nomination, or another category of designation is developed, how would the process of identification and protection be funded in the absence of national advantage? Could Antarctic Specially Protected Area (ASPA) designations be used to protect multiple places distributed on specific areas (such as on the Byers Peninsula ASPA)—if so how would they be identified, nominated, and managed? Could the requirement for management plans be expanded to cover all categories of protected designation under the Antarctic Treaty System, including cultural heritage sites—if so, who would be the responsible manager in the absence of national advantage?

It is worth pointing out in relation to these questions that within the Environment Protocol the recognition of outstanding natural values is based on scientific assessment of values in an Antarctica-wide context, with little scope for national storytelling. This suggests that the Antarctic Treaty System might be flexible enough to extend this value-based assessment process to cultural heritage, and in doing so develop the necessary tools to deal with the stateless heritage status of the sealing sites.

While the nomination process for Historic Sites and Monuments listing remains in the hands of state parties, it would not be impossible for the Antarctic Treaty System to agree expanding the mandate for parties in unison to take a more systematic approach to identifying cultural heritage sites. If this were to occur, the criteria for Historic Sites and Monuments listing could be updated and improved. The criteria as they currently stand reflect a particular focus on the Treaty's raison d'être, science, and scientific knowledge. They also display an emphasis on the exploits of individuals (not groups), feats of endurance, and somewhat dated concepts reflecting the master narrative nature of Antarctic historiography: important men doing heroic things. The only existing criteria that could be easily applied to sealing sites, without conceptual gymnastics, are those relating to a site being representative of an activity important for developing knowledge about Antarctica; being able to produce such knowledge of human activities through further study; and being a symbolic or commemorative value for people of many nations. With some modification of the wording of other existing criteria, sealers and whalers as groups (and other subaltern groups in Antarctic history) could be seen as being associated with the history of geographical exploration and knowledge of Antarctica (currently limited to the association of "a person"). Sealer occupation of the South Shetland Islands could be seen as an unusual illustration of human adaptation to the Antarctic environment, though this is currently limited to "a notable feat of endurance achievement." Sealer shelters and associated landscapes could also be seen as outstanding examples of a type of technological ensemble or landscape which illustrates a significant stage in human history, though the current criteria are more limited, to "particular technical, historical, cultural or architectural value in its materials, design or method of construction."[47] Some of the ideas behind these suggested extensions of criteria draw from those for the World Heritage List.

The potential to use the Antarctic Specially Protected Area designation to protect cultural heritage opens up an opportunity to better incorporate the idea of cultural landscape that has entered the Antarctic Treaty System policy arena within the last decade. The clearest expression of this is the description of the Mawson's Huts Antarctic Specially Protected Area (2014, combining earlier designations). This covers the entire area of Cape Denison in Commonwealth Bay and was identified as a cultural landscape having both important physical remains, such as the huts and surrounding artifact scatters and food caches (also designated as an Historic Site and Monument) in an evocative natural setting, and the visual symbolism it provides of the challenges facing humans in the occupation of the continent. "In designating the entire area as an Antarctic Specially Protected Area, Cape Denison's unique 'sense of place' is protected, with Mawson's Huts and Boat Harbour as the focus of the visual catchment."[48] In 2018 "cultural landscape" was included in the *Guidelines for the assessment and management of heritage in Antarctica*, developed for the Antarctic Treaty Consultative Parties, as one of the attributes of a site that should be considered in its description and documentation. The cultural landscape approach has great potential for better recognition and protection of sealing sites, which very often comprise multiple small shelters and work sites scattered within a landscape that links them, gives them additional meaning, and enhances their understanding.

Sealing sites on the South Shetland Islands had multiple national authors, and in this regard, they may be viewed as the earliest expression of the international nature of the territory that is a keystone of the Antarctic Treaty. Sealers were not only multi-national, but they were also very largely anonymous people taking part in a collective enterprise. They were not hired for their outstanding exploring skills (except the captains) or scientific knowledge, and this clearly illustrates that the history of Antarctica was not only created by prominent people or acknowledged heroes. This perspective could help produce a more plural history of the Southern continent and create stronger ties between the region and ordinary people from all over the world. Considering that Antarctica is not a territory populated by native people, and that the possibility of visiting Antarctica for most people is somewhat remote, this could create a sense of identity encompassing the region, countering the feeling of what otherwise seems to be the extreme "otherness" of the territory.

The recognition of the multiple national authorship of sealing sites promotes the production and reproduction of a different story to the one traditionally told by dominant narratives of the history and sciences in Antarctica. This story does not attempt to segment in any way contributions to historical processes by nations. On the contrary, it gives an interesting chance to highlight the interconnectedness of human activities in the region, and from the region to the globe. Considering Thomas Adam's perspective on transnational history, it could be said that the history of Antarctic sealing and the authorship of related sites entailed a constant influx of people and materials making nationalistic distinctions "difficult if not obsolete."[49]

As has been said, it is hard to reconcile sealing sites with the values of science and nature conservation that underpin the Antarctic Treaty System. However, the widely distributed presence of sealing sites on the South Shetland Islands accounts for the early achievements of sealers' exploration: systematically sailing in Antarctic waters; charting the archipelago and surrounding seas; and making observations of the area that were later utilized by navigators, explorers, and researchers. While sealing operations were clearly not guided by environmentalist principles, sealing sites might act as a cautionary tale of the risks of the uncontrolled exploitation of resources. The logic of looking at the counter-conservation side of history is paralleled in the World Heritage List which includes places of memory where dark episodes of human history occurred, such as Hiroshima and Auschwitz-Birkenau. Similarly, the World Heritage List includes sites of mining and industrialization and their associated landscapes that draw attention to the nature of past resource extraction and industrial processes that helps form the perspective from which modern environmental controls developed. These include areas and landscapes such as the copper mining landscape of Cornwall in the United Kingdom, the coal mining landscape of the Nord-Pas de Calais Basin in France, the Völklingen Ironworks and Zollverein Coal Mine in Germany, and the sites of the Meiji Industrial Revolution in Japan. Recognizing the other side of the historical coin—in the case of Antarctica the history of exploitation of nature rather than its conservation—gives us pause to reflect on the nature of world history, and the worthy aims enshrined in the Antarctic Treaty.

Beyond the question of improving the assessment and listing mechanisms that might apply to sealing sites is one about the willingness of state parties to embrace a wider vision of the history of Antarctica, and specifically their role in the submission of Historic Sites and Monuments, Antarctic Specially Protected Area proposals, and related management plans. As we have shown, in the current situation state parties are unlikely to nominate, much less to manage, sites that do not in some way trigger national interests. In the majority of cases Historic Sites and Monuments are proposed by a single party, or sometimes multiple parties, who then undertake their management in various combinations.

The relationship between the proposal of a Historic Site and Monument and undertakings to manage it can be complex. Proposals for listing in the past often appear to be based on national territorial claims, sometimes with multiple claimants combining in the process. Then another party agrees to joining the undertaking to manage the Historic Sites and Monuments because it was originally associated with the site's history, or because it is close to a research station it operates. As examples, many sites in the Antarctic Peninsula area have been proposed jointly by Argentina and the United Kingdom, which have overlapping territorial claims to the area. They are then joined in agreed management by the creator of the historic site, such as Sweden. In the Ross Sea region, many sites were proposed by New Zealand, the United Kingdom, and Norway in combination, reflecting a mix of countries creating the sites (United Kingdom and Norway) and the current inheritor of the British territorial claim, New Zealand. Norway's participation in proposing Heroic-Era huts is perhaps reflective of their historical rivalry with the British in that period, the non-survival of their own main historic site (Amundsen's Hut), and their interest in collaborative commemoration of the events. The management is taken on by New Zealand and the creating country.

It should also be recognized that the undertaking of management for the great majority of Historic Sites and Monuments does not impose a major commitment to funding—the conservation and management of the seven surviving Heroic-Era huts aside, almost all the remaining Historic Sites and Monuments require little or no major conservation works. They do require monitoring of condition over time, and action when required to protect them from clear risks such as animal or human damage, but these are not onerous roles in the context of the overall commitment required to maintain an Antarctic presence.

The challenge in expanding the Historic Sites and Monuments list to reflect a more systematic assessment of heritage values across Antarctica, short of a major policy change of the mechanisms for heritage identification within the Antarctic Treaty System, will be to convince parties to invest time and resources in collaborative efforts to both propose and assist in the management of Historic Sites and Monuments and Antarctic Specially Protected Areas. While the input to research and management of a wider range of sites would not bring the overt benefit of highlighting the party's history of involvement in Antarctica, it may have a wider benefit in the party being seen to be fostering the multinational collaborative ethos that underpins the Antarctic Treaty System and achieving a more systematic identification and protection of Antarctica's cultural heritage.

FINAL WORDS

The traditional way of telling stories in Antarctica is in the context of national activity in the interests of furthering exploration, science, and knowledge. Hence the sites of the Heroic Era, the interwar explorations, and the International Geophysical Year and the subsequent early years of the Antarctic Treaty are easy to recognize as heritage. These sites support national prestige in the Antarctic Treaty System context. The sealing sites do not advance national stories or prestige, and so there is little incentive to own the sites—they do not get proposed as Historic Sites and Monuments or get actively managed by a state party. The gaining of prestige within the Antarctic Treaty System is a clear continuation of what historian Adrian Howkins has dubbed "environmental imperialism"—the use of the ability to master environmental knowledge for subtle or not-so-subtle national positioning.[50] The sealing sites of the South Shetland Islands are not recognized within the Antarctic Treaty System as being significant cultural heritage places because no state party to the Treaty regards their history as beneficial to their Antarctic image. They are literally "stateless heritage." In this chapter, we have proposed the expansion of the Antarctic Treaty System mechanisms for the identification and management of these and a range of other neglected heritage sites. Such a move would bring the Treaty into line with other national heritage and World Heritage regimes that generally post-date the drafting of the Treaty. Whether the state parties making up the Antarctic Treaty System will ever see this as a priority remains to be seen.

NOTES

1. Briton Cooper Busch, *The War Against the Seals; A History of the North American Seal Fishery*, Montreal: McGill-Queen's University Press, 1985.

2. Rubén Stehberg, *Arqueología Histórica Antártica: Aborígenes Sudamericanos en los Mares Subantárticos en el Siglo XIX*, Santiago: Centro de Investigaciones Diego Barros Arana, 2003; Andrés Zarankin and María Ximena Senatore, *Historias de un Pasado en Blanco: Arqueología Histórica Antártica*, Belo Horizonte: Argumentum, 2007; Michael Pearson and Rubén Stehberg, "Nineteenth Century Sealing Sites on Rugged Island, South Shetland Island," *Polar Record* 42, no. 4 (2006): 335–347. Andrés Zarankin, Michael Pearson, and Melisa A. Salerno, Archaeology in Antarctica, London: Routledge, 2023.

3. Charles Orser Jr., *A Historical Archaeology of the Modern World*, New York: Plenum, 1996.

4. Philipp Robinson Rösner, *Freedom and Capitalism in Early Modern Europe: Mercantilism and the Making of the Modern Economic Mind*, Cham: Palgrave Macmillan, 2020.

5. Andrés Zarankin and María Ximena Senatore, "Archaeology in Antarctica: Nineteenth-Century Capitalism Expansion Strategies," *International Journal of Historical Archaeology* 9, no. 1 (2005): 43–56.

6. A. G. E. Jones, "The British Southern Whale and Seal Fisheries," *The Great Circle* 3, no. 1 (1981): 20–29; Busch *The War Against the Seals*.

7. Marcelo Mayorga, *Pieles, Tabaco y Quillangos. Relaciones entre Loberos Angloestadounidenses y Aborígenes Australes en la Patagonia (1780–1850)*, Santiago de Chile: Ediciones de la Subdirección de Investigación, Servicio Nacional del Patrimonio Cultural, 2020.

8. Rhys Richards, "New Market Evidence on the Depletion of Southern Fur Seals: 1788–1833," *New Zealand Journal of Zoology* 30, no. 1 (2003): 1–9.

9. Jorge Berguño, "Las Shetland del Sur: El Ciclo Lobero. Primera Parte' y 'Segunda Parte,'" *Boletín Antártico Chileno* 12, no. 1 (1993): 5–13; 12, no. 2 (1993): 2–9.

10. A. Howard Clark, "The Antarctic Fur-Seal and Sea-Elephant Industry," in: George Brown Goode (ed.), *The Fisheries and Fishery Industries of the United States*. Section V—History and Methods of the Fisheries, Washington, D.C.: Government Printing Office, 1887, 400–467; Robert Burton, "From Shoes to Shawls: Utilization of 'South Seas' Fur Seal Pelts in late 18th and early 19th Century England," in: Robert Keith Headland (ed.), *Historical Antarctic Sealing Industry: Proceedings of an International Conference in Cambridge 16–21 September 2016*, Cambridge: Scott Polar Research Institute, 2018, 87–93.

11. James Kirker, *Adventures to China: Americans in the Southern Oceans 1792–1812*, New York: Oxford University Press, 1970.

12. Anthony B. Dickinson, *Seal Fisheries of the Falkland Islands and Dependencies: An Historical Review*, St. Johns: International Maritime Economic History Association, 2007, 13.

13. Stehberg, *Arqueología Histórica Antártica*, 2003.

14. Angela McGowan, "On their Own: Towards an Analysis of Sealer's Sites at Heard Island," *Papers and Proceedings of the Royal Society of Tasmania* 133, no. 2 (2000): 69; Melisa A. Salerno, "Sealers Were not Born but Made: Sensory Motor-Habits, Subjectivities and Nineteenth-Century Voyages to the South Shetland Islands," in: José Roberto Pellini, Andrés Zarankin, and Melisa A. Salerno (eds.), *Coming to Senses. Topics in Sensory Archaeology*, Newcastle-Upon-Tyne: Cambridge Scholars Publishing, 2015, 77–104.

15. Conon Fraser, *The Enderby Settlement; Britain's Whaling Venture on the Subantarctic Islands 1849–1852*, Otago: University Press, 2014; Michael Pearson, "Charting the Sealing Islands of the Southern Ocean," *The Globe: Journal of the Australian and New Zealand Map Society* 80 (2016): 33–56; Beau Riffenburgh, "Enderby, Messrs," in: Beau Riffenburgh (ed.), *Encyclopedia of the Antarctic* vol. I, London: Routledge, 2007, 380–381.

16. John R. Spears, *Captain Nathaniel Brown Palmer: An Old-Time Sailor of the Sea*, New York: The Macmillan Company, 1922.

17. Mayorga, *Pieles, Tabaco y Quillangos*, 49.

18. Michael Pearson, "'Knowing' the South Shetlands: The Role of Sealer's Charts," *Shima* 14, no. 1 (2020): 108–132; James Weddell, *A Voyage Towards the South Pole, Performed in the Years 1822–24*, London: Longman, Rees, Orme, Brown & Green, 1827.

19. Kenneth J. Bertrand, *Americans in Antarctica, 1775–1948*, New York: American Geographical Society, 1971, 34–35.

20. Michael Pearson, "Living Under their Boats: A Strategy for Southern Sealing in the Nineteenth Century—Its History and Archaeological Potential," *The Polar Journal* 8, no. 1 (2018): 68–83.

21. Thomas W. Smith, *A Narrative of the Life, Travels and Sufferings of Thomas W. Smith . . .* , Boston: Wm. C. Hill, 1844, 159–161; Edouard A. Stackpole, *The Voyage of the Huron and the Huntress: The American Sealers and the Discovery of the Continent of Antarctica*, Mystic: The Maritime Historical Association, 1955, 45–46; Robert Fildes, "A Journal of a Voyage Kept on Board Brig *Cora* of Liverpool Bound to New South Shetland," 1–41. Public Records Office Series: Adm. 55, Admiralty and Secretariat. Log books etc. Supplementary, Series II, explorations. PRO AJCP reel 1599, piece 143, 1820–21.

22. Michael Pearson, "Australians Sealers in the Antarctic Region—1820–22," *The Great Circle: Journal of the Australian Association for Maritime History* 40, no. 2 (2018): 105–121.

23. Paul Basu and Wayne Modest, "Museums, Heritage and International Development: A Critical Conversation," in: Paul Basu and Wayne Modest (eds.),

Museums, Heritage and International Development, Abingdon and New York: Routledge, 2015, 1–32.

24. Pamela Erskine-Loftus, Victoria Penziner Hightower, and Mariam Ibrahim Al-Mulla, "National Representations or Representations of the Nation: Museums, Heritage, Identity and Narratives," in: Pamela Erskine-Loftus, Victoria Penziner Hightower, and Mariam Ibrahim Al-Mulla (eds.), *Representing the Nation: Heritage, Museums, National Narratives, and Identity in the Arab Gulf States*, Abingdon and New York: Routledge, 2016: 1–6.

25. Benedict Anderson, *Imagined Communities: Reflections on the Origin and Spread of Nationalism*, London: Verso, 2006.

26. Helaine Silverman, "Contested Cultural Heritage: A Selected Historiography," in: Helaine Silverman (ed.), *Contested Cultural Heritage: Religion, Nationalism, Erasure, and Exclusion in a Global World*, New York: Springer 2011, 1–49.

27. Julia Hager, "700-year old Soot Deposits in Antarctic Ice," *Polar Journal* (web-version October 8, 2021); "Ice Cores and Climate Change," British Antarctic Survey website, March 1, 2014 (https://www.bas.ac.uk/data/our-data/publication/ice-cores-and-climate-change/, accessed September 22, 2022).

28. Denis Byrne, "Western Hegemony in Archaeological Heritage Management," *History and Anthropology* 5, no. 2 (1991): 269–276.

29. The original signatories were Argentina, Australia, Belgium, Chile, France, Japan, New Zealand, Norway, South Africa, the United Kingdom, the United States of America, and the USSR.

30. *The Antarctic Treaty*, Antarctic Conference, Washington, 1959 (https://www.ats.aq/devAS/Meetings/Measure/1?s=1&from=12/01/1959&to=12/01/1959&cat=0&top=0&type=0&stat=0&txt=The%20Antarctic%20Treaty&curr=0&page=1, accessed September 23, 2022).

31. The advisory groups are the Scientific Committee on Antarctic Research (SCAR), the Scientific Committee for the Conservation of Antarctic Marine Living Resources (CCAMLR), the Committee for Environmental Protection (CEP), and the Council of Managers of National Antarctic Programs (COMNAP). These are in turn supported by ten specialist international organizations such as the International Association of Antarctic Tour Operators (IAATO).

32. Minutes of the Antarctic Treaty Consultative Meetings: ATCM 1 Res IX(1961); ATCM 6 (Res 14) (1970); ATCM 7, Wp 011 (1972).

33. ATCM Resolution 3 (2009), amending original criteria adopted in Resolution 8, 1995.

34. The criteria are as follows: a particular event of importance in the history of science or exploration of Antarctica occurred at the place; a particular association with a person who played an important role in the history of science or exploration in Antarctica; a particular association with a notable feat of endurance or achievement; representative of, or forms part of, some wide-ranging activity that has been important in the development and knowledge of Antarctica; particular technical, historical, cultural or architectural value in its materials, design or method of construction; the potential, through study, to reveal information or has the potential to educate people

about significant human activities in Antarctica; symbolic or commemorative value for people of many nations.

35. ATCM Resolution 2, 2018; ATCM Wp 60 rev1, 2021, implementing Decision 1 2019.

36. Robert Headland, *A Chronology of Antarctic Exploration*, London: Quartritch, 2009: 203; David Day, *Antarctica. What Everyone Needs to Know*, New York: Oxford University Press, 2019: 35.

37. Headland, *A Chronology of Antarctic Exploration*, 129.

38. Headland, *A Chronology of Antarctic Exploration*, 225.

39. HSM 74, possibly the wreck of the *Charles Shearer* sealing vessel in 1877.

40. The Protocol on Environmental Protection to the Antarctic Treaty (The Madrid Protocol), 1991: Article 3 (1) of Annex V.

41. ATCM Resolution 3.

42. Management Plan for Antarctic Specially Protected Area No. 126 Byers Peninsula, Livingston Island, South Shetland Islands. ATCM XLIV (2022) Measure 10 (https://www.ats.aq/devAS/Meetings/Measure/760?s=1&from=1/1/1958&to=1/1/2158&cat=0&top=40&type=0&stat=0&txt=&curr=0&page=1, accessed September 26, 2022).

43. Management Plan for Antarctic Specially Protected Area No. 126, section 2, "Aims and Objectives."

44. Michael Pearson, Rubén Stehberg, Andrés Zarankín, María Ximena Senatore, and Carolina Gatica, "Conserving the Oldest Historic Sites in the Antarctic: The Challenges in Managing the Sealing Sites in the South Shetland Islands," *Polar Record* 46, no. 1 (2010): 60.

45. "Historic Sites of Byers Peninsula, Livingston Island, South Shetland Islands, Antarctica," *ATCM* 30 (2007), IP 123.

46. María Ximena Senatore and Andrés Zarankin, "Tourism and Invisible Historic Sites in Antarctica," Paper given to ICOMOS 17th General Assembly session *Heritage Driver of development*, Paris 2011, 599–608.

47. Guidelines for the Assessment and Management of Heritage in Antarctica. ACTM XLI, Resolution 2, Annex (https://www.ats.aq/devAS/Meetings/Measure/677?s=1&from=05/18/2018&to=05/18/2018&cat=0&top=347&type=0&stat=0&txt=&curr=0&page=1, accessed September 23, 2022).

48. Australian Antarctic Division, *Management Plan for Antarctic specially protected area no. 162: Mawson's Huts, Cape Denison, Commonwealth Bay, George V Land, East Antarctica*, 2014 (https://www.env.go.jp/nature/nankyoku/kankyohogo/database/jyouyaku/aspa/aspa_pdf_en/162.pdf, accessed February 4, 2021); Susan Barr and Michael Pearson, "The Polar Regions," in: Carl L. Goetcheus and Steve Brown (eds.), *Routledge Handbook of Cultural Landscapes*, London: Routledge, 2023.

49. Thomas Adam, "Transnational History: A Program for Research, Publishing, and Teaching," *Yearbook of Transnational History* 1 (2018): 1–10.

50. Adrian Howkins, *Frozen Empires: An Environmental History of the Antarctic Peninsula*, Oxford: Oxford University Press, 2017.

BIBLIOGRAPHY

Primary Sources

Australian Antarctic Division. *Management Plan for Antarctic Specially Protected Area No. 162: Mawson's Huts, Cape Denison, Commonwealth Bay, George V Land, East Antarctica.* Kingston: Australian Antarctic Division, 2014.

Clark, A. Howard. "The Antarctic Fur-Seal and Sea-Elephant Industry." In *The Fisheries and Fishery Industries of the United States. Section V: History and Methods of the Fisheries*, edited by George Brown Goode. Washington, D.C.: Government Printing Office, 1887, 400–467.

Fildes, Robert. "A Journal of a Voyage Kept on Board Brig *Cora* of Liverpool Bound to New South Shetland." Public Records Office Series: Adm. 55, Admiralty and Secretariat. Log Books etc. Supplementary, Series II, Explorations. PRO AJCP reel 1599, piece 143. 1820-21.

Secondary Sources

Adam, Thomas. "Transnational History: A Program for Research, Publishing, and Teaching." *The Yearbook of Transnational History* 1 (2018): 1–10.

Anderson, Benedict. *Imagined Communities: Reflections on the Origin and Spread of Nationalism*. London: Verso, 2006.

Barr, Susan, and Michael Pearson. "The Polar Regions." In *Routledge Handbook of Cultural Landscape Practice*, edited by Carl L. Goetcheus and Steve Brown. London: Routledge, 2023.

Basu, Paul, and Wayne Modest. "Museums, Heritage and International Development: A Critical Conversation." In *Museums, Heritage and International Development*, edited by Paul Basu and Wayne Modest. Abingdon and New York: Routledge, 2015, 1–32.

Berguño, Jorge. "'Las Shetland del Sur: El Ciclo Lobero. 'Primera Parte'" *Boletín Antártico Chileno* 12, no. 1 (1993): 5–13.

Berguño, Jorge. "'Las Shetland del Sur: El Ciclo Lobero. 'Segunda Parte.'" *Boletín Antártico Chileno* 12, no. 2 (1993): 2–9.

Bertrand, Kenneth J. *Americans in Antarctica, 1775–1948*. New York: American Geographical Society, 1971.

Burton, Robert. "From Shoes to Shawls: Utilization of 'South Seas' Fur Seal Pelts in Late 18th and Early 19th Century England." In *Historical Antarctic Sealing Industry: Proceedings of an International Conference in Cambridge 16–21 September 2016*, edited by Robert Keith Headland. Cambridge: Scott Polar Research Institute, 2018, 87–93.

Busch, Briton Cooper. *The War Against the Seals; A History of the North American Seal Fishery*. Montreal: McGill-Queen's University Press, 1985.

Byrne, Denis. "Western Hegemony in Archaeological Heritage Management." *History and Anthropology* 5, no. 2 (1991): 269–276.

Day, David. *Antarctica. What Everyone Needs to Know*. New York: Oxford University Press, 2019.

Dickinson, Anthony B. *Seal Fisheries of the Falkland Islands and Dependencies: An Historical Review*. St. Johns: International Maritime Economic History Association, 2007.

Erskine-Loftus, Pamela, Victoria Penziner Hightower, and Mariam Ibrahim Al-Mulla. "National Representations or Representations of the Nation: Museums, Heritage, Identity and Narratives." In *Representing the Nation: Heritage, Museums, National Narratives, and Identity in the Arab Gulf States*, edited by Pamela Erskine-Loftus, Victoria Penziner Hightower, and Mariam Ibrahim Al-Mulla, Abingdon and New York: Routledge, 2016, 1–6.

Fraser, Conon. *The Enderby Settlement; Britain's Whaling Venture on the Subantarctic Islands 1849–1852*. Dunedin: Otago University Press, 2014.

Hager, Julia. "700-Year Old Soot Deposits in Antarctic Ice." *Polar Journal*, October 8, 2021, available online: https://polarjournal.ch/en/2021/10/08/700-year-old-soot-deposits-in-antarctic-ice/ (accessed September 23, 2022).

Headland, Robert Keith. *A Chronology of Antarctic Exploration*. London: Quartritch, 2009.

Howkins, Adrian. *Frozen Empires: An Environmental History of the Antarctic Peninsula*. Oxford: Oxford University Press, 2017.

Jones, A. G. E. "The British Southern Whale and Seal Fisheries." *The Great Circle* 3, no. 1 (1981): 20–29.

Kirker, James. *Adventures to China: Americans in the Southern Oceans 1792–1812*. New York: Oxford University Press, 1970.

Mayorga, Marcelo. *Pieles, Tabaco y Quillangos. Relaciones entre Loberos Angloestadounidenses y Aborígenes Australes en la Patagonia (1780–1850)*. Santiago de Chile: Ediciones de la Subdirección de Investigación, Servicio Nacional del Patrimonio Cultural, 2020.

McGowan, Angela. "On Their Own: Towards an Analysis of Sealer's Sites at Heard Island." *Papers and Proceedings of the Royal Society of Tasmania* 133, no. 2 (2020): 61–70.

Orser, Charles, Jr. *A Historical Archaeology of the Modern World*. New York: Plenum, 1996.

Pearson, Michael. "Australians Sealers in the Antarctic Region—1820–22." *The Great Circle: Journal of the Australian Association for Maritime History* 40, no. 2 (2018): 105–121.

Pearson, Michael. "Charting the Sealing Islands of the Southern Ocean." *The Globe: Journal of the Australian and New Zealand Map Society* 80 (2016): 33–56.

Pearson, Michael. "'Knowing' the South Shetlands: The Role of Sealer's Charts." *Shima* 14, no. 1 (2020): 108–132.

Pearson, Michael. "Living Under Their Boats: A Strategy for Southern Sealing in the Nineteenth Century—Its History and Archaeological Potential." *The Polar Journal* 8, no. 1 (2018): 68–83.

Pearson, Michael, and Rubén Stehberg. "Nineteenth Century Sealing Sites on Rugged Island, South Shetland Island." *Polar Record* 42, no. 4 (2006): 335–347.

Pearson, Michael, Rubén Stehberg, Andrés Zarankín, Maria Ximena Senatore, and Carolina Gatica. "Conserving the Oldest Historic Sites in the Antarctic: The Challenges in Managing the Sealing Sites in the South Shetland Islands." *Polar Record* 46, no. 1 (2010): 57–64.

Rhys, Richards. "New Market Evidence on the Depletion of Southern Fur Seals: 1788–1833." *New Zealand Journal of Zoology* 30, no. 1 (2003): 1–9.

Riffenburgh, Beau. "Enderby, Messrs." In *Encyclopedia of the Antarctic I*, edited by Beau Riffenburgh. London: Routledge, 2007, 380–381.

Rösner, Philipp Robinson. *Freedom and Capitalism in Early Modern Europe: Mercantilism and the Making of the Modern Economic Mind.* Cham: Palgrave Macmillan, 2020.

Salerno, Melisa A. "Sealers Were Not Born But Made. Sensory Motor-Habits, Subjectivities and Nineteenth-Century Voyages to the South Shetland Islands." In *Coming to Senses: Topics in Sensory Archaeology*, edited by José Roberto Pellini, Andrés Zarankin, and Melisa A. Salerno. Newcastle-Upon-Tyne: Cambridge Scholars Publishing, 2015, 77–104.

Senatore, María Ximena, and Andrés Zarankin. "Tourism and Invisible Historic Sites in Antarctica." Paper Given to ICOMOS 17th General Assembly Session *Heritage Driver of Development*. Paris, 2011, 599–608.

Silverman, Helaine. "Contested Cultural Heritage: A Selected Historiography." In *Contested Cultural Heritage: Religion, Nationalism, Erasure, and Exclusion in a Global World*, edited by Helaine Silverman. New York: Springer, 2011, 1–49.

Smith, Thomas W. *A Narrative of the Life, Travels and Sufferings of Thomas W. Smith . . .* Boston: Wm. C. Hill, 1844.

Spears, John R. *Captain Nathaniel Brown Palmer: An Old-Time Sailor of the Sea.* New York: The Macmillan Company, 1922.

Stackpole, Edouard A. *The Voyage of the Huron and the Huntress: The American Sealers and the Discovery of the Continent of Antarctica.* Mystic: The Maritime Historical Association, 1955.

Stehberg, Rubén. *Arqueología Histórica Antártica: Aborígenes Sudamericanos en los Mares Subantárticos en el Siglo XIX.* Santiago: Centro de Investigaciones Diego Barros Arana, 2003.

Weddell, James. *A Voyage Towards the South Pole, Performed in the Years 1822–24.* London: Longman, Rees, Orme, Brown & Green, 1827.

Zarankin, Andrés, and María Ximena Senatore. "Archaeology in Antarctica: Nineteenth-Century Capitalism Expansion Strategies." *International Journal of Historical Archaeology* 9, no. 1 (2005): 43–56.

Zarankin, Andrés, and María Ximena Senatore. *Historias de un Pasado en Blanco: Arqueología Histórica Antártica.* Belo Horizonte: Argumentum, 2007. Zarankin, Andrés, Michael Pearson, and Melisa A. Salerno. Archaeology in Antarctica. London: Routledge, 2023.

Chapter 10

Aerospatial Heritage Sites

A Borderless, Transnational Heritage of Valued, Meaningful Sites at Altitude

Ryan N. Sisak

Despite the mostly outer-space setting of the missions of the Space Race by the United States and the USSR, and the more than fifty years of heritage conservation efforts aimed at them, not a single location in outer space has been recognized or designated as a heritage site. Yet this conceptual gap in the heritage discipline and field is not due to a lack of effort, initiative, or imagination. For in less than four years following the Apollo 11 moon landing mission by the United States, its launch site "at the Kennedy Space Center was listed on the [United States] National Register of Historic Places."[1] And in the decades that have followed, numerous parties have made strong cases for designating and protecting historic sites and objects of American spaceflight. From the "24 recommended resources contained in . . . the Man in Space Theme Study"[2] by Harry Butowski, to the more recent scholarship and conservation work by Lisa Westwood, Beth O'Leary, and Milford Donaldson, the material culture of American space programs has received thorough and creative attention. In their recent book *The Final Mission: Preserving NASA's Apollo Sites,*[3] Westwood, O'Leary, and Donaldson discuss prior efforts and challenges to achieving US National Historic Landmark designation for Tranquility Base (the site of the first human lunar landing in 1969 by the American Apollo 11 mission) and O'Leary and Westwood's successful campaigns for inscription of the objects and structures at Tranquility Base onto the historical and cultural registers of both California and New Mexico around 2010. And in 2006, O'Leary and a team of students successfully inscribed Tranquility Base "as a historic archaeological site as part of . . . [the] database in the [State of New Mexico] Laboratory of Anthropology."[4]

Still, all of these heritage sites and objects recognized or advocated for exist only on Earth or the Moon—none are in outer space.

Those cases, though, represent only a fraction of the conservation and designation efforts aimed at the material remains of Apollo 11 alone. In "2001, the Lunar Legacy Project approached both the federal agency, NASA, and the federal preservation authority, the Keeper of the National Register of Historic Places . . . proposing that the [Tranquility Base] lunar site become a National Historic Landmark."[5] This effort failed to gain acceptance for a number of legalities, including perceived discord with the Outer Space Treaty and lack of jurisdiction.[6] Additionally, For All Moonkind, Inc., an international nonprofit organization that works toward the preservation of history and human heritage in outer space, has been working to include Tranquility Base on their "For All Moonkind Registry,"[7] simultaneously participating as an observer organization with the United Nations Office for Outer Space Affairs Committee on the Peaceful Uses of Outer Space.[8] Quite plainly, efforts to

Figure 10.1. Apollo 8 Photograph "AS08-13-2329." Though not the infamous Earthrise photo taken moments later and in color, this is the first and unedited photograph of the Earthrise event. *Source*: By courtesy of NASA/Johnson Space Center.

Aerospatial Heritage Sites 225

conserve and designate Apollo 11 sites and objects have been exhaustive. Yet other space heritage projects still abound.

Alice Gorman, a prominent space archaeologist, has recognized aerospace objects or sites as heritage, on Earth, in orbit, in outer space, and on celestial objects including the Moon.[9] Recently, Gorman has embarked (with Justin Walsh) on the "first archaeological study of a space habitat... [that explores] how material culture shapes human experiences of the space environment" on the International Space Station.[10] Gorman's work includes roughly two decades of research and advocacy, recognizing the heritage status of objects in orbit, arguing for their conservation, and emphasizing the link between satellites and their orbits as an essential component of their heritage value.[11] Such orbital settings constitute an intangible, spatial aspect of those satellites' heritage character. Similar to how places become heritage sites, these orbits have come to form *heritage paths*. But despite these intrepid ideas

Figure 10.2. This Is the Crater That Armstrong Avoided by Flying Over It, After Assuming Manual Control. He would later take this photograph (AS11-40-5955) while on his moonwalk. Note the depth, rockiness, and overall unsuitability as a possible landing site. *Source*: By courtesy of NASA/Johnson Space Center.

about space heritage, researchers have yet to ideate *heritage sites in outer space*.[12]

Much of the focus, instead, has been on navigating the legalities of designating Tranquility Base a US National Historic Landmark or including it on the World Heritage List. Several master's theses have explored these legal issues in detail, in addition to *The Final Mission*. Ralph Gibson Jr. (a student of Beth O'Leary) argued for National Historic Landmark status for the objects and structures at Tranquility Base,[13] and Joseph Reynolds acknowledged Gibson Jr.'s arguments and presented a legal precedent by which Tranquility Base could achieve international designation by "properly present[ing] the dangers at the Apollo Lunar Landing Sites";[14] this is similar to the approach used to add "'Old City Jerusalem and its Walls' to the World Heritage List."[15] By focusing the campaigns for Tranquility Base on the risk of loss to the lunar site (by damage or decay), this kind of argumentation could enable circumvention of the issue of *national ownership*—a precondition for World Heritage listing.[16]

Thus, with such imaginative inquiries into space heritage, from novel ideas about what is considered heritage (such as sites on the Moon and objects in orbit) to the various legal issues that have entangled its conservation, two key questions arise: Are there sites in outer space that have been valued as heritage? And if so, what management actions should be taken given their location beyond the physical and legal realms of national boundaries? This chapter shall demonstrate a linkage of heritage value for sites in outer space and elucidate the transnational nature of this *borderless* heritage.

A LONG-STANDING HERITAGE— UNRECOGNIZED AND OVERLOOKED

There are two overarching reasons why human spaceflight heritage sites have been restricted to Earth and the Moon. First, recognition and designation of space heritage has been focused mainly on attributing inherent value to historic things and places—this is how the National Register of Historic Places and World Heritage List inscription processes work.[17] Second, most of these things and places have had a well-defined material correlate. These two patterns have, therefore, steered space heritage work along the lines of historic preservation and archaeology. But for things and places with a more immaterial character, there has been little consideration that they, too, are also heritage. Thus, a *discursive boundary* has existed between the tangible and intangible—with most recognized space heritages starkly on the tangible side.

Gorman, though, has shifted how value is assigned to space heritage and stretched the boundaries of what constitutes heritage. For Gorman, "heritage is about things from the past which are significant to people in the present, and which they want to keep into the future."[18] Gorman explicitly refers to people rather than governments or authorities. John Carman also follows in this track, writing that "not only can the category of heritage include any object, it can include anything at all—not only the physical but also the ideational."[19] Gorman also views heritage as a *discourse*—one in which an *unvalued* object, place, memory, or practice is *not* heritage, no matter how old or historic it is.[20] Gorman's views on heritage seemingly echo Carman's ideas on heritage sites, in that "what makes them heritage . . . is that they represent intangible qualities we value."[21] These notions are similar to those of Laurajane Smith, who in an earlier, signal work, emphasized the intangible nature of heritage, such that "all heritage is intangible . . . [and] the tangible or pre-discursive . . . [is not] the self-evident form and essence of heritage."[22] Accordingly, Westwood, O'Leary and Donaldson have also argued that even in the absence of an official heritage designation, it "does not imply that a site not meeting such criteria is not important to any given person or group."[23]

Despite the diversity of things conceived of as space heritage, from sites on Earth and the Moon, to objects in orbit among the "spacescape,"[24] they are all either places on a celestial object or just an *object in space*, but not a particular *place in space*. And though certainly boundary-breaking, Gorman's spotlights on various intangible space heritages, such as satellites' orbits and community aboard the International Space Station, are rather rare postulates. Research into the intangible aspects of space heritage is terribly scarce, and of the works that have been written, the majority have noted either a material or archaeological regard for what is considered heritage. Consequently, untethered, pure places at altitude, have yet to be considered within the heritage literature.[25]

Given the conceptual strides in heritage studies and its subdiscipline of space heritage, recognition of sites in outer space *as heritage* should be evolutionary. For when Gorman recognized the *orbit* of Vanguard 1 (the oldest satellite still orbiting Earth, launched by the United States)[26] as an ineluctable part of its heritage character and value,[27] a "quasi-immaterial"[28] *path of travel* was identified as a critical element of its *heritage status*. Edward Casey had commented years earlier about the very significance of "pathways between"[29] places—what are essentially "heritage paths." It would seem, then, that a more marginal *conceptual boundary* could be easily crossed: one that separates the concepts of paths and places. Therefore, if the value, meaning, and significance of a place (even as path or region), regardless of its location is clearly demonstrated, then it should be recognized *as a heritage site*. Whether such places lie on Earth, the Moon, or suspended in outer space is an irrelevant concern. Any valued, meaningful place can be a heritage site.

Another issue, though, has kept heritage sites in outer space theoretically hidden. The generally *intangible character* of places in outer space is rather dissimilar to the character of typical heritage sites. Most heritage sites occupy a tangible, touchable place—even the lunar site of Tranquility Base. But places in outer space occupy a near-true vacuum, filled with minuscule amounts of gasses, radiation, charged particles, dark energy, dark matter, and occasionally micrometeoroids and space debris.[30] And though surely physical in nature, such aspects of outer-space places are generally insensible. Not much of what is described here is *discernibly tangible or visible*, and though the space heritage literature has acknowledged the *intangible nature* of heritage valuations,[31] its focus has remained mostly within the discursive confines of tangible, material heritage.[32] Stemming from the obsession with tangibility in heritage management, heritage sites in outer space have remained unseen behind the conceptual boundary of tangible and intangible places.

What, then, has caused such a tangible-intangible boundary to form? Since the earliest space heritage conservation efforts, there has been a broad reliance on structures, solutions, and organizations operating firmly within the "Authorized Heritage Discourse."[33] Accordingly, most research on and advocacy for such heritage has analyzed legalities and proposed management schemes that rely on various management authorities. And though some have presented an international approach, invoking organizations such as the World Heritage Committee (which manages the World Heritage List)[34] and other United Nations organizations, proposals such as World Heritage listing would require national authorities (such as the United States National Register of Historic Places) to first designate the place or structure of interest.[35] Yet such a designation would also require domestic ownership.[36] But given that ownership of space is prohibited by international treaty, domestic ownership or designation of "sites or paths in outer space" is not possible.[37] Thus, only a *land-based* site or structure, rather than a site or path in outer space, could be a "place . . . of interest." This boundary of *materiality*, then, is deeply rooted in heritage management bureaucracies that depend upon *national boundaries*. And it is the resultant interplay of all these boundaries that has inhibited the very ideation of heritage sites in outer space.[38] Without a physical site to be owned, managed, or saved from destruction, there is little incentive for state authorities to develop an interest. Consequently, the value and meaning of places in outer space can only be determined by considering them a *heritage without national boundaries*.

It is for this reason that suggestions like drafting a new treaty or amending existing agreements to accommodate unorthodox space heritages feed the same bureaucratic cycle that has marginalized such unorthodox heritages until now,[39] a cycle that continually reframes heritage authorities as indefinitely necessary.[40] Such schemes would likely act to sustain the obsession with materiality and national ownership that has kept hidden the very awareness of significant places in outer space from humanity's cultural consciousness. Thus, only an assessment of unofficial, personal accounts could truly establish the heritage value of places in outer space.

A UNIQUE METHODOLOGY FOR AN UNCONVENTIONAL HERITAGE

What places in space, then, have been valued as heritage, and by what means is this known? At the minimum, five places in outer space "have historically held meaning for, and been valued by, those who experienced [them]."[41] And as such, these places were experienced by Frank Borman, James Lovell, and William Anders of Apollo 8 (the first human mission to circumnavigate the Moon), and by Neil Armstrong and Buzz Aldrin of Apollo 11 (the first human landing on the Moon). And though not explicitly referred to as heritage sites by the astronauts themselves, the places known as Translunar Injection (where humans first left Earth orbit and ventured to the Moon), Lunar Orbit Insertion (where humans first entered lunar orbit) and Earthrise (where humans first saw Earth emerge above the lunar horizon) from Apollo 8, and Powered Descent Initiation (where the final phase of humanity's first Moon landing began) and Program 66 (where Armstrong assumed Manual Control to complete the first Moon landing) from Apollo 11 have been valued as such.[42] Yet given their nature as places at altitude, these places have been aptly named *Aerospatial Heritage Sites*.[43] This term acknowledges the sites' distinctive nature as valued, meaningful places located in aerospace.

Developing an understanding, however, of why such places have been valued required an amalgam of methodologies. Given that the aim was to determine the significances ascribed to the Apollo sites in space, a phenomenological approach was needed to gather an "understanding and description of things as they . . . [were] experienced by a subject."[44] In this case, the subjects were the five Apollo astronauts. And though some phenomenologies consist of revisiting landscapes, the issues of celestial positions and rotations would likely not allow for the same vistas that were initially seen.[45] Thus, experiencing the same "spacescape" would be unlikely. But another issue, though, posed a greater challenge to revisiting the Apollo sites: due to the technological requirements of spaceflight, space travel is physically, financially, and technologically extremely prohibitive. And only the United States National Air and Space Administration (NASA) has ever sent astronauts beyond Earth—a feat not reattempted since the end of the Apollo program in 1972. Thus, a physical revisiting was not really a viable option.

Still, though, even if such a revisiting was indeed feasible, new observations of these places would not yield the kinds of impressions applicable to understanding their heritage status. Any newly ascribed value or meaning would have been applied outside of the contexts that historically hung over the missions, and despite the futility of returning to sites above Earth and the Moon, it was possible instead to compile a "synthetic"[46] accounting of significance. Given that phenomenologies are about "observation . . . [and] mediated experiences of landscape,"[47] firsthand accounts were vital. "There is," as Christopher Tilley asserts, "no substitute for personal experience, for being there."[48] Therefore, a "discourse analysis"[49] of the transcripts of every recorded utterance from the Apollo 8 and Apollo 11 missions, formed the basis of a *"synthetic phenomenology of place and landscape* [original emphasis]"[50]—one that aimed to describe the astronauts' "experiences as fully as possible."[51] This was the only way to uncover the *original significance* of the Apollo sites in space.

Therefore, what about the Apollo sites in space has been valued and what meanings have the sites held, to the extent that their status as a *heritage without national boundaries* is discernible? And furthermore, how do certain Apollo sites exemplify elements of transnational history? These questions, accordingly, guide and frame my arguments. This chapter will demonstrate how the Apollo sites have been valued as *borderless places*, how the meanings ascribed to them draw on the *transnational history* of the Space Race, and how recognizing these sites as primary examples of *Aerospatial Heritage Sites* would liberate sites like them from the various organizations whose authority and schemes rely upon the dominance of *national boundaries*.

UNCOVERING SIGNIFICANCE BY REVISITING THE PAST

In order to convey what has been significant about the Apollo sites, each site was synthetically revisited by reexamining the astronauts' experiences.[52] For the sake of clarity, each site was initially investigated in the chronological order of its visit but then reinforced by statements made in the decades that followed each mission. For the first Aerospatial Heritage Site (Apollo 8 Translunar Injection), there were few recorded utterances at the time of the maneuver. Apart from technical transmissions regarding initiation of the engine burn, cutoff and trajectory readings, there was little indication of local awareness by the Apollo 8 crew, no mention of being in a special place.[53] But given that "grasp of one place does allow . . . [for] grasp [of] what holds, for the most part, in other places of the same region,"[54] examination of the most proximal data available with respect to the event of Translunar Injection, provides insight into the crews' earliest experiences of the region where it occurred. When the crew first reacted to seeing Earth, approximately twenty-six minutes post Translunar Injection, they were immediately flush with excitement at viewing Earth from what was then the highest altitude achieved by humans. After Borman exclaimed "what a view,"[55] Lovell and Anders became totally engrossed with photographing this novel sight for approximately fifteen minutes. As the sphere of Earth came fully into view, Borman framed the event's historical significance by gloating to Michael Collins (the Capsule Communicator in Houston, and future Apollo 11 astronaut), "tell Conrad he lost his record."[56] And though Borman was referencing a record from Gemini VIII (an earlier American mission during the Space Race) that had already been broken (soon after the Translunar Injection event), his comment was not really an indication of an awareness of achieving a great altitude. Given that the record-breaking moment had occurred about a half hour earlier,[57] his "Conrad" comment was spurred instead by a *perception of altitude*—derived from their new vista and place high above Earth. Borman, thus, valued this region for the *historical awareness* it afforded, and Anders and Lovell valued the post-Translunar-Injection area as a special place that yielded an unseen magnificent view of Earth.

Alternatively, though, it might seem that the place of value was not where Translunar Injection had occurred, but a region much farther along their path than where they had precisely left Earth orbit. But when interviewed for the documentary film *Earthrise* almost fifty years later,[58] the astronauts of Apollo 8 connected their distant sighting of Earth and the history they achieved, to the *event and place* of Translunar Injection. Anders added context to his reminiscence, characterizing the moment as "when we went into orbit and then injected to the Moon," and though Lovell reflected on the same events that did not begin until at least twenty-six minutes after Translunar Injection, he drew the memories together into a single event, adding, "this was the first time that we actually escaped from the Earth." Borman further united the sighting and translunar events, by expressing how the astronauts failed to convey "in its entirety, the grandeur of what we had seen." Lastly, Anders added to his remembrance of going into orbit and injecting to the Moon, by emphasizing how they "were the first ones to see it in color . . . from that altitude." For Anders, Lovell and Borman, there was no distinction between the *place* of Translunar Injection (which NASA defined as a single coordinate, altitude, and time)[59] and the *place* of their first-ever sighting. For them, Translunar Injection was a single event at a singular place, despite encompassing a vast region; a place defined by them and *not* by NASA. And given how "place . . . is inseparable from the concrete region in which it is found,"[60] this singular place was more a region than a location. For the Apollo 8 crew, then, Translunar Injection eventually became "a set of relational places linked by paths, movements and narratives . . . [and] sedimented with human significances;"[61] shaped by personal, philosophical, and historical meanings.[62] For them, the official coordinative location of Translunar Injection became *just a part of* a boundless region of space, associated with the same name, but *as the same place.*

Following several days of transit from Earth to the Moon, Apollo 8 entered the Lunar Orbit Insertion maneuver. Once completed, humans had begun orbit of another celestial body for the first time. But about seven minutes prior to Lunar Orbit Insertion (achieved only when the engine burn was complete), the Apollo 8 crew became the first humans to see the Moon up close. In that moment, two of the three astronauts were immediately struck with awe, remarking on the Moon's craters, mountains, and shadows in proximity; twice Anders exclaimed "fantastic"[63] and even "oh, my God!"[64] But despite the excitement, Borman remained staunchly mission focused, and even redirected Anders and Lovell back to their scheduled tasks. But in addition to these sights prior to entering orbit, they also *felt* their deceleration, both during the burn and through Lunar Orbit Insertion.[65] Such sensing and perceiving of movement, "solidified"[66] their understanding of this path to orbit, and helped form future "spatial stories, [and] forms of narrative understanding."[67] This only becomes evident, though, through analysis of how this movement was remembered several decades later.

As recounted in *Earthrise*,[68] though, Borman and Anders recalled Lunar Orbit Insertion as not just an event at the location at which it was achieved (at the termination of the burn),[69] but as an orbital path colored by their experiences. Accordingly, this path began where they "came into the shadow of the Moon" (as described by Anders), and terminated where they reacquired visual of the lunar surface (after the burn maneuver).[70] Anders, during the *Earthrise* interview, described a hair-raising experience that "brought up an animalistic feeling." But, for Borman, Lunar Orbit Insertion was the difference between achieving lunar orbit or failing the mission and a swift return to Earth, and though they would have seen the far side of the Moon, regardless of achieving orbit,[71] Borman attributed its sighting to the success of the Lunar Orbit Insertion, thus enabling them to see "a portion of the Moon that human eyes had never seen before." For him, the primordial sighting was a "poignant moment." Thus, in the case of Lunar Orbit Insertion, the Apollo 8 crew ascribed significance to a particular place in space, and just like Translunar Injection, the place of Lunar Orbit Insertion meant much more *as a path* than as a location. Bracketed by moments before and after the maneuver, Lunar Orbit Insertion's path was unbounded by NASA's definition[72] of where the event had occurred. Here, again, the boundaries of this specific place in space were redefined and redrawn by the Apollo astronauts.

Nearly seven hours following Lunar Orbit Insertion and without warning, the Apollo 8 crew was greeted with an awesome view. During their fourth orbit of the Moon, Earth was seen rising above the Moon's horizon for the first time. Bearing from right to left, the home planet suddenly and unexpectedly emerged. As evidenced in the capsule recording transcript,[73] all three astronauts expressed urgency at capturing high-quality photographs of the sight. Anders (who first saw the event) and Lovell were demonstrably expressive during this time. Yet of important note, the color photograph (ubiquitously known as Earthrise) would eventually become a widely and internationally disseminated image.[74]

Unsurprisingly, though, in their *Earthrise* interviews,[75] all three astronauts confirmed their astonishment. They spoke in existential terms, expressing memories of thoughts about being "here" with Earth over "there," and how "over there" "was everything we held dear," and though these memories were more explicitly recalled by Borman, Anders and Lovell echoed the same sentiments. Yet despite having redirected Anders and Lovell earlier in the mission to refocus on their tasks (ahead of Lunar Orbit Insertion), he now noted *his interest* in the events, recalling, "it all struck us immediately—get that picture!" But then he commented further about their role in the famous pictures, saying, "we had never had any discussion of taking an 'Earthrise' picture, before the flight or during the flight." Thus, according to Borman, the "Earthrise" photography was a series of unplanned actions, taken only because of the crew's initiative. As he remembered it, their decision making, and not NASA's, was responsible for the otherworldly images.

Additionally, the language used by the crew in the film *Earthrise*,[76] further nuanced their recollection of *where they were* during the Earthrise event. Thorough analysis reveals a mention of their distance to Earth, and a contrasting description of the gray lunar surface set against the rising, colorful Earth. Such language evidences an awareness of landscape, and a realization that the lunar one was local, with the Earthly one far-off. They were acutely aware of being in a *unique and specific place*. Lovell intimated such local awareness, saying, "when I was around the Moon, and I saw the Earth . . . I personally thought that everybody would like to have that view, as we did, to see the Earth as it really is." For Lovell, Earthrise provided an authentic view of Earth. And though Borman did list "our country" as one of the things they "held dear," he immediately juxtaposed the notion by asking, "how in the world could [Earth] . . . exist in this vast universe of nothing?" His amazement was mostly directed at concepts of place that transcend national boundaries such as the world, Earth, and the "vast universe." Lovell, too, felt that "it gave a contrast, it said that 'hey, here are people looking from a different planet, looking back at what is our home.'" And though he simply misspoke by referring to the Moon as a planet, the image of Earthrise held significant meaning for him: seeing Earth from another heavenly body and being present in a rather unique place. For him, Earthrise *was a place* that put home in perspective, not his country. Thus, Lovell, too, has valued the place of Earthrise for ideas that also *transcend national boundaries*.

Roughly six months later, in July of 1969, Apollo 11 was tasked with the first human Moon landing, and although Apollo 11 repeated many of the flight maneuvers from Apollo 8 and Apollo 10, it truly distinguished itself from prior missions when it began the final approach (known as Powered Descent Initiation) to the Moon's surface.[77] Yet despite limited utterances during the first phase of Powered Descent, what Armstrong and Aldrin (the two astronauts who landed on the Moon) said suggests an awareness that the lateness of Powered Descent Initiation would force them to "land long," that Earth was visible above the lunar surface, and that unexpected computer alarms required their attention.[78] Accordingly, when debriefed during post-flight quarantine, Armstrong recounted that "the computer was a little bit confused at what our downrange position was. Had it known where it was, it would have throttled down later . . . so that we would still hit the right place."[79] Thus, not more than ten days after the Powered Descent (and eventual landing), Armstrong implied an awareness of having been in a specific place at altitude, shortly after descent initiation. When interviewed at the Apollo 11 post-flight press conference,[80] Armstrong again referred to Powered Descent Initiation as a place: "where you are over the surface of the Moon at the time of ignition." Here he made "a direct connection between overshooting the targeted landing area"[81] and the location of Powered Descent Initiation. Aldrin, too, made similar connections in his own response to a question during this conference. He used the word "where" five times, both to describe the same place of descent initiation, and also for the eventual landing site. For both astronauts, this place at altitude where Powered Descent began, was linked to the eventual site of Tranquility Base.

After a few minutes, toward the end of the Powered Descent, Armstrong visually interpreted their trajectory via the landing point designator (a scale in the window), and as revealed in the capsule transcript,[82] concluded the area was safe. As the only one regularly looking out the window,[83] he stated, "that's not a bad-looking area." But soon thereafter his assessment changed, as he acted to extend the landing across a treacherous, threatening landscape. Five seconds after noting "pretty rocky area," he said, "I'm going to," and then took manual attitude control (of the Lunar Excursion Module) seven seconds later. Then, following his assumption of Manual Control, he said, "looks like a good area here," and soon followed with "gonna be right over that crater . . . I got a good spot." Ahead of Manual Control the initially acceptable surface soon became dangerous; but following Manual Control, the ground appeared good again. Thus, the place and time of Armstrong's Manual Control acted as a *spatiotemporal boundary*—a boundary that is central to Armstrong valuing his Manual Control as a unique place at altitude.

Furthermore, the post-flight debriefing illuminates more about the meaning of Manual Control for both Armstrong and Aldrin.[84] When probed by a reporter, Armstrong linked Manual Control with where he was "when crossing the top of the crater and the boulder field." He also explained that he took over to "look for a satisfactory landing area," which confirmed they were facing a poor landing spot. Manual Control, however, was also linked to their fuel situation. Armstrong recalled that he "was also reluctant to slow down my descent rate anymore than it was or stop because we were close to running out of fuel;" this is supported by Armstrong's query (as recorded) of "how's the fuel?"[85] Yet as noted in the capsule transcript commentary[86] and in *First Man: The Life of Neil A. Armstrong*,[87] the drama of the fuel situation was eventually demystified—they landed with nearly one minute of fuel. Armstrong later downplayed this challenge, claiming "it didn't really matter."[88] Thus, determining whether Manual Control held meanings related to running out of fuel required further analysis. For Armstrong, though, Manual Control still meant that he was able to avoid dangers on the Moon's surface and in turn, find a suitable landing area.

It is important to consider, however, Armstrong's pattern of minimizing perils of life-endangering events. As recounted in the book *First Man*,[89] his tempered, balanced conclusions are coated in equanimity. Thus, his assertion that the fuel crisis "didn't really matter" is rather predictable, and to the commentators of the Apollo 11 landing transcripts, he even provided technical reasoning as to why he did not really worry about running out of fuel.[90] But regarding reflective memories, it is known that "individuals' discourse about their experiences and thoughts may change over time, such that it becomes structured differently . . . if they are contacted at another phase of their lives."[91] In this way, only one year before his death, at the Certified Practising Accountant Australia 125th Anniversary Gala Dinner in 2011,[92] he dwelled on the fuel crisis, saying, "I'm running low on fuel." There, during his narration of a simulation of the lunar landing,[93] Armstrong added, "get a thirty second fuel warning, need to get it down on the ground, here, before we run out." Here, Armstrong directly stated meaning of his Manual Control, saying, "so I took over manually from the computer, the autopilot, and flew it . . . to try to find a smoother, more level landing spot."[94] For him, it was about finding an acceptable place to land. This is supported by his interview later for the same event, whereby he recounted:

> The computer showed us where it intended to land and it . . . was a very bad location . . . not a good place to land at all. So . . . I took over manually and flew

it like a helicopter out to the west direction, got into a smoother area with not so many rocks . . . found a level area and . . . was able to get it down there safely before we ran out of fuel.[95]

Here, though, the supposedly settled fuel crisis still carried meaning and remained an unshakable part of his lunar landing reminiscence. Thus, since the Apollo 11 landing, to more than four decades later, Armstrong valued his Manual Control of the Lunar Excursion Module as a critical set of actions that culminated in a safe and successful lunar landing.

Still, though indiscernible from the capsule recording transcripts, post-flight debriefing and post-flight press conference, Aldrin, too, valued Powered Descent Initiation as a place. But just four years following the mission, as recounted in Aldrin's 1973 autobiography *Return to Earth*, Powered Descent Initiation did not mean much more than as a planned and insensible maneuver; only instruments confirmed its commencement.[96] But forty years after the Apollo 11 mission, in a more recent autobiography,[97] Aldrin remembered that "our hearts pounded in anticipation of the 'Powered Descent' to the lunar surface," and that upon receiving permission to commence initiation, "Neil nodded as we acknowledged the implications." Here the event took on greater significance: initiation was anticipated as Armstrong and him acknowledged the undertones of the moment. But Powered Descent Initiation held more meaning still for Aldrin, recalling, "inside my helmet, I was grinning like we had just won the biggest race of all time. In eleven minutes we were going to set the Eagle down for a landing unlike any other."[98] Here it is clear how the moment of descent initiation came to act as a *temporal boundary*. It demarcated time so that eleven minutes from initiation, the first human landing on another celestial body would occur. Yet Aldrin also recognized the nature of initiation as a place at altitude, noting that "downward we were going, and rapidly, too. I could see the moonscape seemingly rising toward us."[99] Thus, this place at altitude, valued as the departure point for the final approach to the lunar surface, held meaning for Aldrin as a *spatial boundary* as well.

Additionally, though, and consistent with Armstrong's views, Aldrin, too, viewed Manual Control during descent as crucial to negotiating the dangerous, inhospitable landscape. In Aldrin's *Return to Earth*, Aldrin emplaced the event:

At an altitude of five hundred feet, Neil took over manually . . . [and] we immediately saw that the area of the moon where our computer intended to land was rather more strewn with rocks than we had anticipated. The area beyond it however, was quite clear. Neil extended our trajectory and thereby changed our touchdown point. . . . The slight change caused our flight to last quite a few seconds longer and used a great deal more fuel.[100]

For Aldrin, then, the fuel crisis and the extension of their trajectory and touchdown point were intimately connected events. In Aldrin's *Magnificent Desolation*,[101] evidence abounds of spatial awareness, remarking, "we checked our position relative to the surface . . . at an altitude of only 2,000 feet;" such emplacing continues throughout his accounts. Regarding altitude and descent rate callouts, he clarified that he was "letting Neil know that we were a mere 750 feet above the surface and descending at twenty three feet per second," and remembered Armstrong's callout of "pretty rocky area." Though he also described the cratered, rocky primary landing site, he valued Armstrong's Manual Control as "good" and "a split-second decision to fly long to go farther than we had planned to search for a safe landing area." He thus echoed Armstrong's concern with landing safely, and through use of the word "split-second" confirmed that Manual Control acted as a *temporal boundary*, and that the decision to assume Manual Control allowed them "to go farther than we had planned" begot it then as a *spatial boundary* as well. Thus, by synthesis of his accounts, Aldrin also valued Armstrong's Manual Control as a particular place at altitude that demarcated both time and space, and thus favorably affected the outcome of the Moon landing.

WHY DOES THE PAST, PRESENT, AND FUTURE OF AEROSPATIAL HERITAGE SITES MATTER?

The places (locations, paths, and regions) at altitude that encompassed Translunar Injection, Lunar Orbit Insertion and Earthrise (all during Apollo 8), and Powered Descent Initiation and Armstrong's Manual Control (both from Apollo 11) should be recognized as primary examples of Aerospatial Heritage Sites. These places have held various significances for the astronauts who visited them, from the time of their first visit and still decades later. As NASA and other space agencies (including national agencies and commercial companies) prepare to send a diverse roster of astronauts to the Moon, Mars and possibly beyond, newer and more inclusive, international heritages will be born in outer space. It is conceivable, then, that similar to the Aerospatial Heritage Sites of Apollo 8 and Apollo 11, the astronauts of the first all-female spacewalk[102] would still find value and meaning in that historic event. But the unique character of events at altitude requires a novel approach to recognizing such heritage sites—and as such, innovative interpretations. If newer, more inclusive heritages at altitude will be claimed, then the Aerospatial Heritage Sites established herein and others like them cannot be ignored.[103] If what will come is to be also recognized, then what has already come before must be recognized first; precedent must be respected.

Therefore, given that Aerospatial Heritage Sites are not about visitable heritage sites but instead about revaluing the reminiscences that have breathed them into life, the oral histories and phenomenological accounts are the indispensable threads of this heritage fabric.[104] These kinds of sites are constituted by memories, and though their physical, relative places in outer space are important (including the paths and regions that emanate from certain coordinates and altitudes above Earth and the Moon), those places in space are not really the same as when they were first visited;[105] but from a heritage standpoint, that fact is irrelevant. The Aerospatial Heritage Sites presented herein have been valued for what they represent, far more than what their physicality implies—because "space does not and cannot exist apart from the events and activities within which it is implicated . . . [and spaces] are [only] meaningfully constituted in relation to human agency and activity."[106] Only, then, by the actions, experiences, and agency of the astronauts, beyond national duty, that occurred in borderless places valued for their *transcendence of national boundaries*, have these sites become "spatial impressions with temporally inscribed memories."[107] These meaningful places have been burned into the astronauts' memories and consequently reshaped their identities;[108] they have become ineluctable parts of who they are.

Of great significance, though, is how some of these sites have been valued as *transnational boundaries*, and for the other sites, they too have been valued for reasons that redefine their *boundaries*—upending their definition as point coordinates at altitude,[109] as defined by the national authority NASA. For Armstrong and Aldrin of Apollo 11, Powered Descent Initiation and Armstrong's Manual Control (Program P66) were valued as *spatiotemporal boundaries*. For Borman, Lovell and Anders of Apollo 8, Translunar Injection, Lunar Orbit Insertion, and Earthrise were valued as places sewn together across regions and paths that extended far beyond any singular location in space.[110] For the Apollo 8 crew, "the act of moving . . . [was] as important as that of arriving."[111] Thus, these transnational boundaries have acted to transform these heritage sites—from authorized heritages officially valued by the United States, to now borderless, personal heritages as recognized by the astronauts.[112] Not for official, *national reasons*, but for personal, *transnational reasons* instead, and given the boundary of materiality that sustains bureaucratic reliance on national boundaries, this is incredibly significant.[113] It suggests that these heritages might indeed survive without an authorized management; a true embodiment of heritage without national boundaries.

Finally, though, the Aerospatial Heritage Sites exhibited herein are patent, borderless heritages. As the Outer Space Treaty declares, no nation shall claim ownership over space or celestial bodies, and "States Parties to the Treaty shall regard astronauts as envoys of mankind."[114] Although the objects and site of Tranquility Base have been added to state registers, efforts to secure their (and other lunar sites') inclusion in the World Heritage List have so far been officially denied.[115] But this is unsurprising. World Heritage inclusion relies upon national boundaries and authorities, and the international approval such designation implies belies its reliance on national, material ownership. World Heritage Sites are far from being borderless. But as a quasi-immaterial and borderless heritage of spatial impressions with temporally inscribed memories, Aerospatial Heritage Sites require safeguarding of their constitutive memories and interpretation of their unique places in space.

Thus, the character of Aerospatial Heritage Sites as *significant places at altitude* requires creative interpretation. Ideally, geographic information systems and audiovisual simulations should play a central role. These kinds of technology are useful for depicting events and places in three-dimensions. Currently exemplary interpretations exist of both Earthrise and Armstrong's Manual Control.[116] They feature audiovisual simulations and are either synced with capsule recordings and narrated or use Google Earth and Google Moon to depict interactive visuals and geodetics. These interpretive modes respect the nature of such sites as locations, paths, and regions suspended at altitude. Just as Stonehenge has been interpreted as a vast heritage site extending across a broad cultural landscape, with its cursi, barrows, and famed stone circle,[117] so too must Aerospatial Heritage Sites be envisioned. Consider how the flight path of the tragic United 93 (of September 11, 2001) has been interpreted to acknowledge much more than just the final site of loss; the memorial encourages visitors to envision the aerospatial nature of passengers' unfathomable acts of courage.[118] Still, other memorials around New York City also encourage visitors to look toward the skyline to bear witness to the grave human loss.[119] Thus, when appropriate, ground level monuments should also be used to draw visitors' attention skyward to memorialize events at altitude. These are important considerations in the context of recognizing new heritage sites at altitude. Future places at altitude are likely to be deemed significant and these interpretations can act to guide those that might come.

Beyond being borderless, transnational boundaries, these Aerospatial Heritage Sites are also *transnational heritages*. The astronauts of Apollo 8 and Apollo 11 framed Earth in stark relief. For the Apollo 8 crew, their reminiscence several decades later was rather existential—there was little mention of country or nation, and just a few years after the Apollo 11 flight, Aldrin reflected that "intellectually one could realize that there were wars on earth, but emotionally it was impossible to understand such things. The thought occurred and reoccurred that wars are generally fought for territory or are disputes over borders; from space the arbitrary borders established on earth cannot be seen."[120] For Aldrin, then, national borders were simply cognitions, and not something experienced while traveling in space. Still, forty years after his Apollo 11 flight, Aldrin noted the transnational quality of his experiences—such that despite Armstrong's disapproval for transmitting their communications during Powered Descent, he said: "I'm glad I left the mike on. Millions of people on Earth listened in between Mission Control in Houston and us as we descended."[121] For him, then, the events of Powered Descent Initiation and Armstrong's Manual Control (and eventual landing) were *universally* relatable. Even Michael Collins (Capsule Communicator at Mission Control Houston during Apollo 8's Translunar Injection, and Apollo 11 astronaut who remained in lunar orbit during Powered Descent and landing) remarked more than fifty years after the Apollo 8 flight, how he regretted the lack of tribute at the moment of Translunar Injection—and how he had even expected the Pope to make a statement.[122] Understandably, though, the Apollo astronauts did view their missions at times in *national terms*. But most significances attributed by them to the events and places in space have been mainly colored by values and meanings that transcend national boundaries.

Of final note, however, is how the five Aerospatial Heritage Sites explored herein draw some significance from the *transnational history* of the Space Race. Consider that shortly after the launch of Sputnik (the first artificial satellite) in 1958, the official American view of "spaceflight represented . . . the ability to influence other nations through intangibles such as an impressive show of space capability. It granted to the nation achieving it first . . . an authenticity and gravitas not previously enjoyed among the world community."[123] These were the "feelings . . . [of cultural inferiority that are] a precondition for intercultural transfer to occur"[124]—a hallmark quality of transnational history.[125] Yet despite the fact that the American public was generally unafraid of Sputnik's launch, it is what drove the United States' official reactions to Sputnik, up to and including the founding of NASA;[126] additionally, the "feelings . . . of . . . inferiority" that circulated at the time, were likely promulgated by politicians.[127] Still, American answers to Soviet advances in space were driven by an intercultural transfer of values, as the United States government believed that expansion of its space program could demonstrate "the use of state power for public good."[128] Likewise, this was similar to Soviet aims for Sputnik and other Soviet space programs. But official US actors did not merely seek programs on par with the Soviets.' The American program "experience[d] significant mutations and transformations . . . which were determined by the actions of those involved in the transfer as well as the needs and expectations of the receiving culture."[129] For when President John F. Kennedy announced in 1961 a future American moon landing, the United States was unequipped to reach that lofty goal. But it was the "feelings . . . of cultural inferiority" that fed American space programs and thus ignited in them a "significant mutation and transformation."[130] Without the official intercultural transfer of valuing preeminence in space, from the Soviets to the Americans, as a means to promote state power for public good, the United States might not have engaged in a manned Space Race at all. But these transnational influences were directly tied to some of the Aerospatial Heritage Sites established herein. The decision to send Apollo 8 (instead of a later Apollo mission) to the Moon was spurred by a fear that the USSR would arrive there first.[131] This very element of transnational history will forever be linked to the heritage sites of Apollo 8.

CONCLUSION

In the end, Aerospatial Heritage Sites are really about heritage that transcends every aspect of national boundaries. From the heritage management authorities that rely on such schema, to the borderless nature of sites in space, Aerospatial Heritage Sites demonstrate how various transnational meanings may lay hidden beneath the surface of what have otherwise been nationally ascribed heritages. Seen here is how heritage without national boundaries is less about heritages that are unassociated with such boundaries, but instead, are valued for reasons that *dissociate* them from national boundaries. There is no denying that the Apollo missions explored were official, American ventures that culminated in the planting of an American flag on the Moon (during the first moonwalk on Apollo 11). But as shown throughout this chapter, incredibly unique places in outer space have been valued over the decades since their visit, and not for official, American reasons, but for personal, transnational ones. Discovering heritages without national boundaries requires looking in between the layers of established national heritages, not just simply outside of them. Such heritages remain hidden because of the dominance of national boundaries, both as precondition for their recognition, and as incentive for their management. Reliance on such boundaries acts to bury the new kinds of sites exposed herein. With innovative interpretations and exhaustive accountings, the unusual threads of this heritage fabric can be preserved and disseminated. This new kind of heritage represents an opportunity to redefine the places humans value without national boundaries.

NOTES

1. Harry A. Butowski, *Man in Space: National Historic Landmark Theme Study*, US National Park Service, US Department of the Interior, 1984.

2. Butowski, *Man in Space*.

3. Lisa Westwood, Beth L. O'Leary, and Milfred W. Donaldson, *The Final Mission: Preserving NASA's Apollo Sites*, Gainesville: University Press of Florida, 2017.

4. Westwood, O'Leary, and Donaldson, *The Final Mission*, 178.

5. Westwood, O'Leary, and Donaldson, *The Final Mission*, 149.

6. Westwood, O'Leary, and Donaldson, *The Final Mission*, 149–150.

7. For All Moonkind, Inc., "Declaration of Objectives and Activities Regarding Cultural Heritage in Outer Space" (https://www.forallmoonkind.org/about/the-declaration/, accessed July 23, 2021).

8. UNOOSA, "Committee on the Peaceful Uses of Outer Space: Observer Organizations" (https://www.unoosa.org/oosa/en/ourwork/copuos/members/copuos-observers.html, accessed July 23, 2021).

9. Alice Gorman, *Dr Space Junk vs The Universe: Archaeology and the Future*, Cambridge and London: The MIT Press, 2019.

10. ISS Archaeology, "About" (https://issarchaeology.org/about/, accessed July 24, 2021).

11. Alice Gorman, "Heritage of Earth Orbit: Orbital Debris—Its Mitigation and Cultural Heritage," in: Ann G. Darrin and Beth L. O'Leary (eds.), *Handbook of Space Engineering, Archaeology and Heritage*, Boca Raton: CRC Press, 2009, 381–397.

12. Ryan Sisak, "Aerospatial Heritage Sites—A History of Value and Meaning for Places in Relative Space," Master's Dissertation University of Birmingham, 2020, 1–15.

13. Ralph D. Gibson Jr., "Lunar Archaeology: The Application of Federal Historic Preservation Law to the Site Where Humans First Set Foot Upon The Moon," Master's Thesis, New Mexico State University, 2001.

14. Joseph P. Reynolds, "One Small Step: An Analysis of International Space Law and How it Effects Historic Preservation," Master's Thesis, Clemson University, 2012, 62.

15. Reynolds, "One Small Step," 62.

16. UNESCO World Heritage Centre, "World Heritage List Nominations" (https://whc.unesco.org/en/nominations/, accessed July 5, 2020); Westwood, O'Leary, and Donaldson, *The Final Mission*, 189; Reynolds, "One Small Step," 8–9.

17. U.S. Department of the Interior, National Park Service, Cultural Resources, National Register, History and Education, "How to Apply the National Register Criteria for Evaluation," (National Register Bulletin, 1997), i–50; UNESCO World Heritage Centre, "The Criteria for Selection" (https://whc.unesco.org/en/criteria/, accessed April 16, 2022).

18. Gorman, *Dr Space Junk vs The Universe*, 12.

19. John Carman, "Where the Value Lies: The Importance of Materiality to the Immaterial Aspects of Heritage," in: Laurajane Smith and Emma Waterton (eds.), *Taking Archaeology Out of Heritage*, Newcastle upon Tyne: Cambridge Scholars Publishing, 2009, 197.

20. Laurajane Smith, *Uses of Heritage*, London and New York: Routledge, 2006; Carman, "Where the Value Lies"; Rodney Harrison, "What is Heritage?" in: Rodney Harrison (ed.), *Understanding the Politics of Heritage*, Manchester: Manchester University Press in association with the Open University, 2010, 5–42.

21. Carman, "Where the Value Lies," 197.

22. Smith, *Uses of Heritage*, 3.

23. Westwood, O'Leary, and Donaldson, *The Final Mission*.

24. Alice Gorman, "The Cultural Landscape of Interplanetary Space," *Journal of Social Archaeology* 5, no. 1 (2005): 85–107.

25. Sisak, "Aerospatial Heritage Sites," 7, 12.

26. National Aeronautics and Space Administration, NASA Space Science Data Coordinated Archive, "Vanguard 1" (https://nssdc.gsfc.nasa.gov/nmc/spacecraft/display.action?id=1958-002B, accessed April 17, 2022).

27. Gorman, "Heritage of Earth Orbit," 390.

28. Sisak, "Aerospatial Heritage Sites," 6.

29. Edward S. Casey, "How to Get From Space to Place in a Fairly Short Stretch of Time: Phenomenological Prolegomena," in: Steven Feld and Keith H. Basso (eds.) *Senses of Place*, Santa Fe: School of American Research Press, 1996, 40.

30. Federal Aviation Administration, United States Department of Transportation, "The Space Environment (4.1.2)" (https://www.faa.gov/about/office_org/headquarters_offices/avs/offices/aam/cami/library/online_libraries/aerospace_medicine/tutorial/media/III.4.1.2_The_Space_Environment.pdf, accessed July 8, 2021).

31. Carman, "Where the Value Lies."

32. Sisak, "Aerospatial Heritage Sites," 1–15.

33. Smith, *Uses of Heritage*.

34. UNESCO World Heritage Centre, "The World Heritage Committee" (https://whc.unesco.org/en/committee/, accessed July 5, 2020).

35. Westwood, O'Leary, and Donaldson, *The Final Mission*, 189.

36. Westwood, O'Leary, and Donaldson, *The Final Mission*, 189–191.

37. Westwood, O'Leary, and Donaldson, *The Final Mission*, 189; Gibson Jr., "Lunar Archaeology," 9, 11, 19–21; Reynolds, "One Small Step," 5, 8–9, 15, 46.

38. Sisak, "Aerospatial Heritage Sites," 1–15.

39. Westwood, O'Leary, and Donaldson, *The Final Mission*, 191–192; Reynolds, "One Small Step," 62.

40. John Carman, "What Sustaining Heritage Really Does," *VITRUVIO International Journal of Architectural Technology and Sustainability* 4, no. 1 (2019): 1–10.

41. Sisak, "Aerospatial Heritage Sites," 15.

42. Sisak, "Aerospatial Heritage Sites."

43. Sisak, "Aerospatial Heritage Sites," 15.

44. Christopher Tilley, *A Phenomenology of Landscape: Places, Paths and Monuments*, Berg and Providence: Oxford, 1994, 12.

45. Christopher Tilley, *Interpreting Landscapes: Geologies, Topographies, Identities; Explorations in Landscape Phenomenology 3*, London and New York: Routledge, 2010, 25.

46. Tilley, *Interpreting Landscapes*, 30.

47. Tilley, *Interpreting Landscapes*, 24.

48. Tilley, *Interpreting Landscapes*, 24.

49. Sisak, "Aerospatial Heritage Sites," 16–17, 19.

50. Tilley, *Interpreting Landscapes*, 27, 30; Sisak, "Aerospatial Heritage Sites," 23–24.

51. Tilley, *Interpreting Landscapes*, 24.
52. Sisak, "Aerospatial Heritage Sites," 16–44.
53. W. David Woods and Frank O'Brien, "Apollo 8 Day 1: The Green Team and Separation" (https://history.nasa.gov/afj/ap08fj/03day1_green_sep.html, accessed September 1, 2021).
54. Casey, "How to Get From Space to Place in a Fairly Short Stretch of Time," 45.
55. Woods and O'Brien, "Apollo 8 Day 1."
56. Woods and O'Brien, "Apollo 8 Day 1."
57. Woods and O'Brien, "Apollo 8 Day 1."
58. *Earthrise*, directed by Emmanuel Vaughan-Lee (2018; Go Project Films, 2018) (https://www.nytimes.com/2018/10/02/opinion/earthrise-moon-space-nasa.html?referringSource=articleShare, accessed August 18, 2021).
59. Robin Wheeler, "Apollo Lunar Landing Launch Window: The Controlling Factors and Constraints" (https://history.nasa.gov/afj/launchwindow/lw1.html#TLI, accessed December 28, 2019); Woods/O'Brien, "Apollo 8 Day 1"; Lunar and Planetary Institute, "Apollo 8 Mission: Mission Overview" (https://www.lpi.usra.edu/lunar/missions/apollo/apollo_8/overview/, accessed December 29, 2019).
60. Casey, "How to Get From Space to Place in a Fairly Short Stretch of Time," 31.
61. Tilley, *A Phenomenology of Landscape*, 34.
62. Sisak, "Aerospatial Heritage Sites," 31–34.
63. W. David Woods and Frank O'Brien, "Apollo 8 Day 3: Lunar Encounter" (https://history.nasa.gov/afj/ap08fj/12day3_lunar_encounter.html, accessed September 1, 2021).
64. Woods and O'Brien, "Apollo 8 Day 3."
65. Sisak, "Aerospatial Heritage Sites," 34–36; Jeffrey Kluger, *Apollo 8: The Thrilling Story of the First Mission to the Moon*, New York: Henry Holt and Company 2017: 197.
66. Tilley, *A Phenomenology of Landscape*, 27.
67. Tilley, *A Phenomenology of Landscape*, 28.
68. *Earthrise*.
69. National Aeronautics and Space Administration, *Apollo 8 Press Kit* (Release no: 68-208, Washington, D.C.: National Aeronautics and Space Administration, 1968), 16 (https://history.nasa.gov/afj/ap08fj/pdf/a08-presskit.pdf, accessed September 22, 2022).
70. *Earthrise*; Woods and O'Brien, "Apollo 8 Day 3."
71. Apollo 8 was launched on a circumlunar free return trajectory. See: National Aeronautics and Space Administration, *Apollo 8 Press Kit*, 14b.
72. Wheeler, "Apollo Lunar Landing Launch Window."
73. W. David Woods and Frank O'Brien, "Apollo 8 Day 4: Lunar Orbit 4" (https://history.nasa.gov/afj/ap08fj/16day4_orbit4.html, accessed September 3, 2021).
74. Nadia Drake, "We Saw Earth Rise Over the Moon in 1968. It Changed Everything," *National Geographic*, December 21, 2018 (http://www.national-geographic.com/science/2018/12/earthrise-apollo-8-photo-at-50-how-it-changed-the-world/#close, accessed May 25, 2020).

75. *Earthrise*.
76. *Earthrise*.
77. National Aeronautics and Space Administration, *Apollo 10 Press Kit* (Release no.: 69-68, Washington, D.C.: National Aeronautics and Space Administration, 1969) (https://www.nasa.gov/specials/apollo50th/pdf/A10_PressKit.pdf, accessed September 22, 2022).
78. Eric M. Jones, "The First Lunar Landing" (https://history.nasa.gov/alsj/a11/a11.landing.html, accessed September 4, 2021).
79. Mission Operations Branch, Flight Crew Support Division, NASA, *Apollo 11: Technical Crew Debriefing (U)*, Vol. 1, Houston: Manned Spacecraft Center, 1969, 9-17–9-18 https://www.hq.nasa.gov/alsj/a11/A11TechCrewDebrfV1_ALSJ.pdf, accessed September 22, 2022).
80. Eric M. Jones, "The First Lunar Landing: Part VI" (https://history.nasa.gov/ap11ann/FirstLunarLanding/ch-7.html, accessed September 3, 2021).
81. Sisak, "Aerospatial Heritage Sites," 40–41.
82. Jones, "The First Lunar Landing."
83. James R. Hansen, *First Man: The Life of Neil A. Armstrong*, New York: Simon & Schuster 2005, 441–475.
84. Mission Operations Branch, Flight Crew Support Division, NASA, *Apollo 11*, 9-18–9-29.
85. Jones, "The First Lunar Landing."
86. Jones, "The First Lunar Landing."
87. Hansen, *First Man*, 473–474.
88. Hansen, *First Man*, 474.
89. Hansen, *First Man*.
90. Jones, "The First Lunar Landing."
91. Ana Caetano, "Personal Reflexivity and Biography: Methodological Challenges and Strategies," *International Journal of Social Research Methodology* 18, no. 2 (2015): 227–242.
92. Peter Aylward, "Neil Armstrong Narrating His Apollo 11 Moon Landing," July 30, 2013, video, 4:27 (https://youtu.be/Qqe7-rFRrkc;MEM-TEK, accessed September 4, 2021); MEM-TEK, "GoneToPlaid's Apollo Web Site" (http://apollo.mem-tek.com/, accessed September 4, 2021).
93. Aylward, "Neil Armstrong Narrating his Apollo 11 Moon Landing"; MEM-TEK, "GoneToPlaid's Apollo Web Site."
94. Aylward, "Neil Armstrong Narrating his Apollo 11 Moon Landing"; Sisak, "Aerospatial Heritage Sites," 44.
95. Slartibartfast, "An Audience with Neil Armstrong," November 12, 2018, video, 49:54 (https://youtu.be/KJzOIh2eHqQ, accessed September 6, 2021).
96. Buzz Aldrin and Wayne Warga, *Return to Earth*, New York: Open Road Integrated Media, Inc., 1973, 204.
97. Buzz Aldrin with Ken Abraham, *Magnificent Desolation: The Long Journey Home from the Moon*, New York: Harmony Books, 2009, 14.
98. Aldrin and Abraham, *Magnificent Desolation*, 14.
99. Aldrin and Abraham, *Magnificent Desolation*, 14.

100. Aldrin and Warga, *Return to Earth*, 205.

101. Aldrin and Abraham, *Magnificent Desolation*, 19.

102. "NASA Astronauts Complete the First All-Female Spacewalk," *The New York Times*, October 18, 2019 (https://www.nytimes.com/2019/10/18/science/space/nasa-female-spacewalk.html, accessed September 22, 2022).

103. Examples include: the first human spaceflight and orbit by Yuri Gagarin on Vostok 1, the first female spaceflight by Valentina Tereshkova on Vostok 6, and other notable feats from the United States Mercury, Gemini, and Apollo missions of the Space Race.

104. Tilley, *A Phenomenology of Landscape*, 24, 27, 33.

105. Tilley, *A Phenomenology of Landscape*, 27, 33.

106. Tilley, *A Phenomenology of Landscape*, 10.

107. Tilley, *A Phenomenology of Landscape*, 31.

108. Smith, *Uses of Heritage*, 2.

109. Wheeler, "Apollo Lunar Landing Launch Window"; Woods and O'Brien, "Apollo 8 Day 1"; Lunar and Planetary Institute, "Apollo 8 Mission"; NASA, *Apollo 11 Mission Report* (1971) (https://www.hq.nasa.gov/office/pao/ History/alsj/a11/a11 MIssionReport_1971015566.pdf, accessed September 22, 2022).

110. Tilley, *A Phenomenology of Landscape*, 15.

111. Tilley, *A Phenomenology of Landscape*, 31.

112. Casey, "How to Get From Space to Place in a Fairly Short Stretch of Time," 34; Sisak, "Aerospatial Heritage Sites."

113. Carman, "What Sustaining Heritage Really Does"; Smith, *Uses of Heritage*; Carman, "Where the Value Lies"; Harrison, "What is Heritage?"; Harrison, Fairclough, Schofield, and Jameson Jr., "Heritage, Memory and Modernity"; Carman, *Archaeology and Heritage*.

114. "Treaty on Principles Governing the Activities of States in the Exploration and Use of Outer Space, Including the Moon and Other Celestial Bodies," opened for signature January 27, 1967, *United Nations Treaty Series*, vol. 610, no. 8843, 205–300 (https://treaties.un.org/doc/Publication/UNTS/Volume%20610/volume-610-I-8843-English.pdf, accessed September 22, 2022).

115. Westwood, O'Leary, and Donaldson, *The Final Mission*, 149–150.

116. NASA Scientific Visualization Studio, "Earthrise in 4K" (https://svs.gsfc.nasa.gov/4593, accessed July 30, 2021); NASA Video, "Apollo 11 Landing Profile," May 17, 2013, video, 4:44 (https://youtu.be/In5xf5DHiM4, accessed May 10, 2021).

117. Mark Bowden, Sharon Soutar, David Field, and Martyn Barber, *The Stonehenge Landscape*, Swindon: Historic England, 2015.

118. The History Underground, "Flight 93: First in the Fight on 9/11 | History Traveler Episode 163," September 11, 2011, video, 19:11 (https://youtu.be/EBIKMdTPaU4, accessed September 11, 2011). See the brochure map: National Park Service, "Maps" (https://www.nps.gov/flni/planyourvisit/maps.htm, accessed September 8, 2021).

119. See: NJ 9/11 Memorial Foundation, "Empty Sky, New Jersey 9/11 Memorial Foundation" (https://nj911memorial.org, accessed September 11, 2021); National

September 11 Memorial & Museum, "Tribute in Light" (https://www.911memorial.org/visit/memorial/tribute-light, accessed September 11, 2021).

120. Aldrin and Warga, *Return to Earth*, 197.

121. Aldrin and Abraham, *Magnificent Desolation*, 14.

122. PBS NewsHour, "What Apollo 11 pilot Michael Collins feared most during critical NASA mission," July 17, 2019, video, 10:05 (https://youtu.be/UQ5rangYxng, accessed August 5, 2021).

123. Roger D. Launius, "An Unintended Consequence of the IGY: Eisenhower, Sputnik, the Founding of NASA," *Acta Astronautica* 67, no. 1–2 (2010): 260.

124. Thomas Adam, "New Ways to Write the History of Western Europe and the United States: The Concept of Intercultural Transfer," *History Compass* 11, no. 10 (2013): 885.

125. Thomas Adam, *Intercultural Transfer and the Making of the Modern World, 1800–2000: Sources and Context*, Houndmills and New York: Palgrave Macmillan 2012, 1–7.

126. Launius, "An Unintended Consequence of the IGY," 254–258.

127. Launius, "An Unintended Consequence of the IGY," 258.

128. Launius, "An Unintended Consequence of the IGY," 262.

129. Thomas Adam, "Transnational History: A Program for Research, Publishing, and Teaching," *Yearbook of Transnational History* 1 (2018): 1–10.

130. Smithsonian National Air and Space Museum, "The Moon Decision" (https://airandspace.si.edu/exhibitions/apollo-to-the-moon/online/racing-to-space/moon-decision.cfm, accessed September 18, 2021).

131. Kluger, *Apollo 8*, 107–109.

BIBLIOGRAPHY

Primary Sources

Aeronautical Chart and Information Center, United States Air Force. "Edition 1 LM Descent Monitoring Chart – Sheet 2: 16 July 1969 Launch Date—Landing Site no. 2," available online: https://www.hq.nasa.gov/office/pao/History/alsj/a11/A11_LDP_00-09.jpg (accessed August 9, 2020).

Aldrin, Buzz, and Ken Abraham. *Magnificent Desolation: The Long Journey Home From the Moon*. New York: Harmony Books, 2009.

Aldrin, Buzz, and Wayne Warga. *Return to Earth*. New York: Open Road Integrated Media, 1973.

Aylward, Peter. "Neil Armstrong Narrating His Apollo 11 Moon Landing." July 30, 2013, video, 4:27, available online: https://youtu.be/Qqe7-rFRrkc;MEM-TEK (accessed September 4, 2021).

Bennett, Floyd V. *Apollo Experience Report—Mission Planning for Lunar Module Descent and Ascent*. Washington, D.C.: National Aeronautics and Space Administration, 1972, available online: https://www.hq.nasa.gov/office/pao/History/alsj/HSI-45202.r.pdf (accessed September 16, 2022).

Butowski, Harry A. *Man in Space: National Historic Landmark Theme Study.* US National Park Service, US Department of the Interior, 1984.

Jones, Eric M. "Apollo 11 Lunar Surface Journal," available online: https://history.nasa.gov/alsj/a11/a11.html (accessed September 4, 2021).

Jones, Eric M. "The First Lunar Landing: Part VI," available online: https://history.nasa.gov/ap11ann/FirstLunarLanding/ch-7.html (accessed September 3, 2021).

Le Conte, David. "Photographing Apollo 8's Orbit Toward the Moon," available online: https://airandspace.si.edu/stories/editorial/photographing-apollo-8s-orbit-toward-moon (accessed July 14, 2020).

Miller, Todd D., dir. *Apollo 11.* 2018; Neon and CNN Films, 2019, Hulu.

Mission Operations Branch, Flight Crew Support Division, NASA. *Apollo 8: Technical Debriefing.* Houston: Manned Spacecraft Center, 1969, available online: https://www.ibiblio.org/apollo/Documents/Apollo8-TechnicalDebriefing-Martin-1.pdf and https://www.ibiblio.org/apollo/Documents/Apollo8-TechnicalDebriefing-Martin-2.pdf (accessed July 24, 2020).

Mission Operations Branch, Flight Crew Support Division, NASA. *Apollo 11: Technical Crew Debriefing (U), Vol. 1.* Houston: Manned Spacecraft Center 1969, available online: https://www.hq.nasa.gov/alsj/a11/A11TechCrewDebrfV1_ALSJ.pdf (accessed July 24, 2020).

NASA. "Armstrong Hosts NASA 50th Anniversary Documentary." August 25, 2012, video, 1:27:10, available online: https://youtube.com/watch?v=3TrNN_eTau0 (accessed June 20, 2020).

NASA. *NASA's Recommendations to Space-Faring Entities: How to Protect and Preserve the Historic and Scientific Value of the U.S. Government Lunar Artifacts.* 2011, available online: https://www.nasa.gov/sites/default/files/617743main_NASA-USG_LUNAR_HISTORIC_SITES_RevA-508.pdf (accessed May 14, 2020).

National Aeronautics and Space Administration. *Apollo 8 Press Kit.* Release no: 68-208. Washington, D.C.: National Aeronautics and Space Administration 1968, available online: https://history.nasa.gov/afj/ap08fj/pdf/a08-presskit.pdf (accessed July 24, 2020).

National Aeronautics and Space Administration. *Apollo 10 Press Kit.* Release no.: 69-68. Washington, D.C.: National Aeronautics and Space Administration 1969, available online: https://www.nasa.gov/specials/apollo50th/pdf/A10_PressKit.pdf (accessed July 24, 2020).

One Small Step to Protect Human Heritage in Space Act. Public Law 116–275. *U.S. Statutes at Large* 134 (2020): 3358–3361.

PBS NewsHour. "What Apollo 11 Pilot Michael Collins Feared Most During Critical NASA Mission." July 17, 2019, video, 10:05, available online: https://youtu.be/UQ5rangYxng (accessed August 5, 2021).

Slartibartfast. "An Audience With Neil Armstrong." November 12, 2018, video, 49:54, available online: https://youtu.be/KJzOIh2eHqQ (accessed September 6, 2021).

"Treaty on Principles Governing the Activities of States in the Exploration and Use of Outer Space, Including the Moon and Other Celestial Bodies." Opened for

Signature January 27, 1967. *United Nations Treaty Series* 610, no. 8843, 205–300, available online: https://treaties.un.org/doc/Publication/UNTS/Volume%20610/volume-610-I-8843-English.pdf (accessed September 6, 2021).

UNESCO, Intergovernmental Committee for the Protection of the World Cultural and Natural Heritage. *Operational Guidelines for the Implementation of the World Heritage Convention*. 2019, available online: https://WHC.unesco.org/document/178167 (accessed May 15, 2020).

UNESCO. *Records of the General Conference, 31st Session, Paris, 15 October to 3 November 2001, v. 1: Resolutions*. Document code: 31C/Resolutions + CORR, 2002, available online: https://unesdoc.unesco.org/ark:/48223/pf0000124687.locale=en (accessed June 5, 2020).

Vaughan-Lee, Emmanuel, dir. *Earthrise*. 2018; Go Project Films, 2018, available online: https://www.nytimes.com/2018/10/02/opinion/earthrise-moon-space-nasa.html?referringSource=articleShare (accessed August 18, 2021).

Williams, David R. "Apollo 11," available online: https://nssdc.gsfc.nasa.gov/planetary/lunar/apollo11info.html (accessed April 30, 2020).

Woods, W. David, and Frank O'Brien. "The Apollo 8 Flight Journal," available online: https://history.nasa.gov/afj/ap08fj/index.html (accessed September 3, 2021).

Woods, W. David, Ken MacTaggart, and Frank O'Brien. "The Apollo 11 Flight Journal," available online: https://history.nasa.gov/afj/ap11fj/index.html (accessed September 6, 2021).

World Heritage Committee. *Large Complex Serial Transnational Nominations and the Need for Nomination Strategies*. Decision Code: 41 COM 8B.50, 2017, available online: https://whc.unesco.org/en/decisions/6922/ (accessed May 9, 2020).

Secondary Sources

Adam, Thomas. *Intercultural Transfer and the Making of the Modern World, 1800–2000: Sources and Context*. Houndmills and New York: Palgrave Macmillan, 2012.

Adam, Thomas. "New Ways to Write the History of Western Europe and the United States: The Concept of Intercultural Transfer." *History Compass* 11, no. 10 (2013): 880–892.

Adam, Thomas. "Transnational History: A Program for Research, Publishing, and Teaching." *Yearbook of Transnational History* 1 (2018): 1–10.

Andermann, Jens, and Silke Arnold-de Simine. "Introduction: Museums and the Educational Turn: History, Memory, Inclusivity." *Journal of Educational Media, Memory & Society* 4, no. 2 (2012): 1–7.

Bainbridge, William S. *The Meaning and Value of Spaceflight: Public Perceptions*. Cham: Springer, 2015.

Banks, Marcus. *Visual Research Methods in Social Research*. London: Sage, 2001 (accessed July 9, 2020).

Bowden, Mark, Sharon Soutar, David Field, and Martyn Barber. *The Stonehenge Landscape*. Swindon: Historic England, 2015.

Caetano, Ana. "Personal Reflexivity and Biography: Methodological Challenges and Strategies." *International Journal of Social Research Methodology* 18, no. 2 (2015): 227–242.

Carman, John. *Archaeology and Heritage: An Introduction*. London and New York: Continuum, 2002.

Carman, John. "What Sustaining Heritage Really Does." *VITRUVIO International Journal of Architectural Technology and Sustainability* 4, no. 1 (2019): 1–10.

Carman, John. "Where the Value Lies: The Importance of Materiality to the Immaterial Aspects of Heritage." In *Taking Archaeology Out of Heritage*, edited by Laurajane Smith and Emma Waterton. Newcastle upon Tyne: Cambridge Scholars Publishing, 2009, 192–208.

Casey, Edward S. "How to Get From Space to Place in a Fairly Short Stretch of Time: Phenomenological Prolegomena." In *Senses of Place*, edited by Steven Feld and Keith H. Basso. Santa Fe: School of American Research Press, 1996, 13–52.

Chazelle, Damien, dir. *First Man*. 2018; Universal Pictures, 2018, iTunes.

Creswell, John W. *Qualitative Inquiry & Research Design: Choosing Among Five Approaches*. Los Angeles: Sage, 2013.

Drake, Nadia. "We Saw Earth Rise Over the Moon in 1968. It Changed Everything." *National Geographic*, December 21, 2018, available online: http://www.nationalgeographic.com/science/2018/12/earthrise-apollo-8-photo-at-50-how-it-changed-the-world/#close (accessed May 25, 2020).

Federal Aviation Administration, United States Department of Transportation. "The Space Environment (4.1.2)," available online: https://www.faa.gov/about/office_org/headquarters_offices/avs/offices/aam/cami/library/online_libraries/aerospace_medicine/tutorial/media/III.4.1.2_The_Space_Environment.pdf (accessed July 8, 2021).

For All Moonkind, Inc. "For All Moonkind—Home," available online: https://www.forallmoonkind.org/about/the-declaration/ (accessed July 23, 2021).

Gibson, Ralph D., Jr. "Lunar Archaeology: The Application of Federal Historic Preservation Law to the Site Where Humans First Set Foot Upon the Moon." Master's Thesis, New Mexico State University, 2001.

Gisler, Monika, and Didier Sornette. "Exuberant Innovations: The Apollo Program." *Society (New Brunswick)* 46, no. 1 (2008): 55–68.

Gorman, Alice. *Dr Space Junk vs The Universe: Archaeology and the Future*. Cambridge and London: The MIT Press, 2019.

Gorman, Alice. "Heritage of Earth Orbit: Orbital Debris—Its Mitigation and Cultural Heritage." In *Handbook of Space Engineering, Archaeology and Heritage*, edited by Ann G. Darrin and Beth L. O'Leary. Boca Raton: CRC Press, 2009, 381–397.

Gorman, Alice. "The Cultural Landscape of Interplanetary Space." *Journal of Social Archaeology* 5, no. 1 (2005): 85–107.

Greenfieldboyce, Nell. "How Do You Preserve History on the Moon?" *National Public Radio, Morning Edition*, February 21, 2019, available online: https://www.npr.org/2019/02/21/696129505/how-do-you-preserve-history-on-the-moon?fbclid=IwAR3AcmNgDP8aVHXsK--y20a0HwF5crCDFU7q8UPQJHs_zan-BQA1QpRMwG0M (accessed July 14, 2019).

Hansen, James R. *First Man: The Life of Neil A. Armstrong*. New York: Simon & Schuster, 2005.

Harrison, Rodney. "What is Heritage?" In *Understanding the Politics of Heritage*, edited by Rodney Harrison. Manchester: Manchester University Press in Association With the Open University, 2010, 5–42.

Harrison, Rodney, Graham J. Fairclough, John Schofield, and John H. Jameson Jr. "Heritage, Memory and Modernity: An Introduction." In *The Heritage Reader*, edited by Rodney Harrison, Graham J. Fairclough, John Schofield, and John H. Jameson Jr. Abingdon and New York: Routledge, 2008, 1–7.

Harvey, David C. "Heritage Pasts and Heritage Presents: Temporality, Meaning and the Scope of Heritage Studies." *International Journal of Heritage Studies* 7, no. 4 (2001): 319–338.

ISS Archaeology. "About," available online: https://issarchaeology.org/about/ (accessed July 24, 2021).

Jeffrey, James. "Apollo 11: 'The Greatest Single Broadcast in Television History.'" *BBC News*, July 19, 2019, available online: https://www.bbc.com/news/world-us-canada-48857752 (accessed May 8, 2020).

Johnson, Nuala. "Memory and Heritage." In *Introducing Human Geographies*, edited by Paul Cloke, Philip Crang, and Mark Goodwin. London: Edward Arnold, 1999, 170–178.

Johnstone, Barbara. *Discourse Analysis*. Hoboken: John Wiley & Sons, 2018.

Kluger, Jeffrey. *Apollo 8: The Thrilling Story of the First Mission to the Moon*. New York: Henry Holt and Company, 2017.

Koren, Marina. "The Soviet Space Program Was Not Woke." *The Atlantic*, July 26, 2019, available online: https://www.theatlantic.com/science/archive/2019/07/space-race-soviet-union-nasa-valentina-tereshkova/594871/ (accessed July 27, 2019).

Launius, Roger D. "An Unintended Consequence of the IGY: Eisenhower, Sputnik, the Founding of NASA." *Acta Astronautica* 67, nos. 1–2 (2010): 254–263.

Lunar and Planetary Institute. "Apollo 8 Mission: Mission Overview," available online: https://www.lpi.usra.edu/lunar/missions/apollo/apollo_8/overview/ (accessed December 29, 2019).

Lunar Reconnaissance Orbiter Camera. "What Armstrong Saw: Simulation 1." July 10, 2019, video, 4:07, available online: https://youtu.be/YPXitv2CRJs (accessed May 10, 2020).

MEM-TEK. "GoneToPlaid's Apollo Web Site," available online: http://apollo.mem-tek.com (accessed September 4, 2021).

NASA Scientific Visualization Studio. "Earthrise in 4K," available online: https://svs.gsfc.nasa.gov/4593 (accessed July 30, 2021).

NASA Video. "Apollo 11 Landing Profile." May 17, 2013, video, 4:44, available online: https://youtu.be/In5xf5DHiM4 (accessed May 10, 2021).

National Aeronautics and Space Administration. "17. Acronyms and Abbreviations," available online: https://www.nasa.gov/pdf/140648main_ESAS_17a.pdf (accessed June 10, 2020).

National Aeronautics and Space Administration, NASA Space Science Data Coordinated Archive. "Vanguard 1," available online: https://nssdc.gsfc.nasa.gov/nmc/spacecraft/display.action?id=1958-002B (accessed April 17, 2022).

National Park Service. "Maps," available online: https://www.nps.gov/flni/planyourvisit/maps.htm (accessed September 8, 2021).

National September 11 Memorial & Museum. "Tribute in Light," available online: https://www.911memorial.org/visit/memorial/tribute-light (accessed September 11, 2021).

NJ 9/11 Memorial Foundation. "Empty Sky, New Jersey 9/11 Memorial Foundation," available online: https://nj911memorial.org (accessed September 11, 2021).

NPR. "Special Series: The Apollo 11 Moon Landing, 50 Years Later," available online: https://www.npr.org/series/738145345/apollo-11-50th-anniversary-coverage (accessed July 8, 2020).

Reynolds, Joseph P. "One Small Step: An Analysis of International Space Law and How It Effects Historic Preservation." Master's Thesis, Clemson University, 2012.

Siddiqi, Asif A. "American Space History: Legacies, Questions, and Opportunities for Future Research." In *Critical Issues in the History of Spaceflight*, edited by Steven J. Dick and Roger D. Launius. Washington, D.C.: NASA, 2006, 433–480.

Sisak, Ryan. "Aerospatial Heritage Sites—A History of Value and Meaning for Places in Relative Space." Master's Dissertation, University of Birmingham, 2020.

Smith, Laurajane. *Uses of Heritage*. London and New York: Routledge, 2006.

Smithsonian National Air and Space Museum. "The Moon Decision," available online: https://airandspace.si.edu/exhibitions/apollo-to-the-moon/online/racing-to-space/moon-decision.cfm (accessed September 18, 2021).

Smithsonian National Air and Space Museum. "Space Race," available online: https://airandspace.si.edu/exhibitions/space-race (accessed July 6, 2020).

Sørensen, Marie Louise Stig, and John Carman, eds. *Heritage Studies: Methods and Approaches*. Routledge: London and New York, 2009.

Stone, Robert, dir. *Chasing the Moon*. 2019; American Experience, 2019, available online: https://www.pbs.org/wgbh/americanexperience/films/chasing-moon/ (accessed July 8, 2019).

Taylor, Ken, and Jane Lennon. "Cultural Landscapes: A Bridge Between Culture and Nature?" *International Journal of Heritage Studies* 17, no. 6 (2011): 537–554.

The History Underground. "Flight 93: First in the Fight on 9/11 | History Traveler Episode 163." September 11, 2011, video, 19:11, available online: https://youtu.be/EBIKMdTPaU4 (accessed September 11, 2011).

The Los Angeles Times, 2019.

The New York Times, 2019.

The Wall Street Journal, 2019.

Tilley, Christopher. *Interpreting Landscapes: Geologies, Topographies, Identities; Explorations in Landscape Phenomenology 3*. London and New York: Routledge, 2010.

Tilley, Christopher. *A Phenomenology of Landscape: Places, Paths and Monuments*. Oxford: Berg and Providence, 1994.

Tilley, Christopher. "The Power of Rocks: Topography and Monument Construction on Bodmin Moor." *World Archaeology* 28, no. 2 (1996): 161–176.

UNESCO World Heritage Centre. "The Criteria for Selection," available online: https://whc.unesco.org/en/criteria/ (accessed April 16, 2022).
UNESCO World Heritage Centre. "The World Heritage Committee," available online: https://whc.unesco.org/en/committee/ (accessed April 24, 2022).
UNESCO World Heritage Centre. "World Heritage List," available online: https://whc.unesco.org/en/list/ (accessed July 5, 2020).
UNESCO World Heritage Centre. "World Heritage List Nominations," available online: https://whc.unesco.org/en/nominations/ (accessed April 24, 2022).
UNOOSA. "Committee on the Peaceful Uses of Outer Space: Observer Organizations," available online: https://www.unoosa.org/oosa/en/ourwork/copuos/members/copuos-observers.html (accessed July 23, 2021).
U.S. Department of the Interior, National Park Service, Cultural Resources, National Register, History and Education. "How to Apply the National Register Criteria for Evaluation." National Register Bulletin, 1997.
Waterton, Emma, Laurajane Smith, and Gary Campbell. "The Utility of Discourse Analysis to Heritage Studies: The Burra Charter and Social Inclusion." *International Journal of Heritage Studies* 12, no. 4 (2006): 339–355.
Westwood, Lisa, Beth L. O'Leary, and Milfred W. Donaldson. *The Final Mission: Preserving NASA's Apollo Sites*. Gainesville: University Press of Florida, 2017.
Wheeler, Robin. "Apollo Lunar Landing Launch Window: The Controlling Factors and Constraints," available online: https://history.nasa.gov/afj/launchwindow/lw1.html#TLI (accessed December 28, 2019).
Wilson, Charles Reagan. "American Heavens: Apollo and the Civil Religion." *Journal of Church & State* 26, no. 2 (1984): 209–226.

Index

Note: Page locators in italics refer to figures.

Aapravasi Ghat, 150
Abenaki people, 130–35
Aborigines, 99
absolutism, 194
Abu Simbel temple, 3
Acadia, 125
Accra (Ghana), 82
Adam, Thomas, 2, 8, 213
Adriatic, 53, 57–60, 63–65; Dalmatian, 62
Aegina (Greece), 105
Aenon, Chief, 136
Afghanistan, *15*
Africa, 6, 11, 145, 153, 157
Afro-American Bicentennial Corporation (AABC), 150–52
Afro-American Institute for Historic Preservation and Community Development, 150, 152
Agorsah, Emmanuel K., 147
Agrafiotis, Andreas, *105*
Aitysh/Aitys, art of improvisation, *15*
Akko (Israel), 39, 44–46
Alaska, 7
Al-Ayyala, a traditional performing art of the Sultanate of Oman and the United Arab Emirates, *15*

Albania, 8–*10*
Alberta, 4, 5
Aldrin, Buzz, 229, 234–39
Alexander the Great, 39
Algeria, *12*, *16*
Allemang, John, 124
"Allies, Adversaries, and Kin in the African Seminole Communities of Florida," 147–48
Alnôbaiwi, 134
Alnobark: Wearing Our Heritage, 133
alpinism, *13*
Al-Razfa, a traditional performing art, *15*
Al-Taghrooda, traditional Bedouin chanted poetry, *16*
American Civil War, 150
American Revolution, 152
Americas, 5, 145–46
Amsab-Institute of Social History in Ghent, 91
Amundsen's Hut, 214
Ancient and Primeval Beech Forests of the Carpathians and Other Regions of Europe, 8, *10*, 25
Anders, William, 229, 231–33, 238
Andorra, *15*

255

Antarctica, 5–6, 11, 23, 26, 195–216
Antarctic Peninsula, 23, 204
Antarctic Seas, 206–7
Antarctic Specially Protected Area (ASPA), 209–15
Antarctic Treaty (1961), 23, 200–1, 203–208, 210, 213–14, 216; Protocol on Environmental Protection, 202, 205–6, 209–11
Antarctic Treaty Consultative Meetings, 204
Antarctic Treaty System, 11, 23, 200, 204–6, 210–13, 215–16; List of Historic Sites and Monuments, 11, 200, 204–7, 209–12, 214–15
anthropogeography, 176
anthropology, 170
Antioch: Principality of, 30; Siege of, 36
Antoniou, Depy, *105*
Apalachicola National Forrest, 150
Āpharoja, Sulatānā, 147
Apollo 8, *224*, 229–34, 237–41
Apollo 10, 234
Apollo 11, 224–25, 229–31, 234, 236–41; moon landing, 223, 226, 229, 234–37, 240–41
Apollo program, 230
Apollo sites, 229–30
Aptheker, Herbert, 148
Arabic calligraphy: knowledge, skills, and practice, *12*
Arabic coffee, a symbol of generosity, *15*
archaeology: British, 40–41; French, 40–41
Architectural Work of Le Corbusier, 6–8, *10*, 25, 87, 203
architecture: Gothic, 34, 42; Romanesque, 34
Argentina, 4, *9–10*, *16*, 23, 85, 87, 91, 196, 204, 210, 214
Armenia, *13*
Armenians, 32, 44
Armstrong, Neil, *225*, 234–40

Arnaud, Fanny, 55–56, 67
Arsuf (Israel), 39
Artisanal Talavera of Puebla and Tlaxcala (Mexico) and ceramics of Talavera de la Reina and El Puente del Arzobispo (Spain) making process, 11, *13*
art of crafting and playing Mbira/Sansi, the finger-plucking traditional musical instrument, *12*
art of crafting and playing with Kamantcheh/Kamancha, a bowed string musical instrument, *14*
art of dry stone walling, knowledge and techniques, *14*
art of glass beads, *13*
art of miniature, *12*
Ashkelon (Israel), 39
Asia, 6, 11; Central, 203
Assmann, Jan, 172, 174
Assyria, 2
Athens, 98, 103, 105
Athens Charta for the Restoration of Historic Monuments, 2–5, 18, 98
Atlantic Ocean, 124
Auschwitz-Birkenau, 214
Australia, 4–6, 11, 23, 81, 87, 90–91, 99, 196, 204
Australian Convict Sites, 87
Austria, 8–*10*, *13–14*, 22, 58, 180
Authorized Heritage Discourse (AHD), 21, 99–100, 102, 110–12, 228
avalanche risk management, *14*
Azerbaijan, *12*, *14–15*

Baba, Mount, 104
Babylonia, 2
Bahrain, *12*, *13*, 18
Bajra, Ismail, 64
Balkans, 21, 62, 64–65, 67, 97–113; Western, 101
Balkan Wars of the 1910s, 112
Baltic song and dance celebrations, *16*
Banff National Park, 4
Barre, Vermont, 90

Index

Basu, Paul, 175
Bay of Biscay, 124
Bear Waters Gathering in Muskoka, 129
Beaudreau, Sylvie, 135
Beaufort, castle of, 38–39, 47
Beirut, 39
Beit Govrin, 37
Belarus, 7, *9*, *13*, 180
Belfries of Belgium and France, *9*
Belgium, 8, *9*, *10*, *12*, *14*, *16*, 87, 90
Belgrade, 57, 66
Belize, *16*
Belvoir, castle of, 38
Benin, 7, *9*, *16*
Bermuda, 11
Białowieża Forest, 7, *9*
Bitabagw, 131, 135
Bitola (North Macedonia), 103–7, 109–10; National Library, 107–8
Black Seminole, 146
Black Women Oral History Project, 150
Blaenavon Industrial Landscape, 77, 89
Blaine, Washington, 5
Blanchegarde (Israel), 37
Blaudruck/Modrotisk/Kékfestés/Modrotlač, resist block printing and indigo dyeing in Europe, *14*
Blue and John Crow Mountains World Heritage Site, 146, 155–58
Bocheński, Adolf, 168
Bodrum (Turkey), 31
Boissevain-Morton, Manitoba, 4
Bolivia, *10*, *16*, 87
Bordeaux, 90
Borman, Frank, 229, 231–33, 238
Borque, Bruce, 133
Bosnia and Herzegovina, 10
Boston University, 170
Bouillon, Godfrey of, 40
bourse du travail. *See* workers' assembly hall
Bourse du Travail in Bordeaux, 90
Brazil, 3, 6, *9*, 210
Brigham Young University, 169
British Columbia, 5, 7

British Slavery Abolition Act, 152, 155
Broken Hill (Australia), 77, 90
Broken Hill Trades Hall, 77, 90
Brook, Melody Walker, 130
Brooks, Douglas, 136
Brouage (France), 124
Bruncevic, Merima, 18
Brussels, 81, 84
Buenos Aires, 85
Bulgaria, 8, *10*, *14*, 68, 103–5
Bull, Henryk, 207
Burj el-Hazna, 44–45
Burkina Faso, 7, *9*, *16*
Burlington, Vermont, 123, 129, 133–34
Butowski, Harry, 223
Byers Peninsula of Livingston Island, 199–*200*, 209, 211
Byzantine chant, *13*
Byzantine Empire, 32

Caesarea (Israel), 39
Cahiagué, 128
California, 223
Cambodia, *15*
camel racing, a social practice and a festive heritage associated with camels, *12*
Cameroon, *10*
Canada, 4–7, *9*, 11, 18, 24, 82, 91, 101, 123, 125, 127, 131, 133, 135–37, 146, 151; English, 127; French, 125, 127; Parks, 128–29; Register of Historic Places, 151
Canton, 198
Cape Denison, 212–13
Cardinal Stefan Wyszyński University, 170
Caribbean, 11, 147
Carman, John, 227
Cartier, Jacques, 125
casa del popolo. *See* workers' assembly hall
casa del pueblo. *See* workers' assembly hall
Casa Garibaldi in Istanbul, 82

Casey, Edward, 227
Castellum Regis (Israel), 37
Caves of Aggtelek Karst and Slovak Karst, *9*
Central African Republic, *10*
Central Suriname Nature Reserve, 146, 148–49
Ceramics of Talavera de la Reina, 11
Certified Practising Accountant Australia 125th Anniversary Gala Dinner (2011), 235
Chace, Nicholas, 130
Champlain, Samuel de, 21–22, 123–37; voyage of, 124, 130
Champlain College, 129; Republican Club, 130; Student Government Association, 130
Champlain Monument, 128–30, *132*; Working Group, 128–29
Champlain Quadricentennial, 123–37; Commission, 123–24
Champlain Society, 124
Champlain Tercentenary, 123, 126, 135
Champlain Valley, 123–24, 134–35; National Heritage Partnership, 137
Chile, *10*, *16*, 23, 87, 196, 204, 207, 209
China, 6, *10*, *12*, *16*, 125, 198
Chippewas of Rama First Nation, 128, 129
cholera, 171
Choüacoet, 125
Clarke, Steve, 129
Clermont-Ferrand (France), 32
Climent of Ohrid, 62
Clinton, Hillary Rodham, 123
Clinton County, 133–34
Clinton County History Through the Eyes of Its Children, 133–*34*
Clute, Penelope, 131
coal mining landscape of the Nord-pas de Calais Basin, 214
Cold War, 19, 203
Cole Harbour Meeting House, 152
Coliath (Syria), 37
Collegium Polonicum, 178

Collins, Michael, 231, 240
Colombia, *10*
colonialism, 11, 101, 130, 135–36, 197; French, 41, 137, 150; Iberian, 11
Colonies of Benevolence, *10*, 87
Columbia, *14–15*, 87
Commonwealth Bay, 2112
Congo, 4, *10*, *12*
Congolese rumba, *12*
Constantinople, 32
Copenhagen, *83*, 84, *85*, 90
Cornec, Julie, 147
Costa Rica, *9*
Côte d'Ivoire, 7, *9*, *16*
Council of Europe, 98, 101-102
Covert, Jay, 130
Crac des Chevaliers, 38, 39, 47
Cradley Heath, 82
craftsmanship of mechanical watchmaking and art mechanics, *12*
craft techniques and customary practices of cathedral workshops, or Bauhütten, in Europe, knowhow, transmission, development of knowledge, and innovation, *13*
Creative Europe program, 99, 101–102, 111
creolization, 145
Croatia, 8, *10*, *14–15*, 19–20, 25, 53, 55–56, 65–69; National and University Library, 57, 67; Socialist Republic of, 53, 57; State Archive, 57; Tourism Board, 66, 69; Tourism Master Plan for, 67; Tourism Museum, 57, 67;
Croatian Democratic Union (HDZ), 67
Crusader fortifications, 19, 33–48
Crusades, 6, 31–48; history of, 19
Cultural Heritage, Transnational Narratives, and Museum Franchising in Abu Dhabi, 18
cultural practices and expressions linked to the balafon of the Senufo communities, *16*

cultural practices associated to the first of March, *14*
Curaçao, 11
Curonian Spit (Lithuania), *9*
Cypriots: Greek, 43; Turkish, 43
Cyprus, *13–15*, 19, 25, 31–33, 35, 37, 42–44, 48; division of, 44; Kingdom of, 37, 40
Czechia, *10*, *14*, *15*, 89

Dale, Amanda, 129
Dallmann, Eduard, 205
Dalmatia, 58, 62, 66
Danish Workers Museum. *See* Workers Museum in Copenhagen
Dann, Kevin, 136
Danube River, 104, 109
Darache, Captain, 125
Dark Vein, 105–6
Dartmouth, Nova Scotia, 152
Date palm, knowledge, skills, traditions and practices, *13*, 18
Deception Island, 207–*8*
Democratic Republic of the Congo, *12*
Denmark, *12*, 24, 77, 87, 90
Diouf, Sylviane A., 148
Dodecanese, islands of, 40
Donaldson, Milford, 223, 227
Dubrovnik, 19, 53–54, 56–57, 59–61, 63–69; destruction of, 65
Dugua, Pierre, 125
Durmitor National Park, 61

Earthrise, *224*, 229, 231, 233–34, 237–39
Earthrise, 232–33
Ecuador, *10*, *15–16*, 87, 204
Edessa, County of, 31
Edificio de la Confederación General del Trabajo de la República in Buenos Aires, 85
Education, Audiovisual and Culture Executive Agency (EACEA), 103, 111
Egypt, 2–3, *12–13*, 18

Elafiti Islands, 64
Elephant Island, 209
Elephant Point, *201*
Elnu Abenaki Tribe, 130–31, 133
El Puente del Arzobispo Making Process, 11
Endangered Archaeology in the Middle East and North Africa (EAMENA), 35
Erzgebireg/Krušnohoří Mining Region, *10*, 89
Estonia, 7, *9*, *16*
Eurasia, 25
Europe, 3, 6, 11, 20–21, 31–32, 34, 61–62, 64–65, 67–68, 80–81, 90–91, 97, 103, 111, 158, 203; Eastern, 62; Mediterranean, 63–64; Southern, 63; Western, 58
European Commission, 98, 103
European Cultural Heritage Onstage (ECHO), 6, 20–21, 97–113
European Union, 98, 101, 110–11, 113
European University Viadrina, 22, 169, 177–78, 181–82
European Year of Cultural Heritage 2018, 98, 102

Falconry, a living human heritage, 11, *14*, 25
Famagusta, citadel of, 37
Fanning, Edmund, 198
Fausto, Florestano di, 46
Fertö/Neusiedlersee Cultural Landscape, *9*
The Final Mission: Preserving NASA's Apollo Sites, 223, 226
Finish Labor Museum, 91
Finland, 7, *9*, *12*, 90
First International Congress of Architects and Technicians of Historic Monuments, 2–3
First Man: The Life of Neil A. Armstrong, 235
First Seminole War, 150
Fischer, David Hackett, 126

Fiskovič, Cvito, 58
flatbread making and sharing culture: Lavash, Katyrma, Jupka, Yufka, *14*
Florida, 146, 149–52, 157–58; Black Heritage Trail, 151; Humanities Council, 151; Public Archaeology Network, 151–52; Purchase, 150; Spanish, 149–50
Flynn, 133
folkets hus. *See* workers' assembly hall
Folkets Hus in Motala, 90
For All Moonkind, Inc., 224; Registry, 224
Fort Gadsden/Prospect Bluff Historic Sites National Historic Landmark, 146, 149–52, 159
Fort Negro, 149–52
Foucault, Michel, 175
France, *9–16*, 18, 24, 59, 87, 90, 124–26, 204, 214
Frankfurt am Main, 82, 90
Frankfurt an der Oder, 22, 169, 177
Franks, 33, 36, 38, 40
French Austral Lands and Seas, 11
Frontiers of the Roman Empire, *9*

Gambia, *9, 16*
Gaza: castrum of, 37; Strip, 31
Gemini VIII, 231
genealogy, 22, 167–86
genetics, 170
"geographies, emotional," 176
geography, 176; historical, 170, 176
Georgia, 150–51
Germany, 6, 8–*10*, *13–14*, 18, 22, 82, 87, 89–90, 169, 177–78, 181, 207, 214; West, 84
Gewerkschaftshaus. *See* workers' assembly hall
Gewerkschaftshaus in Frankfurt am Main, 82, 90
Ghana, 82, 91
Ghent, 77, 90–91
Gibraltar, 11
Gibson Jr., Ralph, 226

Giovine, Michael A. di, 61
Glacier National Park, 4–5
Glasgow, 170
Global Strategy for a Representative, Balanced and Credible World Heritage List, 86
Google Earth, 239
Google Moon, 239
Gorham's Cave Complex, 11
Gorman, Alice, 225, 227
Gough and Inaccessible Islands, 11
Gravé, François Du Pont, 125
Great Britain. *See* United Kingdom
Great Law of Peace, 126
Great Spa Towns of Europe, *10*
Greece, *13–15*, 19, 25, 31–32, 35, 44, 48, 59, 68, 98, 103–5, 109
Greek Civil War, 101
Greenlee, Marcia M., 150
Groulx, Patrice, 125
Gruevski, Nikola, 68
Guatemala, *16*
Guidelines for the assessment and management of heritage in Antarctica, 213
Guinea, 7, *9*
Gule Wamkulu, *16*
Gulf of Mexico, 147

Hagia Sophia, cathedral of, 42
The Hague Convention of 1907, 98
Halbwachs, Maurice, 172
Hale, Charles Harold, 127
Hall, Derek, 67
Hall, Melanie, 18
Hall of Trade Unions in Accra, 82
Hansen, Marcus L., 174
Hardof-Jaffe, Sharon, 170
Harrison, Rodney, 55
Hart, Diana, 171
Haudenosaunee, 126
Heber, Carl, 131
Hector Whaling Station, 207
Heisse Jr., John W., 129
Helsinki, 77, 84, 90

Henderson Island, 11
Henry II, 42
heritage, 202–3, 227, 238, 241;
  Aerospatial, 6, 23–24, 223–41;
  African American, 150–51; Crusader,
  31–48; cultural, 1–3, *9–10*, 20, 25,
  58–61, 63, 67–68, 97, 112, 129, 149,
  155–57, 177, 186, 201–2, 204, 2121,
  215 (intangible, 1–18, 25, 98, 100,
  155–58, 226–28; tangible, 1–2, 6–18,
  24, 98, 100, 157, 226–28); dark,
  21, 97–113; familial, 168–69, 184;
  maroon, 22, 145–59; micro, 186;
  natural, 3–4, *9–10*, 58–59, 61–63, 68,
  100, 129, 149, 155–57; stateless, 23,
  195–216
heritage of Dede Qorqud/Korkyt Ata/
  Dede Korkut, epic culture, folk tales
  and music, *14*
heritage of Mercury. Almadén and
  Idrija, *10*
heritage sites, 6, 11, 17–19, 23–25,
  55–57, 61–63, 65, 68, 69, 146, 158,
  195, 211, 216, 223–25; Aerospatial,
  24, 223–41; cultural, 18, 149,
  201, 210–12; maroon, 22, 147–48;
  natural, 3, 7, 149; tangible, 146;
  transnational, 5
Hershkovitz, Arnon, 170
High Coast/Kvarken Archipelago, *9*
Higman, B. W., 147
Hikaye, 17
Hinchey, Maurice D., 123
Hiroshima, 214
Historic Area of Willemstad, 11
Historic Center of Rome, 5, 7, *9*
Historic Town of St. George and
  Related Fortifications, 11
historic urban landscapes, 32, 47
history, 8; cultural, 8; environmental,
  8; family, 167–74, 176, 185; micro,
  169; social, 170
Holocaust, 101
Holy Land, 31–32, 36, 39, 42, 44–45
Holy See, 5, 7, *9*

Honduras, *16*
Horta, Victor, 81
Hospitaller Order of Saint John of
  Jerusalem, 38
Hotel Balkan (Veliki Preslav), 103, 105
house of the people. *See* workers'
  assembly hall
Houston, 231, 240
Hungary, *9*, *14*
Huron Confederacy, 128
Huron-Wendat Nation, 128–29, 136

Ibelin, 37
Iceland, *12*
identity, 168–69, 171–72, 174–76, 184;
  cultural, 173; familial, 174; human,
  174; hybrid, 174–75; personal, 174,
  176; transpersonal, 172
Ilano work songs, *14*
India, 3, *10*, *15*, 87, 153
Indian Ocean, 145–46, 153
Indian Residential Schools Settlement
  Agreement, 129
Indonesia, *13*
industrialization, 77–78, 89, 197, 202
Inter Alia nongovernmental
  organization, 98, 103
Inter-American Court on Human Rights,
  145
International Council on Monuments
  and Sites (ICOMOS), 3, 86, 98, 101
International Geophysical Year of
  1957/58, 203, 215
International Peace Garden, 4–5
International Peace Park, 7, 24
International Space Station, 225, 227
Invisible Yet Invincible, 147
Ioannina (Greece), 105
Iran, *12–14*
Iraq, *12–13*, *15*, 18
Islam, 31
Israel, 17–19, 31–32, 35, 37, 39, 41, 45,
  47–48; Antiquities Authority, 17
Istanbul, 82
Italianization, 46

Italian-Turkish War of 1911, 46
Italy, 5, 7–*10*, *13–15*, 25, 59, 68, 203

Jackson, Andrew, 150
Jaffa (Israel), 39
Jamaica, 22, 146–47, 151, 155–59; Action Plan for Safeguarding the Maroon Heritage of Moore Town, 156; Conservation and Development Trust, 156
Japan, 3, *10*, 87, 214
Jerusalem: City of, 17, 31–32, 38, 45; Islamic Waqf of, 17; Kingdom of, 31–33, 37, 39, 41, 44–46; Partition of, 17
Jesuit Missions of the Guaranis, *9*
Johannesburg Trades Hall, 82
Jordan, *12–13*, 17–18, 24, 35, 38, 41, 47
Josic, Bojan, 109

Kaimaktsalan, Peak of, 104
Kaimanston, 149
Kambel, Ellen Rose, 149
Kankurang, Manding initiatory rite, *16*
Katyn Massacre, 101
Kazakhstan, *10*, *13–15*
Kearns, Christa, 25
Kekulé, Stephan, 183
Kennedy, John F., 240
Kennedy Space Center, 223
Kerak, castle of, 38–39, 47
King George Island, 206
Kluane/Wrangell-St. Elias/Glacier Bay/ Tatshenshini-Alsek, 7, *9*
Knights Hospitaller, 31, 36, 40, 44–46
Knights Templar, 36, 44
Knin (Croatia), 66
knowledge, know-how, and practices pertaining to the production and consumption of couscous, *12*
Koasek of the Koas, 131, 133
Koasek Traditional Band, 131
Kohav Hayarden (Israel), 38
Kohn, Margaret, 80, 82
Konstantin, Kiril T., 109

Kos, island of, 31
Kosovo, 101–102
Kotor (Montenegro), 19, 53–54, 56–57, 59–61, 63–65, 67–69
Kristensen, Leonard, 207
Kuwait, *12–13*, 18
Kwinti, 148–49
Kyrenia, castle of, 37
Kyrgyzstan, *10*, *13–15*

labor lyceum. *See* workers' assembly hall
labor movement, 6, 20, 77–92
labor temple. *See* workers' assembly hall
labor union hall. *See* workers' assembly hall
Lafrenz, Samuels K., 18
Lagoons of New Caledonia, 11
Lake Champlain, 21–22, 124, 132–33, 136–37; Basin Program (LCBP), 136–37; Committee (LCC), 136
Lake Champlain Voyages of Discovery: Bringing History Home, 131
Lake Nasser, 3
Lake Prespa, 60
Landscapes of Dauria, *10*
language, dance, and music of the Garifuna, *16*
Lateran Treaty, 5
Latin America, 6
Latvia, 7, *9*, *16*
Law of the Third Generation, 174
League of Nations, 3
Leahy, Patrick J., 123
Lebanon, *12*, 19, 32, 35, 37–39, 41, 47
Lemieux, Rodolphe, 127
Le Morne Brabant, 153–55, 158
Le Morne Cultural Landscape, 153–55, 158
Le Morne Cultural Landscape of Mauritius, 146
Lepore, Jill, 169
Lesotho, 7, *9*

Levant, 34-35, 40-41
Liberal Peace Framework, 102
liberty hall. *See* workers' assembly hall
Limes, 203
Lithuania, 7, *9*, *16*, 180
Liverpool, 88
Livingston Island, *201*
Ljubljana, 61
London, 198
Lorenzo Big Canoe of the Chippewas, 127
Louisiana, 146; Purchase, 199
Lovell, James, 229, 231–34, 238
Lowenthal, David, 100
Lunar Excursion Module, 234, 236
Lunar Legacy Project, 224
Lunar Orbit Insertion (Apollo 8), 229, 231–33, 237–38
Lusignan, Guy de, 42

Macedonia, Socialist Republic of, 53, 57, 60, 62-63
MacKay, Fergus, 149
Magnificent Desolation, 237
Maine State Museum, 135
maison du people. *See* workers' assembly hall
Maison du Peuple in Brussels, 81, 84
Majlis, a cultural and social space, *15*
Malawi, *12*, *16*
Malaysia, *12–13*
Mali, *16*
Maloti-Drakensberg Park, 7, *9*
Mamluks, 38
Manastir. *See* Bitola
Manhattan, 137
Manual Control (Apollo 11), *225*, 229, 234–40
March, Vernon, 126
Margat, castle of, 39
Marimba music, traditional chants and dances, *15*
Maritime Mercantile City of Liverpool, 88
Maroonage and the Maroon Heritage in Mauritius, 147

Maroon Heritage: Archaeological, Ethnographic, and Historic Perspectives, 147
Maroon Heritage of Moore Town, 146, 155–58
Maroons, 5, 22, 145–59; assimilation, 146; communities, 148–49; culture, 146–47; migration, 157–59; society, 146
Mars, 237
Martinique yole, 11
Master Plan of Rome, 5
Mauritania, *12–13*, 18
Mauritius, 22, 146, 152–55, 157–58; Environmental Protection Act, 154; Le Morne Heritage Trust Fund Act, 154; National Heritage Fund Act, 154; Wildlife Fund, 153
Mawson, 195
Mawson's Huts and Boat Harbour, 213
Mawson's Huts Antarctic Specially Protected Area, 212
M'Bow, Amadou Mahtar, 60
McFarlane, Andrew, 207
McLellan, Hugh, 131
Mediterranean, 41–43, 48, 59, 63, 65–66; Eastern, 31–33, 47
Mediterranean Diet, *15*, 25
The Meeting, 136
Meiji Industrial Revolution, 214
Melbourne, 77, 90
memory, 176; communicative, 172; cultural, 173; documentary, 173; family, 173, 184; oral, 173
men's group Colindat, Christmas-time ritual, *15*
mercantilism, 197
Mexico, 3, *10*, *13*, 147
Middle East, 17, 35
migration, 176, 180
migration studies, 170
mining landscape of Cornwell, 214
Missisquoi, 131, 133
Mobilizing Heritage: Anthropological Practice and Transnational Prospects, 18

Mohawk, 131
Moldova, 8–9, *14–15*
Moller, Sabine, 173–74
Monfort, castle of, 39, 47
Mongolia, *10*, *14*, *16*
Montana, 4–5
Montenegro, *10*, 19–20, 53–54, 60, 65, 68–69; Earthquake of 1979, 60, 63–64; Socialist Republic of, 53, 57, 63–65; Tourism Board, 68–69
Monte San Giorgio, *9*
Montreal, 136
Moon, 2, 24, 224–35, 237–38, 241
Moore Town, 146, 155–57, 159
Moranda, Scott, 59
Morocco, *12–15*, 18, 25
Mosi-oa-Tunya/Victoria Falls, *9*
Motala (Sweden), 90
Mount Nimba Strict Nature Reserve, 7, *9*
Mozambique, *16*
Mračno Naslede/Dark Heritage, 105
Munch, Edward, 109
musical art of horn players, an instrumental technique linked to singing, breath control, vibrato, resonance of place, and conviviality, *12*
Muskauer Park/Park Mużakowski, *9*
Mussolini, Benito, 5

Naef, Patrick, 55
Nahodilova, Lenka, 58
Nahuel Huapi National Park, 4
Nanny, 155
Nanny Town, 158
Napoleonic Wars, 153
nation: branding, 56; building, 54; re-branding, 54–55;
National Air and Space Administration (NASA), 224, 229, 231–33, 237–38, 240; Mission Control, 240
National Endowment for the Humanities, 151
national parks, 4

Nawrouz, Novruz, Nowrouz, Nowrouz, Nawrouz, Nauryz, Nowruz, Navruz, Nevruz, Nowruz, Navruz, *15*
Neisse River, 178
Nelson Independent Labour Party Clarion House, 82
Netherlands, *9–10*, 11, *14*, 87, 148
New England, 21, 126, 135
New France, 133, 135
New Lanark, 89
New Mexico, 223
New York City, 123, 135, 239; Fourth of July Parade, 123; September 11, 2001, 239
New York State, 21, 123–25, 130, 132–35, 137
New Zealand, 5, 81, 91, 202, 204, 214
Nicaragua, *16*
Nicolson, Paula, 177
Nicosia, city of, 42–44
Nidze, Mount, 104
Niger, 7, *9*, *16*
Nigeria, *16*
Nikulin, Dmitri, 159
Nora, Pierre, 176
Nordenskjöld, 195
Nordic clinker boat traditions, *12*
North Africa, 38
North America, 6, 25, 90, 124, 126, 128–29, 133, 136–37, 146, 151, 157–58
North Carolina, 146, 150–51
North Dakota, 4
North Korea, *14*
North Macedonia, *9*, *14*, 19–20, 53, 68–69, 103–5; Tourism Board, 69
Norway, 7, *9*, *12–13*, 68, 156, 204, 207, 214; Funds-in-Trust, 156
Nova Scotia colony, 152
Novi Sad (Serbia), 103–6, 110; raid, 104
Nulhegan Band of the Coosuc Abenaki nation, 130–31, 133
Nunavut, 101

Oceania, 145
Oder River, 177–78
Ohrid, town and lake, 19, 53–54, 56–63, 65, 67–69
Oklahoma, 126
Old City of Jerusalem and its Walls, 17–18, 226
Oldham, John Wesley, 127
O'Leary, Beth, 223, 226, 227
Oman, *12–13*, *15–16*, 18
Ong Chun/Wangchuan/Wangkang ceremony, rituals and related practices for maintaining the sustainable connection between man and the ocean, *12*
Ontario, 21, 125–27, 133; Elementary Teachers' Federation of, 128–29; Heritage Trust, 133
Opatija, 57, 67
Open Space Foundation (Veliki Preslav), 103, 106
oral heritage and cultural manifestations of the Zápara people, *16*
oral heritage of Gelede, *16*
Orillia, 126–29, 136; City Council of, 128
outer space, 11, 23–24, 26, 224, 228; Treaty, 224, 238
Ovide Sioui of the Urons, 127
Owen, Robert, 89

Paasitorni in Helsinki, 77, 84, 90
Pacific Ocean, 6
Pakistan, *14–15*
Palace of Diocletian, 57, 61
Palestine, 8, *12–13*, 35, 45
Palestinian Authority, 17–18, 24
Palmer, Nathaniel, 198
Panama, *9*
Pantun, *13*
patrimonialization, 55
Peace Arch Park, 5
Pelister Peak (North Macedonia), 104

Pendleton, Benjamin, 198
Penetanguishene, Ontario, 136
people's palace *See* workers' assembly hall
Peru, *10*, *16*, 87
Peter the Great, 181
Petrić, Hrvoje, 58
Philippines, *15*
Phillipe Auguste, 40
pilgrimage to the St. Thaddeus Apostle Monastery, *13*
Pingvellir National Park, 77
Piton's cirques and ramparts, 11
Plattsburgh, 123, 130–*32*, 136; Battle of, 136
Plitvice Lakes National Park, 57, 61
Ploner, Josef, 55
Poland, 7, *9–10*, *13–14*, 59, 177–78, 180–82, 185; Germanisation of, 180; Law on National Archival Holdings and Archives, 177; Partitioning of, 22, 180; Russification of, 180; State Archives, 177
Portugal, *9*, *14–15*, 25
Possession Island, 207
Potsdam Conference, 178
Potter Cove, 206
Powered Descent Initiation (Apollo 11), 229, 234, 236–38, 240
practices and knowledge linked to the Imzad of the Tuareg communities, *16*
Prehistoric Pile Dwellings around the Alps, *10*
Prehistoric Rock Art Sites in the Côa Valley and Siega Verde, 9
Prespa Agreement, 105
Pribichevich, Stoyan, 61
Price, Richard, 146
Privredni Vjesnik, 61
Processional giants and dragons, *16*
Program 66. *See* Manual Control
Promotion of Cultural Diversity in Kosovo (PCDK) program, 101
Provo, Utah, 170

Prussia, 22, 180; East, 178; West, 178
puppetry, *15*
Putnik, Vladana, 55

Qal'at al-Shaqif Arnun *See* Beaufort, castle of
Qal'at Hunin, 37
Qal'at Salah El-Din, 38
Qatar, *14–15*
Qhapaq Ñan, Andean Road System, *10*, 87
Quadricentennial celebrations of Samuel de Champlain's arrival in North America, 21
Quebec: City of, 123–25; Province of, 21, 123–27, 133, 135, 137
Queensland, 99

Ramsar Convention on Wetlands, 4
Register of Good Safeguarding Practices, 8
Regulating Transnational Heritage: Memory, Identity, and Diversity, 18
Representative List of the Intangible Cultural Heritage of Humanity, 8
Return to Earth, 236
Reunion Island, 11
Reynolds, Joseph, 226
Rhaetian Railway in the Albula/Bernina Landscapes, *10*, 203
Rhodes: Island of, 31, 40, 46; Kingdom of, 37
Richard the Lionheart, 40, 42, 44
Richelieu, Cardinal, 126
Richelieu River, 135
Rivera, Lauren, 55–56, 67
Roerich Pact of 1935, 98
Rolette County, 4
Roman Empire, 203
Romania, 8, *10*, *14*, *15*
Rome, 5, 7, *9*
Ross Sea, 214
Rotary Club, 5

Royal Geographical Society, 198
Royal National Park, 4
Royal Society, 198
Russia, 6, 8–*10*, 22, 68, 91, 180, 204

safeguarding intangible cultural heritage of Aymara communities, *16*
Samuel de Champlain History Center in Champlain, 135
Sanders, Bernard, 123
Sangha Trinational, *10*
Saone, castle of, 47
Saramaka people, 145
Saramaka People v. Suriname, 145
Sardonis, James, 129–30
Sarek National Park, 4
Saudi Arabia, *12–15*, 18
Saunier, Pierre-Yves, 2, 8, 24
Savorgnano, Guilio, 43
Sayers, Daniel O., 148, 151–52
Schmalz, Timothy, 136
Schumer, Charles E., 123
Scotland, 89
Scott, 195
Scream, 109
Scream 1&2, 109
sealing: companies, 197; industry, 23, 197–98; sites, 195–216
Second Congress of Architects, Conservationists and Technicians of Historic Monuments, 3
II. International, 81
Second Maroon War, 152
Selimiye Mosque, 42
Seminole, 150
Senegal, *9*, *16*, 82, 91
Serbia, *10*, 65, 68, 103–4
Serbian Krajina, 66
Sfera International, 103, 106
Shackel, Paul A., 18
Shashmaqom music, *16*
Shaubak, castle of, 38
Shirt, Luana, 129
Sidon: city of, 39; sea castle of, 37

Silesia, 178
Silk Roads: the Routes Network of Chang'an-Tianshan Corridor, *10*, 87, 203
Sioui, Konrad, 129
slavery, 148, 150, 153, 155
Slovakia, 8–*10*, *14–15*
Slovenia, 8, *10*, *14*
Słubice, 177–78
smallpox, 171
Smith, Laurajane, 99, 227
Smith, William, 197
Smolyan School of Fine Arts, 106
The Socialist, 80
Socialist Labour Hall in Barre, 90
Sociedad Ballenera de Magallanes, 207
Solak, Ljubica Meshkova, *107–8*
Sosa-Stradonitz method, 183
South Africa, 7, *9*, 91
South America, 6, 146
South Atlantic, 11
South Carolina, 150–51
South Indian Ocean, 11
South Korea, *14–15*
South Pacific, 11
South Seas, 197
South Shetland Islands, 23, 195–216
Soviet Union. *See* USSR
space program, American, 223
Space Race, 1, 223, 230–31, 240–41
Spain, 8–11, *13–15*, 25, 59
Split (Croatia), 57, 61
Spring celebration, Hidrellez, *14*
Sputnik, 240
Sri Lanka, 18
St. Louis, 82
Stalin, Joseph, 58
Stari Ras, 61
Stećci Medieval Tombstone Graveyards, *10*
Stevens, Don, 130
Stone Circles of Senegambia, *9*
Stonehenge, 239
Struve Geodetic Arc, 7–*9*, 25

Sudan, *12*, 18
Sumer, 2
summer solstice fire festivals in the Pyrenees, *15*
SUNY Plattsburgh, 137
Surface, 109
Suriname, 22, 145–49, 152, 157–58
Surrey, British Columbia, 5
Svend Foyn Island, 207
Svjetska Baština u Jugoslaviji, 64
Sweden, 4, 8–*9*, *12*, 18, 59, 90, 214
Switzerland, 9–*10*, *12–14*, 17, 87, 203
Syria, *14*, 19, 32, 37–39, 41, 47–48
Sztompka, Piotr, 101

Tadoussac, 125
Taiga, 25
Tainos, 155, 157
Tajikistan, *15–16*
Talamanca Range-La Amistad Reserves/ La Amistad National Park, *9*
tango, *16*
Taputapuātea, 11
Teelock, Vijaya, 147
Tell es-Safi, 37
Teutonic Knights, 36
Texas, 146
Thessaloniki, 105; Documentary Festival (2021), 105
Tilley, Christopher, 230
Tito, Josip Broz, 57–58
Togo, *16*
Torres Strait Islanders, 99
tourism, 53–61, 63–65, 67–69, 153–54, 156, 202
Towards World Heritage: International Origins of the Preservation Movement, 1870–1930, 18
trade union hall. *See* workers' assembly hall
traditional intelligence and strategy game: Togyzqumalaq, ToguzKorgool, Mangala/Göçürme, *13*

traditional knowledge and skills in making Kyrgyz and Kazakh yurts (Turkic nomadic dwellings), *15*
traditional Korean wrestling (Ssirum/Ssireum), *14*
traditional wall-carpet craftmanship, *15*
traditional weaving of Al Sadu, *13*
Tranquility Base, 223–24, 226, 228, 234, 238
transhumance, the seasonal droving of livestock along migratory routes in the Mediterranean and in the Alps, *13*
Translunar Injection (Apollo 8), 229–32, 237–38, 240
tree beekeeping culture, *13*
Trelawny Town, 152
Tripoli, 37; county of, 31, 37
Truth and Reconciliation Commission (Canada), 129
Tschuggnall, Karoline, 173–74
Tsousis, Aristaios, *107*, *108–9*
tugging rituals and games, *15*
Tunisia, *12–13*, 18, 91
Turistkomerc, 66
Turizam, 60–61
Turkey, *12–15*, 59, 82, 91
Turkmenistan, *15*
TWIXTlab (Athens), 103, 105
Tyre, 39

Ukraine, 8–*10*, 91, 180
Ukrainian Labour Temple in Winnipeg, 82
Ulcinj (Montenegro), 64
Uncommon Threads, 133
UNESCO, 3–4, 7–8, 11, 17–20, 22, 24–26, 47, 53–55, 57, 60–65, 68, 79, 86–88, 90, 92, 98, 101–102, 146, 149, 153–58, 202; Convention for the Safeguarding of the Intangible Cultural Heritage, 4, 8, 11, 86, 154–55, 158; digital archive, 57; List of Intangible Cultural Heritage in Need of Urgent Safeguarding, 8; List of Intangible Cultural Heritage of Humanity, 8, 11, 17, 146, 156–58; Masterpieces of the Oral and Intangible Heritage List, 155–56; World Heritage Committee, 62, 154–56, 203, 228; World Heritage Convention (1972), 3–4, 6–7, 17, 86–87, 153, 158, 202–3; World Heritage in Danger, 63; World Heritage List, 6–8, 17, 25, 55, 60–63, 77–79, 86–87, 89, 92, 97–98, 146, 148, 149, 154–56, 158, 203, 212, 214, 226, 228, 239; World Heritage nature preserve, 146; World Heritage programs, 6, 24–26; World Heritage property, 7; World Heritage Sites (WHS), 6–8, 11, 19–20, 25, 46–47, 53, 57, 60–61, 63–65, 86, 149, 157, 239
United Arab Emirates, *12–16*, 18
United Kingdom, 9–11, 18, 23, 24, 41, 59, 81–82, 85, 195–99, 204, 207, 209–10, 214
United Nations (UN), 17, 57, 59, 228; Archives of, 57; Declaration on the Rights of Indigenous Peoples, 145; Development Program (UNDP), 101; International Convention on Biological Diversity, 149; Office for Outer Space Affairs Committee on the Peaceful Uses of Outer Space, 224
United 93 flight, 236
United States, 3–7, *9*, 11, 18, 22–24, 59, 81, 89–91, 101, 123–25, 131, 133–34, 136–37, 146, 148, 150, 152, 157–59, 196–99, 204, 209–10, 223, 227, 238, 240, 241; Congress, 123; Constitution, 126; National Forest Service, 150–51; National Historic Landmark, 151, 223–24, 226; National Park Service, 150, 159; National Register of Historic Places, 224, 226, 228
University of Dundee, 170
University of Strathclyde, 170
University of Vermont, 136; Forums on the Future, 136

Urban II, 32
urbanization, 78
Urtiin Duu, traditional folk long song, *16*
Uruguay, *16*
USSR, 7, 57, 178, 180, 223, 241; disintegration of, 7
Utah, 170
Uzbekistan, *10, 12, 15–16*

Valcour, battle of, 136
Valparaíso, 207
Vanguard 1, 227
Varna Vocational School of Textile and Fashion Design, 106
Vatican City. *See* Holy See
Veliki Preslav, 103, 105–6
Venetian Works of Defence between the sixteenth and seventeenth centuries: Stato da terra-Western Stato da mar, *10*
Venezuela, *14*
Venice, 3, 54
Venice Charter for the Conservation and Restoration of Monuments and Sites, 3–5
Vermont, 123–24, 129–31, 132, 136–37
Vermont Indigenous Heritage Center (VIHC), 134
Vermont Lake Champlain Quadricentennial Commission, 134–35
Victoria Land, 207
Victorian Trades Hall in Melbourne, 77, 90
Victoria Road United Baptist Church in Dartmouth, 152
Viernulvier. *See* Vooruit
Viet Nam, *15*
Virginia, 146, 151
Virunga National Park, 4
Vojvodina, 104, 110
Vojvodina Civic Center (Novi Sad), 103, 106
Völklingen Ironworks, 214
Volkshaus. *See* workers' assembly hall
Vooruit in Ghent, 77, 90
Vujanović, Filip, 68

Waaden Sea, 87
Wakefield, Sarina, 18
Wales, 89
Walsh, Justin, 225
W-Arly-Pendjari Complex, 7, *9*
War of 1812, 152, 199
Warsaw, 170
Washington DC, 150
Washington State, 5
Waterton (Alberta), 5
Waterton Lakes-Glacier International Peace Park, 7, *9*
Waterton Lakes National Park, 4–5
Weddell, James, 199
Weik, Terrance, 147
Welzer, Harald, 173–74
Wendat, 126
West Bank, 31
Western Macedonia, 103, 105, 109
Western Tein-Shan, *10*
West Indies, 153
Westwood, Lisa, 223, 227
Whalers Bay, *207–8*
whaling sites, 207–8
Wieliczka and Bochnia Royal Salt Mines, 7
Wijdenbosch, Jules Albert, 148
Winnipeg, 82
Witagron, 149
The Women Workers' Institute in Cradley Heath, 82
Wooden Tserkvas of the Carpathian Region, *10*
workers' assembly halls, 20, 77–92
Workers Museum in Copenhagen, 77, *83–85*, 89, 90
Workers' Union & Association Hall *See* Workers Museum in Copenhagen
World War I, 104, 181, 184
World War II, 55, 58, 63, 81–82, 84, 86, 178, 203
Wyandotte, 126

Xenos, 107–8

Yalta Conference, 178
Yankee Harbour, 207
Yavne (Israel), 37
Yellowstone National Park, 4, 18
Yemen, *12–13*, 18
Yugoslavia, Socialist Federation of, 6, *9*, 19–20, 53–69; Archive of, 57; Civil Wars, 19, 65–66, 68–69; Collapse of, 53–54, 67–69; Tourism, 53–60, 63–64

Yugoslav National Liberation Army, 109
Yugoslav Peoples' Army (JNA), 65–66
Yukon, 7

Zagreb, 57, 61, 66–67
Zambia, *9, 16*
Zerubavel, Eviatar, 168
Zimbabwe, *9, 12*
Zollverein Coal Mine, 214

About the Editors and Contributors

Thomas Adam is professor of political science at the University of Arkansas. From 2001 to 2020 he taught transnational and transatlantic history at the University of Texas at Arlington. He has published and edited more than twenty-five books. He specializes in the study of intercultural transfers and the history of philanthropy. Among his most recent publications are *Deutschland in der Welt* (2021), *The History of College Affordability in the United States* (2020), and *Approaches to the Study of Intercultural Transfer* (2019). Adam is also editor of the book series *Intercultural Transfer Studies*.

Email: tadam@uark.edu

Marie Brøndgaard is museum curator at The Workers Museum in Denmark. She is a practitioner who has worked with visitor experience management in various museums since 2010. She received her BA in Near Eastern Archaeology (2011) with a thesis on the destruction of cultural heritage during armed conflict, which led to her joining the Danish National Committee of Blue Shield. She holds an MA in Cultural Heritage Management from the University of York (2012) and an MA in Tourism from Aalborg University (2015), where the latter extended to an external lectureship. She has worked on a local heritage protection project in the South Welsh Valleys and is now working with the transnational serial nomination of workers assembly halls, a project attempting to locate and document workers' associated buildings internationally for the UNESCO World Heritage List.

Email: mbr@arbejdermuseet.dk

Josef Djordjevski is an environmental historian specializing on transformations of the Eastern Adriatic seaside during the period of Yugoslav socialism. He received his PhD in History from the University of California in San Diego, where he defended his dissertation, titled "A Seaside for the Future: Yugoslav Socialism, Tourism, Environmental Protection, and the Eastern Adriatic Coastline, 1945–2000s." He is currently a postdoctoral fellow at the University of Graz's Dimensions of Europeanization Field of Excellence program.

Email: jdjordje@ucsd.edu

Austin E. Loignon is a visiting instructor of history at Tarleton State University in Stephenville, Texas. He received his PhD in Transatlantic History from the University of Texas at Arlington in 2019, where he was trained by Thomas Adam in the methodology of Intercultural Transfer. His dissertation focused on the health reformer and physician John Harvey Kellogg (the inventor of cornflakes) as a transatlantic agent of transfer between the health reform movements of Europe and the United States. Loignon specializes in transfers within the transatlantic world, European and American tribalism, and Relics and Pilgrimage within European and American societies. He is currently developing his next research project on Transnational Light Therapy and its use and disuse within various parts of the world.

Email: austinloignon@icloud.com

Izabella Parowicz is senior researcher at the Heritage Studies Program of the European University Viadrina in Frankfurt (Oder), Germany, and coordinator of the postgraduate course "Strategies for European Cultural Heritage." As a two-time Marie Skłodowska-Curie Postdoctoral Fellow funded by the European Commission, she has carried out research projects at the University of Malta and the European University Viadrina. She is a specialist in the field of management and marketing of cultural heritage with particular emphasis on marketing of conservation services; a genealogist with thirty-five years of experience; and a lecturer in genealogy at the Department of Cultural Studies. As the initiator and manager of the project "To Read the Illegible," she coauthored materials for the self-study of neo-Gothic handwriting and old Russian handwriting.

Email: parowicz@europa-uni.de

Nikos Pasamitros is visiting research fellow at the Department of Political Science and International Relations (PSIR) of the University of the

Peloponnese. He holds a PhD in International Studies (Panteion University of Athens), a MSc in Environmental Sciences–Environment and Art (University of the Aegean), a MA in International Conflict Analysis (University of Kent in Brussels), and a BSc in Political Science and History (Panteion). He is a founding member of the Inter Alia NGO. In 2018–2019, he was the cultural heritage supervisor of the ECHO project and a text-writer of the creative documentary "Dark Vein." In 2019–2022, he was the coordinator of the ECHO II project artistic activities. From 2022 on he is the heritage supervisor of ECHO III: For Memory's Sake. Nikos has also worked as a researcher for the Kosovo Foundation for Open Society (KFOS) and the Institute of International Economic Relations (IIER).

Email: pasamitros@interaliaproject.com

Michael Pearson is a former heritage manager, consultant, and researcher, who now works as an independent scholar in Australia. He received his doctoral degree from the Australian National University in 1981. In 2013 he was made an Officer of the Order of Australia for his achievements and services in the areas of cultural heritage conservation, research, and teaching. He has worked extensively in historical and industrial archaeology, heritage planning, and world heritage internationally for over four decades, and has undertaken extensive research in the Antarctic, with many published articles and books. He and Melisa Salerno are coauthors, with Andres Zarankin, of the forthcoming book *Archaeology in Antarctica*, to be published in 2022.

Email: mike.p@ozemail.com.au

Shelley-Anne Peleg is a specialist on cultural heritage (intangible and built) and conservation procedures of the cultural built heritage (archeological sites and historical cities) with a focus on the Old City of Akko. She is a fellow researcher and lecturer in the Department of Israel Studies at the University of Haifa, and a lecturer at Kinneret College. She completed her PhD at the University of Haifa in which she presented the connection between intangible and tangible heritage in Historic Urban Landscapes in Israel. Her research was based on twenty-five work years at the Israel Antiquities Authority, during which she served as the director of the International Conservation Center–Citta' di Roma (situated in the Old City of Akko). She is the founder of Hands-on-Heritage, which initiates various programs for public outreach in all fields of heritage.

Email: shelleypeleg@gmail.com

Anastasia L. Pratt is associate professor of history and public history at SUNY Empire State College. Since 2008, she has also been the Historian for Clinton County, NY. She received a BA in History from SUNY Plattsburgh (1998) and both an MA (2001) and PhD (2007) in American Culture from the University of Michigan. She combines her interest in public and local history work through her research and has published several books about Clinton County's history. In 2009, she worked to contextualize local commemorations of Samuel de Champlain's explorations, seeking to offer a more complete and inclusive history.

Email: Anastasia.Pratt@esc.edu

Melisa A. Salerno is a researcher at the Multidisciplinary Institute of History and Human Sciences, National Council of Scientific and Technical Research in Argentina (IMHICIHU-CONICET). She received her doctoral degree from the University of Buenos Aires, Argentina, in 2011. She has worked on several case studies in historical archaeology with special emphasis in nineteenth-century Antarctica. Her research interests include the life of "invisible" groups, power and identity dynamics, and embodied practices and experiences.

Email: melisa_salerno@yahoo.com.ar

Ryan N. Sisak is a professional educator with Carrollton Farmers-Branch Independent School District in Irving, Texas, and an emergent heritage professional and researcher. He received his MA in International Heritage Management from the University of Birmingham, United Kingdom (2020), and his BA in Humanities from Florida State University (2009). His dissertation "Aerospatial Heritage Sites—A History of Value and Meaning for Places in Relative Space" first established the concept of heritage sites in outer space by focusing on the valorization of five sites from both Apollo 8 and Apollo 11. His main current research interests are military heritage and history, with a particular emphasis on World War II and the use of military history to analyze current strategic issues. Sisak currently provides exhibit and curatorial consulting to a war museum in North Texas, with an emphasis on applying heritage interpretation theory and museum industry standards.

Email: rns838@alumni.bham.ac.uk

Barry L. Stiefel, PhD, is associate professor at the College of Charleston's Historic Preservation and Community Planning program, which is part of the Department of Art and Architectural History. Dr. Stiefel is interested in how local preservation efforts affect regional, national, and multinational policies within the field of cultural resource management and natural heritage conservation. He has completed numerous publications, including ones that address sustainability in heritage preservation; cultural-ethnic architectural history; historic transportation mobility; human-centered historic preservation; community-building through historic places; diversity, equity, and inclusion in historic preservation; and preservation education.

Email: StiefelB@cofc.edu

Ingram Content Group UK Ltd.
Milton Keynes UK
UKHW010617010523
421006UK00003B/41

9 781683 933786